BUDDHIST HIMALAYA

To

My European Masters

H. W. Bailey

Walter Simon

Giuseppe Tucci

BUDDHIST HIMALAYA

Travels and Studies in quest of the origins and nature of Tibetan Religion

David L. Snellgrove

Orchid Press

David L. Snellgrove
BUDDHIST HIMALAYA
Travels and studies in quest of the origins and nature of Tibetan Religion

First edition, Bruno Cassirer, London 1957

Second edition, Himalayan Book Sellers, Kathmandu 1995

Third edition, Orchid Press, Bangkok 2011

ORCHID PRESS
P.O. Box 1046,
Silom Post Office,
Bangkok 10504, Thailand
www.orchidbooks.com

Cover image : Bhaktapur, Nepal

ISBN: 978-974-524-141-1

CONTENTS

	List of Illustrations	vi
	Preface to the Second Edition	xi
	Preface to the First Edition	xiii
I	ORIGINS IN INDIA	1
II	TANTRIC BUDDHISM	51
III	BUDDHISM IN NEPAL	91
IV	KINGS OF TIBET	121
V	RELIGIOUS TEACHERS OF TIBET	166
VI	TIBETAN CEREMONIES	212
VII	REFLECTIONS	275
	Appendix: Spiti and Lahul, 1953	283
	Note	303
	Mandalas	316
	On the Spelling of Tibetan and Sanskrit Names	319
	Chronology	321
	Bibliography	323
	Abbreviations	327
	Genaral Index	329
	Tibetan Index	340

ILLUSTRATIONS

Plate

1. *a*. Bodhgaya, the Tree of Enlightenment. *After Page* 36
   b. Sarnāth, the Dharmarājika-stūpa.
2. The Wheel of Existence.
3. Rock-shrines:
   a. Bhaja, *b*. Karla, *c*. Nāsik, *d*. Ajanta.
4. Buddha, summonsing the earth to witness.
5. *a*. Buddha preaching.
   b. Buddha entering the final nirvāna.
6. Decorative motifs:
   a. Horse-riders.
   b. Sun-God and War-God.
7. *a*. Exterior view of caves, Nāsik.
   b. Assembly of buddhas, Nāsik.
8. *a*. Preaching buddha enshrined.
   b. A hall for monks, Kanheri.
9. *a*. Buddha-Heruka. *After Page* 100
   b. Ushnīsha-sitātapatrā.
10. The 84 Siddhas.
11. Detail of the above.
12. A palace-courtyard in Pātan.
13. The Great Stūpa, Svayambhūnāth.
14. *a*. The Great Stūpa, Bodhnāth.
    b. Mongolian Lama of Bodhnāth.
15. Lokeśvara.
16. *a*. The Buddhist temple of Vidyeśvarī outside Kathmandu.
    b. A Hindu temple of Bhadgaon.
17. *a*. Kumārī (by J. Derry). *After Page* 132
    b. Her attendants, Ganesh and Bhairav.

Plate

18. *a.* 'Cauliflowers for sale.' *After Page* 132
b. Pātan.

19. *a.* Neglected heritage.
b. Paśupati.

20. *a.* Sam-yä (by H. E. Richardson).
b. The black chöten, Sam-yä (by H. E. Richardson).

21. *a.* Kyi-bar, Spiti. *After Page* 180
b. The Spiti River.

22. *a.* The Kun-zang Pass.
b. Carrying Tibetan books.

23. Padma-sambhava at Riwalsar.

24. Ancient marble head of a bodhisattva, Gandhola.

25. Tabo: *a.* Decorative motifs, *b.* Vairocana, *c.* Amitābha.

26. *a.* Dankhar, Spiti.
b. Village-festival in the Kulu Valley.

27. *a* Approach to Dankhar.
b. Villagers in Spiti.

28. *a.* Sacred Mountain.
b. Sacred Water.

29. Friends and helpers in Kalimpong. *After Page* 212

30. *a.* Teng-bo-che Monastery.
b. Effigy of the previous head-lama.

31. *a.* The monk of Lug-lha receives a visitor.
b. The monks of Jiwong despatch a bandit.

32. *a.* Grinding corn.
b. Opening a jar of barley-beer.

33. *a.* Jiwong Monastery.
b. Houses of the monks.

34. *a.* The boy-lama of Jiwong and his preceptor.
b. Effigy of the previous head-lama of Rongphu.

Plate

35. *a.* Carving printing-blocks. *After Page* 212
b. Chopping dried mutton.
36. 'The Union of the Precious Ones.'
37. *a.* 'The Universal Saviour.'
b. Page of text.
38. Ceremonial requirements:
a. Vajra, *b.* Ritual vase, *c.* Butter-lamp, *d.* Prayer-wheel.
39. *a.* Sacrificial cakes.
b. 'the potion was poured upon the blazing hearth.'
40. *a.* Sounding drum and bell.
b. Blowing trumpets.

MAPS AND OTHER ILLUSTRATIONS

Map of Journeys in Spiti and Lahul, p. 297
Map I. Tibet and Surrounding Countries, following Index
Map II. Western Tibet, following Map I

A small silver Buddha (Amoghasiddbi) p. 50.
Wheel of the Doctrine with garland, p. 120.
Lotus, p. 165.
Crossed vajra (viśvajra), p. 211.
Tibetan script (p. 326) and designs by Parwa Pasang.

PREFACE TO THE SECOND EDITION

I have hesitated for a long time over the republication of this early book of mine which first appeared in 1957. In retrospect it has seemed to me a rather amateurish work, or at least the work of a new-comer giving his first impressions of a vast and complex subject. Indeed it was quite unnecessary for me to warn the reader in the original preface "that in no sense has the last word been written". Inevitably the same applies to my much later work, *Indo-Tibetan Buddhism*, published in 1987, which I intended as an improved replacement of the earlier work. However it is fair to warn the reader of this second edition of *Buddhist Himalaya* that the text remains largely unchanged, whereas my own understanding of much of the materials has quite properly undergone a maturing development in the course of the intervening space of thirty years.

A clear example of this can easily be found in the case of the imposing religious council supposedly held in Lhasa about the year 794 under the order of King Trhi-song-deu-tsen. Following the later Tibetan accounts of this event, I assumed that this great debate, held to decide upon the alternative merits of Indian and Chinese interpretations of Buddhist doctrines, actually took place as described (see pp. 156-8). One should compare with this the more detailed account given in *Indo-Tibetan Buddhism* (pp. 433-6), where other sources are quoted and reasons are given for considering the story largely unhistorical. As another example: judged by my later work, the earlier observations concerning the categories of tantric texts (pp. 202-4), suggesting that they were limited to four categories only, seem to me now to be rather inadequate. At the same time it would be impracticable to rewrite such passages, still retaining the original pagination, and I trust that the reader will accept this new edition as a kind of "period piece" like so-many other early works that have been reprinted over recent years.

I have emended, however, a whole paragraph on p. 130. This is a translation of a very early and rather obscure Tibetan text describing the mythical origin of the early kings. In a revue of my book (published in the *Journal Asiatique* 1958), Professor Rolf Stein kindly suggested some corrections to my translation, which I have now incorporated.

It was perhaps rather rash to state (on p. 92): "The construction of motorable tracks will never be practicable so that greater Nepal will continue to remain largely ignorant of the ways of the outside world." All those who have visited Nepal since 1956 will know that a large number of motorable roads have in fact been constructed. I was there myself in 1956 when the road from the Indian frontier to Kathmandu was first opened. Since then the road from Kathmandu to Tibet, the road from Kathmandu to Pokhara and down to the Indian frontier at Bhairawa, as well as the so-called East-West Highway have all been constructed. However it remains true that the greater part of Nepal can still not be reached by motor-transport and probably never will be. The cost of maintaining the existing roads, constructed with the greatest difficulty across such mountainous terrain, is already enormous. I have therefore asked the printers to amend the text from "never be practicable" to "hardly be practicable". A few other minor changes to the text have been incorporated, and since all the illustrations have had to be reprinted from the original negatives, I have found it necessary to make a few changes here as well.

When I first arrived in Kathmandu together with my companion Pasang in early 1954 the only motorable roads were in the Kathmandu Valley itself. No service by air was then available. A small railway existed from Raxaul on the Indian frontier to Amlekhganj, some forty kilometres inside Nepal, and from there one took to one's feet, spending one night in a rest-house en route and finally descending the next afternoon into what then really seemed a quite magical valley at a point near Balaju. Here at last some rare motor transport was available, all such vehicles having been carried in across the mountains by the same route that we had followed.

I recall that a reviewer of this book when it first appeared observed that there was very little description of travel and that it might equally well have been written from ones desk despite its sub-title "Travels and Studies in quest of the origins and nature of Tibetan religion". This is a fair criticism and in response I add as an appendix to this second edition the account of the journey through Spiti and Lahul which I made in the early autumn of 1953. It was subsequent to this journey when I was spending the winter of 1953-4 in Kalimpong that I made the acquaintance of Pasang Khambache Sherpa who accompanied me to Solu-Khumbu in early 1954 and so became my faithful companion on all subsequent Himalayan travels (except those in Ladakh) up to the year 1979. By then he was already senior official of the Nepalese Ministry of Agriculture, primarily responsible for experimental fruit growing at higher altitudes, and so no longer free to travel with me without special permission. Our long 8-month tour of north-western Nepal (1956) is described in my *Himalayan Pilgrimage*, and a brief account of our very difficult sojourn in Dolpo (1960-61) is given in my *Four Lamas of Dolpo*. In 1967 we visited Bhutan together, and in 1978 and 1979 we made shorter tours within reach of Pasang's main base at Marpha in the upper Kali Gandaki Valley. Now with the advancing years we are content to meet for a few days in Kathmandu or Pokhara, whenever I have occasion to pass through Nepal.

Other books are dedicated to Pasang and I see no reason for changing the dedication of the present work. Of the three "European Masters" only Professor Sir Harold Bailey, who taught me Sanskrit at Cambridge over the years 1946-9 survives. Walter Simon, then Professor of Chinese in the University of London (School of Oriental and African Studies) encouraged me in my then new interest in Tibetan literature and religion, while

Giuseppe Tucci with whom I studied in Rome in the early 1950s readily provided the guidance and inspiration which only such a great master of all things Tibetan could then provide.

David Sneligrove
Torre Pellice
27th November 1993

PREFACE TO THE FIRST EDITION

Most books that use the name 'Himālaya' in their title are concerned with the adventures of mountaineers, and so it is but fair to warn the reader that there are here recounted no exciting tales of risks rewarded or of catastrophic and cruel defeat.[a] We have shared but the incidental joys of mountaineering, the long approach-marches through the lower valleys with their rushing torrents and across the foot-hills clad in rhododendrons, red and white and pink. We have toiled through desolate places and camped contentedly far from the amenities and conventions of modern western life. We have gazed enraptured upon great snow-peaks with their impregnable pinnacles of ice. The memory of those journeys through Sikkim and Nepal and on the wild and rugged confines of western Tibet have remained so vivid throughout the writing of this book, that one might easily have swelled its pages with descriptions of this ideal life. But there are matters of more serious import, which were the object of these travels.

In an historical appreciation of Tibetan Buddhism it is impossible to ignore this enormous mountainous expanse of the Himalayas. It preserves, especially in the Nepal Valley, important traces of the later Indian Buddhism, which has provided the substance of much of Tibetan religion. It was through that country and the western passes that Buddhism was painstakingly transferred to Tibet from central India and Kashmir,

[a] Himālaya (with a long accented vowel in the second syllable) is the correct Sanskrit term, meaning *Abode of Snow*, which is used vaguely and poetically for any high mountain. The Tibetans also use the vague term k'ang-ri, *Snow-Mountains*, and they like to refer to their own country as the *Snowy Land*. The anglicized forms, Himalayas and Himalayan (usually accented on the third syllable), are merely convenient terms for geographical reference. Since it is now scarcely possible to combine these two forms, viz. the correct Sanskrit with its literary and poetic associations and the matter-of-fact English derivatives, I use one or the other, depending upon the context.

and there still exist important archaeological remains, dating from this period of transfer, especially in the west.

Lastly the Himalayas can still testify to its activeness, for these regions which once saw the passage of Buddhism to Tibet, have now become dependant on Tibet for the very life of their religion. The source in India has long been dead, and only the Tibetans possess the living traditions which can enliven the ancient places. It will be found that short as this work is, the scope is very wide. It has been necessary to resume in an introductory chapter the origins of Buddhism in India itself and the developments that prepare the way for the later Buddhism which is our special interest. On early Buddhism and the Mahāyāna several useful works are available, but as they are specially concerned with the presentation of these phases, they sometimes fail to draw attention to elements and tendencies, which only find fulfilment in later times. Moreover this later period, viz. from the eighth century A.D. onwards, is often passed over as if it were nothing more than a degeneration of the earlier periods without any special value of its own. Thus this book represents the first attempt to relate Tibetan religion to its origins in any comprehensive manner. The account here given is based upon all available information as well as my own researches. Every section has been brought into relationship with the journey which is relevant to it and is illustrated accordingly. Thus the first chapter dealing with the Buddhism of India is related to the visits made to some of the ancient Indian sites. The introduction of Buddhism into Tibet is connected with travels on the confines of western Tibet. Present-day Tibetan Buddhism is demonstrated by reference to the monasteries of Shar-Khumbu in eastern Nepal. All these journeys were made during 1953 and 1954, during which time I was occupied in learning as much as possible about the Tibetans and their culture and religion, as it is found in the Himalayan regions. The subject-matter of one chapter, which centres around Lhasa, lies beyond the range of my personal experience, and I am therefore grateful to Mr. H. E. Richardson who worked on some of this material during his long residence there, for having looked through this part of my manuscript. For the means to travel and pursue these absorbing studies I am immeasurably indebted to the School of Oriental and African Studies in the University of London. I am mindful also of the opportunities for fruitful discussion with my colleagues there, who although they may remain nameless, have contributed much to the forming of my views on the most varied matters. It will be clear from the list of references at the end of my work, to which other scholars I am specially indebted, but I must mention in particular Professor Tucci, whose extensive travels and monumental publications, which cover the whole field of my own research, are a constant source of inspiration.

It has not been my intention in a diffuse work of this kind to argue any particular thesis, but rather to illustrate the origins and nature of Tibetan Buddhism with the material which is now at my disposal. By the time this book appears in print, I shall be in other Himalayan Buddhist regions in west Nepal, and so the reader should be warned that in no sense has the last word been written. Compared with the classics, oriental studies generally are in their infancy, but it would be absurd (even if it were possible) to withhold the publication of general summaries until every relevant branch of research had been pursued and studied.

There is considerable interest both in Buddhism and in Tibet, and Buddhism has suffered much at the hands of would-be exponents of her tenets, who possessing no first-hand knowledge of the texts and little enough of the historical and cultural background against which they must be interpreted, have not hesitated to make pronouncements on the subject *ex cathedra*. Books on Tibet are generally reliable so far as they go, for they have usually been written by those who have visited the country. But very few of these travellers have possessed the necessary preliminary knowledge or indeed the inclination to write in detail on the subject of Tibetan religion. Now one can but regret their lost opportunities, for who knows how long it will be before Tibet is accessible again. My own general estimate of the nature of this religion is in the last resort derived not so much from the careful study of texts and balanced weighing of evidence, as from direct perception into the personalities of a few Tibetans, whom I have known closely. In this respect orientalists may well have a considerable advantage over the students of the western classics, for it is still possible for us to meet with genuine representatives of the ancient traditions. Perhaps one should say just possible, for before this century is finished, there may be none left at all.

D. L. Snellgrove,
Lecturer in Tibetan,
The School of Oriental and African Studies,
University of London.

NOTE

The writing of Tibetan terms in a work such as this presents serious problems, and it is possible that I shall displease the scholar by my phonetic renderings without having yet simplified them sufficiently to satisfy the general reader. To the scholar I would submit that it is unreasonable to expect those who are unacquainted with Tibetan to master its curious combinations of compound consonants. A Tibetan index is provided for his special use. I would beg the general reader to refer to my notes on Spellings (pp. 299–300), so that his criticism may be tempered by sympathetic understanding. Certain technical terms cannot be avoided, but the General Index should give direct access to the meaning.

I thank Mr. J. E. S. Driver for correcting the final proofs during my absence in Nepal.

I

ORIGINS IN INDIA

Bodhgaya

It was at Bodhgaya some 2,500 years ago that the Śākya-Sage gained buddhahood and so this place may provide us with an obvious starting-point. The Buddhists themselves have never conceived of an absolute beginning for their doctrine. This Buddha, unique in our world-age perhaps, was none the less the successor of the previous buddhas of past world-ages, and he in turn would be followed by others who are yet to come. Even so, Bodhgaya is the eternal starting-point; it is here beneath a pipul-tree that all great buddhas gain buddhahood, for this is the centre of the universe, the indestructible 'Diamond Seat' which alone is preserved from universal conflagration at the end of the world-age. Just as from this point the universe will emerge anew, so the true doctrine will in due course be discovered and spread once more. It is therefore necessary from the start to clarify the use of the term *buddha* for those who are not accustomed to the idea of many buddhas. Gotama of the Śākya Clan was a buddha, not *the* Buddha, and in order to distinguish him from the many other buddhas who will be mentioned, we must know him by his proper appellation, the Śākya-Sage. As such he was known in the earliest times and still is known in Buddhist countries today. It may be objected, of course, that after all he was the only historical Buddha, and for practical purposes still is the only Buddha in some Buddhist lands, notably Ceylon, Burma and Siam. But even in these lands he must be regarded properly as one in a series, while in other countries, India, Tibet, China and Japan, he counts for little amongst the other buddhas and their active counterparts. It has been doubted whether the accounts of his life contain anything of historical worth and even whether the Śākya-Sage was an historical character at all. If the traditional accounts alone be our standard of judgement, he has no greater claim to historical reality than Padma-sambhava, whom the Tibetans call 'the Second Buddha'. At least we are sure of the century in which this second Buddha lived and of the period of his arrival in Tibet.[a] Nevertheless the Śākya-Sage starts the doctrine for us, whether we are believers fortunate enough to be born within the duration of his doctrine (there are alas world-ages in which no buddha manifests himself) or whether we are just scholars, seeking the origins of a religion which is still professed by a large part of mankind and which at least demands our interest and our admiration. Thus it is at Bodhgaya that we begin.

The village lies some six miles south of the modern town of Gaya in Bihar, about 250 miles north-west of Calcutta, and, what is more relevant to us now, about half that distance from Benares, for already 2,500 years ago Benares was an important city, probably frequented then as now by beggars and religious cranks, by propounders of doctrines old and new. About eighty miles away to the north-west of Gaya are the ruins of Rājgir, the ancient capital of Magadha in the earliest days of Buddhism.[b] It was this small kingdom of Magadha that during the third century B.C. became the centre of the first Indian Empire and it seems to have been largely under the patronage of its kings that Buddhism began to develop into a universal religion. Magadha is the heart of Buddhist India, but now only ruins remain to tell their tale. The followers of Islam penetrated to this region in the eleventh and twelfth centuries and with iconoclastic fury destroyed the great places of Buddhism and put its followers to the sword. At that time the 'Diamond-Seat' (*Vajrāsana*) was the site of a vast monastery, which also served as one of the great universities of those times. Remote as this

[a] By the eighth century A.D. the use of the term 'second' in such a context is a mere convention, for all buddhas are envisaged as essentially one in buddhahood.

[b] Magadha corresponds approximately to modern Bihar.

period may seem from the twentieth century, Buddhism was then almost as old to India as Christianity is now to Europe, and throughout this long period, the actual site of the enlightenment of the Śākya-Sage had remained in fact the centre of the Buddhist world. There is no doubt concerning the identity or this place. It is vouched for by the great Emperor Aśoka, who visited the famous tree, or rather its lineal descendant, during the second half of the third century B.C. (pl. 1*a*). At this time the place was already a famous place of pilgrimage and probably had been so ever since the last days of the Sage. It continued to grow in importance and archaeological traces date back to the time of Aśoka. The most circumstantial account of this place as of all Buddhist India has been preserved for us in the travel accounts of the Chinese pilgrim-scholar, Yuan Chwang, who came here in the seventh century.[1] It was then a flourishing concern, housing many hundreds of monks and students, comparable only with the similar institutions that continue in Tibet to this day. But the onslaught of Islam made an end of Buddhism in India, and from the thirteenth to the nineteenth centuries all continuity was lost. The 'Diamond-Seat' was still properly the centre of the universe, but it was no longer in fact the centre of the doctrine. Its significance had become purely mythical. Thus we find a Tibetan writer of the last century making a distinction between the physical (karmic) centre and the religious centre of the universe, a sadly necessitated accommodation to the actual condition of the doctrine. He is commenting on the prerequisites for the leading of the religious life: one must be a human being, one must be born in the centre of the world, one's faculties must be complete, etc. But the centre of the world can no longer apply to Magadha alas, and thus he comments: 'When the text says *centre of the world,* we have to distinguish between a karmic and a religious centre. The first is at the centre of the southern continent, the Diamond-Seat of India. It is the place where the thousand buddhas of the Perfect Age gain buddhahood, and even at the time of universal emptiness it is said that this place is free from harm and destruction and is left, as it were, in space, a vessel from which sprouts the Tree of Enlightenment.[a] It is the physical centre of the chief places of the holy land. But as for the religious centre, this applies to where the Buddhist doctrine now abides. Wherever it is not found, that is a barbarous land. Thus from the time a buddha appeared in the world and for as long as the doctrine continued to exist in India, the karmic centre and the religious centre were one and the same. But now that the Diamond-Seat in India has been seized by heretics and the doctrine there has been destroyed, so far as the idea of a religious centre is concerned, it is just a barbarous place. Conversely although in the time of this Buddha, Tibet was a barbarous country, for there were few humans there and the doctrine was unknown, yet afterwards the number of humans gradually increased, the doctrine made a start there—and in spite of all vicissitudes the true teachings of the buddhas remained unchanged, so that Tibet is now the religious centre.'[b]

But since the last century the site has been reconstituted and the pilgrims have returned. The King of Burma erected a new temple on the site of the old and the Archaeological Department of the British-Indian Government has restored some of the ancient railings, a large number of small votary stūpas, several images and even the Diamond-Seat itself. This is a sandstone slab, now placed once more beneath the pipul-tree, which one may reasonably assume to be a lineal descendant of the original tree of enlightenment. But the site is still in heretic, viz. Hindu, possession. Near-by the Tibetans have built a small monastery, and it is strange now to see in this completely Indian setting a building so typically Tibetan with white-washed walls and brightly painted curling eves. In the main temple is a vast image of Maitreya, the buddha who is next to come. The monks belong to the 'Virtuous Order' which was founded by Tsong-kha-pa, the greatest of Tibetan lamas, in the late

[a] Universal emptiness refers to the condition of voidness which follows upon the general conflagration at the end of each world-age.

[b] *Kun-bzang-bla-ma*, folio 14a.

fourteenth century. Probably few visitors to this place reflect that these outlandish fellows, who despite the heat of central India are still addicted to their buttered tea and still not over-fond of too much washing, represent a firm line of continuity between the Buddhism of central India in the twelfth century and their own Buddhism today.

The Nature of a Buddha

Attempts have been made to explain the historical reality of the Śākya-Sage away as myth. Such an interpretation, however, is quite unhelpful, for it remains completely out of contact with the historical origins that we are attempting to understand. It has been well said: 'The elaboration of a coherent doctrine, the organization of a religious community according to the rules of strict discipline are not just the work of astrologers and mythologists, for they require the calculated intervention of one or several personalities, existing in flesh and blood.'[a] But when we seek to know something certain of this man of flesh and blood, it is then that our perplexities begin. Some of the relevant texts have been translated and discussed by Dr. E. J. Thomas in *The Life of the Buddha as Legend and History*. His conclusions are non-committal and wisely so. Others have not been so guarded, and have attempted to produce a genuine biography, based upon a careful selecting of the texts in the Singhalese (*pāli*) Canon, accepting the factual, rejecting the miraculous. From these attempts there emerges, it is true, a perfectly plausible historical figure, the events of whose life may be resumed in a few words. A young man of royal family is so affected by the vanity of life and all that it contains, that abandoning his parents, his wife and child, he flees to the forest and seeks a spiritual guide. The guides he finds, cannot take him far enough, and he turns alone and unguided to the practice of severe austerities. These prove completely fruitless. Then he remembers that as a boy he has once experienced a condition of mindful happiness and so he resolves to place himself in this

[a] E. Lamotte, *La Légende du Buddha*, *RHR*, 1948, p. 39.

condition again and if possible to progress from there.[2] In this he succeeds; progressing from stage to stage, he achieves the end of his quest, and knows that he is a buddha, an enlightened one. He gains followers, whom he leads along the way, which he himself has trodden alone, and so great becomes their number, that a properly constituted order is formed. At the age of eighty he leaves this life, passing into a condition of complete *nirvāṇa,* which he has been qualified to enter ever since his achieving of buddhahood.

In India, past and present, there is little of the unusual in such a life as this, and so it fails entirely to explain the extraordinary success of his doctrine; it is this which is of chief interest to the historian. We may as well draw attention at once to those elements in the story, which endow it with historical reality. First there are the many references to established place-names, of which four have chief importance, the Lumbini Grove near Kapilavastu, where he was born, Bodhgaya, where he achieved enlightenment, the deer-park outside Benares, where he preached the first sermon, and Kuśinagara, where he finally passed into complete nirvāna. These places have all been identified with certainty and there is no doubt that they represent very early traditions, which fix the main events of his life to the actual ground. If his life were mere myth, one would not expect him to be born amongst the Śākya clan. It would have been easy to invent a dynasty more worthy of a universal 'conqueror'. If it had been a matter of just asserting the pure nature of his birth, myth could easily have arranged for him to be born on a lotus, much in the manner that Padmasambhava, 'the Second Buddha', was born later. But it must have been known that he was born of the wife of the Rāja Śuddhodana, and so legend, setting to work at a secondary stage, had to resort to more cumbersome means of indicating his natal purity.[a] He descends into her womb from the

[a] For a precise elaboration of this argument see A. Foucher, *La Vie du Bouddha,* p. 32 ff. This work is of capital importance for relating the events of the legend to the actual sites.

heavens and she remains free from any thought of man. He is born from her side as she supports herself against a tree in the Lumbini Grove. This place is marked for us by the pillar of the Emperor Aśoka discovered at this place, of which the modern name is Rummindei, just within Nepal's Indian frontier. Thus the site is fixed with certainty from the third century B.C., and as it is unlikely that the spot was invented for the benefit of Aśoka, one may assume that it already represented a well-established tradition. It seems that the occurence of his death can be fixed with even greater certainty. Not only is the actual site of the final nirvāna at Kuśinagara (modern Kasia) identified, but it is also likely that a certain stūpa (funeral-mound) at Piprawa in the same area contained the ashes of the Śākya-Sage. The site was excavated in 1898 and a casket was found inscribed with a script which appears to be pre-Aśokan: 'This deposit of relics of the blessed Buddha of the Śākyas is of Sukiti and his brothers with their sisters, their sons and their wives.' This may well be linked with the traditional account of the funeral rites, found in the texts. He died near Kuśinagara and after some dispute the ashes were shared with seven other cities, who laid claim to them, Magadha, Vaiśālī, Kapilavastu, Allakappa, Rāmagrāma, Pipphalivana and Pāvā. So originally eight funeral-mounds, enshrining the shares of the relics, were built. Of these one may have been found.[a]

So there is no need to doubt the historical reality of the Śākya-Sage, whatever uncertainties may attend the writing of a full biography. For this the chief difficulty consists in the fact that it is impossible to separate the historical person from his mythical religious setting. There is a development of the various legends that embellish the accounts of his life, but one cannot simply remove all strange and miraculous elements and present a person who is in himself a sufficient explanation for the immediate success and the particular development of the

[a] see E. J. Thomas, *Life*, p. 161, and de la Vallée Poussin, *L'Inde aux temps des Mauryas*, p. 144.

doctrine. Even in India an ascetic surrounded by a following of monks and faithful lay-folk, would have remained this and no more, a sage like countless others. It is sometimes suggested that it is all too easy for a man to become eternized in India to the stage of quasi-deification, and in our times Gandhi has been quoted as an example. This may be so, but only in so far as the man can be identified with some idea which makes a wide appeal. In Gandhi's case it was the cause of national independence and his memory remains a sacred one, so long as the cause is remembered. But here we have something clearly on a vaster scale, which for 2,500 years has retained a hold on almost half of mankind. The idea which he represented and the ideal which he typified is made clear both in the monuments and in the texts. Variations may appear in different times and places, but the theme remains the same. It is this theme that has provided Buddhism with its continuity and its universality, namely the idea of a buddha, without which Buddhism would never have become distinguished from the many other religions that India has produced.

Unless we are prepared to rest content with a biography of the Śākya-Sage which is based on a selective choice of passages, it is important to realize that the early texts, as they stand, and the existing archaeological evidence in no way permit the reconstruction of the life of a normal man. Reason may well suggest that a normal man must stand behind this example of a buddha which is presented to us, but it is quite another matter to find him. Any such attempt must leave the religious and mythical implications to one side, and without these nothing in the religious sphere can be explained at all. Even when dealing with normal human greatness, history is unable to go to the root of the matter, although the man concerned may be well known from contemporary records. No one can finally explain why Napoleon or Alexander the Great was successful. We may know the attendant circumstances, but not the inherent causes of a man's activity. Thus even if we possessed a contemporary biography of the Śākya-Sage, it is unlikely that we should be able to understand better the source of his success which is to be sought as much in his contemporaries and in his followers as in himself. It is because they believed in him, that his doctrine spread, and they have left testimony of their belief in stone and in the written word. It would be indeed of interest to know to what extent he identified himself with their belief, but that we can never know, and the absence of that knowledge does not prevent us from following the course of his religion through the centuries.

A buddha, although in his last life a man in appearance like other men, is of rare occurrence. His buddhahood is the fruit of continuous striving through innumerable previous births and the belief in rebirth is an essential part of the Buddhist world-view.[3] When his course is fully run, that is to say, when he has achieved perfection of morality, concentration and wisdom, his buddhahood in what will now be his last birth, becomes inevitable. His final achievement is thus predestined, by no higher power, but by force of his own acts in the past. In theory, as was soon realized, there need be no limit to the number of those who were striving, but in the earliest times the followers of the Śākya-Sage were so impressed by the wonder of this difficult and rare achievement, that they considered it almost super-human. In this they went perhaps beyond the requirements of the theory. It would have been sufficient for him to have had a normal human birth, for until he sat beneath the pipul-tree of Bodhgaya, he was still not yet a buddha. But they chose to see his birth as super-human, influenced no doubt by the consideration that it was predestined. It is possible to understand in this sense the title by which the Sage seems to have referred to himself in life, namely as *tathāgata,* he who has *thus come.* There has been some discussion over the meaning of this term, for if analysed grammatically, its meaning is not clear, as it might equally well mean *thus gone.* It seems, however, that such a term could only properly be applicable after the final nirvāna, whereas if we are to trust the texts, it was used by the sage himself during his lifetime. A more subtle interpretation would be *thus achieved,* where *thus* stands for the ineffable conception of enlightenment, and indeed later on the term *thus-ness* (*tathatā*) is commonly used in this sense. In any case this title *tathāgata* is used as a synonym for *buddha,* and comes to be applied to any being of this rank, historical or not. In the case of the sage, however, to whom this term was first applied, some special connotation was seemingly intended, and *thus come,* in fact, *come as expected,* and so predestined, seems the most plausible interpretation. Whether this is so or not, it was as such that the Śākya-Sage was regarded by many. He was already perfect, some imagined, before he descended to the womb, and so his life on earth was a mere display for the benefit of all living beings. This of course is in any case the implication of many of the legends of his life, and in so far as they repeat these legends, all early schools, even the Theravādins (the present *hīnayānists* of southern Asia) subscribe to this view.[a] In some cases it became the accepted view, seemingly amongst another school, the Lokottaravādins, who were *believers in the supramundane idea,* which is the meaning of their name. Another related idea, which is properly non-Buddhist, is that of the great man, the hero, who may be recognized in infancy by thirty-two physical marks; well-set feet, long fingers, soft skin, etc. In the case of the Śākya-Sage the presence of these signs was said to indicate either a universal monarch or a buddha. The term 'conqueror' (*jina*), which also became the title of Mahāvīra, the leader of the Jains, was also applicable to the Sage. These various terms became almost clichés and were applicable to any buddha, as was the term *tathāgatha.* As we shall see, later on the expression 'possessed of the thirty-two major marks and the eighty minor marks of perfection' became part of the traditional description of the Five Buddhas of Space, who are in essence cosmologic-meditational forms and so without need of human form.[b] It is

[a] Although nowadays the Buddhists of southern Asia refer to themselves quite happily as followers of the *hīnayāna* (inferior way), the Tibetans have by no means forgotten the sense of opprobrium attached to this name.

[b] see *Buddhist Texts,* p. 249 ff.; also p. 210 below.

possible to see in these various tendencies to deify a buddha a degeneration of the true teaching, for which the credulous lay-folk, as opposed to the monks, have been responsible. But it is artificial to set up any real distinction between monks and lay-folk, and totally misleading to go one stage further, and explain away the Great Way, the Mahāyāna, as a degeneration, for which popular notions were responsible. The monks themselves are fervent enough in praise of their master, so there seems little need to blame the lay-supporters. In all schools there may have been a few who doubted the value of this devotion, but their opinion has counted for little. A buddha is essentially one who has achieved the fruit of his strivings through innumerable past lives. It is the telling of these tales of past activities in other lives, which fills so much of the sculptured stone on early monuments. Either born as animal or man, the would-be buddha is ever sacrificing his life for the sake of others. There are large collections of these tales in all the extant canons, and so texts and stones may vouch for one another. In stone there is no sculptured testimony earlier than the second century B.C. and the texts were probably committed to writing even later, but both are clearly based on much earlier traditions and in any case they represent the earliest Buddhism that we know.

Thus there were already two ways in which people migh conceive of the Śākya-Sage. From the first he presented himself as a perfected buddha, for it was as such that his followers met with him. Secondly it was accepted that his perfection was the result of altruistic striving through many births. Thus he is both the sage who has seen existence to its end and the hero who strives untiringly for the welfare of others. Both these aspects of a buddha are part of the earliest known Buddhism.

A being who is set on buddhahood, is known throughout all his lives of striving as a *bodhisattva*. The original meaning of this term may possibly have been *set on enlightenment*, but the sanskritized form, now in current use in European works on Buddhism, means *enlightenment-being*. The Tibetans when they later came to translate the term, understood it as *hero of the thought of enlightenment*. In any case the intended meaning is clear enough. Thus there was a tendency for the term *buddha* to imply quiescent wisdom, and *bodhisattva* altruistic activity. Some schools stressed the need of one rather than the other, and thus there gradually developed that division between the Buddhist schools into the Lesser Vehicle and the Great. In the following chapter more will be said on this subject, but it is of importance to make it clear from the start that this double development exits in Buddhism from the earliest times. It is easy now to regard the Great Vehicle as the later development simply because it continued to develop. As is well known, it replaced many of the older texts by new ones, but often in order to give better expression to old ideas which required re-emphasis. There is little in their teachings, which is not a logical development of what had gone before. To what extent the other schools, ridiculed as lesser, developed their doctrines, we cannot tell. They continued to exist in India up to the last (thirteenth century), but of their later history we have but the slightest knowledge. The one surviving school is that of the Theravādins of Ceylon, Burma and Indo-China, but their development was cut short very early by their separation from the Indian mainland. They represent an early phase of Buddhism, but they cannot be taken as the full measure of all that Buddhism stands for.

The Nature of Enlightenment

The experience of the sage, as he sat beneath the tree, is fundamental to Buddhism. It is the *alpha* and *omega* of the doctrine. Without it there would have been no buddha and thus no doctrine to teach, and unless there had been followers ever confident of its final realization, there would be no one to continue the doctrine. Buddhism did not spread because of a gospel, or because of the good news that its followers brought. It spread by means of an experience, which was tested and proved at every stage. We need but to know the nature of this experience, and we shall know the secret of the strength of the doctrine itself. Unfortunately the texts help scarcely at all in this crucial matter. The term that most commonly occurs to describe it is *nirvāṇa,* which means 'blowing out', 'blowing away', 'extinction' or 'disappearance', and indeed the simile of a lamp which is extinguished is often used to illustrate the process.[a] In what way the Buddhist trance distinguished itself from other kinds of early Indian yoga, no one has ever shown satisfactorily.[4] Yet it claims that its goal is the one and only condition of the deathless state, the final end of craving, the one and final extinction of passion, of wrath, of stupidity. We must renounce the task of plumbing the significance of nirvāna, simply because it evades all definition. Nevertheless much may still be learned from the events of Bodhgaya, for tradition continued to be more interested in the positive powers of a buddha than in the state of deathless calm that he had achieved for himself. We can also learn how the Buddhists have conceived of life and all that it contains, matter of the greatest relevance to any study of Buddhist developments. But the experience of the Śākya-Sage, which started the doctrine and which has remained its final goal ever since, the *raison d'être* of the doctrine cannot be summarily defined.

The earliest accounts describe it in terms of a threefold knowledge: knowledge of his own previous births, knowledge of the births and deaths of all other beings and knowledge of his release from the whole process. The knowledge of release was elaborated into a twelvefold causal nexus which he in his wisdom had now overcome. Traditionally, however, this scheme became the incentive to the religious life and it is still unfailingly represented in the porch of every Tibetan Buddhist temple. Such a representation is shown on pl. 2 and thus the Buddhist conception of existence may be shown by its description.

A monster, the Lord of Death (*Māra* in Sanskrit, *gShin-rje* in

[a] *Buddhist Texts,* p. 92 ff. and E. J. Thomas, *Early Buddhist Scriptures,* p. 97 ff.

Tibetan), is shown clasping a circle in his teeth and between his arms and legs. The circle represents all phenomenal existence and it is held by Death, for all that lives must die, and live and die again. It is from this dreadful fate, from deliverance from the circle, that Buddhism offers release. Around the edge of the circle are twelve small inset pictures. These represent the twelvefold causal nexus which binds living beings to the misery of the inner circle. At the time of his enlightenment, the sage is supposed to have first worked backwards through the series, beginning with the idea of death, for if once a man were free of death, he would be free of the whole circle. As each concept occurs to his mind, he seeks the previous conditioning concept, going back as far as he may go.

Death is illustrated by a man carrying a corpse to its place of disposal.

The necessary condition of death is birth.

Birth is represented by a birth-scene.[a]

The necessary condition of birth is growth, the whole process of becoming.

The process of becoming is represented by a pregnant woman.

The necessary condition of the process of becoming is the act of appropriation.

The act of appropriation is represented by a man grasping fruit from a tree.

The necessary condition of the act of appropriation is desire.

Desire is represented by a drinking scene, for the Sanskrit term used here for *desire* is *thirst*.[a]

The necessary condition of desire is the sense of feeling.

Feeling is represented by a man with an arrow in his eye.

The necessary condition of feeling is contact.

Contact is represented by a kiss.

The necessary condition of contact is the possession of senses and the spheres of sense.

[a] On our example of the wheel the birth-scene (representing Birth) and the drinking-scene (representing Desire) have been mistakenly transposed.

The senses are represented by a house with many windows.

The necessary condition for the operation of the senses is the existence of personality.

Personality is represented by a boat on a journey.

The necessary condition of personality is the existence of consciousness.

Consciousness is represented by a monkey plucking fruit.

The necessary condition of consciousness is the existence of elemental impulses.

The impulses are represented by the pots which a potter is making.

The necessary condition of these impulses is absence of knowledge.

Absence of knowledge is represented by an old blind woman.

Attempts have been made to discover a logical sequence of ideas from this ill-sorted list, both by early commentators and by European scholars. But no general relationship between the terms can be found, which will relate in the same manner any two consecutive terms. The list is best understood as it is first presented to us, as a spontaneous searching back and back into the origins of death and rebirth, and apart from the stimulation and satisfaction of desire which maintains the process, and the existence of the mental and physical components of which a personality with his active senses is formed, no origin can be found beyond absence of knowledge.[5]

At the centre of the circle are depicted a cock, a snake and a pig, representing passion, wrath and ignorance. These three at the hub keep the wheel turning, representing, as they do, the essential nature of existence. Around this centre there is a small inner circle. In the left half monks and lay-folk are moving upwards on their way to happy rebirths. In the right half naked figures are being dragged downwards on their way to woeful rebirths.

The rest of the circle, which is divided into six segments, merely illustrates their possible destinations. The three top segments represent three comparatively happy spheres of existence, the heavens at the top, the realm of the titans to the right and the world of men to the left. The gods must be conceived of as mortals who are spared all the discomforts and unpleasantness of existence, only to be afflicted the more by the thought of the ephemeral nature of their happiness. Historically they represent the gods and godlings of early India, Brahmā, Indra and the rest. On more than one occasion, however, Tibetans have indicated the inhabitants of wealthy western lands as suitable modern prototypes. 'Although they enjoy during their lifetime the utmost comfort and luxury, no thought of the holy doctrine comes to them, for they pass their time in pleasures. Their life lasts a full world-age, yet without it seeming a moment, their time imperceptibly comes to an end and death approaches. As it approaches, the five signs of death manifest themselves. By their own light gods illuminate their surroundings for a league, a mile or some such distance, but now the time has come, the brilliance fades. However gods sit on their thrones, they cannot feel discomfort, but now they do not want to stay there at all, and are unhappy in their discomfort. Their garlands of flowers do not age, however much time passes, but now the flowers die. However long they wear their clothes, no smell attaches to them, but now they become old and smell. No sweat comes from their bodies, but now sweat appears. So they know they will die and are very unhappy. Their god-friends and the god-maidens also know that such a one will die, but they are unable to approach, and throwing flowers from afar, they express good wishes: "When you pass away from here, may you be born in the world of men, and having practised virtue, may you be born in heaven once more." '[a] But it is more than likely that he will fall into one of the hells, which

[a] *Kun-bzang-blama*, folio 67*a*. This quotation should be sufficient to distinguish the Buddhist conception of a god from that in use elsewhere. It becomes, however, only a matter of terminology, for gods in the sense of great beings find their place in the doctrine later on. The term *god* (skr. *deva*, tib. *lha*) is carefully avoided and they are identified with one of the buddha-bodies. See note 11.

the poor fellow knows only too well, and our author assures us that he suffers exceedingly.

Heaven is the reward for the practise of virtue, but good works alone are not sufficient to earn buddhahood. The titans are the traditional enemies of the gods and so were given a place in the circle, although at first they were not included. Quarrelsome jealous people are born in their realm, where they spend their time fighting with the neighbouring gods, who have all the advantages. The wounds of the gods heal at once and for them war is fine sport, but the titans endure all the miseries and butchery of warfare without respite. Death is not allowed them until they have served their time. The chief misery of human existence is knowledge of the certainty of death. There is, however, one overwhelming advantage in being born as a man. It is possible to practise the doctrine, and thus it presents the surest way to buddhahood. These then are the three spheres of happy (or comparatively happy) rebirth.

Of the three places of woeful rebirth the most tolerable is that of the animals, who are to be seen to the bottom left. They either kill one another, or are ill-treated and slain by men. To the bottom right are unhappy spirits, who are tormented in various ways by hunger and thirst and by heat and cold. They are shown with large bellies, which can never be filled and small mouths burning with thirst. Avaricious people are born here. At the very bottom are the various hells, hot and cold, and all equally unpleasant with their different tortures. Still all these torments have their end, and when one's misdemeanours have been paid for, one will be reborn in a happier condition.

Thus the life-process offers nothing but endless misery. Happiness is never real and final, for it must eventually turn into unhappiness. Tradition relates that the sage looked back with his divine eye and saw the continuity of his previous lives going back into a beginningless past; he saw beings dying and being reborn according to the force of their past acts in the various spheres of existence; finally he knew that he was free from the force of sensual desire, of the desire for existence and from the force of ignorance.[a]

There is one other event during the process of enlightenment to which we must refer, for it has remained part of Buddhist iconography until the present day. It was related that Māra, the Lord of Death and holder of the circle of existence, led a personal assault upon the sage, as he sat beneath the tree. First he taunted him about his wasted appearance and tempted him to return once more to the joys of life. Having failed in this, he attempted to disturb his equaniminity by turning the forces of evil against him. Having failed again, he challenged him to produce a witness to his fitness for buddhahood, and the sage, touching the earth with the fingers of his right hand, called upon the Earth as his witness and the Earth quaked in testimony. Likewise in all the stories of his previous lives, the earth by quaking had borne witness to his heroic acts of self-sacrifice. When later a buddha was cut in stone, it was by the 'earth-witness posture' that the moment of enlightenment was typified (pl. 4).

Sarnāth

The ancient deer-park of Benares lies a few miles outside the city. It goes by the modern name of Sarnāth and is now a park of ruins. Most impressive of the ruins is the great cylindrical memorial mound, founded by the Emperor Aśoka. Near-by are the foundations and steps and low-lying remains of a great mediaeval monastery (pl. 1*b*). When Yuan Chwang visited this place in the seventh century, there were 1,500 monks of the Lesser Vehicle. The best of the archaeological remains have been arranged in a pleasant little museum, happily built in a modern Indian style. Far less congruous is a

[a] These three forces (*āśravas*, literally: 'flows') are part of a very early pre-Buddhist technical vocabulary. They become mere clichés in the early doctrinal period as an elaboration of the one fundamental cause of misery, Desire. See Har Dayal, *Bodhisattva Doctrine*, p. 116 ff.

new Buddhist temple, erected largely by subscriptions of European Buddhists. In plan it resembles a small Christian chapel rather than a Buddhist shrine. No way is provided for ceremonial circumambulation of the central image, an essential feature of Indian Buddhist temples in the past and of their Tibetan prototypes today. Around the upper walls the chief scenes from the life of the Śākya-Sage have been painted by a Japanese artist in simple humanistic style. An Indian youth, a modern Buddhist layman, points out from the pictures the main events of the Buddha's life. He represents a new movement which bases itself upon a selective interpretation of some of the early texts. Shorn of its miracles and its obscure philosophizing, Buddhism is presented as a rational way of life for the modern rational man. One may well contrast these modernists with the inmates of the Tibetan Monastery at Bodhgaya, to which reference was made above. The former attempt to restore the original teaching of the Śākya-Sage, freeing it from the 'superstitions and misrepresentations' of later times. It thereby looses all continuity with the past, rejects, accepts, interprets in accordance with a modern rationalist standpoint, and so fails to represent any historical form of Buddhism. The Theravādin tradition of Ceylon has lent itself most easily to this treatment, and it is a little sad when its genuine followers take part in such a modernizing movement. They are not guilty so much of misrepresentation as of wilful suppression of certain essential tenets of their doctrine. The Tibetans on the other hand remain quite unaffected by the views of the modern world. They continue trustingly with the faith and the practice, which is an accumulation of centuries. They have now no thought of exercising critical judgement, of explaining, of justifying. Their monastery is built on the historic site of the enlightenment, but they have no historical sense of the person of the Śākya-Sage. Maitreya is in fact more real to them. For the founding of their order they look back to Tsong-kha-pa; for order and discipline they look to their abbot, and behind him to the Dalai Lama, who founded their monastery. These two kinds of Buddhism represent completely different world-views, which are mutually incomprehensible. It is our task in this chapter to show some of their common antecedents.

The Doctrine

Full enlightenment achieved, the sage made his way from Bodhgaya to Benares. In those days this was a journey of ten days or so, and even in the twentieth century this would still be no unusual hardship to a practiser of the religious life. The first sermon has assumed a traditional form consisting of the four truths and the eightfold path. These have been discussed sufficiently elsewhere and it is unnecessary to do more than to list them here.[a] The truths are (1) the existence of misery, (2) the cause of misery which is desire, (3) the end of misery which is the uprooting of desire and (4) the way of ending misery, which is the eightfold path. The path consists of the right kind of views, intention, speech, action, livelihood, effort, mindfulness, concentration.

These eight can also be grouped under the simpler heading of (1) *good morals,* (2) *mental concentration* and (3) *wisdom,* which we will consider briefly in turn. *Morals* can be simply explained in terms of the ten prohibitions: (1) not to take life, (2) not to steal, (3) to avoid unchastity, (4) not to lie, (5) not to slander, (6) not to insult, (7) not to chatter, (8) not to covet, (9) not to give way to anger and (10) not to doubt. There is another set of ten intended for monks: the first four as above and then (5) not to take intoxicants, (6) not to eat out of regulated hours, (7) not to use garlands and perfumes, (8) not to sleep on broad beds, (9) not to take part in singing, dancing and similar festivities and (10) not to acquire money or jewels. In the regular monastic discipline which was later developed, the number of these rules was vastly extended. In Tibet a set of 258 rules, which was formulated by the Mūla-sarvāstivādin School in north-west

[a] see Har Dayal, *Bodhisattva Doctrine*, pp. 156–60.

India about 2000 years ago, is still in use. In well-ordered monasteries (e.g. Jiwong, see below page 227) it is read twice monthly in a general confession.

Mental concentration involved the use of various techniques of meditation. In general an attempt is made to withdraw the mind gradually from sense objects and conceptual notions, until it is steadied and calm. Simple as this process may seem, it involved months and sometimes years of practice. The type of meditation has always depended upon the type of wisdom which represented the world-view of the practiser. Thus in the case of the early schools no external support was required, for a state of passivity was the goal. All the elements of the life-stream were stilled and nothing took their place. Simple devices were, however, used, such as a flame or a stick in order to assist the development of one-pointedness of mind.[a] Later the goal changed. The practiser now strove to identify himself as the centre of existence. Phenomenal existence is just an imagined form of essential being with which one must oneself become identified. Thus the types of meditation changed as well. This will become less obscure when we go on to discuss the various kinds of wisdom. Here it is only necessary to indicate that mental concentration (if we are to use this term, and it is difficult in English to find a better one) can imply very different processes.

Of the eight items grouped together as the eightfold path, right intention, speech, action, livelihood and mindfulness may be grouped together as morals. These require no special elucidation. Concentration has been briefly referred to. This involves many complicated notions, and much more will be said on the subject in later chapters. Right effort applies to both morals and concentration and presents no special difficulty. There thus remains one item, right views, which belongs to the third category of *wisdom*. It is here that most difficulties are to be found, for the later Buddhists were never finally agreed upon the nature of right views. The omniscience

[a] see de la Vallée Poussin, *Études et Matériaux*, pp. 82–100.

of the Śākya-Sage was not the kind that could settle ultimate questions once and for all. His omniscience consisted of the threefold knowledge, knowledge of his previous births, the divine knowledge which sees all beings dying and being reborn in the various spheres of existence, and the knowledge of his own release. This threefold knowledge was attainable by any of his followers when they had finished their course. A buddha was supposed to possess ten powers,[a] but these are little more than an elaboration of the same threefold knowledge, and contain nothing that a follower could not be expected to acquire. There is no doubt that the early followers thought of the Śākya-Sage as infinitely superior to themselves. Hence the mythical religious developments that we have already discussed. When thought was applied to the matter however, it was realized that he excelled them in only one matter, namely in having gone first and so in being their leader—unless (and it was this thought that produced the Great Vehicle) they had never realized the final nirvāna. They had been fobbed off, as it were, with a state of trance, which was something less, and in order to reach the final goal, where they too would be buddhas, they must run the full course of a *bodhisattva*.[b] This begins to anticipate later considerations, but we wish to emphasize that, however great the respect that was due to a buddha, in no school of Buddhism could he be finally conceived of as possessing higher knowledge, that was not eventually attainable by his followers.

Often the Śākya-Sage was questioned on ultimate matters, but he either preserved silence or evaded the question. Thus he would never say whether the world was eternal or not, whether the self existed or not, whether a monk, who had attained nirvāna, was existent or not. The most the questioner could expect in reply would be the simile of a fire that is extinguished, and more often than not, he would be answered by silence.[6] We may reasonably conclude that the Śākya-Sage did not know and was not interested in knowing, for in the condition of enlightenment which he embodied, all these questions lost their

[a] *Buddhist Texts*, p. 110. [b] *ibid.*, p. 120 ff.

relevance. In his daily activity be compared himself to the good doctor who healed the wound without wasting time to enquire how it had been caused. This view may well have been acceptable, as long as there was a personality such as his available to guarantee it. But the questions would still be asked, and so it was inevitable that different views would be adopted in some of these matters and that disputes would arise in the order.

Before we can examine some of these questions, it is necessary to know how the early Buddhists conceived of existence generally and human personality in particular. The fundamental notion is that of impermanence, for it is this that underlies the fourfold truth concerning misery. As was seen from our consideration of the Wheel of Existence, the process is apparently beginningless and continual. It can end only with nirvāna. Beings are born in various spheres, are conscious of the feelings of pain or pleasure, of the perceptions of sight and sound and so on, and of impulses, such as courage, equanimity, modesty, carelessness, indolence, anger, deceit, etc., which motivate their being. Thus personality was conceived of as five-fold, namely as: (1) body, (2) feelings, (3) perceptions, (4) impulses and (5) consciousness.

Body, like any other substance, consists of the four elements, earth (hair, flesh, nails, teeth, bones, etc., in fact whatever is hard), water (gall, pus, blood, sweat, etc., whatever is fluid), fire ('that by which a man heats himself, consumes himself, worries himself and digests his food') and wind ('in the stomach, in the lower body, that which passes through the limbs and that which is breathed in and out'). These sets of five components and four elements are especially important to our study, as they are employed symbolically in the tantras.

As there is no abiding principle anywhere, the body is not distinguishable from any other matter, all of which may possess sense-data, visual, auditory, olfactory, flavorous or tactile. All these elements are thought of as material. Thus a silent bell will comprise visual and tactile-type elements. When it is struck, the action causes latent auditory-type elements to manifest themselves. On the other hand an eye possesses visual-sense elements, an ear auditory-sense elements and so on. There are thus a total of four gross elements, earth, water, fire and air, and ten subtle elements, five sense elements and five sensation elements. All forms and bodies consist of combinations of these. All these elements are material but conditioned, that is to say, they manifest themselves in dependance on one another.

Mental elements are more numerous and it would be useless to list them all. They represent all mental activities listed as more or less arbitrary groups. There are ten general elements, headed by feeling and perception (two of the components of personality) and including such items as will, sensation, understanding, memory, etc. There are ten good elements, belief, courage, attentiveness, etc., six obscuring elements, ignorance, carelessnesses, indolence, etc., ten vicious elements, anger, hypocrisy, deceit, etc., and so on. Even the notion of impermanence that attaches to all the elements is conceived of materialistically. Thus there are separate elements for origination, continuance and decrepitude. At any one moment one of these three elements must be in collusion with any of the other elements, thus producing its momentary origination, its momentary continuance and its momentary decrepitude prior to its non-manifestation.[7] Such a philosophical system may at first seem difficult to grasp. One has to bear in mind that no difference is felt between what we should call material elements and mental concepts. If a name can be given, the name immediately represents a thing. Indeed these elements of existence might well be referred to as 'things', but the *element* seems to be the generally acceptable term. The Sanskrit term for them is *dharma,* presumably in the sense of an ultimately real thing. For these elements were held to be the only real things in the whole circle of existence. A certain number of these elements manifesting themselves together in mutual dependance would appear as the objects which we think we know. Always present are two elements, known as *pertaining* (*prāpti*) and *non-pertaining* (*aprāpti*). The elements which arise together in accordance with the preceding causes are held together by force of the pertaining-element and those that do not belong are kept away by means of the non-pertaining-element.

A person is therefore just a stream of elements, which holds together thanks to the *pertaining*-element, so long as the *life-duration*-element continues to manifest itself. Homogeneity in such a stream is maintained by a *generality*-element (*nikāyasabhāgatā*). Every element manifests itself just momentarily, but in any such stream the majority of elements that continued to manifest themselves would be the same. The whole of existence is just like the effects produced by a kaleidoscope. Only when one has grasped the idea of this system, does the Buddhist conception of impermanence gain full force.[a]

Neither the Śākya-Sage nor his followers invented this system. They merely accepted the philosophical conceptions of their times, and in those times everything was conceived of materialistically. It is in such a context as this that one has to understand the early Buddhist doctrine of 'no-self' or 'soullessness' as some have chosen to interpret it. To introduce the idea of a soul into such a system would simply mean the addition of yet another material element called soul. Such a soul-element is to be found in some other early Indian philosophical systems, but Buddhism rejected it. The identity of this soul is denied in a way that would be absurd if it were being conceived of in the idealistic manner of later times, let alone in any Christian sense. Thus we read: 'The eye, O monks, is not the Self (soul). That which is not the Self is not mine; that belongs not to me; what I am not, that is not my Self. Thus should one who possesses right knowledge, regard his own being. The nose, O monks, is not the Self, etc.' And so on for tongue, body and mind.[b]

It was generally accepted by the early schools that there was no abiding entity, and this was felt to be a problem. On the

[a] For the complete lists of these elements see Th. Stcherbatsky, *The Central Conception of Buddhism*, upon which this summary is largely based.

[b] *Suttanikāya*, IV 2 (Günther, *Seelenproblem*, p. 50).

one hand it was taught that every act would bear its fruits (and this is the basis of Buddhist morality), and yet there was no person to bear these consequences. Without some conception of a personality the whole doctrine would seem to loose its force. The final life in which buddhahood was achieved was all very well, but how could one really be moved to right action, speech and thought, if one thought in terms of future lives? The symbolism of the wheel would instil no horror in any personal sense, but it could instil horror in its totality. Thus striving would only be reasonable if one strove for the totality as part of the totality, and so we are led to the ideal of the *bodhisattva* as a logical development. But until this ideal was conceived, the problem remained largely unsolved. Indeed a theory of a 'person' (*pudgala*) was developed by one school, the Vātsīputrīyas. They suggested as non-committedly as possible that it was neither eternal, nor non-eternal, neither identical with the five components of personality, nor different from them. But whereas the authority of the master could render acceptable vagaries of this kind, his followers could not put forward such propositions with impunity. The idea of something being neither identical nor different was easily shown to be nonsense by the other schools, and so the *pudgala* remained a sectarian notion. There was, however, one element that was to assume an increasing importance, namely consciousness. This is one of the five components of personality and it was inevitable, for empirical reasons, that it should become the chief of the five.[8]

But there seems to be no doubt that most of the early schools preferred to represent nirvāna as a blank, like space or as a non-manifestation of something which was previously manifest (e.g. a light which has been extinguished). As nirvāna and space and non-manifestation are namable concepts, they were also liable to be listed as elements (*dharmas*), but they differed from all the others in that they were unconditioned, that they became manifest singly and independently in the absence of other elements. This at least was the view of the Sarvāstivādins, who believed as their name suggests, that everything exists. All the elements exist all the time in their self-nature, but they become manifest only in accordance with preceding causes. One has now to translate the progress of a persevering Buddhist into these strange terms. He must understand himself and all that he perceives as things, which possess no self-nature. He and they and the sense-relations that relate them are nothing but the concerted play of conditioned elements. He must learn therefore by continual mindfulness and proper action to bring this interplay gradually under control. Wisdom itself is but an element, but its continual manifestation would prevent the manifestation of elements opposed to it in their self-nature. When by the practice of morals and concentration, only those elements which were not opposed to it, viz. pure elements, manifested themselves, nirvāna was attainable, temporarily during life and finally at death, when the pure elements would finally become non-manifest.

Many objections can be raised against such a system. Although the whole process is conditioned from beginningless time, right thought and right action are held to be a personal responsibility. One can choose in one's folly to go round in the wheel, or one can decide to take action which will bring freedom as its final consequence. Yet there is no person to take this decision. If everything is conditioned from the start, there can be no attaining of something essentially unconditioned, for by reason of its self-nature it is precluded from becoming what it essentially is not. Early Buddhist philosophy was thinking in terms of two planes of existence, both equally real, on the one hand the elements of phenomenal existence (*saṃsāra*) and on the other the elements of nirvāna and space, and there could be no logical connection between them. By no means did all the early schools subscribe to these views, some including in their canon the books that set forth such views, some rejecting them as not being the master's word. It should be mentioned perhaps that the Theravādins of southern Asian countries, the only early sect that has survived to our times and thus the only modern

'Hīnayānists', do subscribe to these views, or rather should do so, if their beliefs are to accord with the contents of their canon.

But other schools of thought were active, and many were the views expressed. All the early sects, however, seem to have been thinking in terms of ultimately real elements. Some, unlike the Sarvāstivādins, did not regard nirvāna as real in this sense, but they agreed on the self-nature of all the other elements. Just as the early Buddhist tirades against a real self seem to imply a wide-spread belief in a soul-element, so the violence with which the doctrine of the real nature of the elements later came to be attacked, suggests that this view was firmly established.

It is at this stage that we pass to doctrines which are generally regarded as later developments. Such a term is likely to be misleading, for it carries with it a suggestion of spuriousness. The propagators of these doctrines were indeed accused of putting aside the master's teachings and writing new ones of their own. It has already been suggested that the Śākya-Sage was not interested in philosophical definition. His early followers therefore did their best to interpret the teachings in terms of the rather crude philosophical conceptions of the time. There is no reason to doubt that many of the sayings in the early sūtras go back to the Śākya-Sage himself, but they have been so mixed with interpolations and pure inventions, many of which merely express the ideas of his followers, that it is impossible to separate the earlier from the later in every case. The section of the canon dealing specifically with philosophical definition (*abhidharma*) is certainly a later production. It was inevitable that sooner or later some schools would no longer be content with the contents of the sūtras as they then found them, either for the reason that they expressed themselves by means of conceptions that were held to be outmoded or that they failed to express the doctrine lucidly as it had originally been intended. Thus although the master had made no pronouncements on the nature of phenomenal existence, fixed views on the subject were not only being held by some schools, but even attributed to the master. In days when textual criticism was unknown, or at best counted for little, there was one solution to the problem, namely to write new sūtras, in which you gave what you believed to be a correct expression of the doctrine, adding a quasi-historical setting, and attributing it to the Śākya-Sage himself. Once begun, there was no end to the producing of texts. To what extent these texts were included in recognized canons by the sects then flourishing in India, cannot be known. By this time the *pāli* canon of the Singhalese Theravadins was largely protected from the incorporation of still later texts by its geographical separation from central and north-western India which seems to have been the centre of these developments. The Indian texts proper have mostly been lost. There is nothing that begins to represent a complete canon; indeed manifold as the texts came to be, it may be that no comprehensive collection ever existed. The texts that were in common use in India from the eighth century on were assiduously collected and translated by the Tibetans, and the piece-meal manner in which they were accumulated, suggests that no one at that time thought in terms of a complete set. Later the Tibetans made their own arrangement of all the texts they had collected. The first section of their canon, the Discipline (*Vinaya*), of which fragments of the Indian original have now been discovered in Gilgit, corresponds generally with the Discipline of the Singhalese Theravadins. The Disciplines of six sects are preserved in Chinese translation. It is certain that these texts underwent little change, for there was little cause for change. The second section of the Singhalese Canon, the Sūtras (discourses) underwent most change and have no corresponding section in the Tibetan canon. In the Tibetan Canon the section that goes by the name of Discourses contains the new sūtras. The third and last section of the Singhalese Canon, which was concerned with philosophical definition (*abhidharma*) clearly had its counterparts in India, for there has come down to us a fourth-century work by one of the greatest of Indian Buddhist philosophers, in which the tenets of the different sects are discussed and those of the Sarvāstivādins defended.[a] But he may well have been their last brilliant defender, for he himself was converted by his brother to the new interpretation of what the true doctrine should be.[b]

The first opposition to the materialistic realism of the early philosophical schools appeared in the form of dogmatic denials of the ultimate reality of anything whatsoever. These denials assumed the form of lengthy discourses, always attributed to the Śākya-Sage, who now generally appears as a supra-mundane being, emitting light-rays in all directions. The instruction is being given for the benefit of bodhisattvas, 'noble sons and daughters' who wish to save all beings. Thus together with a restatement of the philosophical position, the transcendental nature of a buddha is assumed and the career of a would-be buddha is taught as the only really worthy religious life. It would be difficult to give even a close approximation in dating the earliest of these works. They were in use in some schools long before they were written down or assumed any final form, and the mythical and heroic nature of a buddha, which underlay these developments, is a conception that belongs to the earliest times, as has been shown above. It is not this that suggests their comparative lateness, so much as the philosophical teachings that they give, for they must be understood as a reaction against the earlier materialistic theories. Then they in turn prepare the way for a more mature philosophical statement of the doctrine which embraces both the earlier views. Thus in Buddhist philosophy (not in faith and practice be it noted, for these develop somewhat independently) there are three periods to be distinguished, three 'swingings of the wheel of the Law'.[9]

[a] viz. the *Abhidharmakośa* of Vasubandhu, trsl. by L. de la Vallée Poussin (6 volumes, Paris 1923–31).

[b] The old philosophical schemes and terms of reference were never abondoned but merely restated in terms of *Yogācāra* theory. A compendium of this kind was one of the chief fruits of Yuan Chwang's pilgrimage to India (trsl. by L. de la Vallée Poussin, *La Siddhi de Hiuan-tsang* (Paris 1928–9)).

The three periods are these:

(1) *Early Buddhism,* which developed from the fifth century onwards. The elements of existence are regarded as real in a materialistic sense. There are no abiding components for everything is mutually conditioned. Nirvāna is the stilling of the process and is unconditioned by anything whatsoever, There are therefore two spheres of experience, that which is conditioned, namely phenomenal existence (*saṃsāra*) and that which is unconditioned (*nirvāṇa*). They can be given no logical connection, because nirvāna would thereby become conditioned.

(2) *The Doctrine of Relativity,* which is known as the Perfection of Wisdom and developed from the second century B.C. onwards. There are not only no abiding components; even the elements are not real. They are not real just because they are conditioned and cannot exist in their own right. In technical terminology they are said to lack self-nature (*niḥ-sva-bhāva*). Thus although one may speak in terms of phenomenal existence (*saṃsāra*) as conditioned and nirvāna as unconditioned, they are essentially the same in the absence of self-nature which is the essence of everything. Nothing can therefore be predicated about anything in any ultimate sense and philosophical exegesis of any kind whatsoever remains relative and conventional. Its application is practical but not final.

(3) *The Doctrine of 'Mind-Only'*, an idealistic world-view, which perhaps developed from the second century A.D. onwards. Phenomenal existence is conditioned and therefore unreal but in the sense that it is a falsely imagined construction which has its basis in pure consciousness. The falsely imagined construction is produced by the residue of former acts and is therefore a kind of accidental defilement, which may be removed by the right course of practice. Mind may therefore be regarded in three ways, as perfect and undefiled, as manifest in phenomenal existence and hence conditioned, as manifest in phenomenal existence and hence falsely con-

strued. The first represents the view of a perfected buddha, the second the view of philosophical diagnosis and the third the view of the ordinary mortal being who is bound to the wheel of existence. Samsāra is therefore neither the same as nor different from nirvāna. But since the difference comes about either because of the requirements of philosophical disquisition or because of the effects of erroneous views, it is also possible to regard them as essentially the same. This system represents the culmination of Buddhist strivings to achieve a satisfactory philosophical representation of their doctrine, and it solves the problems as well as human minds could hope to solve them in the circumstances. It must be remembered that there were certain generally accepted beliefs which could in no way be rejected and so had to be fitted together into a coherent system. These beliefs always represented the limiting factor. It may be as well to resume them:

(1) Existence is a beginningless process which is also liable to be endless.
(2) Everything is conditioned by everything else. Thus everything is impermanent and so ultimately a source of misery.
(3) There are no abiding entities, no phenomenal objects, no person, no abiding self.
(4) Action (*karma*) produces inevitable results.
(5) A man is responsible for his action. By employing the right means he is therefore able to bring the miserable process to an end.
(6) This bringing to an end may be known as nirvāna, which may represent the state of calm achieved by a monk for his own sake, or it may be known as full and perfect enlightenment, which implies the striving towards nirvāna for the sake of all beings. Thus nirvāna may be individualistic in that it tranquillizes one stream of elements. Perfect enlightenment is universal in that

it only reaches fulfilment when all beings enter nirvāna.

There is no need to write at length of the 'Perfection of Wisdom' and 'Mind-Only' teachings, for description of them and extracts from their texts are now easily available elsewhere.[a] In spite of scholastic disputes between the two schools, they both represent a suitable philosophic justification for the bodhisattva's career. None of the schools pursued a disinterested search for truth. They were explaining and justifying a course of action which would produce certain results. Nāgārjuna, Āryadeva, Asanga, Vasubandhu were practisers of the doctrine first and philosophers afterwards. Their theories lose all value apart from the religion that they represent.

There are certain beliefs connected with the new philosophical teachings which are essential to an understanding of all later developments. The Great Vehicle distinguishes itself from the early schools essentially by a change of world-view. There are no longer two disconnected spheres separated by a veil of mystery. A buddha is no longer conceived of as passing into an ineffable condition of non-manifestation, leaving his followers to find 'islands in themselves'.[b] There is now no real distinction between phenomenal existence and nirvāna, for both have become different aspects of the same mystery. They are still essentially one, whether they are conceived as identical in their absence of self-nature, that is to say, in the voidness of their unpredictability, or whether they are conceived as consciousness in its pure condition and as the same consciousness accidentally defiled. From now on all barriers are swept away. All beings may aspire to buddhahood and all buddhas may respond to faith. The change of world-view implies a different pattern. The world-view of the early schools was lineal thus:

[a] see Conze, *Buddhism*, pp. 130–43 and pp. 160–73; *Buddhist Texts*, pp. 146–80 and pp. 207–17; Th. Stcherbatsky, *The Conception of Buddhist Nirvāṇa* (Leningrad 1923).

[b] see E. J. Thomas, *Life*, p. 146.

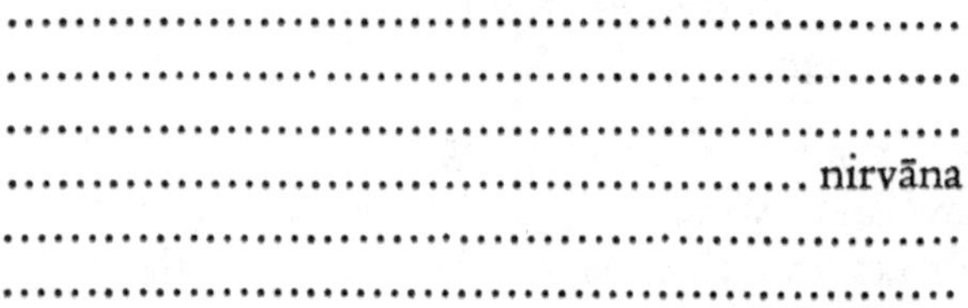

Each dotted line represents a stream of elements stretching both ways into infinity of time. The one that stops short represents nirvāna. It is true that the pattern should be rather more complicated. Some streams will meet and part, influencing one another for a time. In this way a buddha before finally entering nirvāna will influence the streams (apparent personalities) that have met with his, and afterwards these streams will influence others, and so on. As long as some influence remains, the doctrine he preached will have some effect. It is envisaged as an historical process. By contrast the world-view of the new philosophy converges on a point. The subject-object complex bound to senses and spheres of sense resolves itself into the condition of pure consciousness and this is nirvāna. Pure consciousness by the residue of former acts sees itself as the subject-object complex and *saṃsāra* (phenomenal existence) results.

The diagram now appears thus:

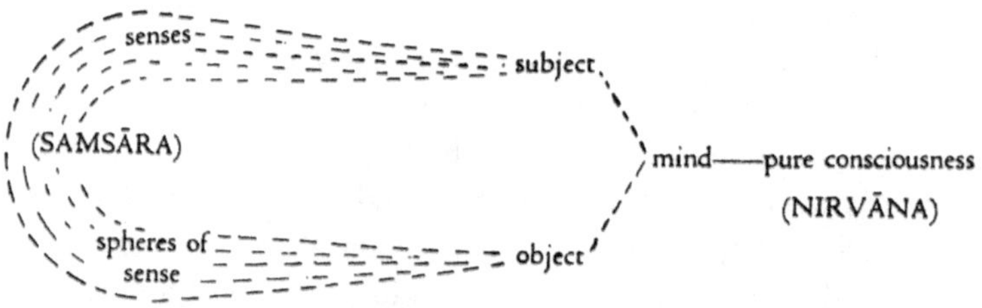

This scheme no longer proceeds along a temporal plane, but operates idealistically. Therefore it coincides very easily with another idealistic pattern which conceives an absolute centre for the universe. Originally this is probably a regal notion, for a king who rules over the four quarters sees his palace as the centre of the world. This may well be the intention of the stage-towers (ziggurats) of ancient Mesopotamia, and it is possible that the idea spread from here both east and west.[10] This was the intention behind the pillars of sovereignty set up by the Mauryan emperors throughout their domains. Likewise the 'Diamond-Seat', the place of the enlightenment *par excellence*, became the idealistic centre of the Buddhist doctrine. Later we shall see how by means of the same idea the funeral-mound became the symbol of the doctrine. This idea allowed many forms of application, and the notions of an undifferentiated absolute and a phenomenal existence, which was in some sense a dispersal of this absolute, lent themselves easily to this pattern. So the diagram now appears thus:

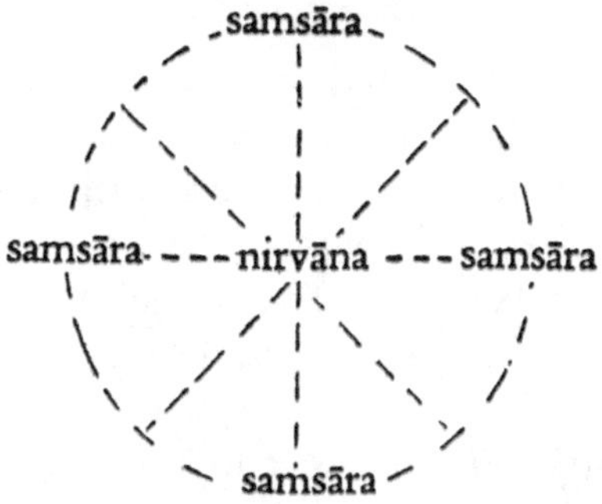

At the same time the traditional omniscience of a buddha assumes a new idealistic significance. As a universal monarch is all-powerful, so a buddha is all-wise. There is no longer need to restrict it to the threefold knowledge or the ten powers, for now it extends through all space. At first it is just the Śākya-Sage who occupies the central position, because at this early stage it was he alone who had a right to buddhahood, but very soon as we shall see, the idealistic scheme out-reached a mere historical personage.

In this scheme the bodhisattva served as link between buddhahood and the refracted state of living beings, for while he toils amongst men or animals his mind is set on enlightenment. From the time that he makes the vow to save all beings he becomes a 'son of the buddhas'. It is the 'thought of enlightenment' (*bodhicitta*) that establishes his relationship with the buddhas, and it is by means of the thought of enlightenment that he will reach his goal.

> 'Do you wish to cross over the myriad sorrows of existence, to soothe the sufferings of living-beings, to taste joys in their thousands of thousands? Then never abandon the Thought of Enlightenment!'[a]

But if men, as bodhisattvas, advance towards buddhahood, buddhas, as bodhisattvas, can come to men's assistance. Our scheme is centrifugal as well as centripetal. Hence it is the idea of the bodhisattva, as heroic saviour, which provides a support in time of trouble. There are two types of bodhisattva, one is a man of flesh and blood, intent on buddhahood; the other an active emanation of a buddha, a supramundane being intent on giving help to men. A practical distinction may be made between bodhisattvas who are human, and bodhisattvas who may be invoked as divinities. There is no real distinction, for both types embody the Thought of Enlightenment and both are intent on the salvation of all beings. In this scheme of things no real distinctions can be made at all. Still later the Thought of Enlightenment was conceived as a germ of buddhahood latent in all beings, and later still in tantric times it was identified in the human body.

At all times the buddhas and the bodhisattvas form a kind of glorified assembly. When new teachings are promulgated, it is in such an assembly that they are heard. When he appears thus, a buddha can be differentiated in form from his condition of complete identity with 'pure consciousness' or 'voidness' on the one hand and from his condition of humanity, as manifest for example in the Śākya-Sage on the other. There was thus conceived an intermediate form of manifestation, known as the Body of Reciprocal Enjoyment. The three 'Bodies' may be listed thus:

[a] Śāntideva *Bodhicaryāvatāra*, I. 8 (trsl. by L. de la Vallée Poussin, *Introduction à la Pratique des Futurs Bouddhas*, Paris, 1907, p. 3).

Plate I

(a) Bodhgaya, the Tree of Enlightenment. (p. 3)
(b) Sarnāth, the Dharmarājika-stūpa and monastery-ruins. (p. 18)

Plate 2

The Wheel of Existence. *(p. 13 ff.)*

Plate 3

Rock-Shrines: *(p. 40 ff.)*

(a) Bhaja. *(b) Karla.*

(c) Nāsik, cave 3. *(d) Ajanta, cave 10.*

Plate 4

Buddha summonsing the earth to witness. Svayambhūnāth, Nepal.
(p. 18)

Plate 5

(a) Buddha preaching. Nāsik, cave 2. *(p. 37)*

(b) Buddha entering the final nirvana. Ajanta, cave 10.

Plate 6

Decorative motifs. (p. 43)

(a) Horse-riders. Pillar-capitals at Bhedsa. (b) Sun-god and War-god. Sculptures adorning the entrance to a monk's cell, Bhaja.

Plate 7

(a) Exterior view, Nāsik. (p. 48)
(b) Assembly of Buddha. Nāsik, cave 2.3 (p. 47)

Plate 8

(a) Preaching Buddha enshrined with attendant bodhisattvas (padmapāṇi) Nāsik, cave 20. (p. 47)

(b) A hall for monks. Kanheri, cave 11. (p. 48)

(1) The Body of the Absolute (*dharmakāya*) which is essentially unmanifest.
(2) The Body of Reciprocal Enjoyment (*sambhogakāya*) which is manifest to bodhisattvas and to the eye of faith.
(3) The Human Body (*nirmāṇakāya*) which is manifest to all men.[11]

This scheme was elaborated to satisfy empiric requirements. It was known that the Śākya-Sage had lived amongst men, that he was identified with the essence of buddhahood (the 'Law') and that now idealistic teachings were promulgated in his name. No practical application was made of it for many centuries, and then at last the Tibetans turned it to good account.

There is a well-defined connection, to be elucidated in Chapter Two, between the Śākya-Sage who preaches his first sermon in the deer-park outside Benares, and the resplendent supramundane buddha who promulgates the later doctrines. This connection is symbolized in stone, for some of the earliest buddha-images show the sage with thumbs and first fingers touching in the gesture of preaching (pl. 5*a*). It is not without cause that the resplendent preaching buddha and the imperturbable buddha of the enlightenment became the two chief ones in later times.

The Cult of the Stūpa

The last great act in the life of the Śākya-Sage was the final nirvāna (pl. 5*b*). Reference has been made above to the ancient site of Kuśinagara, which has been identified with modern Kasia on the Nepal-Indian frontier, and to the funeral-mounds in which his relics were enshrined. In the first instance there was nothing unusual in the use of these mounds. They would have been used to mark the last resting-place of any important personage. Ānanda, the favourite disciple, is supposed to have asked the sage about his burial; he was told that believing laymen, princes and others would see to it, and that it was to be like that of a universal monarch.[a] Nor were the early Buddhists the only religious sect who honoured their master in this way. The Jains certainly made use of the funeral-mound and it is likely that other sects did so as well. The Sanskrit term for mound or heap is *stūpa* and it is by this simple term that the funeral-mounds were always known. There is another Sanskrit word, *caitya,* which is also derived from a word, which means *to heap up,* but this second term began to assume the specific meaning of *shrine.* It is not surprising that the places associated with the main events in the life of the sage, should have become places of pilgrimage and even veneration after his death. Nor is it surprising if the place (or places, assuming we accept the account of the dividing of the relics) where his last remains reposed, became the object of special devotion. All the places of pilgrimage must have been adorned with shrines, and the form they naturally took would be that of the *stūpa.* If there were relics to place inside, so much the better, but if not, at least the form was represented. There are no means of knowing how slowly or quickly this practice developed, but it is certain that by the third century B.C. it was well established. The Emperor Aśoka is credited with having opened the original stūpas in order to share the relics amongst the enormous number of these shrines that he is supposed to have had constructed. The stūpas became increasingly elaborate in design. The central mound was surrounded by a raised pavement for respectful circumambulation and the whole site was enclosed with a railing. The railings that survive are made of stone, but the prototype was probably made of wood. They were pierced by four archways, one at each of the four sides, and these archways provided scope for elaborate carving. It is this carving that provides the earliest archaeological testimony concerning the nature of early Buddhist beliefs, and we learn that the Śākya-Sage was the seventh known buddha, that he like his predecessors had achieved enlightenment beneath a sacred tree, and that his buddhahood was the fruit of heroic acts in former lives.

[a] E. J. Thomas, *Life*, p. 152.

A significant feature of the early sculpture-work is that the buddha-figure never actually appears. It is symbolized by a tree (the enlightenment), a wheel (the turning of the wheel of the doctrine), a stūpa, or the presence may be indicated by foot-prints. Even in the life-scenes preceding the enlightenment, that is to say when he was still a bodhisattva, the Śākya-Sage is not shown. The reasons for his non-appearance have often been discussed but no conclusive solution can be given. According to a naive rationalist theory, he was not represented, simply to indicate his complete disappearance in nirvāna. This is not entirely satisfactory, because there would then be no objection to full physical representation previous to the time of enlighten-ment. Indeed it would be necessary, in order to emphasize the later absence. Foucher suggests that he was not represented, just because it was not the custom, and he produces the in-genious theory of pilgrim-momentos (terra-cotta casts of trees, wheels and stūpas) which came by usage to represent the sage himself. The most satisfactory solution, however, has pro-bably been put forward by Paul Mus. It is clear that the stūpa has become a symbol of the doctrine in general, and of the final nirvāna in particular. The tree and the wheel represent the other two main events in the sage's life, but any of the three can be used to indicate his physical presence. Now a symbol is never used as a mere make-shift. It is employed as a means towards the apprehension of the otherwise inapprehensible. To symbolize a thing is by implication to accord to it existence upon a higher plane. Thus the Śākya-Sage is represented by symbols, not to emphasize his absence, but because it was instinctively felt to be the only means of approaching his true nature. In fact it reveals a conception of him which is in accordance with that of the supra-mundane being in the texts. Monuments and texts are very different mediums: whereas the former may often without difficulty retain their symbolic character, the latter are constantly at the mercy of individualist interpreters and didactic philosophers. 'One is obliged to think that from a certain moment Buddhism was richer in its concrete reality than in its dogma. Taken as a religion it has more substance than as a philosophy, a complete reversal of the current opinion (which for so long has thwarted research) for which it would be according to the *pāli* documentation essentially morals and philosophy, which were then painfully and superficially turned into a popular religion.'[a] There can be no disputing the increasing importance of the stūpa in the development and spread of the doctrine. India was once covered with these impressive monuments, but of the ruins that remain only Sānchi can give anything approximating to an impression of their former grandeur. In those days they were painted and gilded, adorned with umbrellas and garlands; scents and flowers were offered to them and they were circumambulated with devotion and respect. Nor let it be thought that they were merely the refuge of the simple lay-folk. Not only is there archaeological evidence to prove that monks are to be numbered amongst the donators, but as far back as archaeology can go, the stūpa is seen to play an important, if not essential part in Buddhist practice.

Cave-Monasteries

Of the very earliest monastic communities, whose buildings must have been of wood, there is now of course no trace, but from the third century B.C. onwards the dwelling places of these early practisers of the doctrine are preserved in solid rock. The type of rock-formation that allowed the elaborate hollowing-out of these cave-dwellings only exists in certain areas, chiefly in Bombay Province and Hyderabad. Three such sites, in close proximity to one another, are situated about half way between Bombay and Poona. The arrangement is similar in every case. The largest cave of each group is in the form of a long pillared hall with apse-like end, which has been cut so as to leave a simple domed cylinder of stone rising from the floor. There is a passage between the walls and the row of pillars, so

[a] P. Mus, *Borobuḍur*, Introduction, p. 69.

that the *caitya* may be conveniently circumambulated. On both sides of the main hall are smaller caves, arranged in convenient groups, depending on the formation of the rock. Sometimes they are built above one another. Sometimes there are several small cells opening off a larger courtyard. These small caves are hollowed out to form small square rooms, leaving a high platform at one side to serve as the basis for a couch. These are the earliest extant monastic settlements. The inward sloping pillars and the wooden roof-struts of the chaitya-halls indicate their dependence on yet earlier models which were built of wood. Moreover the rock above the entrance is sometimes cut to represent wooden latticed windows of early Indian type and the gaping entrance of the cave was originally screened with wooden lattice work. In the later examples the pillars tend towards the perpendicular, and the stone-work of the entrance-arch itself becomes more ornate. Rock-architecture is seen to come into its own and to lose its dependence on models in another medium. The situation of these caves is always pleasant, but they are probably at their best during and after the monsoon, when the hills appear in luxuriant freshness. The grassy platform in front of such a row of caves is usually a few hundred feet above the general level of the ground and one can see for miles across the flooded paddy fields. It was the practice for those who went forth from home to a homeless state to wander freely for the greater part of the year and only during the season of the rains to settle in one place in comparative comfort; but from the time that the community began to receive regular support from the villages, there must have been an increasing tendency to remain as a member of a more or less fixed community. The rules were gradually relaxed, eventually even by those who strove to resist such relaxation. Decent garments of approved pattern were worn instead of rags.[a] The certainty of regular support gradually made begging unnecessary; monks even possessed wealth and property. Their master him-

[a] see J. Przyluski, *Vêtements de religieux et vêtements de rois*, *JA*, XIII, p. 365 ff.

self had instructed them to follow a middle course, avoiding luxury on the one hand and self-affliction on the other, and thus any relaxation of seeming hardship might be excused as avoidance of self-affliction. The comparatively easy life of the Buddhist monk made him a butt for the followers of other sects, but it probably contributed largely to the success of the doctrine in a worldly sense. It presumably succeeded in preserving a fair balance between genuine religious practice and lay respectability, thus attracting to its ranks men of good family and talent as well as of religious aspiration. From the time of Aśoka onwards its success seems to have been assured and settled communities became a recognized institution. The earliest caves date from this time, and one does not arduously cut temples out of rock in order to use them but four months in the year. Nevertheless whether he dwells alone or in community the Buddhist monk remains responsible to himself or to his chosen master. There is no regular daily office at which he is required to present himself, and if we are to draw any conclusion from the exhaustive detail of the rules of conduct, it would seem that there were many opportunities for transgression. The only regular ceremony was the reciting of the rules of conduct in the form of a general confession, which took place twice monthly at the new and full moon. The chaitya-hall may seem to imply some form of communal worship, and from early times on it may have become a custom to circumambulate every day the simple symbol which represented both the doctrine and the nirvāna of the master. In view of the freedom of practice which has remained so characteristic of the doctrine through the centuries, it is unlikely that its beginnings were very different. In Tibetan monasteries today the temple is used comparatively rarely in spite of the elaborateness of its provisions.

These cave-monasteries represent a long period of development. The three we have so far referred to, namely Bhaja, Bhedsa, Karla, together with a few similar examples, such as an early chaitya-hall at Nāsik, some eighty miles north-east of Bombay, and two such early halls at Ajanta, the most famous of these sites, belong approximately to the period 200 B.C. to A.D. 200. Bhaja represents the earlier date and Karla the later. At Bhaja and Bhedsa the pillars are completely plain, but the Karla pillars have a kind of pot-base and are surmounted by elaborate capitals in the form of elephants with noble couples on them and horses with their riders (pl. 3). Horses and riders are a favourite motif and the massive pillars at the entrance to the Bhedsa caves are likewise adorned. Worthy of special mention are the deep-cut bas-reliefs that cover the walls on either side of one of the Bhaja cave-cells. The sun-god in his chariot is seen on the left and Indra, the god of battle, riding his elephant on the right (pl. 6). These early carvings are purely decorative and if we need any proof of the naive simplicity of the inmates, it is surely here.

The carving on the stone railings and gate-ways of the great stūpas belongs to the same period as these first monastic caves, and as they were popular centres of pilgrimage and thus correspondingly wealthy, there was far greater scope for the sculptors' skill. We have referred briefly already to some of the themes, to the little tableaux illustrating the previous lives of the bodhisattva and the main events of his last life on earth, the recurring themes of the tree and the wheel and the stūpa, which are usually shown with adoring figures around them, men, gods or animals. The craftsmen clearly delighted in portraying contemporary scenes, cavalcades, processions, and especially the sinuous lines of the female figure. Whether they are tree-sprites or just women plucking fruit, they are equally devoid of any religious significance. They had certainly often before been carved in wood for other patrons; now when an order was given for a stūpa-gate to be decorated, the craftsman consulted his patron over his preference for the main designs and worked his own will with the rest. It is interesting to reflect that even the carvings which we consider specifically Buddhist, were at that time not specifically Buddhist at all. The Jains built stūpas and decorated them in much the same way. The symbols of tree and wheel and stūpa were just as much in use by them, and the stories of the 'previous lives' were derived from a common stock of Indian hero- and animal-tales. It is true that these symbols and stories were now associated with the Śākya-Sage, but it is difficult to distinguish between those that were associated with him because they were popular motifs and those that became popular motifs because they were associated with him. Were trees and stūpas worshipped before they came to symbolize two main events in his life? They probably were. Were wheels erected on pillars as a sign of sovereignty before they were used to symbolyze his turning of the wheel of the supreme doctrine? Probably so (pl. 3*c*).

Early sculpture illustrates well the customs and popular beliefs of the time, but nothing can be learned with certainty about the hero in whose honour the work was done.

The Buddha-Image

The buddha-image appeared about the beginning of the Christian era seemingly in the district of Mathurā, about ninety miles south of modern Delhi. Even now some of the best examples can be seen in the museum there. These figures are designated as bodhisattvas. They either stand with legs slightly apart or are seated in the typical posture of meditation. The right hand rests in the one case upon the girdle and in the other palm-upwards upon the lap. The left hand is raised in what is known as the gesture of 'dauntlessness', palm outwards, fingers close together pointing upwards. There is little specifically Buddhist about these figures. It is possible to see in the cross-legged figure with left hand raised in dauntlessness, the bodhisattva, determined to achieve his aim in spite of the assaults of Māra. It may even have been first conceived with this in mind, but neither the posture nor the gesture is new in itself. In the same museum can be seen a nāga-divinity, a Hindu god of war and many other figures with hands raised in just this way. What may be new, however, is the combination of posture and gesture, which suggests both action and tranquillity.

One may compare the early Jain images, which are either standing with arms straight to the sides or seated cross-legged with hands placed together on the lap in the gesture of meditation.

At this period India was connected with the West by the Kushan Empire which stretched from Afghanistan to the valleys of the Ganges and the Jumna. Mathurā came within its orbit. Although the effects of this contact were very great, it is not always possible to specify them in the sphere of purely religious and doctrinal developments. But where sculpture is concerned the effects are still clear for all to see. If Mathurā craftsmen produced the first buddha-figures, it was Gandhāra that enriched the forms and popularized the new conventions. Many examples of this style are to be seen in museums both in India and in Europe, and it is probably the most easily recognizable phase of Buddhist sculpture, just because the humanism of the Graeco-Roman style is such an obvious intrusion. In the fourth century of our era Magadha became again the centre of a new Indian Empire under the Gupta Dynasty, and by this time the Gandhāra style was happily absorbed into the general stream of Indian sculpture. The buddha-figure had now become the fashion and the cave-communities were not slow to make use of it. One of the first and most beautiful examples is an Ajanta cave (no. 10, pl. 3*d*). A stūpa is still the object of devotion but now a standing buddha-figure is superimposed. The right-arm, which is broken, was probably raised in the gesture of dauntlessness. The pillar-capitals and the triforium which they support are richly carved with many small inset buddhas, displaying a variety of conventional gestures, that of meditation (hands together, palms upwards flat on lap), that of preaching (thumbs and first fingers of both hands joined in front of the breast), that of giving (right hand palm outwards pointing downwards) and that of dauntlessness.

Ajanta was a very large settlement with more than thirty caves. Apart from the chaitya-halls, most of the other caves are in the form of large halls some sixty-five feet square. To the sides there are the cells of the monks but at the far end one mounts a platform leading into a shrine-chamber, which contains a preaching buddha seated on a throne. The first turning of the wheel of the doctrine in the deer-park at Benares is indicated by the deer carved on the throne. It is of interest to consider the significance of this buddha who is now chiefly occupied in preaching. The last four or five centuries had seen the appearance of a vast amount of new doctrinal texts, some claiming to be inspired, some the work of commentators and individual authors. This presupposes the existence of much intellectual effort and ability, and it seems that the community was conscious of this fact and rejoiced in it, for what purpose does an image serve if not to reflect and do honour to an ideal? The other favourite figure is that of a bodhisattva, standing and making the gesture of giving. But these never occupy a main position, appearing rather as guardians or onlookers. It is not for them that worship is intended. There seems to be no reason for regarding these caves as specifically mahāyānist; they merely represent the accepted style of the times, and all the Buddhist establishments of whatever order would have used these forms. Nowadays Tibetan Buddhism on the one hand and the Theravādin Buddhism of Ceylon both represent curious extremes of the doctrine, and so suggest extremes of difference between the Great Vehicle and the Lesser. But the four main orders of monks, the Mahāsanghikas, the Sarvāstivādins, the Sammitīyas and the Sthaviras (Theravādins) were all more or less affected by the new ideas which continued to mould the doctrine throughout its 1,800 years of history on Indian soil. There were monks of mahāyānist tendency, but no proper mahāyānist sect. The monastic rule of conduct was the same in every case, and if a monk (or layman for that matter) chose to take the vow of a bodhisattva and direct his life accordingly, that was his affair. He could read mahāyāna-sūtras at his pleasure and dispute with his fellow-monks to his heart's content. We should err greatly if we conceived of the various different philosophical schools as representing different orders in the Christian sense or even as constituted like the Buddhist orders of Tibet. We have for instance no reason to imagine the existence of separate Mādhyamika or Yogācāra monasteries as opposed to Sarvāstivāda ones. These philosophies were merely points of view represented by the inmates of Ajanta, Nāsik, Sānchi or any other of the hundreds of communities established throughout India. True, there would always be a tendency for men to seek for masters who represented the same view-point as they themselves favoured, and coteries would form here and there, but this is a spontaneous regrouping which would occur in any society.

The Nāsik site which in its early days had consisted of just a simple chaitya-hall and the cave-cells of the monks, also underwent this secondary stage of development. The same spacious square halls were cut with shrines at the far side. At first these shrines appear as deeply incised bas-reliefs with a passage cut behind for circumambulation. One such (no. 3) shows in the centre a stūpa with the lion of the Śākyas to one side and the wheel of the law to the other. Two women are in the act of circumambulating it with devotion (pl. 3*c*). Another shows the sage in the posture of meditation seated on the lion-throne. All the later central figures make the gesture of preaching. Some are seated within an inner shrine at the doors of which stand guardian bodhisattvas. The guardian figures in cave no. 20 are holding lotuses in their left while the right hands are raised in the gesture of fearlessness. These figures, known as lotus-holders (*padmapāṇi*), became formalized later and so represented one of the most popular divinities of the last phase of Indian Buddhism (pl. 8*a*). Also at Nāsik are several small caves, not serving as shrines to a larger hall, but simply cut out of the rock so that these preaching buddhas may be multiplied. At their sides stand respectful attendants and one can very easily imagine oneself as present in the midst of such a real august assembly (pl. 7*b*). Nāsik is certainly one of the most pleasant of these early settlements. The caves lie about 400 feet above the general level of the plain. Trees line the path before the caves, and through these trees one looks out into a hazy distance. The place is completely tranquil (pl. 7*a*).

In the hills some twenty miles north of Bombay are the Kanheri Caves, the largest of all these settlements; as there are more than a hundred caves, the monks here must have numbered several hundreds. There is a chaitya-hall similar to the one at Karla and dating from about the second century A.D. It probably represents the earliest of the group. Thereafter monks and groups of monks must have continued cutting out accommodation to their requirements. There is one enormous hall (cave no. 11) which seems to have been intended as a rest-hall for travellers and visitors. Two raised stone platforms run the full length of the hall and served presumably as resting-places. Smaller cells open all around (pl. 8*b*). A few of the caves are carved with deeply cut bas-reliefs inside, and the common motif is still the preaching buddha.

Quite apart from the wonder that these cave-cells and temples evoke in themselves, they possess great value as typical monastic settlements of Buddhist India. The many others, whether built of stone or wood, have long since gone to destruction, leaving but their foundations at the most. The next survivals in direct line of descent are the earliest Tibetan monasteries, and there will be occasion in a later chapter to describe the eleventh-century west-Tibetan monastery of Tabo. It is interesting to reflect how minor are the changes in the dispositions of the buildings and in the activities of the monks. From the texts one gains the impression of vast and sometimes catastrophic changes. How widely different in perspective seems to appear the way of the early disciple and the career of the bodhisattva, yet the outward form of the community does not distinguish these two ways. It is true that at some time in the past the homeless Buddhist ascetics became settled dwellers in a chosen monastery, but this is a change which affects Buddhism as a whole. Likewise the art-forms as they develop become a common expression of the doctrine and a common heritage. We shall now have to discuss the various tendencies conveniently labelled as tantric or ritualistic. These tendencies involve extraordinary practices, which would seem to destroy completely the essential purity of Buddhist practice. Yet the practice of the monks remains essentially as before. Fearful monsters and grotesque couples now adorn the walls and the ceremonies of worship have become more elaborate, but the monks keep the same discipline, they think in the same terms of samsāra and release from samsāra, they learn and copy the texts, they compose new ones, they go into solitary meditation. In essentials all is just as it always has been. When one studies the doctrine from outside, as it were, one is acutely conscious of every new change and development. In this one is encouraged by the protagonists of the different schools themselves, for it is they who split the differences and castigate the views of their opponents. At the same time they are conscious of their unity in one ideal and in the practice of a common code of conduct. The changes come as a logical historical development, and in any one period all are more or less affected by them. Some may attempt to cling to the old conceptions, but even the old conceptions imperceptibly involve the new ideas. Thus the change in meaning which a symbol undergoes, eventually becomes irresistible to all. In the fifth century B.C., for example, the stūpa is the tomb of the master and perhaps the sign of his departure into nirvāna. In the fifth century A.D. it is the essential symbol of the doctrine, the Body of the Absolute common to all the buddhas and from it a buddha-image can become manifest. In the first few centuries of their development, the buddha-images are shown with certain conventionalized gestures which are used because they are found suitable to express the various activities of a buddha, but gradually these different forms become identified with different names, and there can be no going back upon this process, so that all sects just accept them as they have become. Historically Avalokiteśvara is not just a mahāyānist creation, who is set up in some monasteries and denied entry into others. We can impose all too easily our own ideas of religious bitterness and iconoclasm upon a religion which has known little of either within its own ranks. The famous dictum of Aśoka, that 'all which is well spoken is the word of the buddha', applies to all its developments throughout its long history.

A small silver buddha (*Amoghasiddhi*)
Tibetan workmanship

II

TANTRIC BUDDHISM[a]

There is one chief difficulty in achieving a just appreciation of the historical development of Buddhism and that is the geographic division of Buddhism as we see it at the present day. In the sixteenth and seventeenth centuries this division was causing the bewilderment among European travellers and missionaries, who were understandably slow in attributing the religions of Ceylon and Japan to a common source.[12] In India itself Buddhism had been gradually sinking into oblivion since the destruction of the great monastic centres at the hands of the Moghuls. It was not until the first half of the last century that there appeared the two great pioneers of Indian Buddhism, Brian Hodgson, who was British resident in Kathmandu for twenty-five years, and Eugène Burnouf, who was his chief collaborator at the Collège de France. Now after a century of scholastic endeavour it is possible to trace the history of this religion in the land of its origin. Much uncertainty and obscurity remain, especially in the later period, but this does not excuse anyone who professes to write or speak of Buddhism from doing his best to take this whole period into account. For Buddhism is not just the word of one master, promulgated and fixed for all time. It was part of India's religious experience, changing, adapting, developing through the centuries, yet at the same time retaining a certain continuity and independence in

[a] The term *tantric*, popularized in European and modern Indian works, has no basis in any Sanskrit adjectival form. This form of Buddhism is known either as *mantrayāna*, the Way of Spells, or *vajrayāna*, the Adamantine Way. Nevertheless the term is apt, for it characterizes that whole development which is based on the class of texts known as *tantras* (see pp. 54-6). It could be adequately glossed by *ritualistic* and it should certainly not be pervaded by the sense of opprobrium which some writers have attached to it.

its traditions. However far we go back in time, we can never discover such a thing as pure Buddhism, for it inevitably shared its philosophical concepts, its moral and ascetic practices with the rest of the religious life of India. It adopted what came to be its characteristic dogma, *anātmatā*, absence of self-nature, but this weakened neither its adherence to the generally accepted doctrine of rebirth nor its reliance upon the assistance of divine beings. Some monks, it is true, strove to 'be islands to themselves', but there were as many non-Buddhist ascetics who strove likewise, and as devotion developed towards the great Hindu gods, so it likewise developed towards those great beings, the bodhisattvas.

Thus historically, at least, one must conceive of Buddhism as an active living tradition, probably receiving its impetus from a great religious teacher round about the year 500 B.C. (who thought and taught, be it remembered, within the terms of his times) and continuing to enrich and adapt itself on a give-and-take basis for 1,500 years and more. It spread to Ceylon, probably in the third century B.C., and although the connection with India certainly continued for several centuries, Buddhists there remained largely ignorant of subsequent developments in India and have remained so to the present day. At about the beginning of the Christian era it began to spread across central Asia to China and thence finally to Japan. From the eighth century onwards it gradually became established throughout Tibet, but the forms in which it now appeared were very different from those which Ceylon had received a thousand years earlier. Tibet remained in contact with India to the last, and so it was the full inheritor of the Indian Buddhist tradition. Thus the distance that separates Theravādin Buddhism from Tibetan Buddhism today provides some measure of the distance that separated Indian Buddhism of the third century B.C. from Indian Buddhism of the twelfth century A.D. One sees therefore how misleading it may be to speak of Northern and Southern Buddhism, for the difference between the Buddhism of Ceylon, Burma, Siam and Cambodia on the one hand and of China,

Japan and Tibet on the other are not primarily geographical, but historical and temporal. The bond of their unity can still be traced, but only laboriously and with the help of texts and archaeological remains. These are scanty enough, if one relies upon Indian sources alone, for the climate is unsuitable for the preservation of manuscript material and the ancient sites were abandoned for centuries to the callousness of weather and of man. Some of the most important texts have been preserved in Nepal, but in order to gain any real impression of the immense growth of Indian Buddhist literature, we have to turn to the translations preserved in the languages of China, Japan and Tibet. In this labour of faith the Tibetans were certainly the most successful, for they devised a more accurate and consistent means of translation than was possible in Chinese. Also their proximity to Nepal and India rendered possible continuous co-operation between Indian and Nepalese and Tibetan masters, whereas the Chinese translator was often left to translate as he thought best. There will be occasion later to write of the Tibetan Canon in more detail, but it is important now to realize how much we rely upon it for an understanding of Buddhism even for the period preceding the introduction of the doctrine into Tibet itself. The Tibetans translated every Buddhist text they met with, texts which had originated at any time from the fifth century B.C. onwards. The greater part of the texts they found were far later than this, usually from about the first century A.D. onwards. Moreover we can be sure that whatever they did translate still formed part of the Indian Buddhist tradition in the eighth century and later. Therefore the contents of their canon in themselves provide an accurate picture of later Indian Buddhism.

So far as architectural and art forms are concerned, Nepal has preserved the most precious traces of what Buddhist India once was. The pagoda-type temple, which was already characteristic of the India of Yuan Chwang's times, but has now long since been replaced by other styles, was still being built in Nepal in the seventeenth century. Iconographic traditions continue even today and can be traced back directly to old Pāla art of Bengal. All in all there are considerable means at our disposal for a reconstruction of the life and thought of the last centuries of Buddhist India, and an understanding of this period is essential for any just appreciation of Tibetan Buddhism.

The Texts

The texts to which we have chiefly to refer fall into two main categories, known as *sūtras* and *tantras*. The basic meaning of both these words is 'thread (of discourse)', but by and large they have come to be applied to different kinds of literary works. The *sūtras* are mainly doctrinal in character. The earlier ones, such as those that appear in the Singhalese Canon, are historical or quasi-historical in character and represent the Śākya-Sage giving instruction to his followers at Rājgir or Benares or any other of their well-known places of sojourn in Magadha. The later ones present with little serious attempt at historicity a transcendent form of the sage, who gives instructions for the benefit of bodhisattvas in the new philosophical theories, commending the great career of the bodhisattva with its goal of buddhahood for all beings. Although some of the philosophical ideas are abstruse, these texts are all reasonably straight-forward, if often monotonous to the extreme. They all, old and new alike, presuppose much the same sort of religious practice—namely morality, concentration and wisdom—and they differ primarily in the end of their endeavour. The early disciples might hope to gain nirvāna as the fruit of the striving of several lives. The bodhisattva looked forward to innumerable lives of effort and self-sacrifice throughout aeons of time. But all that was said in the previous chapter about the wheel of life applied to both equally, for there was no means of escaping the inevitable retribution for one's acts. All being well, the early disciple would expect to continue to be reborn as a man with opportunities for practising the religious life until his course was run. The bodhisattva on the other hand possessed no such confidence. He must never lose hold of the thought of enlightenment, as expressed in his initial vow, and he was prepared to suffer in any of the spheres of existence for the welfare of all beings. The Mahāyāna is often represented as a way of faith and devotion, but it must not be thought to differ qualitatively from the earlier schools in this respect. The need for faith was stressed from the earliest times and there is no lack of evidence for quite fervid devotion towards the Master. The stūpa and afterwards the buddha-image provided the focal-point of the cult, and as has been emphasized above, these were not restricted to any one school.

The *tantras* make no claim whatsoever to historicity. They are revealed by the Lord (*bhagavān*, about whose forms more will be said below) in a transcendent sphere of existence, and they differ from the *sūtras*, old and new alike, by telling of an entirely different kind of practice, by means of which buddhahood can be gained in this very life. They contain magical spells, descriptions of divinities and sets of divinities arranged for meditational and ritual use, instructions in sacramental worship and in the bestowing of consecrations. These will all be discussed in detail, but their mere enumeration is sufficient to indicate that we are here presented with a very different form of religious practice. These two types of text, *sūtra* and *tantra*, are not entirely isolated from one another. Magical spells appear in several of the *sūtras*, and at least two famous texts, which are known as *sūtras* in the Sanskrit versions that are available to us, were firmly classed as *tantras* by the Tibetans.[a] There was inevitably a certain amount of mingling of the literary material. Some practices which would only gain their full effect as part of the ritual of the *tantras*, were also useful for straightforward devotional practices and so spells found their way into the *sūtras*. Conversely whenever the *tantras* appeal to philosophical considerations, the *sūtras* provide their obvious source. Nevertheless as ways, they are quite distinct, and on my

[a] The *Suvarṇaprabhāsottama-sūtra* and the *Mañjuśrī-mūla-kalpa*.

travels Tibetans have several times asked me: 'Do you follow the *sūtras* or the *tantras?*' In this they are repeating a question which was being asked in India 1,200 years ago. In the later days of Buddhism it was not *mahāyāna* and *hīnayāna* which presented themselves as alternatives, but *mahāyāna* and *mantra-yāna,* that is to say, 'the way of spells', for it was by the use of spells that the ritual was characterized throughout. In these complicated rituals far more than spells was involved, and so we must try to trace the various theories, beliefs and practices, which have come together in some form of coherent whole.

The Transcendent Buddha

More than one reference has been made to the continuity that exists throughout the whole historical development of Buddhism, and it was suggested that this continuity consisted primarily in the idea of a buddha, which has remained generally constant in content in spite of other changes in the doctrine. There is one particular conception of a buddha, which we may dismiss out of hand, namely a buddha as a purely human teacher. This conception is a modern Western creation, and although it has been adopted by quite a number of Buddhists, whether from Ceylon or from Japan, who have come into contact with the West, it still remains no more than an attempted accommodation to present-day rationalist thinking. Before a few Westerners began to suggest otherwise, no Buddhist, Singhalese, Japanese or Tibetan, conceived of a buddha other than as a transcendent being, and his canonical texts, in whatever language they were written, supported him in this view. It is indeed possible that there was a mere man, known as the Sage of the Śākyas, upon whom popular legends and cultural religious ideas centred themselves, but the point we must bear in mind is that it was belief in the supramundane being and not in a man, which accounts for the success of the doctrine in the first centuries throughout India and then later throughout the whole of the Far East. The most significant quality that attached to a buddha was royal dignity. His burial was to be that of a universal monarch and the symbol of his doctrine was the wheel of sovereignty. He was a Great Man, repository of the thirty-two major marks and eighty minor marks of physical perfection. It is usually suggested that the idea of universal dominion entered India from the Middle East with the increase in communications which was one of the more beneficial results of the conquests of Alexander the Great. It is difficult to track down with certainty the traffic in ideas, for who can claim finally to separate the indigenous from the foreign? In India kings were never regarded as divine beings, but the theory would not have been unfamiliar, and it was certainly applicable to those who possessed power of another kind, namely hermits who by their psychic power were thought to be able to coerce the gods. The Śākya-Sage was famed as a wonder-worker as well as a teacher, and with success and fame going hand in hand, he fulfilled all the beliefs and expectations of those times. This inevitably expressed itself in the texts. This process had already begun before his teaching established itself in Ceylon, but in India it continued to far greater lengths. I referred in the previous chapter to the image of the preaching buddha, which appears so frequently at Ajanta, Nāsik and elsewhere, and suggested some connection between these and the appearance of many texts. The early mahāyāna-sūtras, of which *The Lotus of the Good Law* is the best known, are preached by the Śākya-Sage, who now appears as the Lord who shines transcendent at the centre of existence. As transcendent Lord, he turns the wheel of the doctrine. Iconographically this is represented by the thumbs and fingers of the two hands joined in front of the chest, and this is precisely the gesture of the buddhas of Ajanta and Nāsik. At Nāsik these buddhas are seated in what may be called the European posture, and this is also the posture in which the Kushan kings were carved. It is possible that we have here another suggestion of royalty.[13]

In the *Mañjuśrī-mūla-kalpa*, a voluminous text which represents the transitional stage from *sūtra* to *tantra* there is a description of the sovereign-buddha: 'He has the colour of saffron and is like the rising-sun. He holds a great wheel which is turning. He is like a great king with his crown and his decorations, a great being who is crowned and adorned with all adornments. His lower garment is of fine cloth and his upper garment of cloth of various colours. He is bewreathed and handsome, adorned with strands and garlands. He smells a wreath of flowers held in the right hand. He smiles just slightly. He is strong and mighty. Fair he is and handsome, neither young nor old. In his left hand he holds the wheel, wreathed in blazing light, which he is turning.'[14] In this text generally, as in the *Lotus of the Good Law,* it is the Lord Śākya-muni, who occupies the central position, but it is a Śākya-Sage who has little to do with a wandering ascetic.[a] It is not surprising therefore that in the texts that follow, the central figure, although still the Resplendent Lord, no longer goes by the name of Śākya-muni, but by that of Vairocana, which just means resplendent. The continuity is indicated by the preaching gesture, for from now on this pertains to Vairocana. One of the first texts in which Vairocana appears is the tantra *Symposium of Truth of all the Tathāgatas* (*Sarva-tathāgata-tattva-saṃgraha*) where before commencing his teaching, he manifests himself as representing the unity of all buddhas.[b] If we may revert once more to the previous chapter, it will be remembered that reference was made to the change of world-view which took place in the doctrine. Existence no longer proceeded along a temporal plane, but operated idealistically. Buddhas were therefore no longer conceived as following one another in time, but as manifesting themselves spontaneously from an undifferentiated absolute. There appears in the *Lotus of the Good Law* a centripetal arrangement of buddhas with two at each of the cardinal points and intermediate points of the compass. The emanative idealistic

[a] *muni* = sage; Tib. *shā-kya-thub-pa.*

[b] The Tibetan Text is in *Nr. Kj. rgyud,* vol. vii. Of the Sanskrit the opening verses will be found in Indrabhūti's *Jñānasiddhi, GOS,* xliv, p. 81. See also p. 63 fn.

conception of buddhahood characterizes the whole of the *mahāyāna*. The set of five buddhas which is characteristic of the tantras merely conventionalizes this world-view in a form that accords with the several other sets of five. Just as personality consists of five components, so buddhahood is represented by five buddhas, and in accordance with the doctrine of the non-substantiality of everything whatsoever, both personality and buddhahood are equally void of subjective and objective content. This epitomizes the identity of samsāra and nirvāna, the realization of which is the prime object of the tantras. As fivefold the Lord (Vairocana) is no longer transcendent, for he becomes the symbol of the identity of samsāra and nirvāna. Thus in the texts he appears as one when he instructs and as fivefold in the ritual. This mingling of immanence and transcendence forms an essential part of the religious practice of Hinduism and the later Buddhism. One often finds the term pantheistic used of Indian religions, but its use merely reveals unawareness of the subtleties of these doctrines. The Lord, whether known successively as Śākya-muni, Vairocana or Vajradhara, remains preëminent throughout the whole development of Indian Buddhism. Although he may become manifest in any accepted form, he must always be recognized as the same in essence. It is this that is meant, when it is suggested that the continuity of the doctrine consists in the notion of buddhahood.

Other Buddhas and Bodhisattvas

Most of the names of the sixteen buddhas of the *Lotus of the Good Law* have the appearance of being pure invention. Names such as Lion-roar, Lion Banner of Victory, Space-abiding, Eternally Extinguished, can be nothing more than buddha-epithets. They serve no other purpose beyond the perfunctory supplying of the requisite number of names. But there are two among them, placed to the west and east respectively, who became important in the later developments. These are

Amitāyus (Boundless Life) and Akshobhya (Imperturbable). It is not unlikely that the cause of their enduring success is partly the mere succinctness of their names, but rather special associations are also involved. The Buddha *Imperturbable* recalls the moment of enlightenment and the defeat of Māra, who retreats discomfited, leaving the victor unperturbed. When the buddhas came to be distinguished iconographically, his gesture was that of touching the earth with the right hand (earth-witness), thus clearly identifying this particular association. *Boundless Life* on the other hand suggests rather a general attribute of buddhahood, for one may remember that the early texts often speak of nirvāna as the immortal or deathless state. It is typified iconographically by the gesture of blissful concentration, the hands together in the lap resting palm on palm. But there is another association, for this buddha was recognized as identical with Amitābha (Boundless Light). It has been often suggested that the whole idea of buddhahood as light is of Iranian origin, and this is quite plausible, for in the early centuries A.D. when the idea of buddhahood was open to new and developed interpretations, the empire of the Kushan kings bestrode both north-west India and Persia. But when one suggests influence of this kind, it is important at the same time to realize its limitations. According to Iranian ideas, light and good stood in firm contrast to darkness and evil, but it is this very notion of duality, which the Buddhism of this period is most concerned to refute.

> 'There is no difference at all between nirvāna and samsāra,
> There is no difference at all between samsāra and nirvāna.
> What makes the limit of nirvāna is also the limit of samsāra.
> Between the two we cannot find the slightest shade of
>   difference.'[a]

So influence there may well be, but no idea essentially foreign to the doctrine has found its way in. It would be wrong to

[a] see Stcherbatsky, *Nirvāṇa*, p. 77 (Nāgārjuna's *Madhyamakakārikā*, XXV. 19–20.)

think of a god of light entering buddhism in the name of Amitābha. Like the many other epithets, *Boundless Light* was adopted just as an attribute of buddhahood. At the same time it is probably true that the enormous popularity of this particular buddha-name throughout central Asia, China and Japan may be attributed largely to the importance of light in Iranian religion. No such exaggerated development seems to have taken place in India itself, where the buddhas remain not only doctrinally, but also in practice non-substantial, receiving conceptual form only in so far as they are united in the central idea of buddhahood and the person of the Lord. This will become clearer later on when we consider in some detail the fivefold set of buddhas and the interpretations placed upon it.

Whereas in the early sūtras the Śākya-Sage had addressed his disciples and hearers, in the later ones the audience consists of a vast concourse of bodhisattvas, *pratyeka-buddhas* and disciples, rendered the more impressive by interminable lists of names.[a] These names, like the names of the buddhas referred to above, are for the most part pure invention. Nevertheless there are one or two which are important for later developments. Maitreya, the next buddha-to-be, was the first to be named and is the only one known in the Singhalese Canon. His popularity has proved more widespread and more constant than that of any other bodhisattva.[15] The next is Mañjuśrī, who is the foremost of mahāyāna bodhisattvas. He appears in the *Lotus of the Good Law,* fully conversant with the teachings which the Lord Śākya-muni is about to pronounce (whereas Maitreya is not), and throughout the *Mañjuśrī-mūla-kalpa* he is often represented as sovereign-lord. His full name is *Pañcaśikha Mañjughosha,* meaning Five-fold Crest and Gentle Voice. It is likely that the first was the original name and the second just an epithet.[16] But

[a] A *pratyeka-buddha* is the solitary sage of Indian religious life. The Buddhists were willing to include these solitary practisers in their ranks, accounting them as the followers of another Way (*yāna*). The followers of the Mahāyāna classed them with the Disciples (*śrāvakas*) as followers of an inferior way (*hīnayāna*).

as Gentle-Voiced he became associated with the preaching buddha, appearing first as his lieutenant and then afterwards securing recognition as bodhisattva of Wisdom. He became generally known as Mañjuśrī—Glorious Gentle One—and *pañcaśikha* now appeared as the epithet. It caused difficulty and the explanations given betray the arbitrariness for which the Buddhists themselves were responsible. In the *Mañjuśrī-mūla-kalpa* it is understood as a gesture of the hand, representing the power of the bodhisattva. Later when his cult reached China, it was understood as *Mañjuśrī* of the Five Peaks, and so it was assumed that he must have originally come from the China of the Five Sacred Mountains. This legend even reached India, and so still later we find Indians setting out on the long journey across central Asia to China on pilgrimage to the abode of *Mañjuśrī*.[17]

The two next important bodhisattvas, *Avalokiteśvara* (the Lord who directs his gaze downwards) and *Vajrapāṇi* (thunder-bolt in hand) seem to first rise to importance in the *Mañjuśrī-mūla-kalpa*, where they appear to the right and to the left of Śākya-muni, the one as foremost of the gods and the other as foremost of demon-magicians (*vidyādhara*).[a] Mañjuśrī is placed at the centre below Śākya-muni. This arrangement represents the beginning of the idea of sacred lineage which was later to play its part in the general fivefold arrangement. The lineage with which Avalokiteśvara becomes associated is known as that of the *lotus*, presumably because the lotus was a commonly accepted emblem of the gods. The lineage which is represented by Vajrapāṇi was known as the family of the *vajra* (thunderbolt), for this signified the power of powerful beings. The central lineage was known simply as that of the *tathāgata*. These three groups represent the three kinds of divine beings (only one of which was properly Buddhist) which were from now on accepted into the Buddhist fold. Their inclusion was justified by the belief that a bodhisattva might be born in any sphere of existence if it were but for the good of those

[a] see J. Przyluski, 'Les Vidyārāja,' *BEFEO*, 1923, p. 301 ff.

beings. 'These are they who adopt any variety of body and act in accordance with any kind of practice, who do whatever is suitable for converting the minds of living beings and associate themselves with any suitable category. They understand the doctrine of the king of mantras and are perfected in the *dharma*. They appear in the lineage of the *tathāgatas*, of the *lotus*, of the *vajra*, in any lineage on earth or in heaven. Without transgressing their vow, they devote themselves to the giving of instruction. They act without breaking from the family of the Three Jewels.'[a]

It is interesting to speculate why Avalokiteśvara should have appeared as head of the lotus-family. When he is first mentioned in the *Mañjuśrī-mūla-kalpa*, he appears quite insignificantly as one of a list of bodhisattvas: '. . . Dharmeśvara, Abhāveśvara, Sammateśvara, Lokeśvara, Avalokiteśvara, Sulokiteśvara, Vilokiteśvara, etc.' Throughout the whole text the verbal form *avalokya* = 'looking' is used frequently of the Lord Śākya-muni before the discourse commences, and simply because it indicated a well-marked buddha-gesture, this name may have lent itself readily to invocation.[18] Having thus been hypostatized, he would very easily have become the peer of Lokeśvara—'Lord of the World', viz. Śiva. The Buddhists would not have invoked Lokeśvara in the first place, for this would have been tantamount to recognizing a Hindu divinity, but having lighted on their own Great Being, they would willingly accord him overlordship of the world. They entrust to the powerful Vajrapāṇi the task of dealing with Śiva, who is forced into submission and only permitted to live on condition that he will acknowledge the supremacy of Three Jewels, thus becoming the first of those who bound themselves to be defenders of the doctrine.[b] Thus Buddhism developed, part fortuitous, part premeditated, like most human affairs.

[a] *MMK*, p. 9, line 12 ff.

[b] This event is recorded in *STTS*, Part 4 (*Nr.Kj.rgyud* vii, folio 291*b*, ff.). A fragment of Sanskrit text, found by G. Tucci, has been edited and translated by him in *Ind-Tib.*, vol. I, p. 135 ff.

Vajrapāṇi (thunderbolt-in-hand) is a more obvious choice of leader where fierce divinities are concerned. He is also addressed as Lord of the Yakshas, thus implying a connection with still earlier Indian mythology, but he seems to be a completely Buddhist creation. There are several other bodhisattvas with analogous names: Supāṇi (Good Hands), Anantapāṇi (Limitless Hands), Kshitipāṇi (World-in-Hand), Ālokapāṇi (Lamp-in-Hand), Ratnapāṇi (Jewel-in-Hand). The last one in this list also became important later, but only because the jewel was an important religious symbol. Most of those who achieved any particular importance possess names of the kind that would clearly serve as buddha-epithets in invocations: Mahāsthāmaprāpta (Possessed of Great Strength), Sarvanivaraṇavishkambin (Removing all Obstacles), Samantabhadra (Entirely Good). This last name came to be applied later even to the supreme lord (Vairocana/Vajradhara).

The Five Buddhas

Whereas the development of a whole pantheon of buddhas, bodhisattvas and other divinities was largely haphazard, the arrangement of some of these into the sets, which we find in the tantras, was the deliberate expression of the centripetal conception of existence, to which reference has been made above. Moreover far from pandering to popular taste, as they have sometimes been represented, the tantras were essentially secret rituals, which were on no account to be revealed to the uninitiated. 'Reveal nothing to those who have not seen the great circle of divinities (*maṇḍala*), or the bond will certainly be broken!' Such is the admonition given to the pupil before his consecration into *The Symposium of Truth of all the Tathāgatas*. In the *Hevajra-tantra* one is warned that 'should anyone see the book or painting (of Hevajra), one will fail to gain perfection either in this world or the next. To one of our tradition it may be shown at any time, but on a journey the text should be hidden in the hair or under the arm'. This secret which is on no account to be revealed concerns in the first place the mandala itself with its fivefold set of divinities. Although some of the later tantras diverge from it with more elaborate arrangements, the fivefold set remains fundamental to them all, for it represents the simplest expression of the emanative nature of existence and the essential identity of samsāra and nirvāna. It is this that the pupil has to realize within himself by means of the ritual quoted below. The enactment of the rite must be preceded by normal instruction in the symbolism of the mandala with the object of producing understanding of a dialectical kind. The ritual is intended to confirm this understanding in the form of absolute knowledge. The identity of samsāra and nirvāna is expressed by the equation of the simple sets of five, which are listed overleaf. Of these several sets only that of personality stems from the earliest period of Buddhism, but it was not then conceived of in the present centrifugal pattern. It is this personality which is resolved by purification into the condition of buddhahood, which by analogy also assumes a fivefold form. Likewise the three basic evils of existence, desire, wrath and stupidity are extended to five by the addition of malignity and envy. In their condition of purification these become the fivefold buddha-wisdom, Mirror-like Wisdom and the rest.

It is interesting to observe how the original threefold pattern, as typified by the three basic evils, persists behind the fivefold scheme. As has been shown above, the buddha-families were originally three, tathāgata, lotus and vajra, and were devised in the first place as a means of finding place for non-Buddhist divinities within the Buddhist fold. These are also extended to five and by their equation with the five basic evils, it becomes logical to assign to such and such a family those living beings who show a preponderance in their personality of such and such an evil. Nevertheless the old set of three families is remembered in the set of Three Family Protectors, Mañjuśrī, Avalokiteśvara and Vajrapāṇi, who are still commonly invoked in Nepal and Tibet.[a] Likewise of the five buddhas, those who head the same

[a] see p. 116.

THE FIVE BUDDHAS AND THEIR EQUATIONS

Direction	*Colour*	*Family*	*Family symbol*	*Family head*
Centre	White	Tathāgata	wheel	Brilliant *Vairocana*
East	Blue	Vajra	vajra	Imperturbable *Akshobhya*
South	Yellow	Jewel	jewel	Jewel-Born *Ratnasambhava*
West	Red	Lotus	lotus	Boundless Light *Amitābha*
North	Green	Karma	sword	Infallible Success *Amoghasiddhi*

three families, namely Vairocana, Amitābha and Akshobhya, occupy a position of acknowledged preëminence. The three aspects of buddhahood which come to the fore are sovereignty, light and power, which are the primary qualities of these three buddha-families. Although Vairocana is inseparable from the notion of sovereignty, his name actually means brilliance. It is thus significant that in the set of five buddhas of the *vajra-dhātu-maṇḍala* which is found in the *Symposium of Truth* (ch. 2), Lokeśvararāja (King of the Lords of the World) occupies the position which is later unquestionably that of Amitābha. The two later families add no new definition to the nature of buddhahood, for the Jewel-Family of Ratnasambhava duplicates the aspect of sovereignty and the Karma-Family of Amoghasiddhi duplicates the aspect of power. The families are simply made up to five in order to accord with the requirements of the mandala.

The Divinities of the Mandala

The divinities of a mandala always consist of the Lord and his entourage (*gtso-'khor*). Thus the *vajra-dhātu-maṇḍala*, which represents a basic type, consists of Vairocana as central Lord with the other four buddhas as his four aspects at the main points

THE FIVE BUDDHAS AND THEIR EQUATIONS

Buddha gesture	*Type of Wisdom*	*Type of Evil*	*Components of Personality*
Preaching	Pure Absolute	Stupidity	Form
Earth-witness	Mirror-Like	Wrath	Consciousness
Giving	Discriminating	Desire	Feelings
Meditation	Sameness	Malignity	Perception
Dauntlessness	Active	Envy	Impulses

---

of the compass, each of whom is accompanied by attendant bodhisattvas. The act of worship itself is symbolized by eight goddesses, who likewise may be associated two by two with the four directional buddhas. Their names are:

Vajra-Gaity	Vajra-Flower
Vajra-Garland	Vajra-Incense
Vajra-Song	Vajra-Lamp
Vajra-Dance	Vajra-Perfume

The number and the names of the attendant bodhisattvas are not consistent, for there may be two or four in each of the directions, and since the layout becomes purely schematic, few of them remain faithful to their original families. Thus whereas Avalokiteśvara remains firmly in the Lotus-Family, Vajrapāṇi may be found in attendance on Amoghasiddhi. Vairocana as Lord has no need of a special bodhisattva, in that the whole circle forms his entourage. Thus Mañjuśrī moves to Amitābha's family. On the other hand Ratnapāṇi (Jewel-in-Hand), conditioned by his very name, remains faithful to the jewel-family of Ratnasambhava. Since these sets are inconstant, it will clarify nothing to list them here.[a]

[a] For examples refer to the arrangement at Tabo, p. 184, and to the mandala of the Tranquil Divinities, p. 231.

The circle is protected in each of the four directions by a fierce divinity, usually characterized by a hook, a noose, a fetter and a crossed-thunderbolt. They are known as:

Vajra-Hook (*Vajrānkuśa*)	—	East
Vajra-Noose (*Vajrapāśa*)	—	South
Vajra-Burst (*Vajrasphoṭa*)	—	West
Vajra-Fury (*Vajrāveśa*)	—	North

Furthermore each of the families of the four directions is represented vocally by a special spell (*mantra*) and corporeally by a special hand-gesture (*mudrā*). Since in the following ritual the pupil is consecrated as Vajrasattva (*Vajra-Being*), the spell and gesture of the vajra-family will be in use. These spells are not constant, but in the case of the *Symposium of Truth*, from which the extract is taken, they are:

Sattva-vajrī for Akshobhya
Ratna-vajrī for Ratnasambhava
Dharma-vajrī for Lokeśvararāja
Karma-vajrī for Amoghasiddhi.

The ritual is essentially a combination of gesture (*mudrā*), spell (*mantra*) and concentrated thought (*dhyāna*), which corresponds with the common threefold formula of personality, namely Body, Speech and Mind, all of which must play a correlated part in the rite.

The Rite of Consecration

Attention has been drawn to the notion of universal sovereignty which was always associated with buddhahood, and now we come to the logical and practical development of this idea. Just as a man may be consecrated to kingship, so a would-be buddha must be consecrated to buddhahood, and the rite, if properly performed, will be infallibly efficacious. In the sections of the *Mañjuśrī-mūla-kalpa*, which describe this rite, there are constant references to ordinary regal consecration, and it is reasonable to assume that we have here the beginnings of such a ceremony in Buddhist circles. The consecration is performed by means of eight ritual jars, which are first dedicated to Śākya-muni, all buddhas, pratyekabuddhas and early disciples, great bodhisattvas, Mañjuśrī, all divinities, all spirits, all living beings. Afterwards they are placed by the master against the pupil's head. Another important part of the ceremony is the possession by the pupil of the appropriate spell (*mantra*). This is revealed by his being blind-folded and throwing a flower into the circle where the buddhas, bodhisattvas and so on are depicted. 'Wherever the flower falls, he should be given the *mantra* of the (being) there. This *mantra* must be revealed to him as his own. It is connected with him throughout his birth-series, It is the virtuous friend (*kalyāṇamitra*) who will bring him to enlightenment and so act as to perfect completely the all-knowing wisdom of the great bodhisattvas.'[a] At this period, possibly the fifth century A.D., the fivefold scheme had not yet been elaborated. *The Symposium of Truth* represents a considerable development. There are no longer direct references to brahmanical ritual, for the whole practic has been completely coordinated into a buddhist setting. The naive arrangement of the three families (viz. Śākya-muni and Mañjuśrī at the centre with Avalokiteśvara and Vajrapāṇi to either side) is replaced by the centripetal arrangement with a buddha at each point of the compass. Moreover the circle of idealized existence (*maṇḍala*) is now represented in its most elaborate form: a temple-palace with gates to the four quarters, an abode more fit perhaps for a universal sovereign than for the body of all the buddhas. Such symbolism leaves no doubt of the intended nature of buddhahood.[19]

'With a good new thread, well-woven and of the proper length, the mandala should be measured out by a man well-skilled who tries his best. It must be four-sided with four gates and adorned with four portals, hung with four cords and bewreathed with garlands and flowers. Then one should mark the outer circle of the mandala, adorning it with *vajras* and

[a] *MMK*, p. 49, l. 19 ff.

jewels, thus filling the interstices between the four corners and the limits of the gates. Then coming inside this outer ring, one should encircle it with a ring of *vajras* like a wheel. It is equipped with eight pillars and on the inside of these *vajra*-pillars it is adorned with five lunar discs. At the centre of the central disc one should place the buddha-image. Then in the centre of the discs of the buddha-directions one should place the four supreme guarantees.[20] Approaching those four discs with a vajra-tread, one should place there all the four buddhas, Akshobhya and the rest.

In Akshobhya's circle one must place Vajrapāṇi and the rest,
In Ratnasambhava's circle Vajragarbha and the rest,
In Amitāyus' circle Vajralocana (*rdo-rje-spyan*) and the rest,
In Amoghasiddhi's circle Viśvavajra (*rdo-rje-rgya-gram*) and the rest.
On the outer corners of the mandala one should place (the goddesses of) the buddha-offerings.
At the four gates one should place the four guardians.
On the outer edge of the mandala one should place Great Beings (*mahāsattva*).'

'Now first the pupil should make four obeisances to all the tathāgatas.[a] Bending his whole body in the vajra-salutation, he makes obeisance and pronounces this *mantra:*

OṂ I OFFER MYSELF AS THE PLACE OF WORSHIP FOR ALL THE TATHĀGATAS.

MAY VAJRASATTVA, ALL THE TATHĀGATAS, EMPOWER ME.

[a] The names given to the four tathāgatas in these mantras accord with their individual spells as given above on p. 68. They are each addressed as representing all the tathāgatas and at the same time one particular aspect of buddhahood. It is impossible to bring this out fully in the translation. Vajrasattva (Akshobhya) is associated with the place (literally: establishing) viz. the vajra-throne (*vajrāsana*) upon which every buddha symbolically (in the earlier conception—literally) establishes himself. Vajraratna (Ratnasambhava) represents the consummation of buddhahood, conceived as a consecration in a regal sense. Vajradharma (Lokeśvararāja/Amitāyus) represents the promoting (literally: causing to turn) of (the wheel of) the *dharma*. Vajrakarma (Amoghasiddhi) represents the effectiveness of the *dharma* in its tantric form.

Then returning to his former position, he makes the vajra-salutation in front of his breast, and then touching the ground with his forehead in obeisance, he pronounces this *mantra*:

OṂ I OFFER MYSELF FOR CONSECRATION IN THE WORSHIP OF ALL THE TATHĀGATAS.
MAY VAJRARATNA, ALL THE TATHĀGATAS, CONSECRATE ME.

Returning to his former position, he makes the vajra-salutation on the top of his head; then making obeisance flat on his face, he pronounces this *mantra:*

OṂ I OFFER MYSELF FOR THE PROMOTION OF THE WORSHIP OF ALL THE TATHĀGATAS.
MAY VAJRADHARMA, ALL THE TATHĀGATAS, PROMOTE ME.

Then returning to his former position, he brings his hands down from the top of his head, and placing them before his breast, he touches the ground with his forehead in salutation and pronounces this *mantra:*

OṂ I OFFER MYSELF FOR THE ACT OF WORSHIP OF ALL THE TATHĀGATAS.
MAY VAJRAKARMA, ALL THE TATHĀGATAS, ACT UPON ME.

Then he should put on a red upper garment and one should wind a red cloth over his face. Making the hand-gesture which is called *sattvavajrī,* one should recite this *mantra*: SAMAYA HŪṂ. Then one should make him hold the garland of flowers between his two middle fingers, and leading him forward, one again says: SAMAYA HŪṂ. Then as soon as one has brought him to the mandala, one should instruct him in this wise: "Today you are entering the family of all the tathāgatas, and so if I cause you to obtain that knowledge by which all the tathāgatas are perfected, what need be said of other perfections? Since vajra-knowledge of this kind will arise in you, say nothing to those who have not seen the great circle of the divinities, or the bond will certainly be broken."

Then the vajra-master, making the *sattvavajrī*-gesture, which he shows from the inside and the out, places it upon the vajra-pupil's head and says: "This is your vajra-bond. If you tell anyone, your skull will burst apart." Then having empowered (the sacrificial water) with the bond-gesture and with the special *mantra* for the water of the oath, he should get the pupil to drink it. This is the *mantra* of the oath: "To-day Vajrasattva himself has entered into your heart. If you speak of the process, you will split open and burst. OṂ VAJRA-WATER ṬHA."

Then he should instruct the pupil in this way: "Since from to-day onwards, as far as you are concerned, I am Vajradhara, you must do whatever I order you to do. You must not speak ill of me. If you fail to avoid evil, you will certainly fall into hell when you die." Then he commands the pupil to say: "May all the tathāgatas bless me and may Vajrasattva descend to me." Then the master quickly makes the *sattvavajrī*-gesture and gets the pupil to say: "This is the vajra-bond, which is proclaimed as Vajrasattva. Even to-day may the supreme vajra-knowledge descend. OṂ VAJRA-DESCENT A."

Then he makes the wrathful gesture and forming the *sattvavajrī*-gesture, he draws forth its power. He then gets the pupil to recite whatever vajra-verse he pleases that pertains to knowledge of the Great Way. Then (the power) descends, and as soon as it descends, divine knowledge manifests itself, and by means of that knowledge he will know the thoughts of others. He will know all that must come about in the past, in the future and in the present. His mind will be confirmed in all the teachings of the tathāgatas. All his suffering will be at an end. He will be freed of all fears and nothing will harm him. He will be blessed by all great beings and by all tathāgatas. All perfections will become manifest in him. Joy and gladness and gleeful happiness such as he has never known before without special cause will arise in him. At the manifestation of these joys, some will experience profound calm, some will bring all spells to fruition, some all their hopes, and some will arrive at the perfection of all the tathāgatas.

Then making the gesture, he should release it in front of his heart and pronounce this *mantra:* "O VAJRA STAY, BE FIRM FOR

ME, BE ETERNAL FOR ME. EMPOWER MY HEART AND GRANT ME ALL PERFECTION. HŪṂ HA HA HA HA HO." Then he should throw the garland of flowers into the mandala and say: "RECEIVE, O VAJRA, HO." Then wherever it falls, he performs that (particular spell). Taking up the garland, he makes the (appropriate) gesture over his (pupil's) head with that spell, making him say: "OṂ RECEIVE ME, O THOU BEING OF GREAT STRENGTH." One makes the appropriate gesture and that great being makes (the practiser) his own, and so it is quickly done. At the descent (of the divinity), the cloth round the face is removed and the pupil should be made to pronouce this spell:

"OṂ VAJRASATTVA . . .
HE OF ALL EYES, THE VAJRA-EYED, MAKES MANIFEST, SEE SUBLIMITY, HEVAJRA!"

Then he is shown the great circle in due order. As soon as he sees the great circle, he receives the blessing of all the tathāgatas. Moreover Vajrasattva dwells in his heart. Because he is blessed by all the tathāgatas, he will see circles of light-rays of different colours and so on, and phantom shapes and forms, and the great lord Vajradhara himself or the person of one of the tathāgatas will become manifest. Thereafter he will succeed in all things, from whatever needful things he wants to the realization of the nature of Vajradhara or the tathāgatas.

Then after having seen the great mandala he should be consecrated with the sacrificial water of the vajra-blessed jar and with this mantra: "OṂ VAJRA—I CONSECRATE."

Then making the appropriate gesture, one should mark his sign on his hand and say: "To-day the tathāgatas bestow upon you the vajra-consecration. Take this vajra for the sake of the perfection of all the buddhas. OṂ I CONSECRATE YOU LORD OF THE VAJRA. BE FIRM O VAJRA-BOND HŪṂ."

Then with this mantra one gives the name-consecration: "OṂ—I CONSECRATE THEE VAJRASATTVA AND BY THIS CONSECRATION YOUR VAJRA-NAME IS . . . HEVAJRA!" '

(*STTS*, *Nr.Kj.rgyud*, vii, ff. 250*b*–251*b*, 253*a*–256*a*)

The translation of this passage is very much a *tour de force*, but it should suffice as an example of the style and nature of the tantras. The Tibetans, conscious of the mysterious power of the spells, left these untranslated, for the potency was felt to reside in the sound rather than in the sense. Thus for those who are unskilled in Sanskrit (and nowadays most Tibetan monks know nothing of it) these spells are nothing more than a string of meaningless syllables. But at least the Tibetan script lends itself to the transliterating of Sanskrit. The Chinese translators also left these spells untranslated, representing them syllable by syllable with Chinese characters of approximate sound. It is indeed doubtful whether it would be worth the time and toil of any scholar to attempt a complete translation of any tantra from such a medium.

Since magical power, which is represented by the *vajra,* is all important in the tantras, it is inevitably the symbolism of the *vajra*-family that comes to the fore. Thus the buddha who was placed to the centre of the mandala, although properly Vairocana, is here known as Vajradhara (Holder of the Vajra). The pupil is entering the family of all the tathāgatas, but the symbolic gesture employed is called *sattvavajrī* and he becomes identifiable with Vajrasattva, the bodhisattva who is associated with Akshobhya. Thus in the later tantras Akshobhya is placed at the centre, Vairocana taking Akshobhya's place in the east.[a] Vajradhara/Vajrasattva becomes then a sixth and supreme buddha, and all continuity seems to be lost in the line of development: Śākya-muni, sovereign-buddha, Vairocana, to which we referred above (p. 59). In reality, however, the continuity, although unmarked, is still there. At every stage there is only one essential buddha, and perhaps nothing can make this more clear than the directions (already quoted) for laying out the *vajra-dhātu-maṇḍala:* at the centre one places the buddha and in the four directions the guarantees of unity with him (*samaya*). It is imagined that the pupil has a special affinity with one of these guarantees, because of a predominance of

[a] see *Buddhist Texts,* p. 247.

wrath or ignorance or passion or envy or malignity in his nature. Thus:

Akshobhya's *vajra*-family is also called the family of wrath,
Vairocana's *tathāgata*-family is called the family of stupidity,
Amitāyus/Amitābha's *lotus*-family is called the family of passion,
Ratnasambhava's *jewel*-family is called the family of envy,
Amoghasiddhi's *karma*-family is called the family of malignity.

In the mere listing of these equations one is made immediately aware of the fundamental difference between Iranian beliefs in general and the whole Buddhist Mahāyāna. Wrath and the other evils merely represent the nature of *saṃsāra* (phenomenal existence), and since *saṃsāra* and *nirvāṇa* are essentially identical, these five evils are indentifiable with the five buddhas. Good does not overcome evil. Evil is transmuted into good. Buddhahood is but the experimental knowledge of their identity. One must observe, however, that the law of *karma* still applies, for evil will always bear its fruits in hell and good will earn the delights of heaven, for ultimately unreal as both may be, they are real enough to the unenlightened who experience them.

Buddhism moves quite logically from a moral to an entirely amoral viewpoint. The early schools preached morality as part of the necessary means towards nirvāna. One must exercise such personal control that the non-virtuous elements (*akuśaladharma*) cease to manifest themselves (see above p. 27).

The Mahāyāna still preached morality, but they also taught its complete relativity. Charity, righteousness and forebearance are great perfections, but useless for the gaining of buddhahood unless they are permeated with the perfection of wisdom, which is the doctrine of the essential emptiness of all concepts. Moreover the one thing necessary for ultimate buddhahood is the thought of enlightenment (*bodhicitta*), and he who clings to this, will ultimately be saved from the consequences of all his deeds.

The Vajrayāna in its extreme form brutally rejected the practising of virtue as a means to an end, for if the end is realizable here and now, why concern oneself with relative truths? 'In the matter of introducing the pupil to the mandala one should make no distinction between who is suitable and who is unsuitable. And should you ask why, it is because beings, even though they have committed great evil, if they but enter into this great *vajra-dhātu-maṇḍala* and see it, they will be freed from all types of wretched rebirth. Even those beings who cling to wealth and food and drink and desirable things, who take no pleasure in the vow and are not proficient in the preliminaries and so on, even they, by acting in accordance with their understanding and entering the mandala, will bring to perfection what they have in mind.'[a]

The mandala is the sphere of the divinity with whom the practiser identifies himself, thus exercising the power which pertains to the divinity. The acquisition of buddhahood was merely a special application of a general magical practice, for there were mandalas of all sorts and sizes. The tantras refer to rites of all kinds: petrifying, subduing, exorcizing, causing hatred amongst one's enemies, mesmerizing, slaying, propitiating, causing prosperity, bringing rain, winning a woman, finding a thing which was lost and so on. After the higher type of *mantra*-practice, which was illustrated above, it may be useful to have before us examples of a lower kind.

In order to petrify someone 'one should mentally produce the goddess Vajrā, who becoming manifest from the syllable ĀṂ is white in colour. She treads upon a corpse and holds a knife, a skull and the gruesome wand.[b] One should worship her as prescribed, repeating the spell: OṂ HŪṂ SVĀHĀ one hundred thousand times. Then one should write in chalk the syllable MAṂ on a dish of unbaked clay. In the middle of it one should

[a] *STTS*, folio 252*a*.

[b] This is the *khaṭvānga*, a rod upon which three human heads are transfixed, one freshly severed, one decomposed and one already a skull. The rod is topped by a trident. See pl. 23 where it is being held by Padma-sambhava.

place the spell: OṂ HŪṂ MAKE SUCH AND SUCH A ONE STAY HŪṂ SVĀHĀ. Then one must fill it with ashes from a funeral pyre, place another unbaked dish on top to serve as a cover, and on top of this draw the square mandala of the god Mahendra. Then place it on the ground, put you foot on it and repeat the "staying-still" spell one hundred and eight or one thousand times: OṂ HŪṂ MAKE SUCH A ONE STAY HŪṂ SVĀHĀ. Then he will be made to stay.'

In order to cause hatred 'one should meditate on the goddess Vajrayoginī with the syllable U and one should imagine the syllable JRĪṂ dark blue in colour on a solar disc at the heart. One should worship her as prescribed, repeating the spell: OṂ JRĪṂ SVĀHĀ one hundred thousand times. Then one should imagine the two against whom the rite is to be practised as mounted on a horse and a buffalo and as fighting together. One repeats the spell: OṂ JRĪṂ VAJRAḌĀKINI CAUSE SO AND SO TO HATE SO AND SO JRĪṂ HŪṂ HŪṂ HŪṂ PHAṬ and it will certainly cause them to hate one another.'[a]

Of these many rites four were singled out and endowed with some symbolic significance as special powers of buddhahood, namely pacifying, prospering, empowerment and destroying. The rest were never more than simple magic and it might seem that they set the tone of the tantras generally, consecration ceremonies included. Certainly the means employed are identical. One conjures forth the divinity, identifies oneself with him by means of his mystic spell and so appropriates his powers. The five buddhas and their attendant divinities in the mandala each possess their mystic spell. By the throwing of the flower the pupil discovers with which of them he personally has affinity and consequently to which buddha-family he belongs. In his practice he must concentrate upon his own divinity, so that he like the divinity may be consubstantiated in final buddahood. It is easy to forget that Buddhists and Hindus were one and the same people. They practised their religions in the same cultural *milieu*, and so it would be strange

[a] *Yogaratnamālā* (commentary to *Hevajra-tantra*), Part I, ch. 2.

indeed if their beliefs were not analogous and even sometimes identical. Divine beings appeared in Buddhism just because Buddhists themselves believed in them. At first they were called bodhisattvas and given Buddhist-sounding names, but afterwards no one bothered with these artificial distinctions. Sarasvatī, the spouse of Brahmā, was accepted as the spouse of Mañjuśrī, the Buddhist counterpart of Brahmā. Avalokiteś-vara was recognized as Lokeśvara, and so long as his identity with Śiva was ignored, Narteśvara (Lord of the Dance) was equally welcome. So too were Hālāhala, Lokanāth, Nīlakaṇṭha, who were all accepted as forms of Lokeśvara. Then came Jambhala, god of wealth, and his spouse, Vasudharā, the powerful goddess Kurukullā and the savioureess Tārā. Equally welcome were the fierce divinities, Bhairava (the Terrible), Caṇḍa-roshaṇa (Fierce and Wrathful), Śamvara, Heruka and Haya-grīva (the horse-necked God). All these except the last were assigned to the vajra-family, the family of wrath, where they might appear as fierce forms of Akshobhya, implicitly receiving buddha-rank. If it is asked with surprise how such brutish forms should have found so high a place in the Buddhist pantheon, the only proper answer is that Buddhists believed in them, and so a place for them was found. Tibetans will tell one nowadays that they are defenders of the doctrine and so the nature of their duties makes them fierce. But this is only part of the truth. Indians have never conceived of existence as fundamentally good. They have been aware rather of its cruelty and its voraciousness and so they conceived many of their gods accordingly. Nevertheless these fierce beings could only be properly absorbed into a Buddhist tradition in so far as it was possible to bring them into relationship with other members of the pantheon. There thus developed the theory of gentle and fierce aspects of the same divinity and this was quite in accordance with the fundamental teaching of the relativity of good and evil, of samsāra and nirvāna. Since the final truth will reveal the essential sameness of these pairs of concepts, so the devotee must know the single nature in the dual appearances.

Thus the five buddhas came to be paralleled by a fivefold manifestation of the fearful Heruka:

Vairocana	Buddha-Heruka[a] (pl. 9*a*)
Akshobhya	Vajra-Heruka
Ratnasambhava	Ratna-Heruka
Amitābha	Padma-Heruka
Amoghasiddhi	Karma-Heruka.

It is interesting to observe that however great may be the divergence between the Buddhism of the early schools and the stage we have now reached, nothing new has been adopted without first ensuring that it should accord with the doctrinal position. The doctrine itself still remained consciously Buddhist and what is more remarkable still continued to do so, even when feminine partners were introduced into the system. One should note also that Hindu divinities of first rank, Mahādeva (Śiva), Vishnu, the Goddess Kālī, Mahākāla (the Great Black One), Rāhula (god of the eclipse), were permitted entry only in the capacity of defenders of the doctrine. So long as these were kept in their place, it seems that almost any name might find a place in the higher Buddhist circles. Hence there has developed an enormous variety of mandalas to the bewilderment of anyone who attempts to gain a full acquaintance with the gods of Tibetan Buddhism. Nevertheless the fundamental pattern and mental process remain the same.

The central requirement is an appropriate divinity. For normal magical rites this should be the god or goddess who is especially associated with the task in hand. For the attaining of spiritual powers and eventually buddhahood it must be one of the divinities who is associated with the five buddhas in the mandala. Therefore the pupil casts the flower so that he may know with which divinity he is personally associated. In practice, however, a monk often just accepts as his chosen divinity the one who is representative of his order or his monastery. This divinity becomes his guarantor (Tibetan: *yi-*

[a] see p. 205.

dam) and he enters into a condition of union with him by a process of continual meditation.[20]

'Imagine that from the seed in your own heart you send forth a ray, and by means of this ray which is shining black in colour and has the form of a hook, you should draw in the buddhas who are stationed throughout the triple world, and having worshipped them in company with the eight attendant goddesses, you should beseech them saying: OṂ MAY ALL THE BUDDHAS CONSECRATE ME. Then you will be consecrated by those buddhas, all of whom assume the form of Heruka, with the five jars which symbolize the five tathāgatas and contain the five ambrosias. . . . When you have been thus consecrated the Lord of your Family will appear above your head and Heruka is manifest in you. Performing morning, noon and night this meditation which bestows such power, when you arise, you should remain at all times consubstantiated with the divinity.'[a]

It is by constant practice of this kind that the pupil must realize in himself the truth, which was first revealed to him by his master in the mandala. In theory even the initial consecration must accord with the character of the pupil. Thus the *Symposium of Truth*, from which we extracted the description of the *vajra-dhātu-maṇḍala* quoted above, also contains five-buddha mandalas suitable for the lotus and jewel families, in which naturally the symbols of lotus and jewel predominate. But in any studies of the tantras, one must not permit oneself to be bewildered by the mere appearance of diversity.

Feminine Partners

In India, as in many other countries, the gods were often so anthropomorphized as to be represented as marrying and begetting offspring. At least from the times of the epics this was so. But this had no influence upon Indian conceptions of transcendent being, whether conceived as *nirvāṇa* or *brahman*. Nor was it to be expected that ascetics who abandoned their homes

[a] *Hevajra-tantra*, Part I, ch. 4.

for a homeless state, whether Buddhist or Jain or orthodox brahmans, would conceive of a divine being as male and female in character. Their goal in any case was an impersonal absolute, in which all human distinctions and all human passions were annulled. Yet feminine divinities were not unknown even in Vedic times, where they appear as the personification of natural phenomena: Pṛthvī, the earth, Ushas, the dawn, Sarasvatī, the goddess of the river of that name. Most important of all was Vāc, the word. It was through her that Prajāpati, the Lord of all creatures, produced this creation. Later Sarasvatī, possibly because of her fertilizing powers, was identified with Vāc and came to be regarded as the partner of Brahmā. She was then regarded by Buddhists at a later stage as the partner of the peculiarly brahmanical bodhisattva, Mañjuśrī. There is no need for us to follow the development of these different goddesses, for they all tended eventually to accord with one basic form, that of the Great Mother Goddess, in whom they all more or less lost their separate identities. Moreover it is in the type of Mother Goddess that we can so clearly distinguish the Buddhist from the Hindu tantras. We have referred frequently to the general tendency of all accretions to adapt themselves to the already existent tradition, and we observe the same tendency at work now that the Buddhist pantheon is swelled by numerous feminine forms. Whereas in the Hindu tantras the Mother Goddess was typified in the spouse of Śiva and known as Parvatī, Kālī or Durgā, the active blood-demanding partner of a lord who would without her have remained in the deep sleep of the undifferentiating absolute, in the Buddhist tantras the feminine partner is in every case a form of Prajñāpāramitā, the Perfection of Wisdom, the tranquil Void. The rôles are in fact the very opposite of those found in the Hindu tantras. Hence the term *śakti*, 'energy', which is applied to Śiva's partner, is completely inapplicable in the Buddhist tantras.[a] Here she is known usually just as *prajñā*,

[a] I quote a general observation of Prof. Bourda, which although applied by him to another argument, would fit the present one just as well. 'Rien n'est

'wisdom', or as Mother, Yoginī or Symbol (*mudrā*).[21] It is the male partner who represents the energetic element, for he embodies the compassionate activity and skill in means which are the essential characteristics of the bodhisattva. Thus it comes about that all buddhas and bodhisattvas may be represented either as single or as dual. If present their partners partake of the nature of the individual buddha-families. Thus:

> Locanā belongs to Akshobhya's vajra-family and is blue;
> Māmakī belongs to Ratnasambhava's jewel-family and is yellow;
> Pāṇḍuravāsinī belongs to Amitābha's lotus-family and is red;
> Tārā belongs to Amoghasiddhi's karma-family and is green.[a]

Their normal position in the mandala of the five buddhas is at the intermediate points of the compass and in the general process of equating samsāra and nirvāna, they symbolize the four gross elements, earth, water, fire and air. This position presumably precedes their actual partnership with the buddhas themselves and at this later stage it becomes necessary to provide a partner for Vairocana at the centre. This central goddess is with rare exception a complete abstraction, bearing the title of Lady of the Sphere of Space (*Ākāśadhātvīśvarī*) or Lady of the Adamantine Sphere (*Vajradhātvīśvarī*) or She who takes the Lead (*Nāyikā*) or just Absence of Self-Nature (*Nairātmya*).[b] Likewise the partner of the fierce Buddha-Heruka is just named Lady of Wrath (*Krodheśvarī*) and she is particularized in the different directions merely by prefixing to this name vajra-, lotus- or whatever it may be. The great goddesses of Hinduism, Kālī and Ekajaṭā, are accepted

plus difficile . . . que de détruire ou de modifier des affirmations anciennes dont personne n'a cherché à contrôler le bien-fondé. Ces affirmations répétées à plusieures reprises par des personalités plus ou moins réputées, sont considérées, au bout d'un certain temps, comme des vérités acquises; et les travaux se succèdent, reprenant sans cesse une pseudo-vérité, qui provoque de fausses interprétations.' (*Art. As.*, xii, 1949, p. 302.)

[a] see also pp. 114-15.

[b] An exception is Vajravārāhī (p. 210 fn.).

in a purely subservient rôle as defenders of the doctrine and are never permitted to intrude within the mandala.

Thus when sexual symbolism establishes itself in Buddhism, it is immediately identified with the traditional philosophical and doctrinal concepts of the Mahāyāna. Final enlightenment was the realization of the essential unity of an apparent duality, which might be expressed from several different view-points:

samsāra	compassion	subject	consonants
nirvāna	wisdom	object	vowels

Existence is the diversity of *saṃsāra* and *nirvāṇa* and enlightenment is their unity. The career of the bodhisattva is the practice of compassion and wisdom in equal measures and the consummation of his career is their final unity. Subject and object are the two supports of phenomenal existence and their final merging is the end of existence. The mystic syllables and spells consist of consonants and vowels and their proper combination effects the intention of the practiser. A new term becomes current in the sense of final perfection, namely 'two-in-one' (Sanskrit: *yuganaddha,* Tibetan: *zung-'jug*), just because the fundamental pattern of existence was conceived as unity in apparent duality.

The pair compassion/wisdom subsumes all the perfections of the earlier Mahāyāna and so its praises are constantly being sung by the tantric yogins.[a] It represents the essential nature of the inmost buddha Vajrasattva and of the triple buddha-body. This pair is sometimes known as Wisdom and Compassion and sometimes as Wisdom and Means. Compassion and Means are practically synonomous. 'Because one is passionately devoted to all beings who have failed to extricate themselves from a whole flood of suffering, this passionate devotion of which their suffering is the cause is known as Compassion. In that one thereby brings a man to the desired end by a combination of appropriate measures, it is also called the Means.'[b] Hence Wisdom and Means or Compassion represent the foremost

[a] see *Buddhist Texts*, p. 240 ff. [b] *ibid.*, p. 241.

significance with which the coupled figures are endowed. 'Two-fold is the Innate, for Wisdom is the woman and Means is the man.'[a]

More subtle symbolism was also used. The lotus represents wisdom and the vajra represents means. The reader will remember that in the *Mañjuśrī-mūlakalpa* the families of lotus and vajra were placed on either side of the Lord, thus suggesting the general notion of two as manifest from one. These two terms came later to be endowed with a sexual significance, so that the expression 'union of vajra and lotus' could refer as much to the ritual union of the yogin and the yoginī as to the consummation of the bodhisattva's career. For the followers of the tantras these were in any case essentially the same thing. It is the practice of using terms capable of different kinds of interpretation, which render the tantras seemingly difficult to understand. When one has grasped the essential idea however, one ceases to wonder whether one interpretation is to be preferred to another, although in translation it may be necessary to choose one at the expense of the others.

It is not to be pretended of course that the female partners were introduced for the sake of mere symbolism and no more. In some circles they were used for the ritual enactment of the Wisdom/Means union. Indeed it is often assumed that late Indian Buddhism was corrupted precisely by the introduction of sexual ritual. This, however, is quite untrue, for Buddhism seems finally to have remained faithful to its traditions, even when it met with these practices. They had their origin in circles which were neither properly Hindu nor Buddhist and it would be impossible to say how long they had previously continued. The crudity of the beliefs is revealed in the actual texts of the later Buddhist tantras. Thus in the *Hevajra-tantra* we read: 'A man who has been hanged, a warrior killed on the field of battle and one who has been born seven times as a brahmin, of the flesh of these one should partake.'[b] In the company where this verse originated it was no doubt believed that by

[a] *Hevajra-Tantra*, Part I, ch. 8. [b] *ibid.*, Part I, ch. 7.

eating his flesh one could appropriate to oneself the lost years of one whose life had been cut short or the innate power of one so virtuous that throughout seven rebirths he had always been born as a brahmin. What is important to observe, however, is that the very earliest commentators were already interpreting these injunctions in a completely Buddhist sense. It means no more, they say, than the consuming of the notion of a self. Instances of this kind could be multiplied. It seems therefore that the texts themselves reveal a class of yogins who really performed all the rituals referred to and who were at the same time imbued with certain fundamental Buddhist notions, which they were not concerned to distinguish from non-Buddhist formulations. Thus the supreme knowledge is described as 'pure and void like the sky, the essence of existence and non-existence, a mingling of Wisdom and Means', but it is also equated with 'all other things that there are: the universal consciousness, the primaeval man, the Lord, the self (*ātman*), the soul (*jīva*), essence, time, the person.[a] Their experiences, justified as they could only be—by success, were taken note of in the monasteries, where the texts were finally written down and commentaries, always Buddhist in intention, were prepared. It would be quite erroneous to assume that the literal contents of these tantras describe the type of life led by the monks of the great monasteries of Vajrāsana, Vikramaśīla and Nālanda. The references are all to yogins who wander free from all ties, coming together with their fellows only for the seasons and at the places of pilgrimage. Such fellows are still characteristic of the Indian scene.[b] Both Buddhist and Shaivite tradition preserve the memory of eighty-four great yogins or perfected ones (*siddha*). Their biographies are to be found in the Tibetan canon, and although the tales related of them are of no direct historical worth, they portray well enough the general religious setting, in which the actual tantric texts originated. These eighty-four Great Perfect Ones are still

[a] *ibid.*, Part I, ch. 10.

[b] see G. W. Briggs, *Gorakhnath and the Kanphata Yogis.*

revered by the Buddhists of Tibet, for whom they represent the first transmitters of the occult doctrines (pls. 10 and 11). Their central divinity is the Holder of the Vajra (Vajradhara) who was already, as has been shown above, the central buddha of the earlier class of tantras, and thus appearance of continuity is maintained. The period to which these great yogins are to be assigned seems to reach from about the seventh to the eleventh centuries.[a] They form several lines of succession, for since the doctrines were secret, they could only be transmitted from master to pupil. Altogether they represent a strange collection of people, brahmins, kings, scribes, huntsmen, weavers, etc., who abandoning their rank and caste, acquire from their chosen master super-human powers, do good in the world and conduct living beings to heaven. In these popular accounts the goal of perfection seems to be immortality in the form of eternal youth. In fact it was as always the all-resolving trance. This becomes quite clear from the mystical verses of several of these yogins which have been preserved in translation in the Tibetan canon and a few of them even in the proto-Bengali in which they were originally composed.[b] Some of them were monks and even abbots and at the last stage of Buddhism in India one may conceive of the relationship of monks and yogins to be much as it has continued to this day in Tibet. The monasteries are primarily seats of learning and places of worship, whose inmates follow the safe but slow way of the sūtras, namely, the practice of conventional morality, the reciting of texts, performing of ceremonies and immersion into bouts of meditation. There have always been certain natures who remain dissatisfied with such methods and aspire to experience here and now the conviction of permanent release. India and Tibet have always counted amongst the great variety of those who practice religion in one form or another some who are held to have finally reached their goal. Success of this kind is achieved at the price of complete

[a] see Sānkṛtyāyana, 'Recherches Bouddhiques: L'Origine du Vajrayāna et les 84 siddhas', *JA*, 225, 1934, pp. 218–30; also Tucci, *TPS*, I, p. 226 ff.

[b] see 'Saraha's Treasury of Songs', *Buddhist Texts*, p. 224 ff.

renunciation and such men have lived apart from society, even monastic society, and often in complete revolt against it. Hence one will find sometimes a deliberate denial of the value of the conventional religious practices:

'Will one gain release, abiding in meditation?
What's the use of lamps? What's the use of offerings?
What's to be done by reliance on mantras?'
'Mantras and tantras, meditation and concentration,
They are all a cause of self-deception'.

Only one way can lead to complete realization of the truth and that is contact with one who already knows.

'If the word of one's master but enter the heart,
It is like a treasure in the palm of one's hand'.[a]

One easily tends to regard late Buddhism as debased just because from the seventh century there was a marked weakening of the scholastic tradition. But it would be just as plausible to point to a new flowering of religious genius as a result of the new impulse of life which was received from the non-scholastic yogins. In any case we have firm evidence of both trends entering Tibet. On the one hand we have the typical scholar, the Great Translator Rin-chen S'ang-po, about whom more will be said in a later chapter, and on the other the supreme type of yogin, Mila Räpa, who draws his experience direct from the circle of Indian yogins.[b] Both aspects of a religion are necessary if it is to be a vital force, and both were certainly present in India at the time when the religion was transferred to Tibet, where they have persisted to the present day. No one would pretend of course that Tibetan monks are all models of virtue; it matters merely that some are. Nor would one insist that the Indian yogin or the Tibetan näl-jor-pa always possess the knowledge and the powers attributed to them; it matters only that some do bear witness to an extraordinary perfection of

[a] *op. cit.*, pp. 226 and 227.
[b] see W. Y. Evans-Wentz, *Tibet's Great Yogī Milarepa*, O.U.P. (London) 1928.

spiritual equilibrium through the writings they have left us. Probably Saraha on the Indian and Mila Räpa on the Tibetan side present the finest examples.

The Internal Mandala

It is of course extremely difficult to write of experiences and modes of training, which were intended to be secret and which in any case could not be committed explicitly to writing. The basic texts were certainly the tantras, whose unattractive features can easily perturb the modern scholar. But then one must remember that they were not interpreted verbally. The union of the yogin and the yoginī is an internal psycho-physical process, the whole symbolism of which is sexual. Just as in the mundane sphere the union of man and woman produces a consummation of bliss, so the reintegration of the severed personality produces the full awareness of its transcendent unity and concurrently of its unlimited potentiality. As the desired condition is the realization of the essential identity of microcosm and macrocosm, so the whole symbolism is transferred within the body of the yogin. We have referred above to the external mandala as representing the essential identity of buddhahood, personality and phenomenal existence. The body of the yogin is now conceived as representing the unity of Wisdom and Means or in other terms of yogin and yoginī. It becomes the active repository of the process of the realization of the 'two-in-one'. Thus its main arteries are three: the one to the left is known as *Lalanā* and like Wisdom is feminine; the one to the right is known as *Rasanā* and like Means is masculine; the one in the centre is known generally as *Avadhūtī*, sometimes as *Caṇḍālī* or just as the *Yoginī*. The two outside arteries join the central one at its base. The yogin by controlling and stilling his breath through the left and right nostrils induces the psychic energy which flows in the two arteries to unite at the base of the central one. This union corresponds with sexual union, and the psychic energy in the arteries is indeed conceived as blood and semen. Their mingling is the birth of the Thought of Enlightenment, which in the more conventional Mahāyāna practice represented the beginning of the bodhisattva's career. Here the act is endowed with a quasi-physical significance. In the yogin's body there are four psychic centres, envisaged as lotuses, transpierced by the central vein and level with the navel, the heart, the throat and the top of the head. The Thought of Enlightenment must be consciously raised up the central vein, passing the four psychic centres and pervading the body with bliss as it goes. These four stages are related to various other sets of four, which characterize other meditative and ritualistic practices. Thus they are equated with four grades of consecration, of the kind we have considered above; also with four moments and four joys, which in the tantras mark the different stages of the sexual ritual. Perhaps most important of all, they are also equated with the buddha-bodies: at the heart is the *Dharma-kāya*, at the throat the *Sambhoga-kāya*, at the navel the *Nirmāṇa-kāya* and at the top of the head the Self-Existent Body, which absorbs the other three.[a] The texts can be most bewildering when they write of these equations, for everything and anything must be located within the body without regard for apparent contradictions. Also the notion of two-in-one can be envisaged in different manners, for although the chief representation is that of the veins to left and right, the base and head of the body serve the same symbolism. Thus the union of the psychic energies at the base of the central vein brings Caṇḍālī or the Yoginī blazing into life. She rises, finally uniting with her Lord in the head. Thus the mind (represented by the head) is male and the physical (represented by the lower regions) is female, and here we find a scheme which accords properly with the Hindu tantras, but not with the Buddhist. Sometimes the raising of the Thought of Enlightenment suggests the actual passing up the body of the male fluid, as though it were trans-

[a] The technical terms relating to this internal mandala are fully discussed in my Introduction to the *Hevajra-Tantra*.

muted from its coarse condition into the Self-Existent Buddha-Body. These are just different modes of expressing the same experience.

'There is bliss when Caṇḍālī blazes in the body.
There is bliss when the veins Lalanā and Rasanā enter Avadhūtī.
There is bliss when the flow of the Thought of Enlightenment descends from above.
There is bliss when the translucent male fluid pervades from below.
There is bliss from their loving when the white (masculine) and the red (feminine) come together at the centre.
There is bliss from contentment when the body is purified.
Sixfold is the bliss of the experience of yoga.'[a]

When the Tibetans set about systematizing the tantras, they placed in the highest class, namely that of the Supreme Yoga Tantras (*anuttarayogatantra*), those very texts, which seem to prove the most disconcerting to the western reader. Thus two of the most revered, the *Guhyasamājatantra* and the *Hevajratantra*, refer explicitly to the meetings of yogins and yoginīs, to the sexual ritual, to the eating of unpleasant sacramental food. But as the commentaries make clear, they were placed in the highest class, because they were interpreted and practised simply as internal yoga. There remains the interesting problem of how such texts came to be put to a use, which seems to be more successful in achieving results than modern psychology. Perhaps the eighty-four Great Perfect Ones are more deserving of our esteem than their biographies would allow.

[a] B. Laufer, *Aus den Geschichten und Liedern des Milaraspa*, p. 20.

III

BUDDHISM IN NEPAL

In the modern atlas Nepal appears as a country which extends for about 500 miles along the central and eastern Himalayas, perhaps 150 miles across at its widest part. It is thus almost equal in area to England and Wales. Culturally and historically (that is to say, until less than 200 years ago) 'Nepal' refers to one small valley about eighteen miles long from west to east and twelve miles from north to south. Until the Gurkhas consolidated the country within its present frontiers, Nepal in the modern sense was in no way distinguishable from the rest of the Himalayan Range. At the high altitudes of the northern valleys there have always lived people of hardy Tibetan stock, nomads for the most part, who spend the short summer months attending to their scanty crops of barley and buckwheat and wander down the valleys in the winter in search of pasture for their large herds of sheep and goats. Apart from the Terai, a narrow strip of jungle which harbours the most deadly malaria in the world, there is no natural frontier to the south. Thus the plainsfolk of India have always been able to seek refuge in the lower mountain valleys, whenever invaders have threatened their livelihood in the plains. Nepal was practically a closed country until after the last war, and very little is known of the many races of people that go to make up the present political unit. Generally, however, they seem to be the result of the mingling at different times and to a lesser or greater degree of the Tibetan-type of people from the north and the various waves of Indian races from the south. Many of these people have not yet seen such a thing as a wheeled vehicle, for all their journeying is done on foot and most of their carrying is done on their own backs. On the high plateau beyond to the north, the

Tibetans make good use of the horse and the mule, and the usefulness of these animals has been discovered in some Himalayan regions, but not so in Nepal. Often the tracks are so difficult that a pack-animal might well be more of a liability than an asset, and so it is on foot that one must travel. The communities are never more than small villages, strung along the valleys half-a-day or a day's journey apart. Most of these valleys, however, run from north to south, so that in travelling the length of the country one is forced to climb continually out of one valley and down into the next, possibly a day's march or more in each case. The constructing of motorable tracks will hardly be practicable so that greater Nepal will continue to remain largely ignorant of the ways of the outside world.

Right in the centre of this inaccessible country is the small valley which is the Nepal of history. It is rather in the form of an enclosed plain, for it is drained by a large number of small streams which, flowing from all directions, unite as the Bagmati River and make their exit to the south-west. Legend informs us that the great Mañjuśrī himself made this cleft in the surrounding mountains, thus draining away the waters of what was once a great central lake.[a] But as may be remembered from an earlier chapter, Mañjuśrī is too much of a newcomer for work such as this, and in any case the whole story seems to have been borrowed from elsewhere.[b] This little plain is unique throughout the whole Himālaya—a small inlet where the high waters of Indian life and culture have found their way and stayed. The people are known as Newāri, but this name, which is cognate with the name Nepal, indicates their domain as much as a clearly definable race of people; it now refers generally to the culture and inhabitants of the valley prior to the Gurkha conquest of 1768. Before these last usurpers others had come, but eventually they had all been absorbed into a common culture. The Newāri language, which

[a] Landon, *Nepal I*, p. 182–3 and Lévi, *Népal I*, p. 330 ff.

[b] J. Brough, 'Legends of Khotan and Nepal', *BSOAS*, vol. xii, part 2, p. 333 ff.

is still used by these people in spite of the forcefulness with which Gurkhāli has been imposed upon them, is clearly basically non-Indo-European, but whether it is akin to Tibetan or to a proto-Indian language we still know too little to say. In any case there has been much borrowing from Tibetan and the later Indo-European speech of India.

The Gurkhas conquered a far more extensive kingdom than the small areas of mountain tracts surrounding the central valley, which had previously been held by the Newars. Moreover they have succeeded in making their own Gurkhāli not only the official language of the government, but also the *lingua franca* of most of the central and eastern Himalayas, even beyond the actual political frontier. The adjective Nepāli, originally just a phonetic variant of Newāri, has therefore been appropriated quite logically by the Gurkhas to refer to themselves and to their language. By extension of course it refers, at least outside Nepal, to anyone who is a subject of the King, hence to Newars, Gurungs, Tamangs, Sherpas and all others who live within political Nepal. Although these people know very well who are their rulers, there is yet no consciousness of common citizenship. Nor would one expect to find it in communities so scattered and diversified. To them Nepal still means, as it always used to, only the central valley. It never embraces as a single concept the Nepal marked on our maps. These distinguish Nepal from the Nepal Valley, a mere convention devised by the Survey of India.

In the Himalayas things change very slowly and in their understanding of the name Nepal, the people show their recognition of the fact that culturally and historically Nepal always was just this valley. Legend once again connects the early history of the people there with the Indian Emperor Aśoka, and this at least is plausible, for it is well known how concerned he was to spread the Good Law beyond the limits of his own domains. Also the earliest monuments are definitely Buddhist, for they are stūpas similar to those in India, which we have considered above. It is likely therefore that Buddhist communities established themselves in this valley well before the beginning of the Christian era. It seems also that a very special sanctity was associated with Pātan, which at that early period was certainly the chief and perhaps the only settlement there. Four great stūpas were constructed at the four points of the compass and one in the centre of the town. All five are still standing and Pātan may well claim to be the oldest Buddhist city in the world, which has retained its Buddhist character to the present day. It seems likely also that the name Pātan means a royal city, and remembering what was said above concerning the notion of universal sovereignty in buddhahood, one may well wonder what special associations with the idea of a buddha caused Pātan to be thus singled out.[a] It is possible of course that the early Buddhist cities of India, Pāṭaliputra, Vaiśālī, Rājagṛha and Śrāvastī, were marked out with four great stūpas in this way; thus the arrangement at Pātan would be explained as the recognized sign of a Buddhist city, which had been borrowed from earlier models, The Tibetans named this city *Ye-rang*, which means 'Eternity Itself'.[b] It seems strange therefore that the legends give no reason for the esteem in which it was held. Nowadays the visitor is chiefly aware of its glorious middle-age. One of the wonders of all Nepal, indeed of all the world, is the main square of Pātan. On one side stands the old royal palace, the mellowed red of the brickwork surmounted by a harmonious expanse of carved lattices and casements. Opposite stand tiered pagoda-temples with eaves and roof-struts finely carved, conveying an impression of luxuriant fantasy and fairy lightness (pl. 18*b*). Architecturally at least, this is still a monastic city. On all sides there seem to open portals and low archways. One finds oneself within a tranquil little court-

[a] For the meaning of the name *Pātan*, see J. Przyluski, 'La Ville du Cakravartin', *Roc. Or.*, vol. v, 165 ff.

[b] The local Newāri name, which is still in use, is Ya-la (pronounced *Ye-lo* and in some combinations *Ye-long*). There is no doubt concerning the identity of this name with the Tibetan, but one cannot be sure whether they are merely phonetic equivalents or whether the Newāri actually means the same as the Tibetan.

yard, with carved casements all around the upper stories and on just one side another tiered and gilded roof, marking the presence of the divinity in the shrine beneath it. (pl. 16*a*). These court-yards lead one into another, some small and paved with stones, some large and grass-covered. Everywhere are little stūpas. This city was once a place of sanctity and learning, where monks and pundits were glad to come and visit. Some came from India to teach. Others from Tibet came here to learn. Now for several centuries there have been no proper monks and little enough of learning, The descendants of those last monks who broke their vows, live on in these monastic court-yards, preserving the name of monk by means of an empty ceremony and performing for the gods at least the outward signs of the service which is their due. But this anticipates our tale.

When Mañjuśrī had drained the valley, his followers are supposed to have built a great stūpa in his honour, the shrine of Svayambhūnāth, the Self-Existent Lord (pl. 13). This stands on the summit of a prominant hill-top three miles north-west of Pātan and half that distance from Kathmandu which lies just between the two. As there are no means of knowing the date of the original foundation of this stūpa without excavating to its central foundations (and this no archaeologist is likely to attempt to do) it is all but useless to speculate on its age.[a] The site chosen might suggest the period when Buddhism was changing from an historical or quasi-historical basis to an idealistic one, and so bring us to the early centuries of the Christian era. The name of the shrine, if indeed it has remained constant through the centuries, suggests an even later period, for to my knowledge the name 'self-existent' scarcely came to be applied to buddhahood much before the sixth century. It is certainly a characteristic notion of the early tantras. On the other hand this great shrine is traditionally regarded as representing the beginning of Buddhism in the

[a] It is tantalizing to know that early in the last century the whole central portion had to be dismantled for repairs, but there was no archaeologist at hand to profit from this rare occasion (Lévi, *Népal II*, p. 6.).

valley, and in a land where there has been no sudden interruption in the practice of the doctrine and where not a day can have passed without someone having respectfully circumambulated this shrine, it is a tradition not lightly to be brushed aside. As an act of merit a Newar Buddhist will sometimes undertake to visit ceremoniously all the monasteries either in Pātan or Kathmandu (depending upon where he lives), and always he must begin his course at Svayambhūnāth. In its present form this stūpa presents a style well in advance of the four surrounding Pātan, for the proportions have been completely modified. The flattened dome has become a complete semicircle and the squared top-piece (derived from the four-sided balustrade of the earliest Buddhist stūpas) has assumed enlarged and well-balanced proportions. The one umbrella which once crowned the earlier edifice has become thirteen at Svayambhū, which are compressed to appear as tapering gilded rings. Above them is placed a final fully-formed umbrella and on the tip of this a solar disc within a crescent moon. The rings are thirteen so that they may represent the thirteen stages in the advance towards enlightenment, and the sun and moon indicate the final goal in the now familiar terms of 'two-in-one'. The dome has become little more than the foundation for the whole upper portion, which now draws all attention to itself. On each of the four sides of the squared top-piece are depicted the all-seeing eyes of supreme buddhahood, surmounted by an arched flange on which appear the buddhas of the five families—Vairocana above the other four. All that was said above about the essential continuity in the development of the central buddha (the Śākya-Sage—the sovereign buddha—Vairocana—Vajradhara) finds its final expression in the Ādi-buddha, the Primordial Buddha. Every stūpa is his representation and they are his eyes that gaze forth from the dome. It is important to realize that there is nothing essentially new in this formulation. As we have already seen, the one buddha may be conceived as Vairocana, Vajrasattva, any of the four buddhas of the directions, or any chosen divinity (*yi-dam*), who by definition is the guarantee of unity in buddhahood. The term Ādi-buddha merely serves to distinguish the basic idea of buddhahood from secondary buddha-forms. It is probably true that with the impoverishment of learning and the consequent ignorance about even basic notions, Ādi-buddha came to connote a sort of Buddhist Brahmā, a god who existed in time before all other manifested things, but for the present we are concerned with primarily intended meanings.

The wide circumambulatory platform is crowded with little votive stūpas and minor temples. At the head of the steps is a huge vajra resting on an engraved *vajra-dhātu-maṇḍala* and nearby hangs an enormous bell. These are all familiar symbols of the later phase of Buddhism. On the northern edge of the platform are the buildings which presumably once housed the monks, but as at Pātan these have now become the crowded homes of their descendants, and monkeys and pathetic little children play noisily around the shrines. Svayambhū gazes out across the plain indifferent to those who stare and gossip around its massive dome, but the wonderment of the visitor is saddened here by the all too obvious decay of the doctrine (pl. 19*a*). The spell is broken and suddenly one seems to have climbed its many steps in vain. A steep straight flight leads up to the eastern side. When descending one should follow the path that leads down to the saddle of the hill to the north. Here is the little temple of the small Tibetan community. They wear their normal monastic garb of dark-red homespun. As usual they are surprised and pleased to have a European address them in their own language. The temple has been recently and brightly painted by an artist from Shar-Khumbu near Mt. Everest. One is surrounded by the five buddhas and their entourage, who all manifest themselves in their fierce as well as their gentle aspect, each embracing his feminine partner (see p. 229 ff.). The great stūpa above represents the early tantric period, but here in this Tibetan temple one is suddenly brought face to face with that still later phase, of which the words obscenity, demonolatry, are all too freely used. Yet those who keep this temple are monks who keep their vows, read the texts and exert themselves in the religious life. It is the Tibetans who are in fact instilling some new energy into the Buddhism of the Newars. Real Newar monks, still very few in number, are beginning to appear, and the Tibetans are their sponsors and their guides. They have placed their most characteristic mark on the main Svayambhū-stūpa itself, for it is now completely ringed with a framework of wrought metal, in which are set revolving prayer-wheels.

Elsewhere in the valley is another great stūpa, where the interest seems to be so exclusively theirs, that it might almost be regarded as a Tibetan foundation (pl. 14), Its origin is just as vague as that of Svayambhū, and its name, Bodhnāth or just Bauddha, could scarcely be more general in connotation.[22] The Tibetans know it by the name of *Bya-rung-kha-shor*, which, if one accepts the present spelling, can only mean what they say it means: 'It's all right to do it, he said', surely an odd name for a shrine. The Tibetan account of its origin is in the form of a dialogue between King Trhi-song-deu-tsen and Padma-sambhava and by means of the device of the rebirth-theory it is brought into the closest possible connection with the establishing of Buddhism in Tibet. It seems that Avalokiteśvara, saddened at his seeming inability to save all beings from the ocean of the samsāra, stood weeping. Then flicking away two tears, he expressed the wish that they should serve the cause of living beings. These tears were born in heaven as the two daughters of Indra. One of these maidens fell from heaven because of stealing flowers and was born in the human sphere in the Maguta region of Nepal as the daughter of parents who kept chickens. Later she had four sons, one by a keeper of horses, one by a swineherd, one by a keeper of dogs and one by a keeper of chickens. She made money by her chickens, established her sons as house-holders, made even more money, and resolved to found a shrine. She asked the king, who said it was all right to do it (hence the name *Bya-rung-kha-shor*). He kept to his word, even when the people of the country protested at the size of the shrine that a mere keeper of chickens was erecting. She began with the help of her four sons, one servant, a donkey and an elephant, and although she died before it was finished, they completed the work, enshrining within relics of the former Buddha Kāśyapa. By merit and by power of their vows the brothers were born later as the main founders of Buddhism in Tibet: the first as King Trhi-song-deu-tsen, the second as the Pundit Śāntarakshita, the third as Padmasambhava and the forth as Trhi-sh'er of Ba. The animals were disgruntled at what they thought was thankless treatment, so the ass resolved to be born as the wicked minister Ma-sh'ang. The servant counteracted this by being born as the good minister Padma K'ang-tsen of Gö. The elephant then resolved to be born as the wicked king Lang-dar-ma. A friendly crow then decided to be born as Päl-gyi-dorje of Lho-lung.[a] The only significant point in this story is the firm linking of the stūpa with Tibet. One may note in contrast that the Tibetan version of the founding of Svayambhūnāth merely repeats the account of the *Svayambhūpurāṇa* and no attempt is made to appropriate this stūpa also as part of their own past history.[23]

Bodhnāth is situated five miles or so to the north of Pātan and by the side of the main trade-route leading in from Tibet, which may well be the reason for the choice of site. It is encircled by a ring of picturesque houses, from the windows of which strings of prayer-flags are stretched across to the summit umbrella. Just before my visit it had been repainted and regilded. In design it represents an even later development than that of Svayambhū, for the circumambulatory platform has been incorporated into the general structure, mounting in tiers to the central dome. Therefore it is a sacrilege to use this platform, as it would be tantamount to walking on the stūpa itself.

[a] The parts played by all these will be told in the following chapter. This account of the legend is based on a Tibetan printed text, of which copies are available at the shrine: *mchod-rten chen-po bya-rung-kha-shor-gyi lo-rgyus thos-pas grol-ba*. See also Toussaint, *Padma Thang-Yig*, pp. 238–9. Waddell's translated extracts (*Lamaism*, p. 315 ff.) diverge in certain details.

If the Tibetans were responsible for the building of the present shrine, it might be dated back at the very earliest to the eleventh century, which would also accord with the developed design. But there may well have been a more ancient foundation which only the archaeologist could discover.[24]

All stūpas present this same problem, because they are solid right through, and so any improvements or additions made during the centuries must inevitably conceal completely what was there before. In India it has been possible to excavate to their central foundations, for the neglect of eight centuries or so has robbed these great shrines of their former sanctity and grandeur. In the process of restoration, much could be learned about their origins. Even in Ceylon, which has remained a Buddhist country ever since the founding of the first stūpas there, public opinion is sufficiently enlighted to appreciate the value of scholastic research, so that it has been possible to investigate the shrines without causing offence. But in Nepal, where the stūpas have likewise never ceased to be objects of faith and devotion, the people are still largely unaccustomed to the European and may all too easily become suspicious of his insatiable curiosity. It would be most unwise to start digging into the side of Svayambhūnāth, even with governmental permission. In the case of Bodhnāth, such thoughts scarcely enter the mind, for the whole scene presents itself so firmly in terms of here and now. The surrounding houses are largely filled with Tibetans of whom some are permanent residents, while others are here on pilgrimage. They circumambulate the stūpa, spinning the prayer-wheels as they go. They visit the adjacent temple, make offerings for the general upkeep and for the assistance of the poorer pilgrims. Whether intent on good or evil, the Tibetan is a cheerful fellow, and nowhere probably does this show to greater advantage than at Bodhnāth and Svayambhū.

From the early stūpas of Pātan to the great shrine of Bodhnāth we have spanned a period of 1,000 years and more, and since Nepal seems to have been in constant contact with the

Plate 9

(a) *Buddha-Heruka.* (p.79)
(b) *Ushnīsha-sitātapatrā.* (p.116 *fn.*)

Plate 10

The 84 Siddhas. (pp. 85-7 and pp. 316-17 for key)

Plate 11

Detail of pl. 10
(a) Nāgārjuna and Krishna (Nag-po-pa).
(b) Dharmapa, rDo-ka-ri-pa and Medhenpa

Plate 12

A palace-courtyard in Pātan. The shrine is now occupied by a petty-official.

Plate 13

The Great Stūpa, Svayambhūnāth. (p 95)

Plate 14

(a) The Great Stūpa, Bodhnāth. (p. 98)
(b) A Mongolian lama in his temple at Bodhnāth.

Plate 15

Image of Lokeśvara in the Great Golden Temple (Hiraṇyavarṇa Mahāvihar), Pātan. (p. 102)

(a) The Buddhist temple of Vidyeśvarī outside Kathmandu. *(p. 102)*

(b) A Hindu temple of Bhadgaon, built by Bhūpatīndra Malla (1703)

Plate 16

cities of central India, we may presume that the developments and changes in the doctrine which have been summarized in the preceding chapters, usually had their repercussions in this small mountain valley. In retrospect the Buddhism of Nepal might appear to be predominantly tantric, but this is merely because the later phases have tended to obscure the earlier ones. Also early references are very scanty. The Tibetan historian Tāranātha relates that Vasubandhu, the great Yogācāra philosopher of the fourth century A.D., visited Nepal and died there, but it may be noted that he associates him with the practice of *mantras*. 'Finally surrounded by numerous disciples he travelled to Nepal. There he set up a school of the doctrine and the community increased to great numbers without any set-backs. One day he saw a priest ploughing in religious garb and he was saddened at the thought that the Master's doctrine could so deteriorate. Having given instruction in the doctrine in the midst of the assembly, he recited the *mantra* of Ushnīsha-vijayā thrice forwards and thrice backwards and then he left this life.'[a] Tāranātha's next reference to Nepal relates to a period 350 years later. 'At the time of the seven Pāla kings the doctrine was very active in Magadha, Bengal, in Oḍiviśa and other western districts and in Kashmir. Elsewhere except for scattered communities it was non-existent. In the small country of Nepal it was extremely active. In these places the Mantrayāna and the Mahāyāna were very strong, and though in general there were quite a large number of disciples (*śrāvakas*), all the kings and nobility honoured the Mahāyāna.'[b]

The two well-known Chinese pilgrims of the seventh century, Yuan Chwang and I Tsing, refer to Nepal, although neither of them visited the country. Yuan Chwang was informed that there were about 2,000 monks belonging to the Great and the Lesser Way and that Buddhist monasteries and Hindu temples touched each other. The people were of bad character (presumably just Indian prejudice) but were excellent craftsmen.[c]

[a] Tāranātha, tx. p. 97, tr. p. 125. [b] *ibid.*, tx. p. 155, tr. p. 202.
[c] Watters, *Yuan Chwang II*, pp. 83–5.

The Newars are still good craftsmen and we have already mentioned the many monasteries and temples of Pātan, which may be seen to this day. In the time of Yuan Chwang the pagoda seems to have been the typical architectural style of northern India, and we may presume that like the doctrine itself this mode of building was originally introduced to Nepal from India. Whereas it has almost entirely disappeared from the land of its origin, in Nepal it has survived in profusion. It is the norm for Hindu and Buddhist temples alike, but whereas the former often stand singly by the wayside and in the squares, the latter normally form part of a complete monastic compound (pl. 16). This is approached through a porch-way, on either side of which are usually painted Gaṇeśa and Mahākāla, the two favourite defenders.[25] The main temple faces one across a square courtyard, in which are smaller shrines, sometimes a subsidiary temple, more often numerous little stūpas. The chief divinity, Śākya-muni, Akshobhya or Lokeśvara, reposes in the main shrine behind gilt-bronze or silver doors (pl. 15). On the other sides of the courtyard are the dwellings of the former monks, with window-casements slanting outwards, elaborately adorned with fine wood-carving. There is nothing in the present buildings that suggests great age, but then until 200 years ago these temples and courtyards were still being cared for and renovated. The exquisite wood-carving, which is their chief beauty, was still a living craft. Most of the woodwork one now sees, is probably between 400 and 200 years old, but many of these buildings may have been in use for 1,200 years.

In Pātan there are fourteen great monasteries (*vihāra*) and about a hundred subsidiary ones. In Kathmandu there are eight main ones and about seventy-five subsidiary ones. Their number bears witness to the great strength of Buddhism towards the end of the first millennium A.D. Pātan must have been a kind of vast university-city, differing little in its mode of life from similar towns in mediaeval Europe. In fact its buildings, its traditions, its way of life, must have been modelled on the great monastic universities of central India. Tāranātha's stray references suggest an especially close connection with Vikramaśīla. Nepalese Buddhism was part of Indian Buddhism, for they not only based themselves on the same texts, but they used the same language, Sanskrit. Of the Buddhist Sanskrit manuscripts, which have survived to our times, by far the greater number have been preserved in Nepal. Moreover the present internal arrangements of the Nepalese vihāras, which have remained unchanged through the centuries, can only reflect the last period of Buddhism in India. It is interesting to note therefore that the great non-tantric beings, Śākya-muni, Avalokiteśvara, Akshobhya and Mañjuśrī, continue to occupy the main shrines. The tantric gods, Heruka, Hevajra and Śamvara, are consigned to small temples apart, where women, who are excluded from the main shrines, may approach them. The central symbol of the doctrine continues to be the stūpa, and upon it is superimposed the notion of buddhahood as fivefold. Thus in courtyards, in public squares and by the road-side, everywhere one sees little stūpas, variations upon that single theme, on which Buddhist faith was based. Into the four sides of some of them are inset little images of the buddhas of the four directions, Akshobhya, Ratnasambhava, Amitābha and Amoghasiddhi. Vairocana, the central buddha, is normally not represented, for as Ādibuddha, the whole shrine is his representation. It is important to realize that these five are never regarded as five different gods, or even as five separate buddhas. Brian Hodgson seems to have heard the term *dhyāni-buddha* (buddha of meditation) used in Nepal and although such a compound is odd Sanskrit, it may well have been in use by the Newars. I have never heard it, but it is by no means inapt, for it suggests the transcendent nature of these five buddha-forms. Only Akshobhya is revered separately, receiving the honour which is due to a great god, but his association with Śākya-muni is very close, for he represents essentially the buddha of the moment of triumph over Māra, who is Death and Desire. It was for this reason that he was later recognized as head of the powerful vajra-family when the five-fold scheme was devised, and still later as the essential buddha-body of the fierce tantric gods. Perhaps too much has been written about the degeneration of Buddhism without its being realized that those who consciously introduced these changes were usually attempting to devise a more effective representation of one essential idea. The inmates of these vihāras, or at least the best of them, would have been well aware of the nature of buddhahood and the significance of the symbols employed. Most of them presumably followed the way of the *sūtras*, involving monastic discipline, worshipping at the shrines, the reciting and copying of texts and the practice of mental concentration. The inmates of Bhaja and Bhedsa must have occupied themselves in exactly the same way a thousand years earlier. Their symbolism was by no means so developed and instead of an ornate image they were content with a plain stūpa, but faith and devotion were always the mainspring of their religious life. Tantric practices came as an addition to the life of the monasteries. They were fostered by the yogins, to whom reference has been made in the last chapter, and of whom several came to Nepal. Nāropa, Dārika, Ratnarakshita, Maitripa, are all well-known names to the Tibetan historians. It was from Nāropa that Marpa received the teachings, which he in turn transmitted to Mila Räpa, thus founding one of the chief Tibetan Buddhist orders, the Ka-gyü-pa. It was also in Nepal 200 years earlier that Śāntarakshita had encountered Padma-sambhava and conveyed the invitation of King Trhi-song deu-tsen for him to visit Tibet. These great yogins introduce an uncertain element into the religious practice of their time. Some of them were undoubtedly avowed Buddhists, for they became teachers and abbots in Buddhist monasteries. Others lived entirely apart from all religious institutions, and it is clear from the texts which originated in their circles, as well as from their fanciful biographies, that these masters regarded themselves as free from all sectarian bias, as much Buddhist as Hindu. Thus later the conventional set of eighty-four Great Yogins came to be revered both by the followers of Śiva and by the tantric Buddhists. Nevertheless traditional Buddhism continued to remain quite conscious of its separate identity and the Tibetans who came to India and Nepal in search of true doctrine, took back only those religious texts which bore the mark of Buddhist orthodoxy. The tantras collected in the Kanjur are all consciously Buddhist in spite of their free importation of alien ideas, and they differ markedly from the set of Shaivite tantras, collected and edited by Sir John Woodroffe. But although organized Buddhism could preserve its identity, the religion of the lay-folk could not, and indeed never had. A god or a great ascetic was revered for one thing only, namely his miraculous powers. There will be occasion below to refer to the special case of the yogin Matsyendranāth.

Meanwhile Buddhism in India was entering upon its last chapter. Ratnarakshita was one of the last of the pundits to seek refuge in Nepal and it is of interest to note Tāranātha's brief résumé of this man's accomplishments and activities, for he seems to be typical of the Buddhist scholar of those days. 'The Great Master Ratnarakshita was equal in knowledge with Śākyaśrī (the great pundit of Kashmir) so far as the Perfection of Wisdom teachings and the sciences generally were concerned. In logic Śākyaśrī was more capable, but in mantras the former was said to be more skilled. In the exercise of spiritual and magical power they were considered equal. Ratnarakshita belonged to the Mahāsanghika Order and was Master of Mantras at Vikramaśīla. He had encountered many *yi-dams* (tutelary divinities) face to face, Śamvara, Kālacakra, Yamāntaka and others. On one occasion he heard the sounds of the sixteen aspects of the Void expressed in the music with which the Nāgas and Asuras honour Avalokiteśvara on his holy mountain (Potala). He could impart knowledge through consecration and the *ḍākinīs* came in person to receive the sacrificial cakes.[a] He petrified a mad elephant by fixing his eyes in

[a] Concerning the *ḍākinīs*, see p. 175.

the appropriate glance. He prophesied the downfall of Magadha two years before it happened, and many pupils who believed in him, began from that time on to make their way to Kashmir and Nepal.'[a] In due course 'the whole of the land of Magadha was conquered and many monks were slain at Odantapuri. This monastery and Vikramaśīla were destroyed. In the place of the monastery at Odantapuri the Moslems built a fort. The pundit Śākyaśrī made his way to Jagardala in Oḍiviśa in the east, and having stayed there three years he went on to Tibet. But Ratnarakshita came to Nepal'.[b] From now on Buddhism in Nepal was left to rely upon its own strength and within a hundred years or so the monks had finally capitulated to Hinduism. If one remembers that Nepal means just one little valley, this rapid collapse is not surprising. However, whereas in India Buddhism was ruthlessly destroyed, in Nepal it has been forced into conformity with other traditions, which represent the negation of all its higher striving, so that it has died of atrophy, leaving outward forms that have long since ceased to be Buddhist in anything but the name.

In order to understand how this came about, one must contrast Hinduism and Buddhism in their essential natures. They are often spoken of as though they were two distinct religions, catering for religious needs of different men in analogous ways. But in India they were always somehow complementary to one another. Hinduism came to represent the affirmation of all of man's activities and Buddhism was their denial. This denial first appeared in the Upanishads as part of the religious experience of men who lived in northern India 2,600 years ago, long before either Buddhism or Hinduism as we know them now had taken form. This denial expressed itself as asceticism, a deliberate withdrawing from the world, so that by perfect detachment one might taste tranquillity and calm. It was in this setting that the doctrine of the Śākya-Sage had its origin and it

[a] Tāranātha, tx. p. 191, tr. p. 253.
[b] *ibid.*, tx. p. 193, tr. p. 255. Śākya-śrī arrived in Tibet in 1204. For an account of his activities see Tucci, *TPS*, II, pp. 334–9.

continued to characterize the doctrine of his followers. They may have preached good conduct in the villages (and it was seemingly this that endeared them to the Emperor Aśoka) but in order to be a true son of Gotama one had to renounce all things and become an ascetic. We have already recorded the later development of the doctrine and it will be remembered how essential is the belief in the non-substantiality of all things. Only by holding firm to this, was it possible to revere the great beings, the buddhas and bodhisattvas, and still remain a true Buddhist. To affirm their reality would mean automatically placing oneself amongst the fools or the heretics. Thus Buddhism, if it were to be true to itself, relied always upon the existence of an élite, who were contemplatives and scholars. Since these always congregated in monasteries, the destruction of these places was sufficient to bring the doctrine to an end. But Hinduism is the whole traditional life of India, social and religious. It embraces every possible mode of activity, ascetic and social. Its fundamental notion is that all should play their proper part within the social framework, and with this idea society came to be divided into castes. Hinduism, therefore, provided primarily for the life of men in this world, not because its philosophy is this-worldly, but because most people are concerned with the life of this world. Thus the gods of Hinduism are conceived in the terms which commend themselves to ordinary folk. Here there is no abstraction of a fivefold immanent/transcendent absolute. The supreme being is no longer even Brahman, but Vishnu or Śiva, a god who truly is and who acts. Moreover there was always room for new traditions and new divinities. New traditions could be integrated with the old ones and new gods identified with those already known. Hinduism is perhaps like that characteristic Indian tree, the banyan, which drops roots from its branches and goes on growing where it can. Even when the first roots die, it is still the same tree that goes on growing. Hence so long as it remained within the orbit of Hinduism, Buddhism could never hope to compete for the support of the lay-folk. At the most it could hope that they would be generous to its monks as well as to brahmins and other ascetics. Likewise it is doubtful if any Indian king was ever exclusively Buddhist, for as head of society he was bound to respect Hindu distinctions and provisions. It is not an exaggeration to characterize Buddhism as essentially anti-social. It certainly succeeded in accommodating itself to the requirements of ordinary folk, but only at the cost of compromising its basic tenets. It could do this with safety only under two conditions: firstly it was essential to maintain a strong monastic core and secondly by compromising it must not risk losing its identity. It could then become a religion in the full sense of the term, providing for the needs of all men, whatever their calling. This could happen in Tibet, but never in India, nor as we shall see, in Nepal.

Here Buddhism was placed in an even more delicate position just because the valley is small. India is so vast, that even if Buddhist monks found themselves in disfavour in one region, they could always thrive in another. Even when the Moslems arrived, they could delay the final tragedy by withdrawing ever further to the east. But Nepal is enclosed. The monks in their monasteries were surrounded by lay-folk who were Hindu in sentiment if not in name. Moreover the monasteries of Pātan and Kathmandu are by no means retreats from the world, and thus the monks could scarcely avoid being members of society, or at least being considered as such. With the disappearance of the great monasteries of central India, Buddhism in Nepal was doomed. The monks had no choice but to come to terms with society. That they should have acquitted themselves so well, by worldly standards, is a sure sign of the high esteem in which they were held. Their fellow countrymen wished them no harm; they just regarded them as respected members of society like the brahmins. Thus they were known as *banras* (honourable) and assigned to the highest caste. Their caste system finally received official sanction in the mid-fourteenth century and thereafter true Buddhism was a thing of the past. Oldfield diagnosed the case correctly seventy-five years ago. 'Nothing has contributed so much to the decline of Buddhism in Nepal as the adoption of caste by the Buddhist Newars, and the consequent decay of all the monastic institutions of the country.'[a] Their last concession to society was the abandonment of celibacy. The theories peculiar to tantric Buddhism may have helped to prepare the way for this, but in any case as equals of the brahmins, it was inevitable that they should claim for themselves all equivalent privileges and concessions. One need not suppose that married life was at once universally adopted. The monasteries were certainly well cared for and some tradition of scholarship continued until after the Gurkha conquest. It is also possible that there were some monks in a few of the many vihāras. Thus Buddhism has been dying slowly. One might even extend the simile of the trees. Along the tracks throughout Nepal the banyan and the pipul are often planted in pairs. They provide shade for weary travellers at the resting-places and it is generally believed that they are the masculine and feminine versions of the same tree. The banyan is thought to be feminine because of its lavish productiveness. The pipul, like most other trees, grows only one main trunk. It scatters its seeds abroad and these grow into independent trees. If Hinduism is like the banyan, Buddhism is represented by the pipul. It has scattered its seeds abroad in different countries and these have taken root in different soils. The seed has been self-abnegation, of which the philosophical counterpart is universal non-substantiality, and the trunk has been a sound monastic order. But in Nepal, as in India, both trees have grown together. In India a vicious woodcutter cut the pipul down, but he tired of hacking at the banyan with its many trunks. There remained in Nepal one small pipul-tree, and since no new seeds could now come from the neighbouring country and meanwhile nothing checked the banyan's growth, the pipul was at last surrounded and stifled. The lifeless trunk remains as the relic of a monastic system and the branches are lost amidst those of the banyan.

[a] Oldfield, *Sketches from Nipal II*, p. 131. His observations are in general frank and illuminating.

There is no need to list the many castes into which Newar society is divided, for in this respect we are concerned only with the descendants of the monks.[a] They form the highest of three groups and like all other castes their ranks are closed. They are known as *banra* (honourable) not because they have resolved to lead a religious life, but because they are the successors of those once unworthy monks. Even so, their caste must be confirmed by the performance of the proper ceremony, for from generation to generation the vows must be made and then retracted. As this is an expensive business, parents prefer to wait until they have sufficient sons to make the outlay worth while. Thus when they are brought to make their vows, the children may be any age from a few months to ten years. There will be a large number of them, for all the parents who are members of the vihāra will have agreed together on a suitable day. They will in any case have first taken the advice of an astrologer. Until this time the boys have let their hair grow long. A little bag of white cloth, containing particles of gold and silver and the five kinds of precious stones, is tied to a central strand of hair. Leaving this intact, the oldest *banra* of the vihāra shaves the head of each boy, giving the hair to his paternal aunt. The boys are then given monastic dress and for four days they act as monks. They may not eat meat or salt or onions or tomatoes or rice. Nor may they touch cats or dogs or buffaloes or human beings of low caste. Every day they must beg at seven houses, carrying a staff in the left hand and a begging-bowl in the right. After four days they return to the vihāra, and protest to its head that the rule is too difficult. He pretends to upbraid them, but since he has been through just the same ceremony in his youth, there is no doubt what the outcome will be. They are released from their vows, their normal clothes are returned to them and they resume the life of an ordinary layman, continuing in their now hereditary crafts as workers in silver, gold or crystal, as moulders of bronze images, as wood-carvers, workers in stucco and painters. Indeed things of such

[a] For complete lists see Oldfield, *loc. cit.* and Lévi, *Népal I*, p. 228 ff.

beauty have come and still come from their hands, that one's regret for the decay of the institutions to which they belong, is tempered by wonderment at their individual skills. Moreover they are still a smiling and friendly people, although they often appear saddened and subdued by the long period of subservience to another race. Unhappily in the changed political circumstances of today, their suppressed aspirations may all too easily find misguided expression in the rage of modern party-strife. Nevertheless the traditions of their vihāras continue to supply some form of central stability to their lives, although they are Buddhist in little more than name. These *banras,* as descendants of the original monks, preserve their property rights in the vihāras. The families have so increased through the generations, that it is no longer possible for them all to live within the compound, but their social and religious life centres around the vihāra, to which the family traditionally belongs. It is there that their sons are enrolled into their caste by means of the ceremony described above and they all continue to be responsible by rota for due attendance upon the temple-images. These receive regular daily worship. In the morning offerings are made of flowers, lamps and incense and clothes, cosmetics and food. Rice and milk, butter and honey are suitable for buddhas, bodhisattvas and non-tantric divinities, but flesh and wine are expected by the great tantric gods. Again after sunset they are honoured with lamps and incense. This sort of worship differs in no way from that paid to Hindu divinities, and most of those who perform these ceremonies, conceive of their gods in just the same terms. There are two great festivals during the year of definite Buddhist character, that of the chaityas and that of Akshobhya Buddha. One might add the festival of Śākya-muni, which is the chief celebration of Buddhists in the Theravadin countries, but this does not seem to be generally observed in Nepalese vihāras. There is much sincere devotion amongst the Newars, and private visits to the shrines in the vihāras and especially to Svayambhūnāth are freely made. Also ceremonies are frequently privately instituted, but for these the assistance of the priests is required. Although these priests normally pursue their own crafts like all other *banras,* they represent the élite of the Buddhist community, for they are the vajra-masters (*vajrācārya*) without whose power and guidance no aspirant to the higher knowledge could hope to gain access. Nowadays there is no thought of higher knowledge, for a boy is consecrated as vajra-master just because that is his caste. If the ceremony should be omitted by his parents, he will lose his special caste and become an ordinary *banra.* Nor do most of these vajra-masters even wish to exercise their priestly calling, and even if they do so, they are not expected to be especially learned. The one need is to know how to perform the rites, of which the homa-sacrifice is the most important. The offering of butter and grain, which is poured into the flames of a specially shaped hearth, is an ancient form of Indian sacrifice, which was adopted by Buddhists in quite early times. The first Buddhist text to give detailed instructions for the performance of this ceremony, seems to be the *Mañjuśrī-mūla-kalpa.* Its practice in Nepal does not therefore represent just local Hindu influence, as might at first be supposed. Moreover the same ceremony is still performed by the Tibetans and Japanese.[a]

Buddhism in Nepal has succumbed not because of contamination with non-Buddhist ideas and practices, for these were always present in some degree. It is indeed in its ability to absorb them, that Buddhism has shown its strength elsewhere. It has succumbed, because there is no true élite, none who have abandoned home for a homeless state and whose sole desire is the realization of the inner meaning of the doctrine. There are no monks, but only lay-folk, and so the Buddhism of Nepal represents the religion of the ordinary Buddhist lay-man, much as it must always have been. He could not be expected to grapple with the subtleties of the doctrine. The buddhas are conceived as gods like other gods he knows or knew before. They are real beings, immensely superior in power to mortal

[a] There are four types of homa-ritual, for pacifying, prospering, overpowering and destroying. See p. 258 ff.

living-beings. He supplicates them primarily in order to gain their favour and takes part in their festivals because it is the custom to do so. He is scarcely likely to concern himself with the pedigree of these higher beings, to distinguish in fact what is properly Buddhist from what is Hindu. Indeed his point of view coincides with that of the non-scholastic yogin, who in his pursuit of higher power and knowledge made use of any divinity that might help him to gain his ends. Such indiscriminating belief can be resisted and held in check only by an active community, conscious of its responsibility as the guardian of the traditional doctrines. But in Nepal there was no longer such a community. There were just laymen and yogins.

It is not therefore surprising to discover that the most popular divinity in Nepal is a yogin metamorphosed as a god, namely Matsyendranāth, identified as Lokeśvara. This yogin is listed among the eighty-four great siddhas, and although his biography is a later invention, which was devised to explain his name, Lord Indra of the Fish, tradition is strong in naming him as the master of another yogin, Gorakhnāth. The followers of the latter are still to be found in India and they also are to be associated with another fraternity of yogins, the Pāśupatas, who were active in India at least from the early centuries A.D. onwards.[a] These are followers of Śiva, the great ascetic, who is also known as Paśupati, lord of creatures. We have already suggested that the later tantras originated in the circles of such yogins, and it was for this reason that they were revered as much by the tantric buddhists as by the Shaivites. It is significant therefore that the chief shrine sacred to Hindus in Nepal, is that of Paśupati, while the divinity most favoured by the Buddhists is Matsyendranāth. At this level of belief one can make no absolute distinction between what is Hindu and what is Buddhist. Matsyendra is a national divinity, honoured even by the Gurkhas, and upon the *lingam* of Paśupati is placed once yearly the head-dress of Akshobhya. Paśupati may be Śiva

[a] Briggs, *Gorakhnāth*, p. 218 ff.

and Matsyendra may be Avalokiteśvara, but both are one in Lokeśvara, the Lord of the World, whose favourite abode is on the snow-peaks of the Himālaya. It must have been for this reason that Nepal was a favoured haunt of these yogins, and when traditional Buddhism foundered, they succeeded in leaving their indelible imprint on the little that remained. Even the names of the great Buddhist stūpas, Svayambhūnāth and Buddhanāth, introducing the term *nāth,* Lord, suggest themselves as the names by which the yogins and their followers must have known them. Again the term Ādi-buddha comes all too close to Ādi-nāth, and the latter refers to Śiva. Primaeval buddha or primaeval lord, it is all the same to ordinary lay-folk and to vagrant yogins. Even those little stūpas, representing everywhere the doctrine of the buddhas, all too often assume a form curiously reminiscent of Śiva's *lingam.* Perhaps after all it is a matter for surprise, that the Newar Buddhists of Nepal should have preserved any consciousness of their separate identity at all. That they should have done so, is an indication of the strength of those monastic establishments more than a thousand years ago. At least they preserve the memory of the great beings, in whose honour the tiered pagoda-roofs were raised, Śākyamuni, Mañjuśrī, Akshobhya, Avalokiteśvara, all of whom still receive their share of worship. The set of five buddhas, too abstract a concept for the later times, serves as a mere auspicious device, suitable for painting over doorways.

Of the set of four goddesses, Locanā, Māmakī, Pāṇḍuravāsinī and Tārā, only the last became a general object of devotion. Her mere name, 'Saviouress', was perhaps sufficient to win her adherents, and she comes to rival Avalokiteśvara, the Saviour in popularity. In so far as she belongs to the *karma*-family, her colour is green.[a] But since she comes to be considered a transcendent being in her own right, she may also assume the colour of the central Buddha-family of Vairocana, which is

[a] see above p. 82.

white. Thus it came to be said that there were two Tārās, a green one and a white one.[a]

One may also note in this respect that Avalokiteśvara is white, because he came to be invoked as supreme lord. But his family-colour is properly red, for like the other forms of Lokeśvara, he belongs to the family of Amitābha. Such change in colour represents a weakening of the symbolism which was inherent in the notion of five families. The white Tārā and the white Lokeśvara have nothing directly to do with Vairocana, for whereas he is the supreme buddha-body, they are in essence nothing more than divinities conceived in the Hindu pattern. In much earlier times the transmitters of the sūtras and tantras had filled their introductory chapters with lists of names of bodhisattvas so that the teaching buddha might have an audience worthy of him. The teachers of the mystic doctrines elaborated the fivefold scheme of buddhahood, in which colour played an important symbolic part. Now others who were ignorant of the real nature of a bodhisattva and of the meaning of symbolic forms, who felt only the need for a higher being they could worship, subverted the proper forms. It is sometimes suggested that the Mahāyāna is generally a form of popular Buddhism, but this is a misleading half-truth. In all countries Buddhism has had its true practisers and its popularizers, and these last have always drawn on the religious forms they had to hand. The process inevitably began in India and achieved its full development in Nepal. Under Shaivite influence all the non-tantric male divinities tended to unite in Lokeśvara and the feminine divinities in the Great Goddess Kālī, known generally just as the Lady (*Bhagavatī*). Their most popular forms are Matsyendranāth and the Kumārī, about whom more will be said below. The fact that the Goddess Kālī should have prevailed over Tārā is a final indication of the triumph of

[a] Later on twenty-one forms of Tārā were recognized. They are represented as a mandala of Tārās and are invoked in a form of litany. Concerning the stages of development in the popularity of this goddess, see Tucci, *TPS*, II, pp. 387–91.

Hinduism. Although the white Tārā was always a popular divinity, she had acquired quite valid Buddhist credentials in the course of the centuries. She was accepted as one of the great beings, whereas the Goddess in Indian Buddhism and afterwards in Tibet was never more than a fierce defender of the faith. Tārā and Avalokiteśvara have several features in common. They are both regarded preëminently as saviours. They are both holders of the lotus (*padmapāṇi*). They both possess a triumphant thousand-armed, thousand-eyed form.[a] They are even regarded as partners like that much older pair Mañjuśrī and Sarasvatī. The *mantra* of Mañjuśrī is OṂ VĀGĪŚVARI MŪṂ which might be applicable in the first instance to his partner, for grammatically it is a feminine vocative, saluting the Lady of Speech. It may be that we have here a significant analogy with the well-known *mantra* of Avalokiteśvara: OṂ MAṆIPADME HŪṂ which (if the grammar is classically correct) can likewise only be taken as a feminine vocative, invoking her of the jewelled lotus.[26] One is constantly reminded of this possibility as one travels through Nepal, for once outside the main valley, the commonest shrines are those dedicated to the Protectors of the Three Families (*rigs-gsum-dgon-po*), Mañjuśrī, Avalokiteśvara and Vajrapāṇi. Their three *mantras,* namely the two already quoted with OṂ VAJRAPĀṆI HŪṂ as third, are always inscribed on the stones and sometimes the gods themselves are represented. They must be quite an old trio, going back to the time when there were only three families, those of the tathāgata, the lotus and the vajra, just as they are given in the first chapter of the *Mañjuśrī-mūla-kalpa.* These great beings of the Mahāyāna are all respectfully remembered in Nepal, but it is for Matsyendranāth that popular enthusiasm seems to be reserved.

This transformed yogin is a very composite form of god. His most important function, the yearly bringing of the rains, might well seem a quite unnecessary occupation in Nepal,

[a] In the case of Tārā, I refer to Ushnīsha-sitātapatrā. See pl. 9*b*.

which relies unfailingly upon the arrival of the monsoon in early summer. It is at this season that preparations for his festival are begun. A shrine is erected in a special cart; it is equipped with an archway and hung with flags and banners; the roof is constructed of long bamboos bound together and tapering to a point some fifty feet or more in height. On the summit is placed an image of Vajrasattva surmounted by a gilt umbrella.[a] After ceremonial bathing the image is dressed and placed within the travelling shrine. He is then dragged in slow stages, each taking several days, through the streets of Pātan, accompanied by a smaller cart in which his younger brother Mīnanāth is borne. It is no light feat to drag these two clumsy vehicles with their ill-fitting wheels through the deep-rutted streets, the sides of which have become pools of muddy water in the heavy-pouring rain. If ever an effigy performed his expected function, it is certainly Matsyendranāth. At every stage he is met with offerings of flowers, grain and sweets, which are passed up from under a surging crowd of umbrellas to the priests in the cart. When the carts come to the end of their course, the god is disrobed and carried to a temple outside the town. One significant feature of the disrobing ceremony is the displaying to the people of the shirt which the image wears. The shirt is perhaps a genuine relic or at least it represents the memory of one, and it may well have been originally the centre of the whole festival. It is not unlikely that the followers of this yogin really did preserve his shirt (perhaps his only garment) and that once in later times when the monsoon was delayed, it was brought forth and proved a sovereign remedy. It would have required no more than this for a yearly ceremony to be instituted, and before many generations had passed, Matsyendranāth would be remembered for this alone. The later account of how he was supplicated and brought to Nepal to end the drought, occasioned by his follower Gorakhnāth, bears the

[a] For a detailed description of the car see an article by Lobsinger-Dellenbach, 'La construction du char de procession de Pātan', *Etudes Asiatiques*, 1953, p. 99 ff.

marks of pure invention.[a] It assumes for one thing his identity with Lokeśvara, and this would in any case have been a subsequent development. One may note that the image is red in order to mark this identity, and when the Newars tell one that he is really Avalokiteśvara, this is true only in so far as Avalokiteśvara was himself already identified with Lokeśvara. There would in any case be nothing unusual in a yogin receiving divine honours, for this was characteristic of the master-pupil relationship which was fundamental to tantric practice. Nowadays Gorakhnāth is still regarded as a god by his followers.[b] The above explanation of the origin of the monsoon-festival in his honour is of course pure hypothesis, though quite plausible. The arbitrary manner in which a new custom may become established is illustrated by the case of the little Kumārī.

Two hundred years ago a *Banra* girl of Kathmandu became possessed and claimed to be a goddess. She was judged an imposter and exiled by royal command from the town. Immediately one of the queens was seized by a fit, thus seemingly declaring the genuineness of the child's possession by the goddess. The king, convinced of his mistake, recalled her and instituted a triumphant festival in her honour as amends for his harshness. Two boys, representing Gaṇeśa and Bhairava, were chosen as her guardians (pl. 17). Not only was the festival continued from year to year, but on the children reaching puberty, new representatives of the divinities were sought and so the custom has continued to the present day. Its origins, however, seem to be quite forgotten by the people, and had it first occurred a few centuries earlier, it would be as mysterious to us as the case of Matsyendranāth. This little girl is known as the Kumārī, divine princess, and is popularly regarded as though she were Kālī, the Great Goddess, herself.

It has been suggested that Hinduism and Buddhism have effected a condominion in Nepal, as though both were equally active in some traditional form.[c] In order to realize the present

[a] This legend has been discussed by Lévi, *Népal I*, p. 347 ff.
[b] see Briggs, *Gorakhnāth*, p. 228 ff. [c] Landon, *Nepal II*, p. 212.

abject condition of Buddhism in the country, one should perhaps contrast it with Tibet. There one will find all those later developments, which are usually regarded as representing the complete degeneration of the doctrine, but side by side with them and even through them there manifests itself that higher religious striving, which represents the true life of any religion. Among the thousands of oddly-assorted monks in that country there are always a few who have in truth abandoned everything for the higher knowledge which bears fruit in the good of all living beings. Tibet is still at heart a Buddhist country. But Nepal is Hindu through and through. This is not to suggest that Hinduism itself is to be equated with a debased form of Buddhism, for in all fairness it should be mentioned that the non-Buddhist religious traditions of India all bear witness to the gradual darkening of a former profound religious awareness. Buddhism was not the sole repository of spirituality prior to the Moslem invasions, nor were its true exponents the only ones who suffered. Nevertheless the distinctions made above remain generally valid, for it is possible for Hinduism to retain a form that at least accords with some of its basic tenets, whereas when monasticism comes to an end, Buddhism is cut off at its roots.

The tree, however, has been so slow in dying, that it provides much interesting material for our understanding of the later Indian Buddhism. The styles of shrine and temple represent the India of a thousand years ago. Pātan must be similar in many respects to the great Buddhist university-cities of Magadha, of which all but nothing remains. Particularly informative is the layout of the vihāra with its main temple, central courtyard and surrounding houses of the monks. There is no indication that their practice was predominantly tantric as has been often suggested. Tantric divinities and practices had made their way into the monasteries, but they were primarily the preserve of the yogin who acknowledged no ties. It is also interesting to observe the attraction that these yogins had for the ordinary layfolk and how easily they might become transcendent beings. We shall find the same development in the case of another of their number, Padma-sambhava, who receives divine honours in Tibet to this day. For an understanding of what Buddhism meant to the laity generally in India, Nepal provides a sufficient example. It makes mockery of the whole notion of pure Buddhism as the preserve of any one people at any one time. If pure Buddhism means anything at all, it is referrable to individual belief and practice and so may occur in any country where a Buddhist tradition in any of its forms is sufficiently active.

Finally Nepal represents the end of Indian Buddhism; but long before it began to decline, men from both sides of the Himalayas were active in transferring it piecemeal to Tibet.

Wheel of the Doctrine with garland

IV

KINGS OF TIBET

Once separated from its basic Hindu context, Buddhism was bound to develop differently against different cultural backgrounds. It gained a new strength and independence as the sole representative of Indian spirituality and religious convention, but it was faced with new problems in establishing itself in the midst of other cultures and ideas. Just as its first practisers were Hindus, so its later ones were Kushans, Greeks and Persians, the peoples of Central Asia, Chinese and Tibetans. They all brought their contributions and imposed their own interpretations, and one may well wonder that Buddhism should have preserved so much of its essential character in the midst of such variety. It should, however, be clear from the discussion in the earlier chapters that Indian Buddhism was itself a most luxuriant growth, capable of being all things to all men. It is not without significance that the philosophical texts which appealed most to the Tibetans were the treatises on the Perfection of Wisdom with the doctrine of universal voidness interpreted in a spacial and celestial sense, that the divinities they best understood were those whose disposition was fierce and destructive, and that in the successions of reincarnating hierarchs they developed a special form of the rebirth-theory, for which Buddhist notions alone are not responsible. Yet this could come about without weakening in the slightest the essential core of the doctrine. The greatness and also the popularity of the yogin Mila-Räpa consisted in his ability to express Buddhist doctrine in a purely Tibetan form. The rhythm and the imagery of his verses are of the fresh and rugged style which characterizes all indigenous Tibetan poetry. It is just the religious content that is new.

Early Myths

If we could simply accept the accounts given by the later Tibetan historians of how Buddhism came to their country, the story would be straight-forward enough. They were all writing several centuries after the events they describe, when the benefits of their past cultural relationship with India were so obvious, that it was impossible for them to place in true perspective the earlier non-Buddhist history of their country, even when their traditions preserved clear memories of those former times. This has affected the Buddhists as much as those who claimed to remain faithful to native traditions, the p'ön-pos (*bon-po*), for these only became conscious of themselves as the transmitters of a separate doctrine when Buddhism began to threaten their privileges and their livelihood.[27] Both have therefore codified their scriptures on the Indian pattern, the Buddhists deliberately, the p'ön-pos because they had no choice in the matter. Before texts from neighbouring Buddhist countries arrived in Tibet from the seventh century onwards, there was no model for them to copy, not to mention the absence of an alphabet to write with. This is not to suggest that the Tibetans possessed no cultural heritage of their own before they placed themselves under Indian tutelage, for as in other early civilizations, this heritage existed and was transmitted orally in epic and ballad form. It is only important to observe that those who were later characterized as p'ön-po, are in no sense the special guardians of native traditions, and if we wish to know something of these, we must regard all early Tibetan literature as a fruitful source.

It has been all too easy for many Western travellers to see in Tibetan religion nothing but vain superstition and gross demonolatry, for it is scarcely to be disputed that it does appear in these forms. The inner life of course is hidden. One notes the satisfaction derived from repetitive formulas, from prayer-wheels, especially automatic ones, from the grotesque appearance of so many of their gods and their strange monastic dances. Probably fewer are acquainted with the weird deep-toned refrains which characterize their religious chanting and the gruesome nature of some of the offerings which accompany their prayers and aspirations towards enlightenment. All this should be sufficient to arouse serious interest in their religion quite apart from the strange psychic feats, of which at least one knowledgeable writer believes them capable.[a] When one hears of such happenings, one must remember that the Tibetans are still living (or were until a few years ago) in a world-age vastly different from our twentieth century. Their world is still flat. Virtue practised for its own sake, will still gain its certain reward. Learning and sanctity are still worthy of universal regard. The phenomenal condition is not a self-existent structure, but is dependent on other states of being. Thus he who knows how, may work things to his will for good or evil. In short, the Tibetans still believe in their religion. But to non-believers belief all too often appears as mere superstition. It is rational to believe nothing, but always difficult, if one believes, to know where to draw the line, and so the Tibetans do not draw one.

The writings of their historians, on which we must rely for most of our information, are therefore an extraordinary mixture of fact and fiction. The essential facts can fortunately often be corroborated from independent sources, which generally bear witness to the reliability of the traditions that were recorded.[b] Nor is the fiction without interest to those investigating the psychological basis of religious belief.

The curious story of the origin of the Tibetans has been related elsewhere, but it will be useful to quote an earlier version of it.[c] Although it has received official sanction from Buddhist writers, this legend was merely one of many indigenous accounts

[a] A. David Neel, *With Mystics and Magicians in Tibet*, London 1931.

[b] see G. Tucci, 'On the Validity of the Tibetan Historical Tradition', *India Antiqua* (Leiden 1947), pp. 309–22.

[c] *blon-po-bka'i-thang-yig*, folio 4*a* ff. See also Rockhill, *The Land of the Lamas* (London 1891), pp. 555–61, which represents the version of the *Maṇi-bka-'bum*.

of the origin of mankind.[a] It gained later acceptance, probably because some skilful Buddhist realized how well it might be combined with faith in Avalokiteśvara. In this version, the monkey is merely a pupil of the great god; later on he becomes an actual incarnation. The existence of the primitive pre-Buddhist version is suggested in another quotation, given below (p. 129) where it is of interest to note that it is related with the myth of the origin of kingship in Tibet. 'As for the origin of the Tibetans, according to primitive ideas they should be descended from the serpents, but according to doctrinal notions they are descended from Avalokiteśvara. The Buddha of Boundless Light was abiding in the Paradise of Great Bliss in the western quarter. The most good and excellent Universal Sovereign with chief assistants, thus five in all, appeared as emanations of Boundless Light. As his physical emanation Padma-sambhava appeared. His spiritual emanation Avalokiteśvara was born magically in an *udumbara*-flower which grew in the Milk-Lake in the south-western region. He wore the plumes of a vulture across one shoulder and he was calling out: MANU SARVA CITTA. For three days and nights he stirred up the samsāra in its pit, and he thought to himself: In this realm of samsāra there is not a single living being. But then when he looked from the summit of the Potala Mountain which rises in the eastern quarter, he saw that living beings were in the same wretched plight as before, and (from compassion) his head burst into a thousand pieces. Boundless Light stretched forth his hand, put the many heads to rights and gave his blessing to the Eleven-Headed Lord of Great Compassion, upon the crest of whose topmost head was the effigy of Amideva. "To this samsāra there is no end and no beginning. So be thou active until it be rendered void." Thus Boundless Light ordained. Thereupon there appeared an emanation in the form of a Monkey-King, by name Halumantha, and Tārā sent forth an emanation in the form of the Wrathful Ogress of the Rocks.

"By the strength of the high and mighty Avalokiteśvara, can

[a] see Tucci, *TPS, II*, p. 711 ff.

a monkey-hermit meditate in the Land of Snows and thereby lead many beings to buddha-fields?"–"I can," the monkey promised. So the Mighty Lord instructed that monkey-hermit in the five sections of monastic rules and made him take his vows. The monkey then went to the Land of Snows and settled down to meditate inside a dark cave. Just then the Ogress of the Rocks appeared in his presence and made lustful and lascivious gestures, but although she made tormas[a] for the Earth-Spirit for seven days, the monkey-hermit was unmoved by desire. On the eighth day that Ogress of the Rocks appeared in the form of a very beautiful woman and said: "You and I must set up house." Then she showed her breasts and her sides, but the monkey-hermit struck the ground and sat with his back to her. "I am a disciple of Āryapālo," he said, "and it is not proper that I should offend against the rule of chastity." Then the Ogress was abashed and said: "I shall die in this place." Then for seven days the monkey-hermit was filled with thoughts of compassion and he considered that he might refer the matter to the Mighty Lord. So he went by magic to the Potala Mountain and told the Lord about the Ogress. The Lord said: "You should set up house" and Tārā agreed with this arrangement. When the monkey returned to the Land of Snows, the Ogress said to him: "Alas, O Monkey-King, be attentive and listen. I am of evil works and have been born as the Ogress of the Rocks, but I have feelings of desire for you. If I do not set up house with you, I shall end by uniting with an ogre. Every morning we shall kill tens of thousands of living creatures. Every evening we shall kill thousands of living creatures. Then innumerable ogre-children will be born and this snowy realm of Tibet will become a land of ogres and not of men. Moreover these ogres will eat all living-beings in the world. So you must have compassion on me." She wept with wails of affliction. "If you do not hearken to me and show compassion, I shall end my life here and now, only to be born in the most hellish condition." After such entreaties as this, the monkey-hermit was affected by a

[a] see p. 245 (*gtor-ma*).

bodhisattva's compassion. So they set up house and lived together. Then when nine or ten months had passed, a child was born which was unlike his father and his mother. He stood upright and had a red flat face and no tail. He ate red meat and drank warm blood; he was impure in his ways and would never stay still. He was filled with desire and the other four great evils. He was like a wild monster which no one could tame. When he grew big, he would have eaten his mother, so his father left him in the wood named Peacock-Flock in the south. When a year had passed, he went to see how things were. The fellow had been disporting himself with the monkeys and his breed had increased to about five hundred. Thereafter they increased still more and filled the whole area. In summer they were burned by the sun and afflicted by the rain. In winter they suffered from the snow and the cold wind. They had neither food nor clothes and were very miserable. The father was greatly agitated and the five hundred children depressed. "What shall we eat? What shall we wear?" they cried and waved their arms. The monkey-hermit was greatly affected by compassion at seeing them in this weak condition and he wondered who might be responsible. As I have carried out the word of the Lord, he is responsible, he thought. So he went to the presence of Āryapālo and besought him thus: "Alas, Protector of Beings, Avalokiteśvara. I am thy disciple and have kept my vows as my life, but there came a lascivious ogress, filled with desires, who jeered at me and so I came to be deprived of my vow. O loving protector, since you gave the command, in carrying out your word, we have come to this plight. They have no hair on their bodies and their behinds are like rudders. O, what shall I do, to care for these offspring?" Then the mighty Avalokiteśvara scattered a handful of gold-dust over the land of Tibet, consecrating it as five kinds of grain that it might be food for those households, namely barley and wheat and rice and sesame and peas.'

When we turn to the next important event, the origin of kingship in Tibet, we find the same anxiety to attach their native traditions, however unconvincingly, to those of India.[a] Later writers do not even trouble to reach unanimity over the exact line of descent. It is sufficient that the first Tibetan king be descended from any respectable dynasty, so long as it is Indian. The version which follows comes from the history of Sum-pa Khen-po, who lived in the eighteenth century, and one notes that he was quite aware of the existence of the full version of the Tibetan myth which he distorts.

'The King of Vatsala, Udayana, a hundred armies strong, had a son whose eyes were covered by the lower lids, whose brows were turquoise-blue, teeth jet-white and even, with the marks of wheels in the palms of his hands and webs between his fingers. Fearing that it might be a bad sign, they had him put in a copper box and cast into the Ganges, where he was found by a peasant, who looked after him. According to other accounts the people gave him to a hermit. This last seems to be the most credible version, but however it was, the boy grew up, and hearing how matters stood, was greatly distressed and ran away to the Himālaya Mountains. He arrived on the sacred mountain called Enchantment Peak (*Rol-rtse*) in the snowy range of *Yar-lha-sham-po* in Yar-lung (*Yar-klungs*). Then twelve men, who were worshipping the local divinity, saw him enter the Four-Portaled Plain of the Mighty (*btsan-thang-sgo-bzhi*) and they asked: "Who are you and where do you come from?" "I am a Mighty One," he replied and pointed to the sky, and so thinking that perhaps he had descended from the sky, they decided to make him king and took him with them, carrying him in a palaquin on their necks.[b] For this reason he was called the Neck-Enthroned Mighty One (*gnya-khri-btsan-po*).

According to the notions of the secret magicians (*the-brang*) he is said to have come from the Land of Mu and the P'ön-pos say that he descended from the Land of the Gods in the sky by means of a Mu-cord and so landed on the peak of the holy

[a] see *Bu-tön*, II, pp. 181–2; *Blue Annals*, I, p. 36; Francke, *Ant. Ind. Tib.*, II, pp. 76–7.

[b] Reading *gnya-ba* for *mnyam-pa* in the edition of Sarat Chandra Das.

mountain. But all such talk of coming down from the sky arises from the fact that the P'ön-pos like the sky. It would be a great fault to pursue these falsehoods.'

(*dpag-bsam ljon-bzang*, p. 149.)

It may be hoped that as outsiders we are permitted to pursue these falsehoods a little. Moreover we observe that in the early days of Buddhism in Tibet, that is to say so long as the first line of kings endured, it was not considered unorthodox to pay the sovereign the compliment of divine origin. Presumably it was not yet felt to be a specially p'ön-po notion. In 821–2 the Tibetans and the Chinese, who had been disputing the hegemony of Central Asia for about 150 years, signed a treaty of perpetual friendship and a stone pillar with an incised inscription was set up outside the main temple at Lhasa.[a] In this inscription the reigning king, Räl-pa-cen is given the title of Divine Mighty One of Miracles (*'phrul-gyi-hla-btsan-po*) and is associated with a mythical ancestor named Ö-de-pu-gyel (*'o-lde-spu-rgyal*) 'who descended from the gods of heaven to be the king of men'. In honour of the same event a monastery was founded in the north-eastern frontier region, and fortunately a manuscript containing the invocation that was made on that occasion, has been preserved.[b] The title of the king is Mighty One, God of Miracles and again he is identified with Ö-de-pu-gyel who 'has come from the gods of heaven to be the lord of men' and who 'confirming his dominion in eternity (*gYung-drung*), covers and pervades the eight directions with his great grace'. Even the word used for eternity is one which a later age regarded as specifically p'ön-po, but there is nothing un-Buddhist in the noble sentiments expressed in this invocation, which prays that the king, his ministers and all living beings may attain to buddhahood.

There are thus two names given to the first ancestor in early

[a] This inscription has been edited and translated by H. E. Richardson: *Ancient Historical Edicts etc.*, p. 35 ff.

[b] Ed. and trsl. by F. W. Thomas, *Tibetan Documents*, II, p. 92 ff.

times, one of which was borrowed by later writers for their dynastic inventions, the other for some reason becoming more or less taboo. Little can be gained by speculating on the meaning of these names, for the different spellings used indicate that the Tibetans themselves have long since forgotten the meaning and so devised more plausible versions. Thus the interpretation of 'Neck-Enthroned' was obtained by altering the older spelling *nyag* into *gnya*, both of which would be pronounced the same in a compound-word such as we have here.[a] Likewise Ö-de is written either as *'o-lde* or *'od-lde*. If one could be sure of the correctness of the second spelling, one could translate as 'Divine Being of Light', but for all one knows Ö may be part of a place-name. Pu certainly seems to be, thus giving for Pu-gyel the meaning of Sovereign of Pu.[28]

In any case these two ancestor-kings are completely uncharacterized apart from the one idea of their having descended from heaven by a magic rope. It is not therefore surprising to find them identified as one and the same person.

'In this land of Tibet with its many snow-peaks, there were six who exercised sovereignty before Pu-gyel.

First a black demon (*gnod-sbyin*) held sway and the land was known as the land of devils (*bdud*), as Kha-rag with its many summits.[29] As a result sprites called nyen-po (*gnyen-po*) and cen-po (*bcen-po*) appeared.

Next a devil and an ogress held sway and the country was called land of the two divine ogres. As a result red-faced flesh-eating creatures appeared.

Next the serpents (*klu*) and the powers (*btsan*) held sway and the country was called realm of Tibet with its many parts. As a result grain appeared, active in the waters.

Next the nine brethren, the Unclean Ones (*ma-sangs*) held sway and the country was called realm of Tibet with its six wastes. As a result arrows and spears and weapons appeared.

Next *Za-ram*, who had six lives, held sway and the country was

[a] see Richardson, *AHE*, pp. 48–9.

called the eighteen brigades. As a result horse-riding and the wearing of ear-rings began.

Next the twelve petty-kings held sway and the country was called land of the eight frontier-posts. As a result good manners and polite speech began.

Finally Pu-gyel the Mighty held sway and the country was known as realm of Tibet of the four divisions (*ru-bzhi*).

The Mighty One of Tibet, Ö-de-pu-gyel, came from the gods of heaven to be the lord of men. From the hands of Brahma he passed through the heavenly spheres, sphere of the heavens, sphere of the clouds, sphere of the rain, he came through all nine spheres. To the four brothers known as *rTags-chags Wal-wal* there came the Lord *Yab-la-bDäl-drug*. To him were born those excellent sons, the Seven Brothers. But *Bar-lha-chogs-bdun* caused trouble to his parents and brothers, so his parents expelled him to the land of his maternal uncle. The son of his marriage with the *dMu*-lady *Dem-bcun* was Nya-trhi (*gNya-khri*). Thus is the lineage of the gods of the world (*srid-pa'i iha*) down to his birth.[29] This Lord, the Mighty One, came for the sake of the black-haired folk and of all living beings. He took his seat on the truss and from him the sons who represent the royal lineage were born'.[a]

Although this passage contains several mythological names of which no proper interpretation can be given, the general progression of events is perfectly clear. In the reference to the devil and the ogress we presumably have the earlier non Buddhist version of the hermit-monkey story, quoted above, for his offspring were also red-faced and addicted to flesh-eating. The twelve petty kings who precede the Mighty One are reminiscent of the twelve men who saw Nya-trhi appear on the mountain in the later Buddhist distortion of the legend.

[a] *rgyal-po bka'i thang-yig*, folio 18a ff. This has already been translated by Tucci, TPS, II, p. 732, and also the latter half by Hoffmann: *Bon-Religion*, pp. 245-6.

Thus without immersing oneself uselessly in a maze of cross-identifications and uncertain associations, one can distinguish quite clearly the early beliefs centring around the king as a god who had descended from above, and the very much later Buddhist fabrications, which attempted to derive his ancestry in respectable Indian circles. That these attempts came late, is indicated by the early inscriptions and manuscripts, in which it was not yet felt inconsistent to give glory to the king in accordance with the old mythological pattern and at the same time to pray for his enlightenment in the Buddhist sense. When later on this inconsistency was sensed, the early legends were clumsily altered to suit the new ideas. It is interesting to observe that the p'ön-pos as much as the Buddhists were concerned in making these alterations.[30] Nya-trhi was recognized as the ancestor-king and Pu-gyel was remembered as the supposedly original name of Tibet. It is quoted thus in the *Blue Annals:* 'The ancient name of this country was Pu-gyel, but later it was called Tibet.' In this work the name of the first king is given as Trhi-tsen-po Ö-de, thus solving the problem of the two ancestors by combining parts of their names.[a]

All the sources, early and late, agree that after this first ancestor there were six successors, all bearing the title of Mighty One Enthroned (*khri-btsan-po*). Altogether they are referred to as the Enthroned of Heaven (*gnam-gyi-khri*) and it was believed that their tombs were in heaven, for their divine bodies disappeared like a rainbow, leaving no remains. Some interest attaches to the seventh king, Tr'i-gum-tsen-po, who was the first to lose this power. The omens were misheard by his nurse and so he was misnamed Sword-Slain (*gri-gum*) which adversely affected his destiny.[31] 'He was the son of the De (*lde*) in the form of a man amongst men, possessed of great gifts and powers such as that of passing into the zenith of heaven. Wrath and pride could not prevail upon him, but he wished to vie in a trial of strength. So he said to nine kinsmen on his father's side and three on his mother's: "Could you overpower me as an

[a] *Blue Annals*, p. 36.

enemy or subdue me like a yak?" Each in turn they said it was quite impossible. But when Lo-ngam, the chief groom, answered thus, the king would not allow it, so the groom said: "If you will not allow me to decline, then please give me those treasures of the gods, the lance that throws itself, the sword that strikes of itself, the armour that dons itself, and then I shall be able to do it." Then the king gave him the whole treasury of the gods. Thereupon Lo-ngam, the groom, arrived first at Sham-po Castle in Nyang-ro. When the king had also come there, they prepared for battle in the Grove of Ashes at Nyang-ro. Then the groom said: "I would request you to cut the sacred cord and reverse the ladder of the nine spheres." The king agreed to these two requests. Thereupon Lo-ngam fixed two hundred golden spear-points on the horns of one hundred oxen and loaded ashes on their backs. The oxen fought amongst themselves and the dust was scattered, so that Lo-ngam could prevail in the midst of it. When the Supreme De Zenith-Sovereignty (*bla-lde-gung-rgyal*) would have drawn Tr'i-Gum the Mighty up to Heaven, Lo-ngam produced a monkey from his side and the Supreme De Zenith Sovereignty was hurled back to the enveloping snows of Mount Ti-se and then Tr'i-Gum the Mighty died. They placed him inside a hundred sheets of copper, of which they sealed the openings, and then they let him go in the middle of the Tsang-po River. He arrived at the river's end in the chasm-lair in the bosom of the she-serpent, the long Ö-de P'e-de (*'od-lde-bed-de*).'[a] The son of a faithful retainer eventually succeeded in ransoming the king's body from the she-serpent by giving her a child whose eyes closed from below like a bird's. The two sons of the king built a tomb of earth shaped like a tent. From this time on the kings remained on earth and had their tombs there, for the sacred cord had been cut.

In spite of the inexplicable elements, there are always certain common motifs in these stories which fit together in a general

[a] *Tun-Huang Documents*, tx. pp. 97–8, tr. p. 123 ff. Tucci has translated the version of this story as found in the *rgyal-rabs-gsal-ba'i-me-long*: *TPS II*, p. 733.

(a) Kumārī. (p. 118)

(b) Her attendants, Ganesh and Bhairav. These boys are wearing traditional Newāri dress.

Plate 17

Plate 18

(a) 'Cauliflowers for sale' in the old Pātan Palace.
(b) Pātan, traditionally a Buddhist city (pp. 94-5)

Plate 19

(a) Neglected heritage at Svayambhūnāth. (p. 97)
(b) Paśupati, fundamentally a Hindu city. (p. 113)

Plate 20

(a) Sam-yä. (p. 154)

(b) Sam-yä, the black chöten. Black is the equivalent of dark-blue and corresponds with the eastern quarter.

scheme. Thus mountains occupy a preëminent place in the cosmological conceptions, and it is interesting to find Mount Ti-se (Meru) mentioned as the abode of the Supreme De. Things and places often remain the centre of a cult, even when the original beliefs have long since been forgotten. This may be verified by considering some of our Western customs, and it is nothing unusual if the supposed explanations given by present-day believers differ altogether from those suggested by students of antiquity. Mount Meru is still a sacred mountain, but now as the centre of the enlarged conceptions of Hindu and Buddhist cosmology. It is impossible to distinguish adequately the term *lde* from the more general word for a god (*lha*), but whereas kings were held to be divine in the general sense in which the title *lha* was applied to them, they seem to have been especially embodiments of the *lde*. It will be noticed in the list of historical kings that this term or its diminutive *ldeu* occurs frequently in the royal names. It remains unexplained why the Supreme De should have been powerless before the magic monkey. The Tsang-po is Tibet's main river, identical with the Brahmaputra. The eyes which close from below are a curious feature, but we have met them elsewhere, for they were characteristic of Nya-trhi-tsen-po.

There is one essential feature of the early beliefs which seems to have survived to this day, although its original meaning is forgotten. Until recently a special ceremony was performed in Lhasa every year in which three men from Tsang Province descended a rope stretched down from the roofs of the Potala to an obelisk within the precincts. The event was witnessed among others by Sir Charles Bell, who was informed that it referred to the defeat of the King of Tsang and was intended to prevent this province from rising to power again.[a] While there is no need to

[a] Bell, *Religion of Tibet*, p. 127. The only other accounts of this rope-descent, which are known to me, relate it with the Himalayan districts of the upper Sutlej (Francke, *Ant. Ind. Tib.*, I, p. 4 and A. H. Rose, *A Glossary of the Tribes and Castes of the N.W. Frontier Province*, Lahore, 1911–19, vol. I, p. 345) and also with Srinagar in Garhwal (Moorcroft and Trebeck, *Travels in*

doubt a real connection with this event, it seems likely that far more was involved in the original intention. With the defeat of the King of Tsang by the Mongols (in 1641), the fifth Dalai Lama became the recognized head of Central Tibet. He was a descendant of the ancient royal dynasty of the Yar-lung Valley and it is not unlikely that the ceremony of descending the rope was instituted to assert his preëminence and his continuity with the kings of old. The special significance of such a descent was certainly known in seventeenth-century Tibet, as is witnessed by Sum-pa Khen-po's history, of which the relevant section was quoted above. The term god-king, in spite of its rather un-Buddhist implications, is by no means inapplicable to the Dalai-Lamas. The Buddhists have asserted the association from their side by recognizing the early Buddhist kings as bodhisattvas.

Returning briefly to the legendary accounts, we learn that one of the sons of Tr'i-gum assumed the name of Pu-De Zenith Sovereignty (*spu-de-gung-rgyal*) and established himself on the Tiger Peak of Ching-wa (*phying-ba*) in the Yar-lung Valley. The site of this valley, which is about sixty miles south-east of Lhasa, has been finally confirmed by the explorations of Professor Tucci, and from now on we are sure of being on firm historical ground in our account.[a] It would be satisfactory if we could identify this Pu-De Zenith Sovereign with the mythological ancestor Pu-Sovereign De of Ö (*'od-lde-spu-rgyal*) and regard him as the genuine founder-ancestor of the kings of the Yar-lung Valley, but the various legends provide no basis for such assumption. In any case there now follows a long list of more mythological kings, whose number was conventionally fixed at twenty-seven, followed by another set of four, of whom next

the Himalayan Provinces of Hindustan and the Punjab, 2 vols., London 1841, I, p. 17). The various explanations offered for these rites, such as warding off disaster by a form of transmuted human sacrifice, seem generally inadequate, for the essential article, the rope remains unexplained. The last Dalai Lama has instituted a substitute ceremony of a less dangerous kind. See F. Spencer Chapman, *Lhasa, the Holy City* (London 1938), p. 313 ff.

[a] see Tucci, *The Tombs of the Tibetan Kings*; *idem*, *A Lhasa e Oltre*, p. 114 ff.

to nothing is known. During the reign of the first of these four, a casket containing Buddhist books and a golden reliquary is supposed to have fallen from the skies. Their contents were worshipped, although no one knew what they were. Once again it is useless to speculate whether this represents the first arrival of Buddhism in Tibet.

The Line of Historical Kings

So far we have had nothing but the poetic memories of nomadic warring tribes to guide us. Only when one of these had become firmly established in the fertile Yar-lung Valley and, having gained mastery over their immediate neighbours, began to make contact with outside countries, could Tibet be said to have entered history. This came about in the early seventh century A.D. and from then on, thanks to the assistance given by Chinese historical sources, the reigns of these kings can be fixed with sufficient accuracy. As these dates will serve as a guide-line they are listed here.[32]

s[son] and b[brother] indicate the relationship to the preceding name on the list.

		Date of death:
	Nam-ri-song-tsen	?
s	Trhi-song-tsen, also known as: Song-tsen-gam-po	650
s	Gung-song	?
s	Trhi-mang-long, also known as: Mang-song-mang-tsen	679
s	Trhi-dü-song, also known as: Dü-song	704
s	Trhi-de-tsuk-tsen, also known as: Me-ak-tsom	755
s	Trhi-song-deu-tsen	804
s	Mu-ne-tsen-po	798
b	Trhi-de-song-tsen, also known as: Sä-na-lek	815
s	Trhi-tsuk-de-tsen, also known as: Räl-pa-cen	836
b	Trhi-U-dum-tsen, also known as: Lang-dar-ma	842

It will be noticed that the official titles of these kings are composed for the most part of a few constantly recurring syllables:

trhi (*khri*)	—	enthroned
tsen (*btsan*)	—	mighty
song (*srong*)	—	straight
tsuk (*btsugs*)	—	established
de/deu (*lde/ldeu*)	—	sovereign-being

This has been as much a source of confusion to the native historians as it is likely to be to the present reader, and so the alternatives, representing family-names and nick-names, will be used in the following pages.

These kings lie buried in the Yar-lung Valley, which remained the real heart of the country long after Lhasa had become the capital of a greatly enlarged domain. The one inscription found by Professor Tucci on the actual site of these funeral mounds refers to Sä-na-lek, whose attachment to Buddhism there is no reason to doubt, yet it is conceived entirely in terms of the old mythology. 'The Mighty One, the Son of the Gods, Ö-de-pu-gyel, came from the gods of heaven to be the lord of men. He established the excellent way of the law eternally and it does not change. He established great sovereignty eternally and it does not weaken. Thereafter the kingdom waxed great and the royal helmet is mighty for ever. In accordance with the wisdom of eternity, Trhi-de-song-tsen, the Son of Gods, became lord of men. In conformity with the divine pattern his sovereignty was great and in conformity with the law of heaven his word was mighty, and so by the flood of his profound thought and the model of his excellent commands all was well within and without and the kingdom was great. The manner of this is written on this stone pillar so that all men may know it for ever.[a]

The terms used for 'wisdom of eternity' (*gYung-drung-gi gtsug-lag*) and 'law of heaven' (*gnam-gyi chos*) would by a more

[a] Tucci, *Tombs, tx.* p. 91, *tr.* pp. 36–7.

self-consciously Buddhist age have been classed as p'ön-po and thus as deliberately anti-Buddhist. Their use in the ninth century, however, merely indicates that Buddhism had not yet permeated the institutions of Tibetan society. The early chronicles, discovered near Tun-huang, in what is now the west of Kansu Province in China, make scant reference to Buddhism, although they too were written in this century and in a district where there were a large number of flourishing Buddhist establishments. The only religious rites of any kind referred to in these texts are the burials of the kings, and one may note that when a king dies, he is said to 'pass into the zenith of heaven', exactly the same phrase as was used to describe the divine powers of King Tr'i-gum (p. 131) where the idea of death is not even involved. This is not just a special honorific usage, for high honorific terms are already in use for other members of the royal family as well as for the Emperor of China. The royal cult was in fact so deeply rooted, that it never finally disappeared, merely assuming at last a special Buddhist form in the persons of the Dalai Lamas.

But to be a god and a head of state at one and the same time has always been a rather dubious privilege, for there are men who will willingly concede divinity in another sphere, so long as they may reserve to themselves full authority in the affairs of this world, and it has been a common feature in oriental countries for the chief minister to act as the effective ruler, forcing his supposed master into the position of a mere figurehead and even disposing of him at will. There are certain indications, both in myth (which may often reflect ancient customs) and in fact, that the Tibetan kings were faced with this possibility. Thus we read in the early chronicles that when the prince was old enough to ride a horse, his father departed for heaven.[a] Although he is envisaged as disappearing in a rainbow, there were clearly more practical means of arranging for the disappearance. This was also provided for institutionally by the normal practice of crowning the prince at the age of

[a] *Tun-Huang Documents*, p. 87.

thirteen. But the surest indication of this state of affairs is the actual fate of so many of the kings. Thus Nam-ri-song-tsen seems to have been murdered.[a] Song-tsen-gam-po was a strong enough character to maintain his own position, but it is significant that his son died young (thus the father was able to resume the sovereignty) and he was succeeded by his grandson, who was a mere child. The power now passed entirely into the hands of the chief minister, Tong-tsen of the Gar Clan, who was succeeded in this office by his son Tsen-nya. It was this man who was mainly responsible for the Tibetan victories over the neighbours, to which we shall be referring below. Tsen-nya died in 685 and was succeeded by Trhi-ring who had been associated with him in office and seems also to have been of the Gar Clan. This series of strong ministers left the throne so powerless, that its incumbent appears as a complete non-entity. Dü-song, the great-grandson of Song-tsen, succeeded in gaining the upper hand towards the end of his reign, for we learn that Trhi-ring was disgraced in 698.[b] But the king himself died (whether naturally or not one cannot be sure) in 704, when his successor was only one year old. Thus the initiative inevitably passed to intriguing relatives. The changing of ministers in 725 and then again in 727 and 728 may suggest that the young king was gaining control. But there is evidence of trouble towards the end of his reign and it seems that he too was murdered.[c] Trhi-song-deu-tsen was the first powerful king since Song-tsen. He lived his full life and did much to further the cause of Buddhism. Nevertheless he retired several years before his death and his eldest son was murdered within a year. Sä-na-lek held his own and also did much for the doctrine. His successor had earned the reputation of being even more devoted to the new doctrine, but he too was murdered. The next king was very short-lived and met with the same fate.[d]

[a] *ibid.*, p. 147.

[b] *ibid.*, pp. 39 and 161 ff.

[c] Richardson, *AHE*, p. 22.

[d] A most useful summary of these reigns is that of Petech, *A Study of the Chronicles of Ladakh*. Some of his conclusions now require modification.

This fierce rivalry of jealous clans forms part of the background against which we must interpret the available information concerning the introduction of Buddhism. Equally important is the steady consolidation of Tibetan power and increase of encroachments abroad, which reached their points of highest success in 783 and 821, both marked by the signing of treaties with the Chinese. We must be aware that all this time we are not dealing with countries in the modern sense of the term, but rather with city-states. Just as Nepal meant the Nepal Valley, so the Tibet to which we are referring is essentially the Yar-lung Valley including the neighbouring district up the Brahmaputra and the surrounding feudal dependencies, which under the vigorous action of Nam-ri and Song-tsen were forced into accepting their leadership. It was from these feudal clans that the kings chose their wives and their ministers and there was clearly no lack of scope for bitter rivalry. Nam-ri seems to have initiated the advance to the north by his victories over the Dru-gu, a nomad people, who were probably settled north of the Ch'ang-thang.[a] Song-tsen, not only continued the advance in this direction, defeating the A-sh'a and impressing the Chinese with his strength, but he also extended his power westwards to Sh'ang-sh'ung and southwards to Nepal.[b] Of his four wives, one came from Sh'ang-sh'ung, one from Nepal and one from China, and there is no doubt that these were political marriages. The ministers Gar (whose names were mentioned above) persisted with the advance in the northern regions and so by 670 the Tibetans had wrested from the Chinese the four garrisoned cities of Kashgar, Kucha, Karashahr and Khotan. This conquest was of short duration for the Chinese drove them out again in 692. But in the meantime they had advanced from Sh'ang-sh'ung down the Indus Valley to

[a] Thomas, *Documents*, I, p. 269; Petech, *Chronicles*, p. 51.

[b] *Tun-Huang Documents*, pp. 29 and 147. Concerning the A-sh'a (*'a-zha*), see Thomas, *Documents*, II, p. 34 ff.

present-day Gilgit (*Bru-zha*) and into Baltistān, from where they could make outflanking attacks on the Chinese positions. One may also note the regularity with which Nepal is mentioned as a royal residence from 690 to 723. Fighting with the Chinese, both in Baltistān and again to the north seems to have continued almost uninterruptedly. Nor is there much doubt concerning the object of this warfare. 'At that time the Chinese Empire was very great, for everything as far as Persia was Chinese territory. A great deal of Chinese wealth was being sent westwards and while it was stored at Kva-cu, the Tibetans descended upon it and carried it off. Besides this they gained a large amount of treasure and all the black-haired people were covered with fine silks.'[a] They also brought fire and destruction and they were no respectors of Buddhist monasteries and shrines.[b] For a short period Tibet became the dominant power in Central Asia and it is interesting to observe that the homeland was now all but surrounded by Buddhist countries, a fact which is well illustrated by the travels of Yuan Chwang, who is the most informative of the Chinese pilgrims. He left Ch'ang-an, the Chinese capital, in 630, just at the time when the Tibetans were becoming aware of their strength and only thirty-two years before they were to occupy it. He passed through all the main cities of Central Asia, those to the north of the desert on his way out and those to the south on his way back. In the west he visited Uḍḍiyāna, Kashmir and Kulu, which were all places of prime importance in the history of early Tibetan Buddhism. At this time Kashmir ranked with Magadha as a sacred Buddhist land, and it was the first place of pilgrimage for visitors from Central Asia. The Tibetans, who probably first made serious contact with Buddhism in Khotan and Gilgit, would inevitably have oriented towards Kashmir as a prime source of the doctrine. All these areas had been in close cultural contact with one another long before the Tibetans came upon the scene.

[a] *Tun-Huang Documents*, *tx*. p. 113, *tr*. p. 150.
[b] Thomas, *Documents*, I, p. 202.

THE DEVELOPMENT OF A LITERARY LANGUAGE

In spite of the difficult conditions of travel in the trans-Himalayan regions, long journeys were willingly undertaken, and it would be surprising indeed if the Tibetans had remained ignorant of their neighbours until the time came actually to make war upon them. Our sources tell us only of the Tibetans whose homeland centred around the Yar-lung Valley. Of their neighbours to the west we have no accurate information at all, and we cannot be sure whether they too were Tibetan by race or not.[a] Nor can we know whether Tibetan communities had settled further afield, reaching perhaps even to Khotan, Gilgit and Kashmir. All that is known with reasonable certainty is that about the year 632 Song-tsen-gam-po sent one of his ministers, Sambhoṭa of Thön, to Kashmir, in order to study writing, so that a Tibetan script might be finally agreed upon. This event in itself suggests previous acquaintance with Kashmir or at least knowledge of its prestige as a centre of learning. The fact that Nepal was not chosen would seem to indicate that Tibetan contacts had up to then been with the north-west. Thus an event that is recorded by the later historians as though it were the result of the single journey of a single man, was presumably the result of a long period of contact with these countries, during which the Tibetans felt an acute need of the literary advantages enjoyed by their neighbours. Unfortunately the complete destruction by the Moslems of the Buddhist civilization of Kashmir has removed all evidence which might finally have confirmed the Kashmīri origin of Tibetan writing. Hence doubt has been expressed over a tradition, which in itself is quite probable.[b] The problem is made even more complex by the fact that the earliest examples of Tibetan writing that are

[a] see p. 170 and note 36.

[b] see F. W. Thomas, 'The Tibetan Alphabet', *Festschr. z. Feier d. 200-jähr. Bestehens d. Akad. d. Wiss. i. Göttingen* (*1951*), pp. 146–65. Prof. Thomas argues in favour of the traditional accounts, as against the earlier views of Francke and Hoernle (references given). On the art of early Tibetan writing, see *idem*, *Documents*, II, p. 330 ff.

extant, date from the early ninth century, by which time other influences may have had their effect, especially as by far the greater part of early Tibetan literary activity seems to have taken place in the occupied territories of Central Asia. Some valuable examples of the type of writing used in central Tibet during the same period are provided by the stone-inscriptions, which have been collected by Mr. H. E. Richardson during the years he spent in Lhasa prior to the recent Chinese occupation of the country.

The relationship of the Tibetan language to its script is an unusual one, but this is due only to the extreme conservativism of Tibetan scholars and the fact that their cultural tradition has continued unspoiled to this day. The same might be said of Chinese, but in this case a system of character-symbols is in use, which reflect the earlier phonetic values of the words in a most rudimentary fashion, while the symbolic value which has prevailed, resists change by its inherent nature. There is clearly no incentive to bring the written form of a word into closer relationship with its spoken form, if the former possesses no semblance of phonetic significance.[a]

Languages which employ an alphabet usually keep their spelling more or less in accordance with the prevalent pronunciation. If a language, such as Sanskrit or Latin, becomes static as the acknowledged expression of a particular religious and cultural tradition, the spoken language separates itself (like Hindi and Italian) and in due course develops its own written forms. Nothing similar has occurred in Tibet, where the only available written forms are those which are traditionally ascribed to the ingenuity of Sambhoṭa of Thön 1,300 years ago. The situation is aggravated by the fact that Tibetan is a monosyllabic language, liable to lose easily the initial and final consonants. Thus we now find most of its words equipped with an elaborate system of unpronounced consonantal prefixes and with final consonants, many of which merely have the effect

[a] Thus one might argue the benefit of revising the spelling of the word *eight*, but one accepts the symbol 8 without question.

of modifying the quality of the preceding vowel. This process of linguistic decay is most marked in the central provinces and it is surprising to observe that it is already causing uncertainty in some of the ninth century manuscripts mentioned above. Sambhoṭa is supposed to have fixed the alphabet and the system of spelling on his return to the capital, and if he recorded the language as he heard it then and there, one is led to wonder at the rapidity with which it diverged from his standard. He is also said to have composed a grammar in eight parts, of which two have been learned and recited to this day, for they still serve as chief guide to the young Tibetan who is learning to spell.[a] This grammar primarily consists of rules for the correct use of the unpronounced prefixes and suffixes, which are still nowadays a serious difficulty to the beginner. It is only surprising that they should have been so in Sambhoṭa's time, unless he was introducing forms which were already slightly archaic or based upon a type of Tibetan spoken elsewhere. There is nothing to rule out the possibility that other Tibetans in the north-western region had devised an alphabet before he finally established the official one, so that his spellings would then have been conditioned by what were already recognized forms.[b]

In spite of the great differences which distinguish the modern spoken language of central Tibet from eastern and western dialects, there exists a recognized system of reading the sacred texts, which is learned by all Tibetan monks. This comes very close to the speech of central Tibet and makes no pretence at preserving the phonetic values of ancient spellings. It might be

[a] Ed. and trsl. in two different versions by J. Bacot: *Les ślokas grammaticaux de Thonmi Sambhoṭa,* and by J. Schubert: *Tibetische Nationalgrammatik.* The basic text in each case consists of sixty-five brief verses attributed to Sambhoṭa, elaborated by the commentary of a traditional grammarian, who is always at pains to demonstrate the absolute validity of the great master's concise generalizations. See also G. Morichini, 'Review of Shôju Inabo's *Classical Grammer of Tibetan', East and West* (Rome), vi (1955), part 2, pp. 172–5.

[b] see G. Uray, 'On the Tibetan Letters *Ba* and *Wa*', *Acta Orient. Hung.*, vol. V (1955), pp. 101–21, where the argument is led into the general field of the Tibetan alphabet as a whole and similar conclusions are drawn (p. 121).

suggested that it is universally imposed by a powerful central authority, but Lhasa has only been universally powerful for the last two hundred years or so, and then this pronunciation is remarkable in the very details in which it diverges from Lhasa Tibetan. Taking into account the extraordinary conservativism of Tibetan religion, one may well surmise that this method of reading stems from a much earlier period, probably from the time of 'the second spreading of the doctrine', viz. from about A.D. 1000 onwards. This 'classical' pronunciation and Sambhoṭa's grammar accord so well together, that it is difficult, although not impossible, to envisage the court-language of his day as very different from that which one hears in the temples today.

The Introduction of Buddhism

Later historians regard the fixing of an alphabet as the most important event in the reign of Song-tsen-gam-po, but they also honour him as the founder of Tibetan Buddhism, indeed as a special incarnation of Avalokiteśvara, who had assumed this form with the intention of benefitting Tibet. It certainly seems that the Khotanese, who earlier had cause to lament the destruction of their temples and shrines at the hands of the 'red-faces', were later able to rejoice in having in Song-tsen-gam-po an ardent protector of the Good Religion.[a] It is reasonably certain that the first Buddhist temples were erected in central Tibet during his reign. They were presumably simple rectangular structures of dried mud-bricks, possibly with a chö-ten on each of the four sides and surrounded with a mud-brick wall, much as they are still to be seen in the poorer districts of Tibet, which have not been graced with the more lavish structures of later times. At least three well-known temples may reasonably be dated back to this earliest period, although they have been destroyed and rebuilt since. One is the Trhan-tr'uk (*khra-'brug*) Temple in the Yar-lung Valley, which is mentioned in several

[a] Thomas, *Documents*, I, pp. 79 and 294.

ancient texts and was visited by Professor Tucci in 1948.[a] The others are the two well-known temples at Lhasa, the Trhül-nang (*'phrul-snang*), which has now become the cathedral-church of Tibet, and the Ra-mo-che Temple.[b] These are both supposed to have been built originally to enshrine buddha-images brought by the Chinese and Nepalese Queens, that of Buddha the Prince, which was placed in the Trhül-nang Temple and those of Akshobhya, Maitreya and Tārā, which were brought from Nepal and placed in the Ra-mo-che Temple. Whether these images really are of such early workmanship is open to doubt, but no qualified visitor seems yet to have had the opportunity of scrutinizing them carefully. The image of Buddha the Prince is now the centre of pilgrimage at Lhasa, but the strength of the tradition of its origin is no guarantee of accuracy. As will be seen, Buddhism practically disappeared from central Tibet after the murder of Räl-pa-cen, and when it eventually returned, pious sentiment would willingly have associated the main image in the central temple with the earlier period. It was said that during the eclipse of the doctrine, it had been buried and later retrieved, but the supposed burial of precious objects and texts is all too common a story, when the genuine nature of the items is in need of vindication. The Tibetans are usually quite unquestioning in matters of religious devotion. They will believe anything which redounds to the greater sanctity of a place or object, such deliberate faith being considered of great spiritual value.

It is related that:

'There once lived in Kong-po a foolish fellow named Jo-wo-Ben and he went to visit the image of the Precious Prince at Lhasa. It chanced that no attendant was to hand and he went right up to the image. Seeing the food-offerings and the butter-lamps, he said to himself: "It seems that the Precious Prince

[a] Tucci, *Lhasa*, pp. 116–17.

[b] *ibid.*, pp. 77–8; Waddell, *Lhasa and its Mysteries*, p. 363 ff.; Waddell, 'Description of the Lhasa Cathedral', *JRAS*, 1895, pp. 259–83; Spencer Chapman, *Lhasa, the Holy City*, p. 152 ff.

dips his food in this melted butter before eating it and the flame is kept burning so that the butter shall not solidify. If that is how the Prince eats, then I should eat likewise." So dipping some of the cake into the melted butter of one of the lamps, he ate it. "Even though a dog carried off these sacred offerings, you would still smile. Even though the wind causes these flames to tremble, you still smile. You are a good lama. I shall leave my shoes with you, so please look after them. I'll just do a circumambulation for you and then come back", so saying he removed his shoes and left them by the image. While he was away making his circumambulation, the attendant came and was just about to throw the shoes outside, when a voice came from the image: "Ben of Kong-po has left these shoes with me, so don't touch them." Later this fellow returned and taking his shoes, exclaimed: "You really are a good lama. Do come to our place next year. I'll kill an old pig of mine and roast it and brew some beer and I'll be waiting for you." A voice came from the image: "I shall come." Thereupon he returned home and said to his wife: "I have invited the Precious Prince. I don't know just when he will come, so you must not forget that he is always liable to arrive."

One day in the following year his wife had gone to draw water and there in the well was reflected the image of the Prince. She ran home at once calling: "There's someone in the water. Is it not the guest you invited?" The fellow hastened there forthwith and seeing the Precious Prince reflected in the water, he thought: "O dear, the Prince has fallen in." So he jumped in, clutched at the image and really held it and there emerged a form that could be helped out. He led him towards his house and when they reached a large boulder that lay by the way, the image said: "I may not enter the house of a layman," and unwilling to proceed further, he faded away into the boulder. So that boulder, where the Prince manifested himself, is called the Prince's Boulder, and the well in which his image appeared, is called the Prince's Well. Even today the grace one receives there is equal to that of the shrine of the Prince in Lhasa, and people go there to make offerings.

Thus by means of his unshakable faith, that fellow was able to induce the buddha's compassion. Although there would otherwise have been nothing worse than eating the offerings and the butter from the lamps and leaving his shoes in the presence of the Prince, yet by the strength of his faith, it was turned to such merit as has been described.'[a]

Throughout the second half of the seventh century the chief ministers of the Gar Clan were pursuing their conquests in the frontier regions and very little official interest can have been taken in Buddhism. It is noteworthy, however, that Dü-song, who succeeded in asserting his authority towards the end of his reign, is also credited with the founding of some temples.[b] Probably from this time on Buddhism became involved in domestic politics, for while the kings support it, factious relatives and ministers oppose it.

An interesting event during the reign of the next king, Me-ak-tsom, was the arrival of refugee monks from Khotan.[c] If one simply omits all the miraculous elements in the accounts, one learns that they were expelled from their own country by rulers who were hostile to Buddhism, made their way with great difficulty to Tibet and were received there very hospitably thanks to the intercession of the queen who was of Chinese birth. Seven monasteries were built for them and they stayed there in peace for three years. Then skin diseases of various kinds broke out and in A.D. 739 the queen herself died so that the ministers demanded the vagrants should be sent from the country.

Monks from the Gilgit area, many of whom were refugees from regions further west, had also arrived in Tibet. At this time the pressure of the Moslem Arabs was making itself felt,

[a] *Kun-bzang-bla-ma*, folios 123*a*–124*a*.

[b] Richardson, 'Three Ancient Inscriptions from Tibet', *JRASB*, vol. xv (1949), p. 55; Tucci, *Tombs*, p. 14.

[c] Thomas, *Documents*, pp. 55 ff. and 80 ff. Also *Blue Annals*, p. 40.

and since from this time on, persecution was undoubtedly one of the reasons which persuaded Buddhist monks from India to make the difficult journey into Tibet, there is nothing unlikely in all these accounts. The expelling of these refugee-monks may well be associated with the difficulties that the king himself had to face towards the end of his reign. From one inscription we understand that he was murdered by two of his ministers.[a] His son was also in danger and we learn from elsewhere that 'the practice of the Buddhist Law was destroyed and that an order was enacted forbidding the practice of the doctrine both inside the country and out, stating that it was not in order to attend in Tibet upon the gods and religion of Nepal'.[b] Turning to the later historians with their exclusive interest in the fortunes of Buddhism, we find a rather colourful account of the same state of affairs. The new king Trhi-song-deu-tsen was crowned at the traditional age of thirteen (which was in 755, the year of his father's death) but an evil minister Ma-sh'ang Trhom-pa-kye and his associates remained in power. 'They banished those who acted according to the doctrine and made arrangements to send the image of Buddha the Prince back to China. But as 300 men were incapable of moving it, they buried it in sand and turned the temple into a slaughter-house.' Calamities occurred as a result, so they retrieved it and sent it off to Mang-yül, the Tibetan-Nepalese frontier region.[c] The governor there was a certain Säl-nang of the Ba Clan, who was a Buddhist. This man went on pilgrimage to Bodhgayā, Nālanda and Nepal, where he met the famous Indian sage, Śāntarakshita, whom he invited to Mang-yül. He was consecrated by him, receiving the new name Jñānendra (Lord of Knowledge) and subsequently built a temple. He also urged the sage to visit central Tibet, but this was not possible until the evil minister Ma-sh'ang had been removed. This was engineered by Trhi-s'ang of Gö, and Ma-sh'ang was buried alive. So much for the later historians.

[a] see p. 138, fn. c. [b] Tucci, *Tombs*, *tx*. p. 98, *tr*. p. 47.
[c] *Bu-tön*, II, p. 186 ff. Also *Blue Annals*, p. 41 ff.

When we turn to the early chronicles to seek confirmation of this story, we find that the villain Ma-sh'ang trhom-pa-kye is unknown. Trhi-s'ang is recorded, however, as having succeeded a certain Nang-sh'er-s'u-tsen of Ba as chief minister in 763.[a] The next preceding minister is named Kye-s'ang-dong-tsap of Bäl and he is reported as having been disgraced. Unfortunately there is a break in the annals from 747 to 755, but among the entries for 755 one may note that the retainers of two ministers, who are simply referred to by their clan-names of Lang and Bäl, were expelled and their property accessed. Presumably justice had overtaken the two ministers themselves in the meantime, for these two are named in an inscription as having been responsible for the death of Me-ak-tsom and threatening the young Trhi-song-deu-tsen. Thus one is left with the possibility that the evil minister Ma-sh'ang of the later historians may be the same as Kye-s'ang of the early records. It must have been upon this whole series of events that the rather simplified and more dramatic account of later years was based. Perhaps to be buried alive suggested itself as a most suitable end for one who had dared to bury the most precious of images in sand, but in any case the divergence of these accounts serves to illustrate the whole difference of view-point of the early chroniclers and the later historians. The former were still conscious of the clash of forceful and ambitious personalities and the general background of warfare. Buddhism played no part in their calculations. The others conceive of everything they report as either for or against the Buddhist doctrine, and anything that does not bear such interpretation, is not worth recording.

Trhi-song-deu-tsen was later recognized as an incarnation of Mañjuśrī, and there is no doubt that he well merits the full honours which are given him, for his enthusiasm for the doctrine is sufficiently attested by several early inscriptions.

With the hostile ministers removed, the king and his supporters were able to act as they pleased. Śāntarakshita was

[a] *Tun-huang Documents*, pp. 66 and 132.

invited and arrived with his Kashmīri interpreter. He is supposed to have reminded the king of the vow that they had both made in their former lives in front of the stūpa in Nepal. He gave some elementary instruction, but the visit was not a success and he returned disappointed to Nepal. This episode illustrates how small was the progress made by Buddhism since the time of Song-tsen-gam-po. It seems too that it had come mostly from Turkestan and China, for whereas visitors from these parts were generally welcomed and presumably evoked less comment, there seems at first to have been a marked opposition to teachers from Nepal and India, who came as unmistakable foreigners, supported by interpreters and preaching foreign gods. In a passage quoted above (p. 148) the gods and religion of Nepal are singled out for special detestation, when one might have expected the prohibition to refer to Buddhism as a whole, and in the famous edict of 821–2 (see p. 164) Nepal is compared unfavourably with China.

In the meantime, therefore, more was to be gained by visiting Turkestan. Ancient records preserved in this area bear witness to the large number of temples and monastic establishments which flourished there. It is at Tun-huang, the most renowned of these archaeological sites, that by far the greater part of early Tibetan manuscript material was accumulated. The most active Tibetan Buddhist of the period was Säl-nang of Ba (Jñānendra), who has been mentioned above. He now travelled to China in search of texts and was well received at the court. On his return to Tibet, the king sent him to invite Śāntarakshita again, who thus made his second visit, rather unwillingly as may be imagined. On his recommendation another sage, Padma-sambhava, was invited as well. A vast legendary literature later developed around this person, so that it is now impossible to separate the historical element from pure fantasy. It is important to observe, however, that this development took place in central Tibet after the eclipse of the doctrine there, when wonder-working powers were the only type of religious manifestation that continued to hold respect.

In any case a preëminent place is accorded to him only by the followers of one sect, the Nying-ma-pas ('Old Ones') and these only emerged as a self-conscious body in the twelfth century. The impression which one might gain of the religion of eighth century Tibet from some of these later legendary works is completely at variance not only with the testimony of the early inscriptions, to which we shall soon be referring, but also with the comparatively sober accounts of the later Tibetan historians. It would be possible to give a completely erroneous description of early Tibetan Buddhism, if one read into it at this point all the later mythological elements that claim to belong there. The stories of Padma-sambhava's wonderful conversions of local divinities and sprites are the inventions of later times, intended to justify the respect which many Tibetans still felt for their old gods at a time when Buddhism had become the general religion of the land. In a study of Tibetan Buddhism the transcendent Padma-sambhava, hypostasized as the Second Buddha, bodily apparition of the Supreme Buddha Amitābha, is undoubtedly of more importance than the original historical figure, of whom one knows so little with certainty; this importance will be sufficiently illustrated later (ch. 6). Here we only note that these later developments are irrelevant to the early period. The historical teacher seems to have come from Uḍḍiyāna in the west and he may have been the adopted son of a certain king Indrabhūti. It is certain, however, that he was one of the eighty-four Great Siddhas (Perfect Ones) who have been described above. Their biographies reveal how much they appealed as a class to the popular imagination, which always delights in stories of fantastic happenings. In this respect the stories about Padma-sambhava all conform to type. It is interesting to observe how Gorakhnāth, Matsyendranāth and Padma-sambhava, the only three who seem to be still recognized as forms of the supreme being, are related to different religious traditions, which have all been associated in the past. Gorakhnāth is regarded by his devotees as the Supreme God, equal to or even greater than Śiva. Matsyendranāth, the great god of

Nepal, is both Buddhist and Hindu through the identification of Avalokiteśvara with Śiva in the one divinity Lokeśvara. Padma-sambhava is completely Buddhist and related with Avalokiteśvara by their common membership of the lotus-family of Amitābha. It was chiefly through his wonder-working powers that Padma-sambhava impressed the Tibetans, but these were part of the stock-in-trade of all the Great Siddhas. His relationship with Śāntarakshita draws once more attention to the nature of the later Indian Buddhism, which has been discussed in the previous chapters. Tantric forms never replaced the earlier Mahāyāna, but rather worked side by side with it. These two now co-operated with the king in founding the first real Tibetan monastery. Seven Tibetans, the first ever, took the regular monastic vows. The Indian school to which they adhered was that of the Sarvāstivādins, who in the old days had argued that all the elements of existence of past, present and future, really existed. With the development of the doctrine of the non-predicability of anything whatsoever, the earlier teachings had assumed the value of a relative kind of truth, and thus the scriptures of this school, largely in the form of monastic discipline and attendant commentaries, later formed an essential part of the Tibetan Canon, where they were placed together with the Perfection of Wisdom texts. It was this school of Indian Buddhism, which flourished in Kashmir, Gilgit and Khotan, and the Tibetans adopted it not from any selectiveness of their side, but because they were taught to regard it as the best. In this section of their canon they preserve their share of the heritage from the earliest Buddhist times, no more and no less authentic than the texts on monastic discipline (*vinaya*) of that other early school, the Theravādins, which are preserved in the *pāli* of the Singhalese Canon.

The king sent one of his ministers to find a suitable site for the new monastery. He chose a spot in the Brahmaputra Valley close to the castle of the Red Crag (*brag-dmar*) between Yarlung and Lhasa. The description of the place taken from the *Padma Thang-yig*, is so characteristically Tibetan in its strange choice of simile and its delight in wild mountain scenery, that it merits quotation:

'The Lord Bi visited Samyä on the side where lies the lake, and having inspected the ground, he said:

"Mount Hä-po is like a lion, the rose-colour of conch-shell, raised as it were in offering to the sky.
The Me-Yar Hills seem like mules and ponies drinking.
The fair Mount Chim-bu is like a lion, blue as turquoise, raised in offering to the sky.
Mount Shang is like the King on his throne.
This Ge-gye Mountain is like a heap of gems.
The Chim-bu Vale is like an opened lotus.
The Red Crag is like a lion of coral, soaring into the sky.
The Plain of Töl spreads out like an expanse of white silk.
The U-tshä Pool is like a dish of melted butter.
To the south the Tsang-po River is like a turquoise-dragon moving upwards.
In short the Red Crag seems to be watching over the fearful precipices,
And the rising land on all four sides gives consistent order to the four directions
Like the honey-coloured indentations on a tortoise's shell.
That mountain that increases the treasures of the four regions of Tibet,
That Chu-wo Mountain is like a heap of gems.
Perfected masters are always found there,
And places such as U-shang-do and Kar-chung.
Life-giving mountain, rejoicing the Tibetans with longevity.
O District of Tsang where young men seem to be ready-born,
O Mountain, Tiger-Peak of Ching-wa, haughty as an elephant,
Abode of many ministers, so wise.
O Mountain of great festivities—like the strings of a guitar,
O Mountain, which at times is the scene of such trouble for Tibet—mountain black as a wrathful Mongol."

With words such as these he described the layout of the land.'

'Then he came to the tamarisk-grove of Sam-yä and laid the foundations in this tamarisk-grove of the Red Crag.
But the wicked gods and demons of Tibet assembled.
What was built up by day, by night they destroyed.
They did not allow him to build.
Then he calculated wisely and worked out the details and said:
"If we invite pundits, skilled in subduing the gods of the soil, from India, China, S'a-hor and such lands, the king's wish may be fulfilled." '[a]

If we are to trust the descriptions given in the histories, Sam-yä must have appeared as a group of buildings, the like of which had never been seen in Tibet before. It is supposed to have been modelled on the monastery of Odantapuri in central India, but as this place has completely disappeared, there is now no basis for comparison. As it exists now and as it is described in the earliest available text, it appears as a gigantic mandala. Although it has been destroyed and rebuilt several times, it is likely that the original form has been preserved (pl. 20).

'Now as for the way Sam-yä was built, that excellent temple, changeless, self-created: it is spacious and lofty, well laid-out and built of good materials, rich in auspicious gifts, without an equal anywhere. Its roof is three-tiered with four pinnacles above. There are four subsidiary temples and other minor ones with *yakshas* above and below.[33] There are numerous cells—and washing-rooms and a sports-arena. There are four portals and eight shrines for the guardian divinities. There are four chötens and also illuminated chötens and if they are counted, it is said there are thirty of them. One great wall encompasses it around. It all seems to be made with leaf of gold, neatly studded with turquoises. It was scarcely built by men, rather by gods and demons. But it does not seem to have been built, for it seems as though self-created.'[b]

There remain from the eighth century an inscribed pillar

[a] *padma thang-yig*, folio 120*b* ff. (Toussaint, p. 234).
[b] *rgyal-po bka'i-thang-yig*, folio 31*a*.

and bell.[a] The inscription on the pillar contains an oath that the temples of Ra-sa (Lhasa) and the Red Crag and the others shall never be abandoned or lack upkeep, calling to witness 'all gods and non-human beings both of this world and also those who transcend it'. One may note in this connection that very little indeed is heard of local gods and godlings in the early chronicles except in connection with the idea of divine kingship, and when they are mentioned in this way in early Buddhist inscriptions, it would seem to be the gods of Indian Buddhism whom the testator had in mind. The inscription round the bell indicates that it was given by one of the queens of Trhi-song-deu-tsen, to whom the accruing merit is dedicated. Some of these inscriptions and also quotations from them preserved in later histories illustrate very well the sort of Buddhist instruction that was being received in Tibet.

'All beings exist only in so far as they have been born in former times. Having been born, they act either purposefully or foolishly. Thereafter they die. Having died, they are reborn in circumstances good or evil. Now he who has attained to excellence is the Buddha. His perfect expression is the word of the Law. The pointer to virtue is the Monastic Assembly. These permanent places of refuge—these islands—are good. These three jewels are rich in gifts. During the reigns of my paternal ancestors, work accorded with the pattern prevailing in each generation and so truly there were temples new and old. After the Mighty One, my father had passed heavenwards, there were signs and patterns that bore trouble and so this Self-Existent Temple was founded on the seventeenth day of the Spring month in the Sheep Year (A.D. 787). From this time onward the symbol of the Three Jewels is established in Tibet and the practice of the Buddha's Doctrine is not to be destroyed.'[b]

Padma-sambhava left Tibet very soon after the founding of

[a] Tucci, *Lhasa*, pp. 103–4; *idem*, *Tombs*, p. 43; Richardson, *JRASB*, vol. xv (1949), pp. 57–8, and *JRAS*, 1954, p. 167 ff.

[b] Tucci, *Tombs*, *tx.* p. 95, *tr.* p. 44.

the monastery and Śāntarakshita died as a result of being kicked by a horse. Several other Indian teachers are mentioned as co-operating in the translation of texts with the seven newly-ordained monks, but it is one of the latter, a certain Śrī-ghosha, whose Tibetan name was Trhi-sh'er of Ba, who assumes charge.[a] Another important monastic settlement that was founded at this time is the hermitage of Yer-pa, about nine miles east of Lhasa. It is traditionally associated with many of the early Indian teachers and there still survives an ancient bell, which probably goes back to the eighth century. It is inscribed in Sanskrit and Tibetan. The Sanskrit is the common formula:

> 'The elements of existence are all born of causes and the cause of them the Tathāgata has told. Moreover the way of stopping them the Great Ascetic has also told.'

The Tibetan is in the form of an invocation:

> 'Let us hold fast to the excellent religion of the buddhas and act in such a way as to display everywhere deeds of enlightenment; and let us continue also, for all time to come, in the perfect practice of good deeds.'[b]

A far more detailed knowledge of the kind of Buddhism favoured by Trhi-song-deu-tsen, may be derived from the reports of a council which was held in Lhasa about 794. This is not only the most interesting but also the best documented event of his reign.[c] The cause was the ill-feeling which existed between a Chinese teacher, confusingly named Mahāyāna, on the one hand and Śrī-ghosha and those who had been trained by Śāntarakshita, thus representing the Indian school of thought, on the other. Mahāyāna seems to have gained the greater number of converts and so his opponents complained to the king of the heretical nature of his teachings. One observes that the arrival of Indian teachers in some numbers at this time coincides with the period of bitter warfare with the Chinese

[a] He also figures in the Bodhnāth prophecy. See p. 99.
[b] Richardson, *JRAS*, 1954, pp. 166–7.
[c] P. Demiéville, *Le Concile de Lhasa*; *Bu-tön*, II, p. 191 ff.

in Central Asia. It is therefore not unlikely that there were political undercurrents to this indicting of a Chinese teacher. who appears very much on the defensive throughout the whole of the debate.[a]

Jñānendra (Säl-nang of Ba) had withdrawn to a deep cave for solitary mediation and it was only with great difficulty that he could be induced to take part. Even then neither he nor Śrīgosha led the prosecution, for the most renowned of Śāntarakshita's Indian pupils, Kamalaśīla, was summoned from India for this purpose. The main point at issue was whether buddhahood was to be attained to gradually by means of activity or suddenly by means of complete inactivity. The Indians represented the argument for the traditional course of the bodhisattva, who by striving through innumerable lives, perfects his wisdom and his morality. The Chinese represented the case for the silent sage rather in the terms of that special form of Chinese Buddhism, which has been made known in the west under its Japanese name, Zen, chiefly by the writings of Professor Suzuki. One typical example of question and answer at this curious debate may suffice for our brief account:

Question: 'One might say that a buddha does not become a buddha until through immeasurable ages he has satisfactorily cultivated innumerable merits and accumulations of knowledge, and that it is not possible to become a buddha by the mere suppression of false notions. And why? Because if buddhahood were just concerned with these false notions, it would not have been necessary to speak of the Six Perfections or the Set of Twelve Teachings. It would have been enough to speak of the destruction of false notions. But since it is not so, your argument is not reasonable.'

Answer: 'It is because all beings throughout immeasurable ages have been unable to free themselves from the false notions with which their thought has been long impregnated by the three poisons of passion etc., that they are dragged into the flow of birth and death and unable to gain release. According to the

[a] Demiéville, *Concile*, p. 182.

first chapter of the *Sarvadharma-pravṛtti-nirdeśa*, one is called released if one has eliminated every thought of every *dharma*, since these are inapprehensible in so far as they are just objectivized notions. Also in the *Vajrasamādhi-sūtra* the Buddha says: "However little is the spirit kindled, be it only as much as a single thought, the five components of personality are born simultaneously. Let beings but repose their mind in a condition of calm! Let them be established in the vajra-sphere, and they will not have a single thought. This Absolute, this Suchness, contains all the *dharmas*." '

Thus he continues by quoting the *Suvarṇaprabhāsa-sūtra* and the *Lankāvatāra-sūtra*.[a] Whether Mahāyāna was so apt in his quotations during the actual course of the debate, one cannot be sure. To have conducted a debate through the medium of Chinese, Tibetan and Sanskrit with one of the greatest masters of Buddhist logic must have taxed his powers to the full, and in any case judgement against his views seems to have been foreordained.[b] The King declared formally in favour of the Perfection of Wisdom teachings and Mahāyāna withdrew to Tunhuang, where he composed the general summary which has survived to this day. Kamalaśīla was murdered by the supporters of the Chinese faction and Jñānendra seems to have returned to his cave, where he meditated without taking food until he died. Thus the cause of Indian Buddhism seems to have emerged from this successful debate hardly strengthened at all. Trhi-song-deu-tsen probably abdicated in 797 and his successor was murdered after a very brief reign, in the course of which he 'caused four great religious services to be celebrated at Sam-yä and thrice established equality between the rich and the poor'.[c]

Although during the reign of Sä-na-lek Tibet reached the

[a] Demiéville, *Concile*, p. 53 ff.

[b] The discussion seems to have been conducted in written form. *op. cit.*, p. 140, note 5.

[c] *Bu-tön*, II, p. 196. This curious benevolence is reported elsewhere but no satisfactory explanation is offered. See also Petech, *Chronicles*, p. 71.

peak of its power, later historians have very little to say of him except that he greatly furthered the spreading of the doctrine.[a] The two events which are specifically mentioned in this respect, both find confirmation in stone-inscriptions. They are the founding of Kar-chung Temple and the granting of land to a monk named Ting-dzin S'ang-po of Nyang. About the former it is written in an early text: 'He established a *vajra-dhātu-maṇḍala* at Kar-chung. At the centre he built a sovereign-temple (*rgyal-khang*) and at the eight points of the compass chötens containing sacred objects. Even so was this temple with its inscribed stone-pillar. Men of the district were pressed into service and they cut the stone and the wood. On every side a hundred workers laid the foundations in stone and built with wood and clay.'[b] To-day the original name is no longer remembered locally and the only means of identifying it is the inscribed stone. The site has been described and the problem of identity fully discussed by Mr. Richardson. Of interest to us here are the admonitions to the practice of the doctrine which follow the list of royal foundations:[c]

'This founding of shrines of the Three Precious Ones by the generations of our ancestors and this practice of the Buddhist Law is to be held in affection and in no way for no reason whatsoever is it to be destroyed or abandoned, whether because people say that it is bad, that it is not good, or by reason of prognostications or dreams. Whosoever, great or small, argues in that way, you are not to act accordingly. The Royal Descendant of the Mighty One, likewise those who are juniors and those above them, those who rule the realm and those below them, let them choose a spiritual preceptor from among the monks and let them study the doctrine as well as they can understand it, and with all Tibet thus studying the doctrine, let no man cut off the means of practising it, for never shall the

[a] The *rgyal-po bka'i-thang-yig* does him greater justice. See Thomas, *Documents* I, pp. 269–75.

[b] *rgyal-po bka'i-thang-yig*, folio 39.

[c] Richardson, 'Three Ancient Inscriptions from Tibet', *JRASB*, vol. xv (1949), p. 45 ff.

people of Tibet, the aristocracy and those below, have closed to them the door that leads to salvation from the power of their past actions. With this in view we must appoint some of those who are capable from among those of the faithful who have entered upon salvation from the power of past actions, as regular followers of the Lord, and these regular followers of the Lord, being bound to obedience to whatever is prescribed by the religious assembly, shall be appointed to perform the rites and consecrations of the religious assembly and to act as spiritual preceptors. Those who take the vows of monkhood shall act in accordance with what We have permitted in the case of priests, and establishing shrines of the Three Precious Ones in the palace of the Mighty One, they shall perform worship as priests, lacking in nothing and being in nothing neglectful. In short, in the palace of the Mighty One and in the Land of Tibet nothing is to be done, which would be a means of destroying or abandoning the Three Precious Ones.'[a]

The type of Buddhism which is characterized here conforms very well with what we may surmise of the later Indian Buddhism. The monks are regarded primarily as the keepers of the temples and as priests empowered to perform ceremonies. The 'regular followers of the Lord' are not monks, but lay-folk and from them are appointed spiritual preceptors, who perform rites (*karma*) and consecrations (*abhisheka*). One is reminded of the *vajrācārya* of Nepalese Buddhism. 'Bound to obedience' (literally: bound to the authoritative word) seems to refer to the mandate of spiritual authority, for the expression is actually used as a title and is applicable to Ting-dzin S'ang-po, whose inscription we have now to consider.[34]

The Tibetan religious histories are filled with names, to which we can give no real substance, and perhaps the chief value of archaeological remains is their power to evoke the past and thus endow with some historical reality the people whose names are associated with them. Ting-dzin S'ang-po had been the guardian of the prince who was to become Sä-na-lek, and

[a] *op. cit.*, *tx.* p. 52, *tr.* pp. 55–6; Tucci, *Tombs*, p. 50 ff. (*tx.* p. 105).

when his master assumed full power, he continued to give faithful service, for which he was rewarded by the granting to his family of the privileges and royal protection, which are recorded in the inscription. This has been thoroughly studied by Mr. Richardson.[a] It is interesting to observe that a Buddhist priest should at last be able to exercise so much influence in secular affairs, and especially significant that he should belong to the Indian tradition. He was the pupil of Vimalamitra, one of the sages who had come to Tibet during the reign of Trhi-song-deu-tsen. The line of argument adopted by the Indian party at Trhi-song's council and the subsequent vindication of the way of virtuous conduct certainly throw light on the sort of Buddhism that was approved by the king, but there were also other religious practices entering Tibet at this time in the name of Buddhism. Thus of Vimalamitra we read: 'He did not dress in monastic robes, but went about attired as a yogin. The king and his ministers expressed doubt as to whether he was a heretic or a Buddhist.' In order to remove the doubts of the ministers he composed a text called *On the Taking of Refuge in the Three Precious Ones.*[b] One may recall that Padma-sambhava left Tibet soon after the founding of Sam-yä because the ministers were displeased with him. At this time many yogins were coming to Tibet and the powers and practices attributed to them identify them clearly with the type of the *siddha* ('perfect one'). They were skilled in rites of tranquillizing, bestowing prosperity, empowering and slaying, for which they chiefly gained their fame. But they were also concerned with gaining power of a supramundane kind through the medium of their chosen divinity. The texts on which they based their practices were the tantras, many of which were not included in the official Tibetan Canon when it was compiled in the thirteenth century. An important collection of the extra-canonical tantras is represented by *The Hundred Thousand Tantras of the Old Sect* (*rnying-ma'i rgyud-*

[a] Richardson, 'Tibetan Inscriptions at Zhva'i lha-khang,' *JRAS*, 1952, pp. 133–54, and 1953, pp. 1–12.

[b] *Blue Annals*, pp. 191–2.

'bum), a work which seems to be rare, even in Tibet.[a] These tantras are of great interest, for many of them originated in the Gilgit area (*bru-zha*).[b] These early tantras were rejected later on, because they were said to be mixed with indigenous elements. Nevertheless the main divinities referred to are certainly of Indian origin and although local divinities were introduced into the ritual circles (*maṇḍalas*), this has since become a common feature of the practice of all the sects of Tibetan Buddhism. Although the tantras are the most carefully systematized of all Buddhist works, the material on which they draw is such a mixture of heterodox elements, that it would be difficult indeed to decide which are orthodox and which are not. The accounts of the lives of the practisers of these tantras is always unsatisfactory as historical material, because it is regularly assumed that these people were possessed of miraculous powers, enabling them especially to live for extraordinarily long periods or even never to die at all. Padma-sambhava has become the extreme example of this process, but Tibetan historical works are filled with similar legends related of other sages. Ting-dzin S'ang-po was one of these. He was the pupil of the Vimalamitra, who had rendered himself suspect in the eyes of the ministers, and from whom he gained proficiency in a series of mystic practices known as the Heart-Drop (*snying-thig*). The various categories of tantric practice are often obscure, but the Heart-Drop practices are well known among the Nying-ma-pas to this day; they are based upon the psycho-physical exercises of the yogins, to which reference has been made in the last chapter. One is, therefore, nor surprised to learn that 'at the age of fifty-five, his mind having become purified, he disappeared without leaving his physical body behind'. He is said to have constrained a divinity to produce the means for building the temple at Sh'a (*Zhva*), where the stone-inscription still

[a] A copy exists at Rome in Prof. Tucci's library. The only other I have come upon, is at Teng-bo-che in Khumbu.

[b] Some early canonical tantras (*Nr. Kj. rgyud.* xx) are translated from the *bru-zha* language.

stands.[a] While it can generally be assumed that behind the most fantastic of legends there exists some firm historical fact, it is seldom that one can get so firm a hold upon a master of tantric practice. He was a monk (whereas many followers of the tantras in India, Nepal and Tibet were not) and there seems to have been no opposition to his holding a place of influence at court.

Sä-na-lek is the one king, about whom there exists an inscription at the site of the royal tombs at Yar-lung.[b] He is also credited with building a nine-story tower to the south-east of the wall of Sam-yä,[c] and although he is not recognized as a special incarnation, his zeal for the doctrine seems to have been unabated.

The representatives on earth of the Three Family-Protectors (*rigs-gsum-mgon-po*), Avalokiteśvara, Mañjuśrī and Vajrapāṇi are Song-tsen-gam-po, Trhi-song-deu-tsen and Räl-pa-cen, the last of whose reigns we have now reached. Räl-pa-cen has the reputation of being the most slavishly devoted to the doctrine. 'He gave seven households to maintain each monk. The king used to sit in the centre and having tied silk ribbons to the locks of his hair, he caused monks to be seated on them, and so there they were the three of them, monks to the right and left and the king himself in the centre.'[d] It was for this reason that he was nick-named Räl-pa-cen, which means 'the man with long locks'. Still a great deal was achieved during his reign. He built a nine-storied temple at Ön-chang-do, of which, however, little remains,[e] and most important of all, he initiated the great task of bringing order and system into the translation of texts. Those that had been previously translated were retranslated so that they might conform to the accepted type, and from now on the vast bulk of texts were translated from only one language, Sanskrit, thus considerably easing the task of gaining uniformity. All scholars of Tibetan are aware how

[a] *Blue Annals*, p. 192. [b] see p. 136.
[c] *rgyal-po bka'i-thang-yig*, folio 38*b*.
[d] Francke, *Ind. Ant. Tib.*, II, pp. 33–4.
[e] Richardson, *JRASB*, vol. xv (1949), p. 63; Tucci, *Tombs*, p. 15.

completely successful was this undertaking. Stock translations for all technical terms were fixed and regular methods of translating Sanskrit idiom were devised. The Tibetan of the canonical texts has therefore become a kind of shadow of the Sanskrit, so that often the original, which nowadays is seldom available, can be reconstructed without much difficulty. We also learn that 'it was prescribed that the Hīnayāna Scriptures other than those acknowledged by the Sarvāstivādins, and the secret charms were not to be translated'.[35]

It is often said that Buddhism has had the effect of allaying the fiercer tendencies of the peoples who have embraced it. While there are few signs of this where the Tibetan character is concerned, it might be argued that Buddhism has served as a force to make peace between neighbours. In 821–2 the Chinese and the Tibetans made the contract of eternal friendship, to which reference has been made above. It is true that it only lasted about twenty-five years, but it seems that Buddhist priests were largely concerned in initiating it. It has even been suggested that it was part of a deliberate Chinese policy to render their Tibetan neighbours more tractable through the mediation of the representatives of religion. It is also possible that there existed a certain anxiety on the Chinese side with regard to Tibetan contacts with the south. The inglorious defeat of the teacher Mahāyāna may still not yet have been forgotten. Why should this inscription wish to belittle the Nepalese, to whom Tibet already owed a great deal, if not to give some satisfaction to China, who is 'unlike the Nepalese and others in its practice of the excellent religion and the greatness of its sciences'?[a] Perhaps the reader may also be reminded, that it is on this inscription, that Räl-pa-cen, the most devoted of the Buddhist kings, claimed his pagan descent from the mythical ancestor Ö-de-pu-gyel (p. 128).

The king's chief minister was a monk, Yön-ten of Tr'en-ka (*bran-ka*). Scurrilous rumours were first spread about him and finally he was murdered, being succeeded by his vicious brother,

[a] Richardson, *AHE*, *tx*. p. 56, *tr*. 60.

Lang-dar-ma, who made short work of all organized Buddhism.[a] Lang-dar-ma was himself murdered a few years later by a monk, Päl-gyi-dorje, but the doctrine did not immediately profit by this act.

Thus ends the first spreading of the Good Law in Tibet.

[a] *Bu-tön*, II, pp. 197 ff.

Lotus

V

RELIGIOUS TEACHERS OF TIBET

In the last chapter we have told of the Tibetan military occupation of Tun Huang and Khotan, of Thön-mi Sambhoṭa's journey to Kashmir, of Padma-sambhava who came originally from Uḍḍiyāna, of many other expeditions and journeyings to and fro. Vast distances were covered across mountain ranges and through trackless wastes, where danger and privation were the order of the day. Beyond the Himalayas these conditions have not changed at all, and so it is quite possible there, even to-day, to find conditions similar to those experienced by the travellers of long ago. Apart from the mountaineer, who is quite a modern phenomenon, men have undertaken arduous journeys for just three reasons—for gain, for knowledge, for religious merit. Those who open up new routes are usually warriors and traders. In their wake come missionaries, scholars and pilgrims. This applies to the first thousand years of civilization in Europe as well as in Tibet and before the birth of modern man, say five hundred years ago, the ways of east and west were very much the same. There were kings and petty tyrants, traders and peasants, powerful prelates, monks and hermits, scholars and mountebanks, witches and magicians. The rich wore silks and travelled on horseback. The poor wore rough homespun and travelled on foot. It is we who have changed and not the Tibetans, and to understand their ways is to understand the ways of our ancestors. If we go even further back in time, we find that the same means were employed to establish Christianity in pagan Europe as to establish Buddhism amongst the Tibetans. Monasteries and churches were built by small devoted bands. Here the scriptures were copied and learned and the religious arts practised under foreign inspiration. Resistance to the new religion came from indigenous daemonic forces, of which the native priest or magician claimed to have control, and it was over these forces that the missionary of the new faith had to show an even greater mastery before he could hope to wean the people from their earlier beliefs. Some of the mediaeval biographies of Christian saints are very similar in spirit to the lives of some Tibetan sages. Perhaps also we have been too hasty in our desire to rationalize the past; if we really wish to understand other times and other places, it may be as important to know what people believed as what really happened. To-day only the warrior and the trader are really understood. The missionary and the pilgrim have become strange anomalies and the travelling scholar is usually taken for a spy. In our study we move in a world of faith and selfless desire for knowledge quite different from that of present daily experience. Whatever may have been exaggerated in the histories and legends upon which we draw, the faith and devotion of our religious teachers certainly were not.

Kashmir

According to tradition the first of these teachers was Thön-mi Sambhoṭa, who went to Kashmir to learn about alphabets. This was a considerable journey, involving then as now two or three months of travel, well beyond the confines of the Tibet of the early seventh century. Probably the fame of the pundits of Kashmir had already reached the Yar-lung Valley and Sambhoṭa was travelling by recognized trade-routes.

The north-west of India had been more or less Buddhist ever since the third century B.C. when the Emperor Aśoka had sent missions to the Greek rulers on the frontier. From very small beginnings Buddhism had spread widely from the first century A.D. onwards, when under the zealous King Kanishka, originally of barbarian stock, stūpas and shrines were built and a great congress was convened, all very much in accordance with what tradition recounts of Aśoka three hundred and fifty years earlier. There is little doubt that the reigns of these two monarchs had much to do with the success of Buddhism as a world-religion. Aśoka from his capital Pāṭaliputra (Patna) in Magadha caused small Buddhist conclaves to be established here and there throughout the whole of India. It is true of course that the opening up of routes and the consequent increase in trade played as great a part in the process as the Emperor's actual commands, but the traditional historians see fit to give him all the credit. After the disintegration of his empire under his successors, the chief centre of empire developed in the north-west under the foreign Kushan kings, of whom Kanishka is the most famous. It was at this period that Buddhism spread across Central Asia to the Chinese court and west as far as Samarkand, while Kashmir, a term which at this time embraces the whole area of north-west India, became a second holy Buddhist land. When Yuan Chwang passed through it in the early seventh century, probably just before Sambhoṭa's arrival, it had already suffered a great deal from the first Moslem invasions, but although the monks were less and many monasteries in ruins, local traditions seem still to have been quite alive. Between Uḍḍiyāna and the capital of Kashmir were located the sites of many events of the past lives of the Śākya-Sage, for while traditions in central India were too strong to permit in this second Buddhist centre the identification of localities associated with the great acts of his last life, there was no difficulty in discovering here connections with his former lives.[a] Thus there was a stūpa to mark the place where the forbearing hermit Kshānti had remained unperturbed while an unbelieving king had cut off his limbs one by one. There was another where a brahmin had given his life to hear half a stanza of the doctrine, another where a king had ransomed a pigeon's life by giving of his own flesh to the pursuing hawk, another where Indra had turned himself into a great sea-monster and so let the hungry people feed on himself in time

[a] Watters, *Yuan Chwang II*, 227 ff.

of famine, another where King Maitribala had fed five complaining demons (*yakshas*) with his own blood. All these heroes were the Śākya-Sage in his former lives, and however absurd or exaggerated these legends may seem to the modern reader, they were as real to the faithful of those days as the events of Lumbini, Bodhgaya, Sarnāth and Kuśinagara. Indeed the first collections of these stories were not just the work of story-tellers, but were based upon the accounts of pilgrims, who returning home, would sometimes put together all that they had heard on their travels. Thus all the stories listed here and many more besides came to form one great collection, well known in Central Asia, where it was written down in Chinese, and later translated into Tibetan under the title of *The Wise Man and the Fool*.[a] One misses the significance of such compendiums altogether, if one fails to realize that the people of those days not only believed that the events had really happened, but that their actual sites were known. The existence of these sites must have done much to maintain the prestige of the whole country as a Buddhist land. At the same time there were numerous monastic establishments and many scholars of repute. The numbers which the pilgrims give are often contradictory; they seem to repeat round figures, 100, 300, 1000, etc., which had been given to them. But then the modern scholar on his travels, must be prepared for the same vagueness.

Himalayan Tracks

Although no itinerary of Sambhoṭa's journey is preserved, these routes became so well trodden in the subsequent centuries that it is worth our while to identify them, at least in generalities. The area westwards which was directly subject to the Tibetan kings of Yar-lung extended perhaps as far as

[a] Concerning this interesting collection of tales see J. Takakusu, 'Tales of the Wise Man and the Fool', *JRAS*, 1901, pp. 447–61; S. Lévi, 'Le sūtra du Sage et du Fou', *JA*, 1925, part 2, pp. 305–32. For other refs. see P. Pelliot, 'Neuf notes sur des questions d'Asie Centrale', *T'oung Pao*, 26 (1928–9), p. 256.

Mount Kailas.[a] Beyond lay the country which in the early chronicles and annals is known as Sh'ang-Sh'ung. Song-tsen-gam-po had attempted to subject it to his rule, and an uneasy alliance seems to have developed between the two realms. This whole area did not become subject to Lhasa until the seventeenth century; up till then it was largely independent and seemingly very much the better for it, as will be seen. An interesting question is whether the people of Sh'ang-Sh'ung and even further west were already Tibetans by race in the seventh century A.D.[36] They certainly were in the tenth century and nowadays there are no traces of non-Tibetan peoples beyond the main Himalayan ranges until one comes to Lahul, Zangskar and Ladakh in the extreme west.

What most impresses the traveller in these regions, is the vast difference in climatic and natural conditions between India and Tibet (pls. 26 & 27). Wherever the political frontier may be fixed, the true frontier remains unchanged. To the south of the main Himalayan passes the atmosphere is hot and moist and vegetation is luxuriant; it is for these valleys that every summer the monsoon-clouds reserve their heaviest downpours. But to the north, where bare barren hills rise out of flat stony valleys, the only colours are the blue of the sky and the graduated browns and greys of the mountains. There are a few trees only in the villages, and short harsh grass grows high up on the upper reaches, often several hours' climb above the villages, whither the herdsmen must go to graze their yaks, yak cross-breeds (zebus), sheep and goats.[37] The traveller journeys for days through sand and stones and cold torrential water. At times it is depressing; at others a notion of phantasy is produced by weird sentinel-like cones which line the deeply eroded river-terraces, and one feels like a lonely traveller on the moon (pl. 21). The whole region is never less than 10,000 feet high and the villages are often much higher, so the atmosphere is clear with consequent extremes of temperature. The villages exist

[a] On the four divisions (literally 'horns') of Tibet see Thomas, *Documents*, I, p. 281 ff.

wherever a river-terrace of sufficient width to allow cultivation coincides with tributary streams which will provide irrigation. Rainfall is negligible. Much barley is grown, some wheat and buck-wheat, peas, potatoes (a comparatively recent innovation) and turnips. Near the villages, willows, junipers, poplar and firs will grow. There are also apricot-trees, which produce a small but delicious fruit. One may well doubt whether any non-Tibetan people has ever settled in these regions. Linguistically the question is of great importance, for if there were Tibetans speaking other dialects in the west, there would be a plausible theory to explain how classical Tibetan came to be written as it was. Thön-mi Sambhoṭa might then not have been first in the field and might have benefited from the experiments of his predecessors. There were certainly no Buddhists in Sh'ang-Sh'ung. More than a century later during the reign of Trhi-song-deu-tsen, this land seems to have been renowned for it. p'ön-po magicians.

Since Sh'ang-Sh'ung is so vague a name, it is best to use the later names for these areas, some of which were in use probably even then. Guge is the name of the upper Sutlej Valley, which round about A.D. 1000 was to become the chief centre of Buddhism in Tibetan lands.[36] From here one important trade-route follows the Sutlej westwards through the Himalayas to what was then the important Buddhist country of Jālandhara. From Guge another route leads up the Spiti River through the country of the same name. From the head waters of the Spiti one pass, the Kun-zang, leads westwards over to the wild Chandra Valley, thence north-westwards down the Chenab and so eventually to Kashmir (pl. 22). By climbing southwards out of the Chandra Gorge (with a choice of two passes, the Hamta or the Rohtang) one reaches the upper Beas River and the land of Kulu, which in the time of Yuan Chwang was still a Buddhist country. Another pass, the Baralacha of over 16,000 feet, can be gained in two or three days journey from the head of the Spiti River, leading by a choice of route to upper Lahul or northwards to Ladakh. The routes favoured by Buddhist pilgrims were those to the south, leading to Jālandhara, Kulu and Kashmir. From Kashmir one might journey still further west to Uḍḍiyāna (Swāt Valley) which was another famous Buddhist land. Ascending the Indus Valley one would reach *Bru-zha* (Gilgit) and Baltistān. Thence across formidable passes, which seem not to have daunted the travellers of those days, one might reach the Tarim Basin and go eastwards to Khotan.

From the Mt. Kailas region there is a direct route down the Indus through Ladakh, which in those days seems to have been neither Tibetan nor Buddhist, and thence to the Tarim Basin through Baltistān. This was the route used by Tibetan troops in their great outflanking of the Chinese strongholds, but it was one that would have had little attraction for missionaries and scholars. In spite of the difficulties of travel, very close cultural contacts were maintained by all these western Buddhist countries, and even if the Tibetans of the Yar-lung Valley first became aware of the art of writing and of Buddhism in Khotan, it was inevitably to Kashmir, the great Buddhist centre, that their attentions were at once directed. They do not seem to have become properly aware of Nepal until the end of the seventh century, where all their initial cultural requirements could have been met with far less trouble. Thereafter Indian masters were sought and invited in this country and from Vikramaśīla and the other great Buddhist centres in Magadha. But the connection with the west was never weakened and with the destruction of organized Buddhism in central Tibet following upon the murder of Räl-pa-cen, the initiative passed firmly to the west.

Many places in the Nepal Valley still look very much as the Tibetan travelling-scholars must have seen them first 1,250 years ago, but in Jālandhara, Kulu and Kashmir scarcely a trace of anything Buddhist now remains. One realizes by contrast what a miracle of preservation is Nepal.[38] Further west in the regions of Peshawar and Taxila, once Kanishka's capitals, and still further north-west at Bāmiyān there has been no lack of archaeological discoveries to attest the importance of these places in Buddhist history. Nowhere is there any active trace of Buddhism in the west on this side of the Himalayas, except perhaps at a sacred lake set in the foothills some twelve miles east of Mandi (*Za-hor*) which figures prominently in the legends of Padma-sambhava (pl. 23).

Mandi is on the road that leads up into the Kulu Valley, and as the traveller must in any case break his journey up from the rail-head at Pathankot, he may just as well stay the night at Mandi. It is a pleasant little Hindu town with temples and little bathing ghāts flanking the river and with the old Damdama Palace towering imposingly over the central square. The Riwalsar Lake, known as the Lotus Pool (*padma-mtsho*) by the Tibetans, is one of many places in the Himalayan regions, which is sacred both to Shaivites and to Buddhists. Its special interest consists in its legendary connection with Padma-sambhava and this is sufficient to draw vast numbers of pilgrims every winter from all over Tibet. Many of them regard it as his birth-place, but this does not accord with the literary accounts. According to these, the Princess Mandāravā, daughter of King Ārshadhara of S'a-hor, resolved to practise religion and so her father caused her to take her vows in front of Śāntarakshita. Observing that she was a fitting pupil, Padma-sambhava came through the air from Uḍḍiyāna, manifested himself and gave her instruction. This was seen by a cowherd who spread the report that a charlatan was with the princess. The report reached the king and indeed it proved true that a man was in her company. The princess was placed in a pit which was filled with thorns, and Padma-sambhava was led out of the town to a wild spot, tied to the wood of a blazing fire and left there. The smoke did not clear for seven days, so the king went to see the cause. The place had changed into a lake, from the centre of which emerged a lotus and upon it was a boy of eight years. The king was abashed. Padma-sambhava manifested himself and accepted the king's offer of his kingdom and Mandāravā as his bride.[a]

[a] Toussaint, *Padma Thang-yig*, p. 169 ff.; Evans-Wentz, *The Tibetan Book of the Great Liberation*, p. 144 ff.

Thus this little lake near Mandi is the magic lake of the Precious Master's manifestation. A temple in his honour is erected on the bank. It shows no sign of age, but this is scarcely to be expected, as large offerings are received and it is constantly being renovated. Other legendary traces of Padmasambhava exist along the routes listed above. There is the little monastery of Gandhola above the junction of the Bhaga and the Chandra which is associated with his name and is undoubtedly of great age.[39] At Nako in the lower Spiti Valley (Kunāwar) there is a small temple also of great age, built over his supposed foot-print on the rock.[a] Scanty and uncertain as these traces are, they are given greater substance by the strength of popular traditions. The Precious Master is not forgotten and those who know little enough of Buddhist teachings, will still wear his image in a charm-box round their neck. My servant Kal-zang was such a one.

Indigenous Beliefs

That the decay of Indian Buddhism in these western lands has been gradual is indicated by the journals of two Tibetan pilgrims, one of the thirteenth century and one of the early seventeenth century, which have been edited by Professor Tucci.[b] Their destination was Uḍḍiyāna, the land of Padmasambhava, where already in the early seventh century Yuan Chwang had observed that the monks who survived there 'were all mahāyānists who occupied themselves with silent meditation, were clever at reciting their books without penetrating their deep meaning, lived strictly according to their rules and were especially expert in magic exorcisms'.[c] As has been shown in a previous chapter, we know from the texts that originated in this period and in these areas, how many indigenous beliefs were being mixed with Buddhist doctrines. It is from asso-

[a] Tucci, *Ind-Tib.*, III, Part 1, p. 172.
[b] Tucci, *Tibetan Pilgrims in the Swat Valley.*
[c] Watters, *Yuan Chwang I*, 226.

ciation with these beliefs that the name of Padma-sambhava became so famous, for they have proved far stronger than the teachings of the higher religion. Since many elements in Tibetan Buddhism seem to be of western Himalayan origin, there is some confirmation of the Tibetan historical tradition which relates that the first foreign teachings to arrive in the country were p'ön-po and unorthodox Buddhist practices from the west. Especially associated with Uḍḍiyāna is a class of feminine beings known as *ḍākinī*. There is frequent reference to them in the tantric texts, where they appear as the partners of the yogins, flocking around them when they visit the great places of pilgrimage. Their presence was essential to the performance of the psycho-sexual rites and their activities generally are so gruesome and obscene as to earn them quite properly the name of witch. They enter Tibetan mythology in a rather more gentle aspect, and ceasing altogether to be beings of flesh and blood, they become the bestowers of mystic doctrines and bringers of divine offerings. They become the individual symbols of divine wisdom with which the meditator must mystically unite, and although iconographically they retain their fierce and gruesome forms, in such a context witch seems rather a harsh name for them. The Tibetans translated the name as *sky-goer* (*mkha-'gro-ma*), which Mr. Evans-Wentz regularly translates as fairy, but this scarcely does justice to their composite character.[a] They are important in our study because they become one of the members of the new tantric trilogy, which replaces the orthodox one of Buddha-Doctrine-Congregation, in which all new entries to the order had always vowed their faith. The new trilogy is Lama-Yidam-Kandroma, that is to say: spiritual preceptor, tutelary divinity and mystic partner. These three are the Union of the Three Precious Ones, conceived of as embodied in Padma-sambhava himself, and around whom there has developed an extensive and elaborate liturgy.

[a] In modern Nepal the term has come to mean 'prostitute', its earlier religious associations being entirely forgotten. This is typical of the general devaluation of terminology, which we discussed in ch. 3.

Equally important is the cult of the Lords of the Soil (*sa-bdag*) who are pre-eminently mountain-gods, as might well be expected in the Himalayas. Three important ones exist in the west, Kye-phang of Lahul, Jam-la of Spiti and Purgyul of Kunāwar. The idea of Lords of the Soil is probably an importation into central Tibet, for the term is generally used anonymously in Tibetan rituals. When a special identity is given to the god, as in the case of the God of the Plain (*thang-lha*) in the Liturgy of the Universal Saviour (*'gro-ba-kun-sgrol*), this comes about from the adoption of a proper Tibetan divinity. The true Lord of the Soil is never depicted and has no image. His sole symbol is an upright stick, on the top of which may be placed a trident, which is Śiva's borrowed property. To the stick garlands are attached, often in the form of strips of dirty rag, and as a pedestal a pile of stones must serve. Cairns of such a kind are found on the summits of all passes, and the merit seems to be the same, whether one adds stone, stick or rag. Temples may be erected in their honour in or near the villages, but no symbol other than the trident is placed within.[40] This sort of mountain-god involves a far more elementary notion than that of the divine king and his descent on the mountain-top, which was discussed above, and it would be futile to argue any connection. Myths seldom provide the material for responsible deductions. What, however, is clear for all to see, is the confusion which takes place between the chö-ten (stūpa) and the cairn of the mountain-god, so that chö-tens which had been built by the faithful, came to be honoured in a sense that was never intended. All the Buddhist temples in Spiti have chö-tens of a sort before them, out of which protrude the usual sticks with rags appended and often rams' horns thrust amongst them, for the latter are especially detestable to spirits that are ill-disposed.

It is impossible to know the exact relationship that existed between the indigenous beliefs of the mountain folk and those of the wandering yogins. The beliefs of the latter, even when they called themselves Buddhist, were permeated with heterodox elements, so that later on it becomes impossible to tell whether these were of Indian, Himalayan or Tibetan origin. All these elements have been welded together to form the different ritual cycles, which are now represented upon Tibetan altars. While it is true that those who look to Padma-sambhava as the source of their doctrine, have preserved many beliefs that have clearly nothing to do with Indian Buddhism, one must remember that their legends and rituals were not codified until the twelfth and thirteenth centuries, by which time a process of adoption and adaptation, which was only in its beginnings in the eighth century, would have reached its conclusion. All this work of amalgamation is attributed to Padma-sambhava, who thus becomes the great tranquillizer of indigenous divinities and the great converter of the Tibetans, as though it had all happened in the course of a few years. This gives of course an entirely false impression of the first centuries of Tibetan Buddhism, presenting it all as a series of magical feats, when in reality human effort and selfless activity of quite another order were involved. However, when speaking of its nobler aspect, one should remember that the whole time there inevitably continued the less worthy process of adaptation misinterpretation and distortion, so that Tibetan Buddhism appears as it does today, at once the purest and the most debased of Buddhist traditions.

The Kings of Guge

So much destruction, rebuilding and redecorating have taken place in central Tibet, that one must go to the west in order to find undisturbed the monuments of an earlier age. Since with the destruction of organized Buddhism in central Tibet after the murder of Räl-pa-cen, the initiative passed to the western countries, it is of this second spreading of the doctrine (as the Tibetan historians call it), that the Buddhist sites there provide illustration. It will be remembered that Lang-dar-ma was slain by a Buddhist monk in 842, but this action far from strengthening the Buddhist cause, resulted in a period of anarchy and internal strife. Consequently this period appears as one of general gloom in the later historical works. Buddhism was not destroyed by any means, but in the absence of guidance from enlightened leaders, only the more popular and less worthy forms developed. The tales of magical powers that were acquired and the disregard of conventional morality are exactly in keeping with the biographies of the eighty-four Great Siddhas, from whom ultimately all these practices were derived. Although so far as the scholastic tradition is concerned, it is convenient to speak of two spreadings of the doctrine, there seems to have been no break in the transmitting of the yogic practices. Many of these hermits may have been worthy fellows, but they can have done little to establish the doctrine generally amongst the lay-folk of Tibet. It is clear too that the lay-folk regarded them merely as the wielders of special powers, and there must have been many who were prepared to profit from such foolish credulity.

Once again the re-establishing of orthodox doctrine was the work of kings. At the beginning of the tenth century a great-grandson of Lang-dar-ma established himself, seemingly by marriage, as a chieftain in Pu-rang (*spu-hrangs*). From there he conquered the whole of western Tibet from Mount Kailas to Ladakh. After his death this kingdom was divided between his three sons.[a] The historical sources at our disposal disagree on just how the division was made, except that one portion was certainly Ladakh. In any case by the end of the tenth century the son of one of the three brothers had become pre-eminent as king of Guge, holding sway throughout the whole Sutlej Valley at least from the Shipke Pass eastwards, and also possibly over lower Spiti. There follows then throughout the eleventh century a series of kings who were devoted to the

[a] For a full discussion of this dynasty and comparative tables of their geneology see *Tucci, Ind-Tib.*, II, 'Rin-chen-bzang-po e la Rinascita del Buddhismo nel Tibet intorno al mille', p. 14 ff. This work is of capital importance for the whole period under present consideration.

Buddhist doctrine and were determined to establish its true traditions. For in the words of the *Blue Annals:* 'Not withstanding the fact that some of the tantric precepts were to be found in Ü and Tsang (the two provinces of central Tibet) and Nga-ri (western Tibet), tantric practices had become defiled. Meditation on the ultimate reality was abandoned and many coarse practices made their appearance. This was noticed by the kings of Nga-ri (western Tibet) and although they did not voice their objection openly, they sent invitations to numerous learned pundits, who were able to remove these obstacles by placing living beings on the path of purity.'[a]

The first king with whom we are concerned, renounced the throne and took the religious name of Ye-she-ö (Light of Wisdom), being succeeded by his brother, who seems to have ruled for a very short time. He was followed by his son Lha-de (*lha-lde*), who was again rapidly followed by his son Ö-de (*'od-lde*). When Ö-de came to the throne, his great-uncle Ye-she-ö was still alive, although held captive by a barbaric frontier-tribe. Ö-de had two brothers, who took religious names, Ch'ang-chup-ö (Light of Enlightenment) and Sh'i-wa-ö (Light of Peace) and associated themselves with him in the spiritual welfare of the kingdom. The great Indian sage, Atīśa, of whom more will be said below, arrived in Guge in 1042 during the reign of these brothers. One might add that the two sons of Ye-she-ö also took religious vows with their father. Indeed one gains the impression that the whole royal family was intent on one thing only, namely the establishing of Buddhism in their domains. This impression is largely confirmed by the temples and monasteries, founded by them, that are still standing. They worked of course through intermediaries, for their chief function was to provide the inspiration and the funds. These intermediaries were Tibetans who were specially selected for the task, supplied with gold and sent to seek in India the texts and the explanation of their meaning. They were also empowered to invite to Tibet those Indian masters

[a] *Blue Annals I*, 204.

who could be persuaded to come. Of the Tibetan scholars the most renowned was Rin-chen S'ang-po (Good Gem) who lived from 958 to 1055, and of Indian masters, Atīśa, who lived from 982 to 1054. These two so typify the activities of this period, that a brief study of their lives will provide the clearest possible account of this cultural transfer from India to Tibet.

Rin-Chen S'ang-po

Rin-chen S'ang-po was one of twenty-one youths chosen by Ye-she-ö and sent to India. All but two, Rin-chen S'ang-po and Lek-pai-she-rap, died without ever completing their studies. This need be no exaggeration, for it is quite typical of the toll of life and wealth that was taken by these ventures. Tibetans come of a completely different racial stock from Indians, and accustomed as they are to living above 10,000 feet, the climate of India except perhaps for two months in the middle of the winter season, is a torment for them and they succumb easily to disease. Rin-chen S'ang-po studied in Kashmir for many years and also visited central India. The number of his masters is said to have been seventy-five. Most Buddhist scholars were skilled only in one branch of learning, systematic philosophy (*abhidharma*) or mystical philosophy (*prajñāpāramitā*) or logic, monastic discipline (*vinaya*), historical or quasi-historical discourses attributed to the Śākya-Sage (*sūtras*) or special meditational and ritual practices (*tantras*), and even then the texts on which their knowledge was based would be strictly limited. Hence there arose the need to progress from one master to another, seeking copies of the texts, interpretations of them and in the case of the tantras the methods of their practice and actual realization.[41] There were some recognized sets of works, for example the *vinaya* and its commentaries, but there was at that time no complete canon, which needed but to be systematically translated in a scholarly way. Texts were collected and translated piece-meal in accordance with the individual's

Plate 21

(a) Kyi-bar Village (13,700 ft.), Spiti. (p. 170)
(b) The Spiti River winding through its eroded sand-bed. (p. 170)

Plate 22

(a) Crossing the Kun-zang (=Samanta-bhadra) Pass, 15,000 ft., which links the Chandra gorge to upper Spiti. (p. 171)

(b) Carrying Tibetan books.

Plate 23

Image of Padma-sambhava in the Riwalsar Temple. (p. 173)

Plate 24

Ancient marble head of a bodhisattva. This fragment was unearthed near Gandhola. (note 39)

A section of ceiling at Tabo. (p. 188)

(b) Vairocana. Fresco at Tabo. (p. 191)

Plate 25

(c) Amitābha. Stucco-image at Tabo. (p. 186)

Plate 26

(a) *Dankhar, old capital of Spiti (p. 189)*
(b) *Village festival at Gushal at the head of the Kulu Valley. (p. 170)*

Plate 27

(a) Ridge leading up to Dankhar, which may be seen on the summit to the left.

(b) Villagers of Kaze in Spiti, crowding around my camp.

Plate 28

(a) Sacred Mountain. Abode of the 'country-god' of Khumbu.

(b) Sacred Water. The Milk-Lake sacred to LokeSvara (27° 45′N, 86° 36′E) with Peak 22,817 ft. (unnamed). My tent may be seen in the foreground.

aptitude and propensities. The greatness of Rin-chen S'ang-po consists in the fact that he became the head of a whole school of Tibetan scholars and translators, thus rendering possible the co-ordination of the work on a large scale.[a] The type of doctrine favoured by him is that which is still characteristic of Tibetan Buddhism, namely tantric practice with personal realization of the true nature of mystical philosophy as its aim. It is interesting to observe that the only practical reference to the bodhisattva-career concerns the royal dynasty. In the days of Trhi-song-deu-tsen, Śāntarakshita had borne the title *Bodhisattva* and the dispute of his pupil Kamalaśīla with the Chinese teacher, Mahāyāna, was concerned with the justification of the gradual way towards enlightenment, that is to say by altruistic activity throughout many births. It is quite understandable that this method should appeal to Buddhist kings. We are informed that Ye-she-ö was in doubt as to whether the tantras were the true doctrine, and he certainly received the title of *Bodhisattva.*[b] The financing of temples and schools, of foreign travel and costly Indian guests, all productive of much merit, was a more suitable occupation for religious-minded kings than the practising of mystic rituals. That such however represented the religious practice of those whom these kings supported, there can be no doubt. Those who were now one-pointedly intent on the religious life, were concerned with finding the most efficacious means to enlightenment in the course of one life's time. The texts which told of the bodhisattva's slow and noble career were all translated, but their value was that of general edification for the benefit of others, who although religiously inclined, were still immersed in the affairs of this world. Those who now deliberately renounced the world sought a far more rapid fulfilment of their aspira-

[a] Prof. Tucci has listed his collaborators and the texts translated by them. *Ind-Tib.*, II, pp. 39–49.

[b] 'He acknowledged the Vehicle of Philosophy to be the Word of the Buddha, but as concerns the tantras, he was in doubt as to their being the true teaching, since the tantric exorcists indulged in perverse acts, as that of deliverance through sexual ecstasy, etc.' (*Bu-tön II,* p. 212).

tions. Hence there is great preoccupation with the tantric cycles. The scheme employed was the *vajra-dhātu-maṇḍala* (see above pp. 69 ff.) which is described in several important texts, notably *The Symposium of Truth of All the Tathāgatas* (*Sarva-tathāgata-tattva-saṃgraha*), to which we have referred above and which was one of the tantras translated by Rin-chen-S'ang-po himself. One may note that this early group of tantras, which centre around Vairocana and are free of the later sexual symbolism, also found favour in Central Asia, China and Japan, and it seems likely therefore that the source of these texts was in all cases Kashmir.

The route followed by Rin-chen S'ang-po on his travels would have taken him either down the Sutlej Valley to India and thence across difficult foot-hills to the Beas Valley and so north-westwards to Kashmir, or he may have followed the northern route through Spiti and the Chandra Valley. In any case like many Tibetans he was a great traveller, for even if he only founded a proportion of the one hundred and eight temples that are ascribed to him, he must have journeyed far and wide. Locally his name is still remembered as a founder of temples and the Sutlej Valley seems to boast the greater share.[a]

This valley probably provides the easiest route from India to Tibet and here the change of climatic conditions, although gradual, is none the less well marked. In spite of intermarriage in the transitional area, only people of Tibetan stock relish living above 10,000 feet. Spiti provides a cogent example of this fact, for although it can be entered in the west from Kulu and in the east from the Sutlej Valley, it has completely preserved its Tibetan character. Over many of the passes travel is only possible between June and November, for snow and ice clamp down during most of the year and bitter winds blow through the valleys. Thus the season for leaving Tibet is the

[a] The first of these on the way into Tibet by this route is that of Kanam, where the devoted Hungarian scholar, Csoma de Körös lived from 1827–30, working on his summary of the contents of the Tibetan Canon, which still serves as our chief guide to these massive volumes.

very worst one for a Tibetan to arrive in India. Hence travellers from Guge would probably prefer to follow the more arduous route through Spiti, for they would thereby remain the longer in Tibetan territory while still drawing nearer to Kashmir.

Of the temples attributed to Rin-chen S'ang-po one very important one is Tabo in lower Spiti. It consists now of a compound rather less than 100 yards square, enclosed within high mud-brick walls, standing in the flat valley-bottom near the river. Within the compound there is a main temple, oblong in shape, which is entered through an ante-chamber. On either side are two smaller temples and at the far end of the compound is a very small one, standing quite alone. There are ruins of other buildings, presumably once the cells of the monks, and a large number of chö-tens, all in varying stages of decay. All the buildings are constructed of large sun-dried clay bricks. The roofs are flat, braced with wooden struts and supported by wooden pillars. The whole place is in process of sad decay, for the few monks that now care for it, have neither the will nor the means to carry out the necessary preservation. An upper monastery high up on the mountain-side has long been abandoned. The monks now all live in the village, which is about 200 yards upstream, and although no one lives within the enclosure, they readily agreed to my setting up camp there and using the old monastery-kitchen. Morning and evening one member of the community comes to light lamps before the images in the main temple and to intone supplications to Dorje Jik-ch'e (Vajra-bhairava) in the room of the Fierce Protectors, for the monastery belongs to the Ge-luk-pas (Yellow Hat Sect), for whom this divinity is chief protector. Nowhere have the deep tones of Tibetan religious refrain with their accompaniment of drum and cymbals seemed so harrowing as in this ancient all but forgotten site.[a]

The centre of interest is the main temple, for this alone can

[a] It was visited by Francke in 1909 (*Ant. Ind. Tib.*, I, pp. 36–43), and by Tucci in 1933 (*Ind-Tib.*, III, Part 1, pp. 21–115 and plates I–LXII). The latter work represents a complete study of temples in Spiti and Kunavar.

be attributed with certainty to the eleventh century. Inside there is an inscription, of which the opening sentence reads: 'This temple was first founded by the Ancestor the Bodhisattva in the ape-year and now forty-six years later the Royal Descendant the Mighty One Ch'ang-chup-ö, motivated by the thought of enlightenment, has carried out repairs to this temple.'[a] There need be no doubt therefore that Tabo was once a special interest of the two most religious kings of Guge, Ye-she-ö and his great-nephew Ch'ang-chup-ö. But there is something else inside this temple that brings one far closer to the times of Rin-chen S'ang-po than any inscription can do. Set around the walls at about head-height are life-size stucco images of the divinities of the *vajra-dhātu-maṇḍala*. The central divinity, a four-fold image of Vairocana, is set above the altar at the far end of the hall, in the normal cross-legged posture and with two images of Rin-chen S'ang-po placed just below him. The other four buddhas of the directions, each of them flanked by four bodhisattvas, two to the left and two to the right, are set against the side walls. The four buddhas are distinguished from the other images by their generally larger proportions and they are of the appropriate colours and with the proper hand-gestures.[42] Against the wall of entry are set four feminine divinities and just inside the door-way two fierce male ones. Likewise against the far wall are four more feminine divinities with two fierce male ones at the entrance to the passages that lead beyond into the apse. The eight feminine divinities are the goddesses of personified worship, Vajra-gaity, Vajra-garland, Vajra-song, Vajra-dance, Vajra-perfume, Vajra-flower, Vajra-lamp and Vajra-incense. The four fierce male ones are the guardians of the four directions: Vajra-hook, Vajra-noose, Vajra-burst and Vajra-fury.[b]

[a] Tucci, *op. cit.*, p. 146. Ye-she-ö must have died about 1040, shortly before the arrival of Atīśa in Tibet. Assuming he was dead, when Ch'ang-chup-ö carried out the repairs, this would make the earliest date for the founding of Tabo A.D. 996. As an ape-year occurs every twelfth year, one may calculate the next possibility as 1008.

[b] see above, pp. 67-8.

It is unlikely that all these images are originals of the eleventh century, but they are certainly deliberate replacements of the originals. It is doubtful whether there survives anywhere else an ancient temple, laid out as this one is: a complete three dimensional mandala, where there intrudes no image which is not part of the general scheme. One should realize how far removed from any notion of idolatry was the setting up of such a cycle of divinities. No single image has significance in itself. As an integrated whole they represent the manifold human personality transmuted into the ideal condition of buddhahood. This temple does not therefore contain a collection of anthropomorphic gods, but is intended as a symbolic expression of the goal of religious striving and the means that lead to it. There can be no surer sign of the degeneration of the doctrine than the juxtaposition of images and paintings, which have no significant relation the one to the other, and which are placed there purely from sentimental motives. Only in these cases and they are, alas, the more general, might one speak of idolatry in Tibetan Buddhism. But this was clearly not the intention of Rin-chen S'ang-po and his assistants.

There can be no doubt of their preference for the tantric cycles which have Vairocana as their centre. At Nako at the lower end of the Spiti River in another temple attributed to to Rin-chen S'ang-po there is a fine set of stucco images of Vairocana and the other four buddhas.[a] Most important of all from the point of view of the excellence of composition of stucco figures and surrounding frescoes would seem to be the White Temple of Tsaparang, the ancient capital of the Guge Kings, which has been visited and interpreted by Professor Tucci.[b]

But we have not yet finished with the main temple of Tabo. At the far end beyond the fourfold image of Vairocana and past the two fierce guardians, one enters a kind of apse. Here upon a low platform one comes first upon two standing stucco-images of bodhisattvas. Then three steps higher is a large three-sided

[a] Tucci, *op. cit.*, p. 144 ff. and plates LXXV–LXXVI.
[b] Tucci, *Ind-Tib.*, III, Part 2, p. 117 ff. and plates LXX–LXXII.

shrine, wherein is seated a buddha-image in the meditation posture upon an elevated throne formed with two lions standing back to back (pl. 25*c*). Two more bodhisattvas stand one on either side of the shrine. This can be circumambulated for a small passage runs round behind it, the back-wall being painted with innumerable little buddha-figures. This main buddha-image is shown with the hand-posture of Amitābha, and it is indeed as such that the head-monk identified him, naming the attendant bodhisattvas as Khasarpaṇa (a form of Avalokiteśvara), and Mahāsthāmaprāpta, who stand nearest to the throne, and those on the lower platform as Kshitigarbha and Ākāśagarbha. But if it were a normal Amitābha-image, the animals beneath the throne should be peacocks and not lions, for just as the five buddhas have their different colours and gestures and symbols, so they have different vehicles:

Vairocana	*Akshobhya*	*Ratnasambhava*	*Amitābha*	*Amoghasiddhi*
Lions	Elephants	Horses	Peacocks	Harpies

A lion throne was the attribute of the Śākya-Sage before it was inherited by Vairocana (see above p. 47) and like the unqualified title *Bhagavān* (Lord) it belongs essentially to the one transcendent buddha. If then Amitābha is placed upon a lion-throne in the sanctuary of this temple, where Vairocana and the other four buddhas are displayed, it can only be because he is here being honoured as supreme transcendent buddha, in whom the other five lose their identity. We have already referred above to a sixth buddha, known as Vajrasattva or Vajradhara, who was identified as the one transcendent lord in succession, as it were, to Vairocana, and we noted the preeminence of the *vajra* and hence the *vajra*-family in tantric Buddhism. But here it would seem to be the lotus-family with Amitābha at its head, which takes the lead. Once more this is a sure connection with north-western India and Kashmir, whence devotion to Amitābha also passed across Central Asia to China and Japan. By contrast this buddha is of little importance in Nepal, where Akshobhya is the favourite. This may well reflect the situation that existed in Magadha. Of the later importance of the lotus-family in Tibetan Buddhism there is no doubt. Thus Padma-sambhava is conceived of as *nirmāṇa-kāya* of Amitābha (see p. 37), not just as some schematic incidental identification, but as part of the essential basis of Nying-ma-pa ritual. The tutelary divinity of this sect is Padma-Narteśvara (Lotus Lord of Dance) who is a form of Avalokiteśvara and thus *sambhoga-kāya* of Amitābha (p. 235). The popularity of Avalokiteśvara in Tibet is presumably to be explained by the popularity of this divinity (known as Lokeśvara and popularly confused with Śiva) in the Himalayan regions generally. Hence the Dalai Lamas have been recognized as manifestations of this same god and the Paṇchen Lamas, by reason of the greater spiritual excellence which is traditionally attributed to them, are identified with Amitābha. These identifications involve considerable distortion of the theory of the three-fold buddha-body, but they serve the present argument by illustrating how firmly established was the pre-eminence of the lotus-family. As is well known, these two prelates belong to the Ge-luk-pas (Yellow Hats), the reformed sect, which was founded by Tsong-kha-pa. Sensibly enough from the Tibetan point of view Tsong-kha-pa is regarded by his followers as an emanation of Mañjuśrī. It might therefore have been more logical to have assigned their grand-lamas to Vairocana's *tathāgata*-family, to which Mañjuśrī properly belongs, thereby firmly distinguished themselves from the red-hatted followers of Padma-sambhava, whose ways they castigated as so corrupt. But it is Amitābha who is acclaimed by both parties. It is of great interest therefore to find him already accorded first place in Rin-chen S'ang-po's temples.[a]

Around the walls beneath the images of the Vairocana's circle of divinities there runs a series of frescos. Those along the left wall tell in successive scenes the story of the bodhisattva-prince Nor-s'ang and those to the right tell the story of

[a] This is also the intention of a similar image in the White Temple at Tsaparang (Tucci, *op. cit.*, Part 2, p. 122 ff. and pl. XCVII).

the Śākya-Sage. Once again these have not been painted here for the sake of mere decoration, but they represent the advance of the bodhisattva to buddhahood. It is an expression through the time-process (in this case of two human lives) of the transmutation of phenomenal existence into the perfection of buddhahood. According to the mystical philosophy (*prajñāpāramitā*) which is the essential basis of all the tantras, the process of time is only a conventional reality. It has an apparent existence only so long as one remains immersed amongst the false associations of phenomenal things. Thus for the followers of the tantras, who sought realization of absolute truth here and now, the stories of the gradual advance towards buddhahood through a time-process take on a purely symbolic significance. However this may be, the chief interest of these frescos for us is their style, for they clearly reveal their Indian inspiration. The Tibetans invited not only religious teachers, but also craftsmen, who transmitted their traditions of painting and carving to their Tibetan pupils. This had considerable effect upon the whole later development of Tibetan art-forms, for these were already conditioned by Indian and Nepalese styles long before China began to exert an influence in this respect. Sections of the ceilings at Tabo are decorated with motifs which recall at once the caves of Ajanta, graceful human-forms, flowers and birds and twisting garlands (pl. 25*a*). If such exquisite work was being done in western Tibet in the eleventh and succeeding centuries, how much beauty of just this kind must have existed in the India of the preceding centuries! One is saddened at the thought of how fragile is such human skill. Once destroyed by adverse circumstances, an art is lost for ever.

The temples founded during the times of the great religious kings of Guge seem to have been built generally in the plain, which may well be indicative of the safe prosperity that their rule ushered in. Other monasteries in Spiti are built like fortresses on mountain-tops, and as fortresses they have suffered the ravages of war, of which the most disastrous must have been the Dogra invasion of 1834.[a] Dankhar, the former capital of Spiti, is built upon a crest of crags at 12,750 feet. Right on the summit is the old fort, now occupied by the village-headsman, Padma Kün-s'ang. Below it are the ordinary houses, all built of mud-bricks and white-washed in the normal style and descending at an amazingly steep angle (pls. 26 & 27). Towards the river the ridge juts out over a precipice and it is here that the monastery has been built, so that from one side of its court-yard one might easily fall into rocky space. There are two temples, both very small, connected by rough stone steps and a ladder made from a notched tree-trunk. The frescos are good, although in importance they are not to be compared with the early ones at Tabo. They are in a very bad condition and in the lower temple they have disappeared almost completely from one wall. On the right one can make out Padma-sambhava, Vajradhara, Green Tārā and Amitābha. The images on the altar are Śākya-muni flanked by Maitreya and Tsong-kha-pa. In the upper temple are paintings of Śākya-muni, Tsong-kha-pa and the eight Buddhas of Medicine. The Ge-luk-pas (Yellow Hats) began to gain influence in western Tibet in the sixteenth century and it is to this period that all these paintings may be ascribed. They belong to the very last period, in which anything of value was produced in western Tibet. In 1630 the kingdom of Guge disintegrated as a result of the aggressive campaigns of King Senge-nam-gyel of Ladakh and only sixteen years later both Guge and Ladakh were at the mercy of the central Tibetans supported by the Mongolians, who fixed the Tibetan frontier just east of Tabo, where it has remained until today. During the last three centuries this whole region has become more and more impoverished. Guge and Purang have been steadily ransacked by unscrupulous self-seeking governors appointed from Lhasa, while Ladakh and Spiti have been subjected to the ravages of Moslem iconoclasts. It is truly remarkable that Tabo should have been spared this fate. The other important monastery of Spiti, that of Kyi, was

[a] see A. H. Francke, *History of Western Tibet*, p. 137 ff.

completely ravaged, so despite its spectacular situation on a rocky knoll and the large number of monks that still throng there, it contains very little of artistic merit. It has of course been repainted, but in an unseemly garish manner.

The subsidiary temples at Tabo are well worthy of mention, for their frescos like those of Dankhar date from the last period of Guge's greatness. The two immediately on either side of the main temple are adorned with the eight Buddhas of Medicine, a set of divinities which constantly appears in western Tibet. In Tabo alone they are depicted four times over. The chief of the group is the Buddha Master of Medicine (*sangs-rgyas sman gyi bla*) whose function is sufficiently clear. He is invoked in all the medical texts, of which there are a large number in the Tibetan canon. These texts all originated in India and were not specifically Buddhist, but since Tibet and China received their knowledge of Indian medical theory and practice as part of their Buddhist heritage, there was obviously need of a special buddha who had propounded these special doctrines. The names of six others are:

Good Characteristics (*mtshan-legs-pa*)
Immaculate Gem of Excellent Gold (*gser-bzang-dri-med-rin-chen*)
Gem-Moon (*rin-chen zla-ba*)
Thorough-knowing King (*mngon-mkhyen rgyal-po*)
Ocean Melody of the Sound of the Doctrine (*chos-sgra rgya-mtsho dbyangs*)
Most Noble Sorrowless One (*myang-ngan med mchog dpal*)

As the eighth Śākya-muni is added, thus giving a final touch of incoherence to the set. Originally, however, there seem to have been only seven, and possibly Śākya-muni was added by confusion with the set of seven former buddhas.[a] Since he came at the end of this set, it was felt that he should also come at the end of the other. Buddhists must often have been confused by lists of names that were just names and nothing else. Only the

[a] Vipaśyin, Śikhin, Viśvabhū, Krakucchanda, Kanakamuni, Kāśyapa and Śākyamuni.

Buddha Master of Medicine is clearly distinguished iconographically, for he is blue with a begging bowl in the left hand, the right hand pointing downwards and grasping a myrobalan-fruit. The others are not consistently represented. In the temple to the south they occupy the two side walls with Amitābha on the wall opposite the door, as though he were the chief. In the temple on the northern side, however, Maitreya occupies this central position, not as a fresco but as a stucco-image. These associations seem to have no ritualistic or mystic significance, and merely represent the objects of devotion of those who had these temples painted.

The outside temple on the southern side is certainly the finest of all the smaller ones. The central figure opposite the door is Śākya-muni, flanked by Mañjuśrī and Maitreya. On the left hand wall are the Buddha Master of Medicine, Amitābha and Vajradhara. On the right are Vairocana, Tārā and Vijayā. Each is surrounded by his appropriate entourage, so that Vairocana appears once again as centre of a *vajra-dhātu-maṇḍala* (pl. 25*b*). The corresponding temple to the north is similar, although the execution is inferior. The main divinities are the same with the omission of the Master of Medicine and Vajradhara. The little temple at the far western end of the enclosure is the most recent of all. The main divinities are again Śākya-muni flanked by Mañjuśrī and Maitreya, and here for the only time at Tabo do we see Tsong-kha-pa and Avalokiteśvara.

Avalokiteśvara seems to have had no more importance in the Buddhism of western Tibet than in that of China and one may well suspect that this reflected the situation in Kashmir and the north-west generally. This confirms the suggestion made above that he only became a great god by confusion with Śiva, which occurred predominantly in central India and Nepal.[a]

[a] There exists, however, one very important shrine at Triloknāth in the Chenab gorge, where Śiva and Avalokiteśvara are identified in the person of the Lord of the Three-Fold World. For a description of this shrine see J. Ph. Vogel, 'Triloknāth', *JASB*, vol. LXX (1902), Part I, No. 1, p. 35 ff.

This survey has taken us well beyond the life-time of Rinchen S'ang-po, but all the divinities who came to adorn Tabo were part of the Buddhism of Kashmir with which he made contact. Only the little western temple is out of spirit with his times. The centre of his labours was the capital of Guge, To-ling, where he was appointed head-priest by King Lha-de and given the title of Vajrācārya, which then had not the debased significance that it now has in Nepal. When Atīśa arrived in Guge, Rin-chen s'ang-po was a very old man of eighty-four, and the *Blue Annals* would have us believe that it was not until this meeting that he learned to meditate properly. He is generally referred to as the Great Translator and thus it is suggested that he had translated so many texts, that he failed to be aware of the essential significance that was the basis of all of them. It is recounted that when Atīśa visited him in his room at To-ling, he first recited laudatory verses in front of every one of the divinities. 'When he sat down on the mat, the Translator inquired from him: "Who composed these verses?"—"They were composed by me this very instant" replied the Master at which the Translator was filled with awe and amazement. The Master then said to the Translator: "What sort of doctrine do you know?" The Translator told him in brief about his knowledge and the Master said: "If there are men such as you in Tibet, then there was no need of my coming here", and he joined the palms of his hands in a gesture of devotion. Again the Master asked the Translator: "O Great Translator, if an individual is to practise all the teachings of the tantras without rising from his mat, how is he to do it?" The Translator replied: "He should practise each tantra separately." The Master exclaimed: "Rotten is this Translator! Indeed there was need of my coming to Tibet! All these tantras should be practised together." Then he taught him the Magic Mirror of Secret Mantras and a great faith arose in the Translator and he thought: "This Master is the greatest of great scholars." He revised his translations with Atīśa's assistance and after the latter's departure for central Tibet, practised profound meditation for the last ten years of his life.'[a]

This anecdote may not be without its basis in fact, but its chief intention is to give honour and glory to Atīśa, about whom a large number of stories still circulate in Tibet. As a collector and translator of texts, Rin-chen s'ang-po was inevitably interested in their comparative values, but he was certainly initiated into the real meaning of the yoga-tantras, for he in turn conferred initiation on his disciples. Towards the end of his life the task of giving instruction was largely taken over by Lek-pai-she-rap, known as the Junior Translator, who was the one other survival of the twenty-one youths who had been sent to Kashmir long before. During this period a large number of Indian pundits were invited. A certain Jñānaśrī of Kashmir is reported as having come without being invited, and he is of interest to us in that he stayed at Tabo and learned Tibetan, which seems to have been a rare feat. The whole onus of learning Sanskrit and rendering themselves competent in the spoken languages of Kashmir and central India fell upon the Tibetans. When the Indian masters came to Tibet, they were regularly accompanied by an interpreter, and the invitations that are mentioned were rather in the nature of persuasions accompanied by large presents. But Tibetan honorific language conceals this subtle difference.

Atīśa

After much such persuasion the great Atīśa eventually arrived in Guge at the age of sixty. He is presented by the traditional historians as an absolute prodigy of learning. He was a son of a certain King Kalyāṇaśrī of S'a-hor and in his youth experienced a vision of Tārā, which had the effect of setting him on his religious career. He went to Magadha and received initiation into the cult of Hevajra from a yogin named Rāhulagupta, taking the tantric name of Vajra of

[a] *Blue Annals*, p. 249. I acknowledge the great ease of access afforded to this important work by Roerich's recent translation.

Secret Knowledge. Thereafter he travelled placing himself under various masters, especially Avadhūtipa, who is one of the better known of the great yogins.[a] At the age of twenty-nine he took formal vows in a Mahāsanghika community at Bodhgaya, receiving the new name of Noble Knowledge Maker of Light (*Dīpamkaraśrījñāna*). He then studied the canonical works of the four main schools of Buddhism. This involved receiving instruction from a *hīnayāna* teacher, and it is interesting to note that the rules of the bodhisattva discipline did not allow him to spend more than a week at a time with followers of the *hīnayāna*. In this way he passed two years at Odantapuri. Thereafter he studied mystic philosophy and the tantras at the feet of a large number of masters, several of whom were famous yogins, such as the Great Kāṇha, Ḍombhipa, Nāropa and Avadhūtipa. Subsequently he became an elder of Vikramaśīla Monastery. His fame reached the court of the kings of Guge, who at this time were sparing no efforts and no expense to induce the most notable Buddhist scholars of India to visit Tibet. Dīpankara rebuffed all the earlier invitations and his consent at such a late age to make the difficult journey seems to be connected with the sad fate of the Bodhisattva-king Ye-she-ö. He had been captured by a barbarian frontier tribe and held to ransom.[43] It was demanded that either he should renounce his faith in Buddhism or produce gold equal to the weight of his body. This must have happened very late in his life, for it was his grand-nephew Ch'ang-chup-ö who set about collecting the gold. When brought, however, it fell short by the weight of his head. Ye-she-ö said that he would soon die in any case and so it would be better to expend the gold on getting learned masters from Tibet. Thus Dīpankara was again invited and the king's self-sacrifice and the large offering of gold at last persuaded him to set out.[b]

He travelled with his Tibetan escort to the Nepal Valley,

[a] Avadhūtipa, *alias* Maitripa and Advayavajra. A collection of short treatises written by him, has been published by B. Bhattacharyya in *GOS*, No. XL. One concerning the symbolism of the Five Buddhas has been translated by myself in *Buddhist Texts*, pp. 249–52.

[b] *Blue Annals*, p. 241 ff.

visited Svayambhūnāth and founded a monastery called Samatha (Tranquil) with the co-operation of the King Anantakīrti. After a delay of one year, he continued his journey to Tibet, possibly via Mustang.[a] He was met by an advance party sent by King Ö-de and his religious-minded brothers, who offered presents and tea prepared in the Tibetan manner. His reaction to buttered tea seems to have been more favourable than that of most recent travellers, for he is recorded as saying: 'The combination of circumstances is very auspicious. This strange cup of precious substance contains the elixir of the wish-granting tree. What is the name of this drink which you prize so much?' The translator replied: 'Venerable sir, it is called tea. The monks of Tibet drink it. We do not know of tea being eaten, but the leaves are churned and the fluid is drunk. It has many good properties.' Dīpankara observed: 'So excellent a beverage must have originated from the merits of the monks of Tibet.'[b] In fact this drink has been much maligned and very seldom receives the acknowledgement it deserves. Properly strained and churned with butter and salt it is undoubtedly a most suitable drink in the higher altitudes beyond the Himalayas. It would probably never have evoked so much adverse comment, if it had not been called tea, for there is no doubt that it takes the new arrival unawares.

Dīpankara, now known as Atīśa (Great Lord), spent three years in Guge, serving as chief religious guide. He gave instruction in the higher tantric practice which aimed at complete emancipation and accepted the monastic order as the basis of the necessary training. He devised a special form of the *Guhyasamājatantra* with Lokeśvara as the central divinity for the use of the king and wrote a general work on the stages of enlightenment, called *The Lamp of the Path of Enlightenment* (*Bodhipathapradīpa*).

[a] This is assuming that he visited Palpa (modern Tansing), close to the Gandakī River. See S. C. Das, *Indian Pandits in the Land of Snow*, p. 71; Tucci, *Tra Giungle e Pagode*, p. 103.

[b] Das, *Indian Pandits*, p. 72.

By the time of Atīśa's visit Buddhism was again in the ascendant in central Tibet. It can even be claimed that there had been no interruption, for a series of proper ordinations was continued by monks who had fled to Kham (eastern Tibet). Some of these returned first to Sam-yä, and gradually the temples in and around Lhasa were reoccupied and repaired. Moreover another descendant of Lang-dar-ma had established himself in eastern Tsang (the region between central Tibet and the Kingdom of Guge) and his descendants, who were cousins of the Guge kings, also sponsored the propagation of Buddhism. Thus as has often been the case in the history of a religion, persecution had the effect of spreading it over a far larger area.

Atīśa had promised the abbot of Vikramaśīla that he would be absent for only three years, but chiefly as a result of meeting his chosen disciple Drom (*'brom*) he changed his plans and went to central Tibet instead. An excuse for not returning to India was found in the blocking of roads to Nepal as a result of internal feuds there. Atīśa subsequently remitted to Vikramaśīla all the wealth he had accumulated in Tibet, which no doubt had a mollifying effect. An important feature of tantric Buddhism is the special relationship of master and pupil. The texts in themselves were useless unless accompanied by the proper consecration, which only a master, who was himself already initiated into the mystery, could bestow. As the consecration was the door to all-saving knowledge, no adequate return could ever be made to one's master. Hence there are many stories illustrating the absolute devotion of disciples, who committed themselves completely to the mercy of their master. It was also believed that some predestined relationship existed between master and pupil from previous lives. Drom had placed himself under another master, Se-tsün, but when one day he heard the name of Dīpankara mentioned, great faith arose in him and he felt a strong desire to meet him. Similarly Atīśa was advised by Tārā, his tutelary divinity, that he would soon be meeting his chief disciple. It was Drom who persuaded Atīśa to visit Lhasa and arranged for the necessary invitations, for which two other future disciples of his, Lek-pai-she-rap of Ngog and Khu-tön Tsön-drü-yung-drung were largely responsible. These two also had previously studied in Kham and Khu-tön was renowned as a master of mystic philosophy (*prajñāpāramitā*) and was head of a community at Thang-po-che in central Tibet when Atīśa arrived. He was then thirty-four and Drom was forty. One never thought oneself too old to accept the spiritual guidance of another.

'Khu-tön, Ngog and Drom once asked Atīśa: "For someone who sets out to gain release and omniscience, which is more important, the substance of the canonical texts or the precept of a spiritual guide (lama)?"—"The precept of a spiritual guide is more important" he replied. "How is that?" they asked. "Although a man is able to recite all the scriptures (the three receptacles) and knows the characteristics of all the elements, yet when he comes to put all this into practice, unless he is guided by a master's precept, the doctrine and the man will go separate ways."—"So probably one should gather the advice of one's master's precepts and concentrate on keeping the three vows (of a monk) and on practising virtue in body, speech and mind." Atīśa replied: "That would not assist very much." "What should one do?" they asked. He answered: "Even though one keeps the three vows and is of pure conduct, if one does not produce a thought of aversion to the three-fold phenomenal world, it will just be a cause of rebirth. Even though one practises virtue in body, speech and mind day and night, unless one knows how to dedicate it all for the sake of final enlightenment, it will be like the actions arising from false perceptions. However wise one may be, or venerable or capable of giving instruction, if one does not turn one's mind from the affairs of this world, whatever is done, it will just amount to worldly concerns and one will miss the way of the hereafter." Thus did he reply, so greatly did he consider it important that one should be sustained by a lama as one's virtuous guide.'[a]

[a] *Kun-bzang-blama*, folios 18*b*–19*a*.

When later on sectarian differences arose in Tibetan Buddhism, Drom, being Atīśa's favourite disciple, was acknowledged as first of the Ka-dam-pas (*bka-gdams-pa*), which means 'those of the precept'. Nevertheless their views in this respect differed in no way from that of other Buddhists of India and Tibet. Atīśa was very impressed with Sam-yä, where he remained working on translations with the assistance of the interpreter Nag-tsho, who had been with him ever since leaving Vikramaśīla. He also found there many Indian manuscripts, which were no longer to be found in India and expressed the opinion that Padma-sambhava must have obtained them from the realm of the titans (*asuras*). After visiting Lhasa and Yer-pa, he finally settled in Nye-thang. He died here in 1054 and his relics were entombed in a chö-ten.[a]

Non-Celibate Yogins

Another renowned traveller and scholar was Drok-mi (*'brog-mi*), Man of the Steppes.[b] He was despatched to Nepal and India with a quantity of gold under the patronage of those cousins of the Guge kings, who were rulers in western Tsang. Before his departure he was advised to learn monastic discipline (*vinaya*), for it was the basis of the doctrine, to learn mystic philosophy, for it was the essence of the doctrine and to learn tantric practice, for it was the substance of the doctrine. He studied Sanskrit for a year in Nepal under a disciple of Śānti-pa, another of the eighty-four great yogins, and then spent eight years with Śānti-pa himself at Vikramaśīla. This pundit-yogin is the author of an important commentary on the Hevajra-tantra and thus it was in this particular tantric cycle that Drok-mi became proficient, later translating it into Tibetan. He also met a yogin named Prajñendraruci, who belonged to the succession of two other great *siddhas*, Virūpa and

[a] see Bell, *Religion of Tibet*, p. 58, where there is a description of the shrine and a photograph.
[b] *Blue Annals*, I, p. 205 ff.

Ḍombhi-Heruka. From him he received initiation into the practice known as 'Way and Effect' (*lam-'bras*) which employed sexual means for the mystical reintegrating of human personality. On his return to Tibet he settled in the Nyu-gu-lung Monastery, which is just north of the Brahmaputra about twelve days journey from the Nepal Valley if one travels via Kyi-rong. This is the chief route leading from Tibet to India via Nepal and it is a matter of great regret that the region beyond the present Nepalese frontier, which is to the south of Kyirong, has been inaccessible to European scholars. Later Drok-mi was able to invite another Indian pundit, Gayadhara, to Nyu-gu-lung, who in the course of three years passed on to him all the teachings of the 'Way and Effect'. Previously he had not received the basic texts. He paid so large a sum for these teachings, that the pundit promised not to give them to any other Tibetan. Drok-mi seems to have been fully aware of the value of the teachings at his disposal. It was from him that Marpa, who was master of the well-known Mila Räpa, first learned Sanskrit, but he discovered that Drok-mi required large presents in return for the instruction given. Willing as their Indian masters were to receive gifts, one suspects that it was largely the Tibetans who were responsible for introducing commercial ideas into their religion. Quite apart from the perfectly normal (if now slightly outmoded) belief that one should be willing to pay for what one receives, the Tibetans in particular have always been great traders, as much for sport as for gain. Marpa was not at all disgruntled by the unexpectedly high fees demanded of him. He embarked on his own expeditions to Nepal and India, where the same teachings could still be obtained and very much more cheaply.

Drok-mi is important, as he is in a sense the father of the important line of Sa-kya-pa hierarchs. Sa-kya Monastery was founded in 1073 by Kön-cho-gyel-po, who was one of his disciples, and Hevajra has remained their tutelary divinity ever since Drok-mi introduced him to Tibet. The Hevajra-tantra was also one of the most important texts in Marpa's repertoire, for he received very thorough instructions in it from the great yogin Nāropa. He is even supposed to have kept eight consorts in addition to his wife Da-me-ma (*bdag-med-ma*), so that he would always have the proper entourage available for the performance of this tantra. The eight goddesses of this circle are quite distinct from those that appear in the entourage of Vairocana. They are known by the names of low castes: Gaurī, Caurī, Vetālī, Ghasmarī, Pukkasī, Śavarī and Caṇḍālī.[a] Thus they are a systematized representation for the needs of the mandala of the yoginīs, who congregated at the great places of pilgrimage. Da-me-ma (Selflessness) is the name of Hevajra's partner at the centre of the mandala. Marpa is an interesting example of the family-man who is a yogin at the same time. The Blue Annals resume his life thus: 'He seems to have meditated continuously on the Ultimate Reality, but in the eyes of ordinary folk, he reared a family, quarrelled with his neighbours and occupied himself with agriculture and building.'[b] He made money in the accepted manner from the initiations that he was able to bestow, the sole exception being the case of Mila Räpa, from whom he required no payment, but set him to work instead on a series of futile building schemes until the potential effects of his evil *karma* were exhausted. Such was the lot of a chosen disciple.

Rin-chen-s'ang-po and Atīśa on the one hand and Drok-mi and Marpa on the other are typical representatives of the two main trends of the later Indian Buddhism and the Tibetan practices that were based upon them. These may be characterized simply as the practice of the monk and the practice of the yogin.

Through confusion of terms and false comparison with religious practice in the west, considerable misunderstanding of Tibetan religious life is apparent in much of the travel-literature that has appeared in recent years. This is often unavoidable, for the use of any English term involves ideas, which may not appertain to the original Tibetan at all. The word for

[a] *Śmaśālī* may replace *Śavarī* (p. 232)   [b] *Blue Annals*, II, p. 404.

instance, which we translate as monastery (*dgon-pa*) means just a solitary place, but in Tibet it has come to mean any settlement where men or women have gathered together to practice exclusively the religious life. Thus while there are some Tibetan monasteries, which work on a disciplinary system comparable with that of monasteries in the west, the great majority are simply an assembly of temples and privately owned houses, where the inmates practice the doctrine in accordance with their own aspirations. There is therefore a freedom of belief and action, which finds no parallel in Christian establishments. The term monastery ceases altogether to be properly applicable when the community is one of practisers of the doctrine, who are married. Convent should be an unequivocal term, but it carries with it notions of seclusion from the outside world which might again be misleading.[a] Likewise monks, by normal definition, are celibate, and so it is inaccurate and unnecessary to speak of married monks in Tibet. A monk, for which the proper Tibetan term is rap-ch'ung-wa (*rab-byung-ba*), cannot marry without breaking his vows.[b] But a yogin (näl-jor-pa) or a siddha (tr'up-thop) may perfectly well be married. The term *lama* simply means superior, and so the superiors of celibate institutions will be celibate, and the others not necessarily so. Thus a married lama, such as was Marpa, brings no dishonour or scandal to the doctrine. Nor does the fact that it is practised by married men represent in itself any degeneration of the doctrine, for if vows of celibacy are not required in some forms of tantric practice, neither were they required in the classic career of the bodhisattva. At the same time it is undoubtedly

[a] One may also note that in English this term is applied exclusively to a monastic establishment for women, whereas in other European languages (e.g. Fr. *couvent* and It. *convento*) it retains the general sense of any secluded religious community.

[b] The more general term is tr'a-pa (*grva-pa*), which means literally student' and is applicable to anyone who is attached in this capacity to a religious establishment. This term again is often conveniently translated as 'monk', for many tr'a-pa are rap-ch'ung-wa, monks in the proper sense. Others, however, are not, for having completed their studies they may well return to secular life.

true that celibacy often renders possible a single-aimed devotion and purity of doctrine, which easily becomes obscured in a more domestic setting. It is for this reason that Atīśa, Drom and the other Ka-dam-pas and their spiritual successor, the great reformer, Tsong-kha-pa, all upheld celibacy as the ideal religious life. This was not intended to deny to the yogin his positive contribution to Buddhist religious experience.

THE CATEGORIES OF TANTRIC TEXTS

As the tantras represent such a miscellaneous collection of material, not all of them were suitable means for practisers of celibacy, unless some special reinterpretation was evolved. One would expect therefore some division analogous to that of the left and right-handed tantras of Chinese and Japanese Buddhism, but no clear distinction of this kind is made. In accordance with an Indian scheme we find four conventional categories:

Rites of Magic (*kriyātantra*)
Rites of Religious Practice (*caryātantra*)
Rites of Yoga (*yogatantra*)
Rites of Supreme Yoga (*anuttarayogatantra*).

The first category refers to rites of bestowing prosperity, sowing discord, causing death, overpowering other beings, human and non-human.[a] The second refers to ritual worship and the bestowing of consecrations. Both these categories are therefore concerned with activity in the phenomenal sphere. The third category is concerned with the internal realization of the symbolic representation expressed through ritual. The chief example of this class of tantra is the *Symposium of Truth* and it seems to include all those tantras which have Vairocana as the central divinity and which are all definable as right-handed in Chinese-Japanese tradition. The fourth category includes those tantras, which claimed to give supreme realization here and

[a] see p. 76.

now, involving the psycho-physical reintegration of personality through sexual symbolism. The two most important cycles are those of Guhyasamāja and Hevajra. These two last categories therefore aim at realization in the absolute sphere. These divisions would be quite valid if they were referred to the subject-matter of tantras generally, but there is considerable artificiality in assigning a whole tantra to one or other category, for the contents are usually heterogeneous. The Hevajra-tantra, for example, contains material of all four kinds.

Of the tantras that belong to the two higher categories of Yoga and Supreme Yoga, another distinction must be made. There are *yoga-tantras* which are based on the set of five buddhas and *yoginī-tantras* which are based on sets of yoginīs or goddesses, who may number six, eight, nine, fifteen or any number, which will fill the mandala symmetrically. *Yoga* and *yoginī* are not correlative terms, but to our greater difficulty the tantras are not properly systematized and there are no other terms in use. Now whereas the *yoga-tantras* are demonstratively part of the Buddhist tradition and contain nothing that conflicts with regular monastic practice, the *yoginī-tantras* belong originally to the sphere of the tantric yogins and contain references to personalities and practices which could only be recognized as Buddhist by the boldest of reinterpretations. The yoginīs are the feminine partners of the yogins at the places of pilgrimage and in macabre cemetery-settings. The central divinity of their circle is one of the fearful gods, Heruka, Hevajra, Vajraḍāka or Hūṃ-kāra. These are all of the type of Śiva as chief of the yogins, but for the practising yogin they represent the personification of the indestructible all-potent absolute and are thus recognized as fierce forms of Akshobhya. Traditionally the place of origin of all yoginī-tantras is Uḍḍiyāna, the country of Padma-sambhava in the west, for it was here that the ḍākinīs, the yoginīs *par excellence*, were supposed to dwell. From there they are supposed to have spread to central India.[a] Now while it is likely that these feminine counterparts

[a] *Blue Annals*, II, p. 546.

were first accepted into Buddhism in the north-west and that the first tantras of such a kind developed there, the later yoginī-tantras, of which the Hevajra is the chief example, were probably formulated in central India under the influence of Shaivite beliefs. It is significant that during the later spread of Buddhism into Tibet (tenth century onwards), these texts and practices were introduced mainly through Nepal, where Akshobhya is still the foremost of the buddhas, and where his tantric manifestations, Hevajra and Śamvara, still receive the worship due to them in the inner sanctums of the vihāras. By contrast the tantras that were introduced from Kashmir by Rin-chen-s'ang-po and his assistants, were generally of the yoga-class. One important exception is the *Guhyasamāja-tantra,* but this is not a yoginī-tantra, although it belongs definitely to the class of Supreme Yoga. In spite of its references to the fivefold sets of foul substances and different kinds of flesh (cow, horse, dog, elephant and man) which are required in the ritual, and to the physical union of yogin and yoginī, the basic text itself, even without commentaries, has been patently formulated as a practice of conventional yoga, based on the five-buddha system. The supreme all-comprehending divinity is Vairocana as sixth buddha, who is identical with Vajradhara and Guhyasamāja (*gsang-'dus*), who as 'Union of Mystery' seems to be the first of those anonymous entities, who is chosen to represent the notion of essentially-impersonal reflectively-personalized buddhahood. 'The General Union of the Precious Ones' (*dkon-mchog spyi-'dus*) and 'Unity of All the Blessed' (*bde-gshegs kun-'dus*), whom we shall meet in the Nying-ma-pa rituals, are variations of the same theme. Guhyasamāja is therefore neither a fierce form nor regardable as a hypostasis of Akshobhya, as are the other chief tantric divinities. The fierce divinity that belongs to Vairocana's buddha-family is Yamāntaka, 'he who makes an end of death'. He already appears in the *Symposium of Truth* in the rôle of the terrifying tutelary divinity, and it is as such that he is accepted by the Ka-dam-pas and their successors the Ge-luk-pas. It is for this reason that he is now found in the room of the Fierce Protectors at Tabo. He is normally known by the epithet Vajra-bhairava (Adamantine Fearful) and regarded logically enough as the fierce manifestation of Mañjuśrī, in that both are of Vairocana's family. His bull's head suggests an Iranian origin, but in any case his function is quite different from that of Mithra's bull.[a] It endows him with the suggestion of some individual character, which is entirely lacking in Heruka, Hevajra, Vajraḍāka and Hūṃ-kāra.

Heruka is not a single divinity, but rather a type.[b] As was shown above (p. 79), he serves as the fierce manifestations of the buddhas of the five families by merely changing his colours and his symbols of office. His primary colour, however, is dark blue or black, which he retains even as Buddha-Heruka although the *tathāgata*-family is normally white, for since his appearance is universally wrathful, he must show his relationship to the vajra-family, whenever his position is central.[c] In this primary form he is identifiable with any of the fierce divinities of the centre. Thus Hevajra, whose name is derived from the call which is made in the process of ritual empowerment, is merely another form of Heruka, which has become differentiated by the circle of yoginīs, which make up his mandala. Vajraḍāka is another Heruka, who is lord of the ḍākinīs. Hūm-kāra, 'he who makes the sound HŪṂ', is merely an epithet referable to any of these forms, for like Śiva they all enunciate HŪṂ. Śamvara, who now merely gives his name to a tantra based on the set of five buddhas with Heruka as central divinity, is probably derived from the pre-Aryan god of that name, so taking us back to the subsoil of Indian religious experience. It must be confessed that there was no consciousness of this connection on the part of those Indians and Tibetans

[a] For a discussion of Vajrabhairava see Tucci, *Ind-Tib.*, III, Part 2, p. 78 ff. and pl. XXXIV.

[b] see J. Przyluski, 'Heruka-Śambara', *Polish Bul. Orient.*, I (1937), pp. 42–5.

[c] He appears in this form in one of the temples at Chang in lower Spiti together with the whole cycle of fierce divinities. See also ch. 6, p. 232.

who introduced this cycle into Tibet, for Śamvara is translated as Perfect Bliss (*bde-mchog*) and so once more completely depersonalized.[a]

It has been necessary to clarify Heruka's nature, for by reappearing under so many names, he obscures the distinctions that can be made between those tantras that centre on Vairocana and those that centre on Akshobhya. It is an important distinction, for it is to the second group that the yoginī-tantras belong. In origin, far from being schematic groupings of divinities, they appear to be forms of real flesh and blood. The central figure of the circle is the yogin himself, whose intention must be to partake of the nature of Heruka. He surrounds himself by a suitable number of yoginīs for the proper performance of the ritual. They perform the vajra-song and dance. They partake of the sacrament of the five kinds of flesh and the consecrated wine. The yogin embraces each member of the circle and finally unites with his partner at the centre. There need be no doubt from our texts that this ceremony was performed essentially with religious intent and experienced as the union of phenomenal forms in the undifferentiated absolute. That it was open to abuse there is equally no doubt. Thus Atīśa on his arrival in Tibet ordained that it was not suitable to perform the actual practice of the second and third consecrations (viz. *guhyābhisheka* and *prajñā-jñānābhisheka*) except for those who had grasped the final truth.[b] Even so, there are few authenticated examples of actual practice in the Tibetan histories, but this may be because of closely guarded secrecy. An interesting case is that of a woman-practiser named Sh'a-ma (and nicknamed just Mother). She was married at the age of fourteen, but left her husband by pretending to be mad when she was seventeen, and

[a] This cycle is found at To-ling and Tsaparang in Western Tibet. See Tucci, *Ind-Tib.*, III, Part 2, p. 16 ff.

[b] *Blue Annals*, p. 248. The four consecrations are the Guru-Consecration (*ācāryābhisheka*), the Secret Consecration (*guhyābhisheka*), Consecration in the Knowledge of Prajñā (viz. the yoginī) and the Fourth Consecration, which is undefined because it is undefinable. These are discussed in some detail in my introduction to the Hevajra-Tantra.

became the partner of the Translator Ma (*rma*), whom she knew as Heruka. He died at the age of forty-six (1090) when she was only twenty-eight. She performed his funeral rites properly, but within the next three years her spiritual and bodily well-being had gone to nought. She was covered in sores, was oppressed by vulgar passion; animals would not accept her offerings and the ḍākinīs remained aloof from her. She appealed to the Master Dam-pa of Ding-ri, who informed her that she must have transgressed her vow to her own master. In fact she had acted as the partner of other yogins. Dam-pa guided her in the performance of the necessary propitiatory rites and she attended to her master's shrine and gave presents to his relatives. She recovered completely, thereafter sat at the feet of many masters and became perfect in knowledge and active in the welfare of others. She was generally recognized as an incarnation of Tārā, in succession, as it were, to the Chinese wife of Song-tsen-gampo.[a] This story is interesting for the light it throws on the relationship of master and partner. It represented a permanent bond, more permanent in fact than any marriage of those times. Another well-known example was Marpa and his wife Da-me-ma.

At the same time these rituals were interpreted as a process of internal yoga, and were practised by some yogins (such as Mila Räpa) and by the normally celibate monks. They form nowadays the basis of all monastic ritual, as will be seen in the following chapter. There is appended here an evocation of Vajraḍāka and his partner Vajra-Vārāhī (the adamantine female boar), which resumes succinctly the whole process of mental production: first the elements, then the universe, then the protected palace on the sacred mountain, then the divinity and his entourage at its centre. The practiser himself becomes Heruka, achieved by the use of imagined forms.

'With three faces, six arms and dark-blue in colour, clinging to the body of his *prajñā* who is like himself, this

[a] For the full version of this story see *Blue Annals*, p. 220 ff.

lord of six goddesses, who is born of the sound *HŪṂ*, him I salute, and record the process of his evocation.[a]

The yogin should arise early and placing the sacramental jewel in his mouth, should seat himself in the crossed-vajra posture in some suitable spot such as a mountain-cave. Then he should envisage in his own heart upon a solar disc the syllable *HŪṂ*, dark-blue in colour. From that syllable *HŪṂ* he causes rays to shoot forth, which are five-fold in appearance and pervade the whole three-fold world throughout space, and by means of those rays he draws towards himself that lord who dwells in his palace in the highest heaven and whose various attributes will be described below, together with all yogins and gurus and buddhas and bodhisattvas who appear no larger than sesame seeds, and having gathered them in front of himself, he draws those rays back into the seed within his own heart. Then drawing them forth from his heart he should worship with different kinds of worship, both external and internal, the lord and the yogins and gurus and buddhas and bodhisattvas, and it should be done in the way prescribed. Then in their presence one should recount one's faults, vow to commit wrong no more, rejoice at such merit as has accumulated, make the three-fold refuge, rouse up the thought of enlightenment, expel the concept of a self, and having made prayer and supplication in this manner, one should meditate upon the four *brahma*-abodes of love, compassion, joy and equanimity.

Then one pronounces the formula:

'*OṂ All things possess the adamantine nature which is knowledge of the void.*

'*OṂ I possess the adamantine nature which is knowledge of the void.*'

Realizing the meaning of this mantra which comprehends the true essence of all things, he is established at that instant in an indeterminable manner in the perfect knowledge (*samādhi*) of light which is unborn and unending. Then because of the effectiveness of the vow he has made to save all beings, he

[a] Concerning *prajñā*, feminine partner, see above pp. 81-2 and note 21.

arises from the condition of light and regarding everything like a dream or illusion and intent on saving the world, he conceives the nature of Heruka.

First he envisages one upon another the mandalas of the four elements: that of air which has the shape of a bow, is dark-blue in colour and arises from the syllable *YAṂ;* that of fire which has the shape of a triangle, is red in colour and arises from the syllable *RAṂ;* that of water which is round and white and arises from the syllable *LAṂ;* that of earth that is square and yellow and arises from the syllable *VAṂ.*

Then upon these he imagines Mt. Meru, which arises from the syllable *SU.* It is made of the seven kinds of precious stones and is square (at its base) with eight (surrounding) peaks.

OṂ May the ground become as the vajra, firm as the vajra HŪṂ
OṂ Vajra-rampart HŪṂ VAṂ HŪṂ
OṂ Vajra-trellis HŪṂ PAṂ HŪṂ
OṂ Vajra-canopy HŪṂ KHAṂ HŪṂ
OṂ Vajra Web of Arrows TRAṂ SAṂ TRAṂ
OṂ Vajra Ring of Flames HŪṂ HŪṂ HŪṂ

Having provided the six (protective devices) by means of these mantras, he should envisage in their midst a four-sided palace. In the centre of this he should envisage a wheel with six spokes which rests upon a many-petalled lotus and is surrounded by a chain of vajras, lotuses and wheels. In the centre of this he should envisage, resting in the heart of a lotus, a solar disc which arises from the syllable *RAṂ,* and here he sees the syllable *HŪṂ,* dark-blue in colour, which is the essence of Vajrasattva and which rests in the middle of a cup formed by a lunar and a solar disc. All this he envisages as transformed into the Lord Vajraḍāka who arises from that syllable *HŪṂ.* He is embraced by Vajravārāhī and possessed of great bliss; he embodies the five transcendent wisdoms, Mirror-like Wisdom and the rest, and is in all things just as described. He has six arms and three faces, the front one dark-blue, the right one yellow and the left one green. Each face has three eyes. He possesses the thirty-two major and eighty minor marks of physical perfection. In the two hands that embrace his *prajñā* he holds a vajra and a bell; in another two he holds aloft a human skin; in the remaining left hand he holds a *khaṭvānga* and a skull and in the right he holds a trident. He is resplendent with adornments and garlands of skulls; he wears the six symbolic ornaments and round his thighs a garment made of a tiger's skin; his knotted hair is adorned with a crossed vajra and a half-moon. He stands with one leg advanced and the other retracted and treads upon the head and the left ear of Bhairava-kāla-rātrī who rests upon a solar disc upon a many-petalled lotus. He is the true nature of samsāra and nirvāna. Vajra-Vārāhī is like her lord in the matter of colour and arms and so on, but instead of a human skin she holds a bow and arrow, and clasping the two knees of her lord, she is affected with the highest joy.[a]

Next he should envisage the six goddesses on the six spokes going from the left in this order. On the eastern spoke is the first goddess Śrī-Herukī who arises from the syllable *PHAṬ* and is dark-blue in colour. Then comes the second goddess Vajra-bhairavī who arises from the syllable *HŪṂ* and is yellow in colour. Then comes the third goddess Ghoracaṇḍī who arises from the syllable *HAṂ* and is red in colour. Then comes the fourth goddess Vajra-bhāskarī who arises from the syllable *HA* and is green in colour. Then comes the fifth goddess Vajra-raudrī who arises from the syllable *HRĪḤ* and is reddish-black. Then comes the sixth goddess Vajra-ḍākinī who arises from the syllable *OṂ* and is white. These goddesses have one face and four arms. With two hands they are sounding drums and bells and with the other two they are holding aloft human skins. They have three eyes and are terrible in appearance with their

[a] Vajra-vārāhī, the Adamantine She-Boar, is the only goddess who reincarnates in a recognised series. She regularly appears as the abbess of Samding Monastery on Lake Yam-drok, for a description of which see Waddell, *Lamaism*, p. 274 ff.

hair loosed and their bodies naked, for they wear only garlands and tiaras of skulls and the five symbolic adornments. They stand upon corpses and solar discs in a dancing posture. They are the bearers of final perfection'.[a]

[a] *Sādhanamālā*, vol. II, pp. 490–2.

Crossed vajra (*viśvavajra*)

VI

TIBETAN CEREMONIES

If the tracks that lead through the Himalayas to Tibet from the west bear witness to the great achievements of the past, those that lead out from the east testify no less to the activity of more recent times. This is but part of the general outward expansion of Tibetan Buddhism which followed upon the final establishing of central power at Lhasa. Its effect in the west has already been noted. With the disappearance of Buddhism in India and its gradual extinction in Nepal, the Tibetans really have come to regard their country as the centre of the Buddhist world. The general ignorance of present-day Tibetan scholars where Sanskrit is concerned, although a matter for regret, is quite consistent with their estimate of Tibetan religion. For this is now for them the classic form of Buddhism, and without any second thoughts or sense of self-consciousness they have established their extra-territorial communities in India and Nepal, where the texts are read and even printed and the proper ceremonies performed all in the sacred language of classical Tibetan. Conscious of the strength of their own tradition, they have felt no need to learn of other forms of Buddhist doctrine and to argue their non-validity. They know from their own scriptures that the Theravadins whom they see at Bodhgaya, are following an inferior path, and there the matter ends. Except for this central point of contact at Bodhgaya, the vast expanse of 'pagan' India has forced these two Buddhist traditions completely apart, and active as the Tibetans have been in spreading the doctrine, they have found sufficient scope in Himalayan areas where people are predominantly of Tibetan stock.

The first country in the eastern Himalayas to receive Bud-

Plate 29

Friends and helpers in Kalimpong. (p. 213)

(a) *Lop-s' ang Pun-tsok, a most gifted Tibetan sholar.*

(b) *The wood-carver, Pasang Sherpa, the most faithful assistant.*

(c) *The Mongolian lama, Ge-she Wang-gyel; Thar-Chin, editor of the Tibetan Newspaper, his wife and her brother, Ring-dzin-wang-po.*

Plate 30

(a) Teng-bo-che Monastery. (p. 214)
(b) Effigy of the previous head-lame, flanked by a chöten, enshrining his relics.

Plate 31

(a) The solitary monk of Lug-lha receives an unexpected visitor.

(b) The monks of Jiwong dispatch a captured bandit under guard. *(p. 215)*

Plated 32

(a) The miller's daughter supervises the grinding of our grain. The mill operates by water. (p. 215)

(b) Pasang, assisted by our servant Kami, opens a jar of barley-beer. The scene is a Sherpa kitchen. (p. 215)

Plate 33

(a) Jiwong Monastery. (p. 217)
(b) Houses of the monk, Jiwong (p. 219)

(a) The boy-lama of Jiwong and his preceptor, Nga-wang YOn-ten. *(p. 218)*

(b) The boy's predecessor, the previous lama of Rong-phu. An effigy at Jiwong.

Plate 34

Plate 35

(a) Carving printing-blocks. (p. 220)
(b) Chopping dried mutton. (p. 216)

Plate 36

'The Union of the Precious Ones'. (p. 228 and p. 315 for key)

(a) 'The Universal Saviour'. (p. 237 and p. 318 for key)

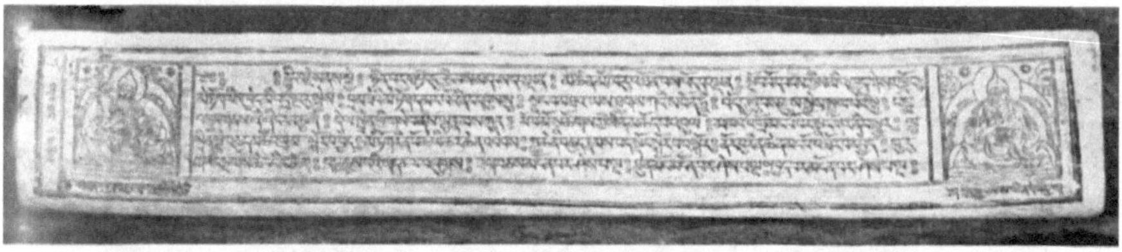

(b) Page of Tibetan text (original size 21″ by 3½″)

Plate 37

Plate 38

(a) vajra. *(b) ritual vase.*
(c) butter-lamp. *(d) prayer-wheel.*

(a) Tormas arranged for the ceremony of 'The Unity of All the Blessed'. (p. 247)

(b) 'the potion was poured ladle-full by ladle-full upon the blazing hearth'. (p. 261)

Plate 39

Plate 40

(a) Sounding drum and bell.
(b) Blowing trumpets. (p. 275)

dhism from the Tibetans was Bhutān. To-day there seem to be more than a thousand monks, predominantly of the Ka-gyü-pa Order, who are well provided for by the King and his chief ministers. Small communities of the Nying-ma-pa Order came to be established in the neighbouring country, Sikkim, from the end of the seventeenth century onwards, but they have long since passed their prime and nothing more can be expected of them during the prevailing spate of political preoccupations, which are in general hostile to any serious form of religious practice. Gangtok, the capital, remains a colourful outpost of Tibetan cultural life and possesses a fine temple, which is well maintained by the traditional rulers. This route between Tibet and India, which leads from Gyantse through Phari to Sikkim or direct to Kalimpong on the Indian frontier, has developed during the last fifty years into a most important trade-route, and since many Tibetans now congregate in Kalimpong, it serves during these modern times of political barriers as the best centre for Tibetan literary studies (pl. 29).

Shar-Khumbu

Another region, which received Buddhism at about the same time but where by contrast it is still extremely active, is Shar-Khumbu of the upper Dudh-kosi Valley along the approaches to Mount Everest. The doctrine was established there by Sanga Dorje (*gsang-ba rdo-rje*), the fifth in the series and the most renowned of the incarnating lamas of Rong-phu Monastery on the other side of Mount Everest.[a] It is recounted that 'aspiring with devotion to the company of the victorious repository of wisdom, the Father Padma-sambhava, he triumphed over all attachment to the reality of this world, and flying in a south-westerly direction, he left the imprint of his

[a] The correct name of this monastery is *rDza-rong-phu*, 'Clayey valley-head'. It is thus named in the official history and is so called locally. On the maps it appears as Rong-buk.

foot upon a rock. Then flying further, he descended on the great rock of Teng-po-che in Khumbu and there too he left his mark. There are stories of his sojourn in these parts. This is the place where they have recently built a new monastery. Having gained power over the five elements in such a way, he was known as Sanga Dorje, the second Urgyen (Padma-sambhava). At that time he had many brilliant pupils both in Shar-Khumbu and in Rong-phu'.[a] These indentations on the rocks are still shown at Pang-bo-che (scarcely south-west of Rong-phu it is true) in upper Khumbu and at Teng-bo-che, where there now stands the most imposing three-storied temple, which was built thirty-eight years ago (pl. 30). Pang-bo-che with its far smaller temple is certainly the older site and there is much local tradition that relates it with its founder. The villagers indicate a spring, now dried up, where Sanga Dorje used to draw his water, and the trees that stand in a semi-circle in front of the village are supposed to have sprouted from the hairs of his head, which he cropped and scattered. Most precious memory of all, however, is the casket containing his eyes, tongue and heart (representing Body, Speech and Mind) which is kept in the temple. The now famous 'head' of the yeti (*gYa-dred*) is also kept here and that too is traditionally connected with Sanga Dorje. It is said to be the scalp of the friend of a yeti, whom the lama had subdued to his service in the typical manner of hermits.[44]

Three days journey to the south there is the monastery of Tr'ak-shing-do, which is even now in its very beginnings. Its head is a monk of Teng-bo-che, named Tok-den Tshül-trhim, who was in the habit of spending the winters here in a little hut that he had built. Although he had chosen a lonely spot, well above the houses of the villagers, his presence was altogether too good an opportunity for them to miss. Thus for the last seven years, he has been surrounded by a circle of

[a] Biography of the Tenth Incarnation of Dza-rong-phu (*dus mthar chos smra-ba'i btsun-pa ngag-dbang bstan-'dzin nor-bu'i rnam-thar 'chi-med bdud-rtsi'i rol-mtsho*), fol. 17*a*.

pupils, several of whom have been to Rong-phu to take proper monastic vows, subsequently returning to make Tr'ak-shing-do their own monastery. Buildings spring up as the need arises and during my stay some of the monks, assisted by villagers, were building a more worthy residence for their lama. To be witness of a process which is typical in every respect of the spread of Buddhism among Tibetan peoples is of enormous interest. It is in just this way that the first simple structures of clay bricks, stone and wood, arose in western Tibet a thousand years ago. The motive is the same zeal for the religious life, which expresses itself in willing unpaid labour and in the bestowing of generous gifts. Nor do these believing lay-folk leave all the practice of religion to the monks, for many of them build for themselves little meditation-shelters well above the villages, where they withdraw from their families to read and meditate alone. It must not be thought of course that these people are all saints and hermits, for they have their full quota of villains and robbers (pl. 31*b*). But most of them lead peaceful lives at home, tending the yaks and zebus, sheep and goats, or winning hard-won crops of barley and buck-wheat from a mountainous soil (pl. 32*a*). The most profitable item of trade is the coarse, tough paper, which is needed for the printing of Tibetan books. The raw material is not available on the far side of the Himalayas, where the greatest demand exists, and so Sherpas and Bhutanese can with ease repay the expenses of a pilgrimage to Lhasa, bringing back carpets, Chinese silks and porcelain, or books freshly printed to their order.

Shar-Khumbu is a composite name, for it includes the two districts Shar-rong (appearing on the maps in the Nepalese form of Solu) and Khumbu. Shar-rong, being to the south, possesses wider and more fertile valleys, and were they but given the opportunity, most English fruits and vegetables would grow here. The term Sherpa (*shar-pa*='easterner') applies vaguely to all people of Tibetan stock, who inhabit these districts. In Khumbu they have complete possession, but in the southern district as the general valley level drops below 10,000 feet, one meets with other people of mixed or entirely non-Tibetan stock. In spite of the proximity of these Nepalese neighbours, the Sherpas have abandoned nothing of their Tibetan heritage. Not only their established religion, but also their local beliefs and superstitions are the same as those recorded of Tibetans elsewhere.[27] Their ceremonies, festivals, clothes and food are all Tibetan in character. They claim, probably justly, to be less guilty of the sin of taking life than their co-religionists on the other side of the Himalayas. This first of Buddhist precepts has always been difficult for the Tibetans, because if they do not eat meat, there is little else left for them to live on. The prohibition is actually against taking life, not against eating meat, and as these are not exactly the same thing, various subterfuges have been employed to minimize the guilt or even to remove it all together. This is probably the weakest spot of their religious practice, as the Tibetans themselves are well aware. For 'especially is there need in the Mahāyāna teachings concerning the bodhisattva's career to act in defence and in protection of all living beings everywhere, and what can possibly be worse than to be so entirely lacking in compassion for the unhappy lot of these creatures who require our protection, as to kill them and make food of their flesh and blood and place it in front of a bodhisattva who should be their protector, and for him to look pleased and fall to with relish'.[a] At least one may claim to the credit of the Sherpas, that the only meat obtained from them in the course of four months was my share of a dead yak which had been killed by wolves and half a sheep's carcass, which was a sun-dried six-months old importation from Tibet (pl. 35*b*). Any sin that was still attached to the corpse of the sheep probably found its just retribution in the act of partaking of its highly tasting flesh. One would not find such strict keeping of the rules outside monastic circles, as other travellers may testify.

[a] *Kun-bzang-bla-ma*, fol. 149*a*–*b*.

JIWONG MONASTERY

Second only to Teng-po-che for the splendour of its main temple, and to none for the pleasantness of its general layout and the excellence of its religious practice, is the monastery of Jiwong, which is built on a ridge at 12,000 feet, high above the little hamlet of Phaphlu in Solu[a] (pl. 33*a*). It merits detailed description for not only may its provisions be taken as typical of all small Tibetan monastic establishments, but it was also the scene of all the ceremonial, which will be described in due course. All the land around Phaphlu belongs to close cousins and their families, having been purchased by the grandfather of the present owners. It was this worthy gentleman, named Sang-gyä Lama, who forty years ago founded this monastery as an act of merit and endowed all members of the community with basic food supplies in perpetuity.

He was personally responsible only for the building of the main temple, for since the inmates build and own their own houses, the original foundation has been growing ever since. An imposing court-yard and gateway which now leads through to the temple was only finished two years ago. Building causes no problems in this country. Stones and wood are available in plenty. Clay serves as mortar and all that is required from outside are nails to hold together the wooden planks of the roofs. But nails are all too often missing and so heavy stones are placed there instead. The resultant building is solid, well-adapted to the landscape and pleasing in appearance. The one discomfort that the foreigner has to suffer comes from the smoke, for chimneys are generally unknown and in any case the smoke is said to preserve the wood-work. Those who can afford it, import glass, but normally the windows consist of light removable frames covered with the tough local paper. Situated

[a] The spelling 'Jiwóng' (accent on second syllable) departs from my rules of phonetic representation, lest the name of this specially favoured monastery be too brutally mispronounced. Tib: *spyi-dbang*, meaning 'Universal Consecration'.

as it is on a high exposed ridge, Jiwong is extremely cold in winter. One small spring provides sufficient water for the thirty inhabitants and as one is just on the limit of the tree-line, wood is available in plenty (a great luxury after the scanty sticks and dried manure of Spiti). The houses of the monks are in effect family-property, where cousins or uncle and nephew or brothers live together. The inmates all come from nearby villages and do not renounce their right to a share of the family wealth and produce by becoming monks. Normally they are all responsible for their own means of livelihood and Jiwong is therefore specially fortunate in the endowment referred to above. The wealthier families contribute as a matter of course a greater share towards the upkeep and improvement of the monastery. One monk, supported by his family, had painted the fine frescoes that adorn the new court-yard and was just building a special school-house. The profit derived from trading ventures will also go partly to the monastery. Regular festivals, —their expense will be mentioned later,—are financed out of the interest on capital which is lent to anyone with firm credentials. All financial matters are in the hands of three monks, who check one another and can only make decisions in unison. Special duties, such as leader of the monks, keeper of the temple, purveyor, cook, are normally on a two-yearly rota-system. No women may sleep in the precincts, the only exception being made unwillingly in the case of the lama's mother, who happens to be a particularly strong character. The lama himself is now (1955) seventeen years old and is recognized as a reincarnation of the Great Translator Vairocana, who was one of the disciples of Padma-sambhava. There has been some doubt about the validity of this reincarnation, for it is a duplication of the present reincarnating lama of Rong-phu (pl. 34). When the last of this series died, two young claimants were put forward and both succeeded in making their case.[a] The Lhasa cabinet, however, which must always make the

[a] The manner in which the reincarnations of these hierarchs are discovered has been often described elsewhere. See Waddell, *Lamaism*, p. 245 ff.

final decision in cases of uncertainty, decided in favour of the Lhasa-born claimant. There was considerable local feeling in favour of the other boy, and when he eventually took refuge at Jiwong and was accorded recognition there as a duplicate reincarnation, no objection was raised at Rong-phu, whither the matter was referred. As Jiwong is outside political Tibet, no one in Lhasa seems to have given another thought to the matter. The boy has been to Rong-phu for part of his education, and should also be going to Min-dröl-ling near Lhasa, the chief Nying-ma-pa Monastery, which Rong-phu and hence Jiwong, regard as the ultimate source of all true doctrine. The strong-willed mother, however, has so far frustrated these intentions, but no doubt this problem will be solved in time, for the monks are ready at any time to build for her and her husband a house in the place of her choice. The father passes his time trading and used to supply me with butter, of which one requires extraordinary large quantities for domestic and religious purposes. The houses of the monks are simple structures, built on the model of the ordinary village-houses, but considerably smaller (pl. 33*b*). There are usually two low-ceilinged rooms on the ground-floor, which are used for storage, from which a dark and awkward staircase leads to the upper compartments. One of these will be the monk's own room, fitted with a wooden case at one end, containing books and images in little alcoves. A short low wooden-platform, covered with home-spun blankets, serves as a couch and meditation seat. Sometimes it is in the shape of a box, in which one can only sleep with the knees drawn up. The other room is the kitchen with its clay-built fire-place, suitable only for boiling and frying. By the side of this is another low platform, where the monk's servant/pupil will sleep. He may be a young relative or any village-boy, who is sent by his parents to obtain instruction in return for the service he renders. This is the only schooling available in the region, and if their parents wish, the boys may go on to Rong-phu later. There is no necessity that he should become a monk. He may even learn the religious crafts of wood-carving and painting and still remain a layman. Perhaps what is most impressive about these people is their strong sense of personal responsibility and their wide freedom of action. The monks are all there on their own responsibility, subject only to their obedience to an older monk, if they choose to ask him to be their master. They meet normally every morning, take tea together, intone prayers, and separate to go about their own affairs, namely attendance on their chosen divinity in their own rooms, invocation and meditation, reading, copying and in some cases composing of texts, laughing and talking together, visiting relatives and acquaintances, either on family affairs or to perform ceremonies in private houses (pl. 35*a*). Part of the year (again the time is self-imposed or imposed by one's chosen master) may be spent in solitary meditation in the hermitage above the monastery. One monk I particularly wanted to see, as he is a renowned painter, was in seclusion during the whole of my stay. He consented to make the drawings required, but it was necessary to make the request through his pupil, who alone might call on him.

The keeper of the temple has the responsibility of morning and evening attendance upon the divinities in the main temple. The monks gather together for general ceremonies only on set feast-days, which are rare, for other special occasions and at the request of one of their members or of any layman, who has some private objective in view. For example a regular feast-day was kept for the previous head-lama, a special ceremony was performed on the occasion of lightning striking down one of the flag-poles (a most inauspicious sign: see pp. 259 ff.) and several parents came to ask for the after-death ceremony to be performed on behalf of children who had died of small-pox, of which there happened to be an epidemic in 1954. In the case of ceremonies performed for private intention, the instigator is responsible for the cost, which is normally between 200 and 300 rupees. This is a large sum in a simple agricultural economy, but no attempt is made to limit it, for much of the efficacy of the rite consists in unregretted giving. Much butter and flour is required for the sacrificial cakes and butter-lamps, vast quantities of buttered tea is served, also cooked rice, unleavened bread, spiced vegetables and whatever fruits and sweetmeats can be obtained. At the end of the ceremony a small monetary present (perhaps five rupees) is given not only to every monk, but to every one else present in suitably graded amounts. A ceremony of this kind lasts for about eight hours. It may in some cases be extended over two or three days. It is of course generally believed that the greater the time and the expense, the more beneficial will be the result. Inevitably notions of family prestige enter into consideration, and the wealthier the family, the more lavish the ceremony. At the same time it is clearly thought that its efficacy depends primarily upon the mental disposition of those taking part. The instigator, who is more properly referred to as the benefactor, can ruin everything by allowing his mind to become affected by any of the 'evils', desire, envy, wrath, malignity or stupidity. Likewise unless the performers are genuinely in contact with the divinities, who are being invoked, they play their part in vain. Thus in general the monks have a dual function, firstly they are contemplatives seeking ecstatic union with their chosen divinity, and through him with all divine forms. Secondly they are priests, bringing their knowledge and religious experience to the assistance of others. The villagers assist and support them entirely on this understanding. Hence in Shar-Khumbu at least, there is a noticeable concern that the monks should be all they are meant to be. A monk who wins the confidence of the villagers, such as the lama of Tr'ak-shing-do or Nga-wang Yön-ten of Jiwong, is in constant demand for his services.

Nga-wang Yön-ten was the most active member of the community. He was preceptor to the young lama, but it was not so much this office as his dynamic personality, which made him take the lead in all matters of action. His family lives at Junbesi, half a day's journey above Phaphlu, and he is one of four brothers, two of whom are monks while two pursue normal worldly affairs. Yön-ten is thirty-five (in 1955) and older than the other monk-brother, whose conduct was so scandalous, that he had been expelled from the monastery by the general assembly of monks long before I knew them. He should of course have been defrocked as well, but there is no secular authority in Shar-Khumbu able to enforce this (as would have been the case in Tibet proper), and so he continued to wear his monk's habit, while pursuing his intrigues among the villagers. The two brothers seem to have been equally forceful characters, the one bent on establishing Buddhist morality or at least respect for Buddhist morality throughout the whole district, the other seemingly delighting in trouble-making for its own sake. Yön-ten had pursued his studies at Rong-phu and Min-dröl-ling, interested himself deeply in classical grammar and literary idiom, on the subject of which he had written several short works. It was by his decision that ceremonies were performed and by his energy that trading expeditions were organized. It was thanks to his intervention that it was possible for me to obtain the books I required. He also organized the capture of a gang of brigands that was active in the neighbourhood (pl. 31*b*). He would discuss his projects with a one-pointedness of mind, which passed through all side-issues and took no account of dangers that he might be running himself, for needless to say, he had many enemies, who have since so distorted his intentions, as to represent him as a dangerous political agitator with designs against the Nepalese Government. He has now fled from Jiwong to its very great loss.

If it should be asked what may induce youths to become monks, the answer can only be personal inclination and encouragement from their families. It is fitting that the elder son or sons should continue to work the family property, while the younger ones follow a religious life. Since in any case they go to the monasteries for their education, it is easy for them to continue in this life, if they have any aptitude for it. Nor except for the vow of celibacy, is the pursuit of normal interests in any way circumscribed. It is a small majority who devote themselves exclusively to religious practice and few again who are literary experts in the canonical and liturgical texts. It is essential only that they should be able to identify themselves with the divine intention by meditation upon its symbolical forms. Thus the liturgical texts and the paintings and images have but one meaning and the outsider, who wishes to know something of their beliefs, must interpret them together. Far from being 'a charlatanism of a mean necromantic order',[a] their mysticism is based upon carefully related complexes of symbolical forms, which are intended to bring a basic order into the confused variety of phenomenal existence. This confused variety exists essentially within the mind and thus it is the mind that must be ordered and controlled. The sexual symbolism and the fierce divinities, which seem to have perturbed some European writers, are an indispensible part of the scheme, unless of course a man is free from sexual impulse and unaware of ferocious tendencies in his nature. The religious process according to this theory is not one of suppression, but of transmutation. It is an experiencing within the individual of the essential identity of samsāra and nirvāna, of form and essence, which has already been discussed above. If indeed one can but grasp the intention of the mandala, one has understood the whole theory of Tibetan Buddhist practice. It only seems to be complicated, because the Tibetans have inherited from India such a vast amount of religious material. The psychological patterns can take so many forms. There may even be apparent contradictions between them. Sets of five buddhas are stretched perhaps to six in order to achieve co-ordination with another existing pattern. A divinity appears as chief in one set and then subordinate in another, or having mastered the symbolism of the colours of the five-families, one is informed that a member of the red family is identical with a blue one. There is no easy way of dealing with this difficulty, except by limiting the material which is under consideration at any one time. This is what is done by the practising monk, who will normally know

[a] Waddell, *Lamaism*, p. 129.

only the divinities of the cycles into which he has been initiated. When he has achieved his goal by means of one of these, there is normally no necessity for him to learn of other cycles. A scholar such as Rin-chen-s'ang-po may have done so, but this was a gradual process covering the whole of his long life, and tradition likes to remember him as having been rebuked by Atīśa for having thought that each tantra was a separate entity.[a]

Another charge sometimes made against Tibetan Buddhism has yet to be countered, namely that it has abandoned the teachings of early Buddhism. This is only true in so far as the rather crude philosophical notions of the *abhidharma*-texts are concerned, and the orthodoxy of these was in any case in doubt from the earliest times. It is undeniable that there has been a development of the basic philosophical conceptions of the doctrine, but this has in general tended towards greater clarification of the aim of the religious practice, which has remained essentially the same. It would be futile to attempt to argue the superiority of the trance of a bodhisattva over that of an early disciple, or that of a Tibetan monk over that of an early Mādhyamika. The tantras were not introduced so much as a new experience, but because they offered surer methods of procedure.

'Because it is free from doubt as to the oneness of purpose, because of absence of difficulty due to its variety of methods and because it is adapted to alert senses, the tantric method is the best.'[b]

At the same time the basic beliefs about the nature of existence and the nature of man have remained practically unchanged. The Wheel of Existence which covers one side of the porch leading into every Tibetan temple, is not intended as mere decoration. 'For if by means of these many examples one thinks on the miseries of existence, then one cannot but cast forth completely all desire for the activities of this world. Unless you abandon completely the doings of this world, even

[a] see p. 192. [b] *Advayavajra-samgraha*, p. 21, lines 12–13.

though you appear to practise the doctrine, it will not be true doctrine.'[a] The whole urge to the religious life, expressed in the words of the meditation which is the normal opening of the religious ceremony, is that which has characterized Buddhism of all periods. The theme is always that of transitoriness, impermanence and consequent suffering.

'It is most difficult to obtain the circumstances of life and the type of character suitable for the practice of the religious life. If a man who has obtained them, does not turn them to advantage by striving towards perfection, how should he obtain them again in a later life?

The world is transitory like the clouds of autumn.
The process of birth and death is like watching a dance.
The life of a man is like lightning in the sky.
Rapidly it goes like water that falls from the precipice.

A king must go when his time has come. His wealth, his friends and his relatives cannot go with him. Wherever men go, wherever they stay, the effect of their past acts follows them like a shadow. Those who are in the grip of desire, the grip of existence, the grip of ignorance, move helplessly round through the spheres of life, as men or gods or as wretches in the lower regions. It is just like the potter turning his wheel.

In the world one is afflicted with old age and with sickness.
One is most of all afflicted by death and there is no protection against it.
Living-beings are always blind when it comes to finding a way out of existence.
They spin round like flies that have got into a pot.'

(Whether this is recited or not, one must meditate on its significance.[b])

It is interesting also to compare the formula of taking refuge,

[a] *Kun-bzang-bla-ma*, fol. 59*b*.
[b] *The Order of Doctrinal Practice* (*chos-spyod-kyi rim-pa thar-lam rab-gsal*), fol. 7*a*–*b*.

which follows immediately upon this initial meditation. Far from being a rejection of the early threefold expression of faith in the Buddha, the Dharma and the Assembly, it represents a logically developed expansion, embracing the new ideas, which had come to enrich Buddhist practice in the course of its duration in India. The lamas (religious preceptors) are equated with the buddhas, for they alone can show the way towards buddhahood. The tutelary divinities are equated with the doctrine, for their meditational forms are the bodily expression of the doctrine. The ḍākinīs are equated with the assembly, for it is in their company that the practiser experiences transcendent wisdom.

'I together with all living-beings who are co-extensive with space
from this time on until we reach enlightenment
go for refuge to our glorious and holy lamas
who embody the basis and whole course of sacred tradition,
for they are of the essence of Body, Speech, Mind, Qualities, Acts
of all the buddhas of the ten directions and the three times;
they are the origin of the whole doctrine in its 1,084 parts;
they are the masters of all religious assemblies.
I go for refuge to all the lord buddhas.
I go for refuge to all the sacred doctrines.
I go for refuge to the religious assemblies.
I go for refuge to the divine circle of the tutelary divinities.
I go for refuge to the ḍākinīs, keepers and guardians of the doctrine who possess the eye of knowledge.
I and all beings, filling space throughout the realm of space
go with devotion for refuge
to our lamas, to our tutelary divinities, to the ḍākinīs,
to the buddhas, to the doctrine, to the religious assemblies.
To the buddhas, to the doctrine, to the religious assemblies
until I reach enlightenment I shall go for refuge.
Whatever merit I gain by the practice of giving and the other perfections,

Let it benefit all beings that they may achieve buddhahood!
I and all other beings are buddhas from eternity.
Let us raise the Thought of Enlightenment that we may know this to be so!'[a]

The Main Temple at Jiwong

Before giving an account of the actual ceremonies, it will be useful to describe the setting in which they take place, for there is nothing on the temple walls, which is not a pictorial representation of the experiences conjured forth by the rituals. The temple is in the form of a simple rectangle with a kind of sanctuary at the far end, to which one mounts by a few steps. Neatly stacked around the walls of this sanctuary are the 108 volumes of the Tibetan Canon and the 225 volumes of the canonical commentaries. These books are placed here primarily as objects of devotion, for they represent the buddha-word. Books in fact possess greater sanctity than images and shrines, for it is by the word that the form is given life. Thus they may be placed above and to the sides of images, but never below them. Set into the central wall of the sanctuary with the books above and around it, is the main image of the temple, Amitābha. Set below and forward of Amitābha is an image of Ṣākya-Muni flanked on each side by eight arhats. These sixteen disciples are the conventionalised representation of the entourage of the Śākya-Sage.[b] It is in front of this assembly that the monks gather twice monthly at the full and the new moon, to recite the ancient text of the confessional (*pratimokshasūtra*). They thus represent an authentic connection with the earliest period of Buddhism.

The main part of the temple is supported by two rows of wooden pillars, between which are placed the seats of the monks facing inwards in two rows. At the head of the rows and in a direct line with the images of Śākya-muni and Amitābha is the throne of the young lama. Anyone entering the temple makes a

[a] *op. cit.*, fol. 7*b*–8*b*.
[b] see Tucci, *TPS*, II, pp. 555–70.

triple obeisance which does for all three at once. The most important item for us are the frescoes. The right wall shows the important sets of divinities known as 'The Union of Precious Ones' (*dkon-mchog-spyi-'dus*) and 'Tranquil and Fierce' (*zhi-khro*). The first of these represents the full manifestation of Padma-sambhava, showing his sacred lineage and his various manifestations (pl. 36). The lineage shows:

> Amitābha as Body of the Absolute,
> Avalokiteśvara as Body of Reciprocal Enjoyment,
> Padma-sambhava as Human Body.

His manifestations appear under two aspects, (1) as the tantric equivalent of Buddha, Doctrine and Assembly, viz.

Lama	Padma-sambhava
Yidam	Guru Tr'ak-po (The Fierce Master)
Kandroma	Seng-ge Dong-ma (The Lion-headed Ḍākinī),

and (2) as his various physical manifestations, eight in number, thus corresponding with the requirements of the mandala:

Lotus-King (*padma-rgyal-po*)	Uḍḍiyāna
Lion of the Śākyas (*shākya-seng-ge*)	Bodhgaya
Lotus-Born (*padma-sambha*)	S'a-hor
Adamantine Sagging-Belly (*rdo-rje grod-lod*) among heretic yogins (*tīrthaka*)	
Thoughtful Coveter of the Best (*blo-ldan mchog-sred*)	Kashmir
Sun-Ray (*nyi-ma 'od-zer*)	Khotan
Roaring Lion (*seng-ge sgra-sgrogs*)	Nepal
Guru Padma-sambhava—among the flesh-eating demons (*rākshasas*)	

In this context Padma-sambhava is considered as the central transcendent buddha and thus the Śākya-Sage has become just one of his manifestations. Under the other various names he is connected with all the other countries, which were important in the early history of Tibetan Buddhism. His central emanation (corresponding with the central image at the centre of the painting) was in Tibet itself. From Tibet he is supposed to have gone to the land of the *rākshasas* where he is still preaching the doctrine.[a]

Beneath him to left and right are his two spouses Mandāravā and the Goddess Ocean of Wisdom (*ye-shes mtsho-rgyal*), who appear in the function of divinities of worship. At the very bottom is the fierce god, Ma-ning, family-defender.

The divinities, known as 'Tranquil and Fierce', represent well-ordered sets of the chief Buddhist divinities, which were introduced into Tibet from India. In no sense are they special Nying-ma-pa divinities.

The tranquil ones consist of two sets:

(1) The *Vajra-dhātu-maṇḍala* with the five buddhas and attendant bodhisattvas and feminine divinities. It corresponds with the set of divinities in the main temple at Tabo, as described above, except that here there are feminine partners for the five buddhas and the attendant bodhisattvas are two in each case instead of four.[b]

(2) The Buddhas of the Six Spheres of Existence:

Name	*Colour*	*Implement*
Indra Lord of Gods	white	guitar
Design of Excellent Weave	green	weapon
Sage of the Śākyas	yellow	bowl and staff
Lion Firm in his Vow	grey	book
King of the Burning Mouth	red	jewelled casket
King of the Dharma	dark blue	wand, whence issues fire and water.

These two sets are completed with a fierce protector and partner for each of the four directions. The totals of the tranquil divinites therefore amount to:

[a] These ten manifestations are listed in the *Padma Thang-yig*, ed. Toussaint, pp. 208–9 and 182. See also Tucci, *TPS*, II, pp. 373–86 and 540–7.

[b] The partners of the five buddhas have been listed on p. 82. The entourage for the buddhas of the directions is still four in each case, for the eight goddesses of worship are paired with the eight bodhisattvas.

A supreme buddha, Samanta-bhadra (see p. 232) and his partner:	2
Five buddhas and their partners:	10
Attendant bodhisattvas and goddesses of worship:	16
Buddhas of the Spheres of Existence:	6
Fierce protectors and their partners:	8

Thus there are 42 tranquil divinities.

Buddha	*Partner*	*Attendant Bodhisattvas and Goddesses*	
1. Vairocana	6. Lady of the Realm of Space		
2. Vajrasattva	7. Locanā	11. Kshitigarbha	19. Vajra-Gaity
		12. Maitreya	20. Vajra-Flower
3. Ratnasambhava	8. Māmakī	13. Ākāśagarbha	21. Vajra-Garland
		14. Samantabhadra	22. Vajra-Incense
4. Amitābha	9. Pāṇḍura-vāsinī	15. Avalokita	23. Vajra-Song
		16. Mañjuśrī	24. Vajra-Lamp
5. Amoghasiddhi	10. Tārā	17. Vajrapāṇi	25. Vajra-Perfume
		18. Sarvanivaraṇa-vishkambin	26. Vajra-Dance

The Buddhas of the Six Spheres of Existence

27. King of the Burning Mouth
28. Indra Lord of Gods
29. Design of Excellent Weave
30. Śākya-Sage
31. King of the Dharma
32. Lion Firm of Vow

Fierce Protectors and Partners

33. Victorious	37. Lady of the Hook
34. Slayer of Death	38. Lady of the Noose
35. Horse-Neck	39. Lady of the Fetter
36. Swirler of Nectar	40. Lady of the Bell

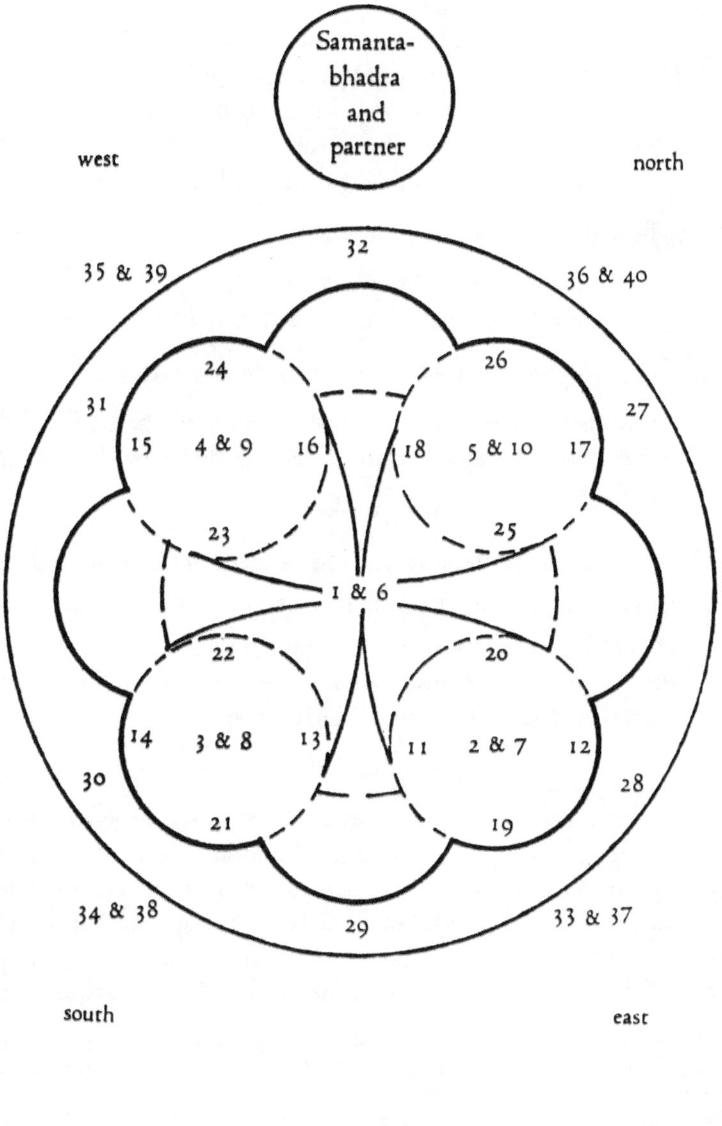
Samanta-
bhadra
and
partner
west
north
32
35 & 39
36 & 40
24
26
31
27
15
4 & 9
16
18
5 & 10
17
23
25
1 & 6
22
20
14
3 & 8
13
11
2 & 7
12
30
28
21
19
34 & 38
29
33 & 37
south
east

The fierce divinities consist of four sets:

(1) The fierce aspects of the five buddhas and their five partners:

The Supreme Heruka and the Lady of Wrath,
Vajra-Heruka and the Vajra-Lady of Wrath,
Jewel-Heruka and the Jewel-Lady of Wrath,
Lotus-Heruka and the Lotus-Lady of Wrath,
Karma-Heruka and the Karma-Lady of Wrath: 10

(2) The eight low-caste yoginīs (see p. 200):

Gaurī, Caurī, Pramoha, Vetālī,
Pukkasī, Ghasmarī, Caṇḍālī, Śmaśālī: 8

(3) The eight animal-headed ḍākinīs (*phra-men-ma*):

Lion-headed, Tiger-headed, Fox-headed, Wolf-headed,
Vulture-headed, Eagle-headed, Crow-headed, Owl-headed. 8

There are four feminine gate-keepers:

Horse-headed, Boar-headed, Lion-headed, Serpent-headed. 4

(4) There are six animal-headed goddesses placed in each of the four quarters and presiding over Tranquil Acts, Prosperity Acts, Consecration Acts and Fierce Acts, with their four animal-headed gate-keepers.[a] 28

Thus there are 58 fierce divinities.

All these divinities and more besides are conceived of as emanating from one supreme buddha, Samanta-bhadra (Universal Goodness). This name, or rather its Tibetan equivalent (*kun-tu-bzang-po*) was a title of the supreme being and one of the earliest p'ön-po adaptations. It was later adopted by those Tibetan Buddhists who claimed to base their traditions on

[a] For the names of these 28 animal-headed goddesses see Evans-Wentz, *The Tibetan Book of the Dead*, pp. 144–6. My lists are based on *The Liturgy of the Union of the Precious Ones and their means of expression in the Tranquil and Fierce Divinities* (*bka rdzogs-pa chen-po yang-zab dkon-mchog-spyi-'dus dang de'i cha-lag zhi-khro nges-don snying-po'i las-byang*).

Padma-sambhava. Its use is attested from about the twelfth century onwards, when the compilers of the supposedly buried texts became active. He is tranquil, as befits his name, but his adamantine nature is indicated by his colour, which is dark blue. He sits in the posture of meditation (like Amitābha) and is always represented together with his partner, who is white. In spite of his distinct iconographical form, he is equated with Amitābha as a name of supreme buddhahood. Thus in an invocation to the three buddha-bodies we find:

'O Supreme Buddha Samanta-bhadra Amitābha,
O Kesar-pāṇi, Guardian of our Land of Snows,
O Lotus-Born of rainbow-form, who dost convert the world,
We beseach you, grant us thy consecration!'

By natural identification of the buddha-bodies, 'universal goodness' and 'boundless light' are epithets of Padma-sambhava, for he too is the supreme buddha-body. Thus all the tranquil and fierce divinities emanate as much from him as as from Samanta-bhadra and the 'Union of the Precious Ones' comprehends them all.

This cosmic body, which may be conceived in these different ways, is also the transmuted form of the meditating yogin. Thus it is said in the liturgy: 'This uncreate mind of my wretched self is the brilliant lotus-body of the Precious Three in Unity'. The tranquil divinities emanate from the heart of Samanta-bhadra and the fierce divinities from his head. But there are three other psychic centres to be considered, before this body is complete, viz, the throat, the navel and the groin.

Thus from the throat emanates Padma-Narteśvara (Lotus-Lord of Dance) with his partner, the Red Ḍākinī. They are surrounded by 'masters of the spell' (*vidyādhara*), who are emanations of the central pair, differentiated by their smaller proportions and the appropriate colours (red inevitably being duplicated in the west).

From the navel there emanates the Ḍākinī of Knowledge,

who is pink, surrounded by the Vajra-Ḍākinī, the Jewel-Ḍākinī, the Lotus-Ḍākinī and the Karma-Ḍākinī, all of appropriate colours.

From the groin comes the fierce divinity Vajra-kumāra (Adamantine Youth) with his partner. He is the defender of all the other divinities.

These sets are brought into relationship with the four-fold buddha-body, thus completing the total cosmic body:[a]

Head	*mahāsukha-kāya* (great bliss)	Fierce Divinities
Throat	*sambhoga-kāya*	Lotus-Lord of Dance
Heart	*dharma-kāya*	Tranquil Divinities
Navel	*nirmāṇa-kāya*	Knowledge-Ḍākinī
Groin		Defender

The whole ritual, which is based upon these schemes, resolves itself into a process of self-identification with this cosmic body. The bewildering variety of divine forms are evoked from the universal void, recognized for what they are, namely the mental product of the practiser, and then returned to their original state, bearing away with them all the mental construction of which they are the symbol and of which phenomenal existence consists. The ritual is nothing more than an exteriorized version of the monk's normal meditation. Its whole effect depends upon knowing the construction of the scheme and concentrating upon the process of its emanation and its dissolution. (*Compare pp. 207 ff.*)

Having dealt with one wall in some detail, the remainder will cause little difficulty. On the left wall are the two chief tutelary divinities, separated by a wide window, beneath which were placed the bolsters and carpets which used to serve as my seat when ceremonies were in process. To the left is Guru Tr'ak-po, who is Padma-sambhava himself in the form of the fierce *yidam*. (He is depicted on pl. 36 bottom left.) 'From the sphere of wrath which is great bliss in its inner nature, there emanates the dark red blazing form of the Union of the Precious Ones.

[a] see p. 89.

He looks sideways to the left and stands with legs apart. With gaping mouth and curling tongue, his teeth bared sharp and white, he feeds on the flesh and blood and pounded bones of enemies and obstructive fiends. He turns towards all directions the fierce gaze of his three red round eyes, causing mighty spirits, both male and female, to tremble and fear. Gales whirl from his nose and the thunder rolls, overpowering, subduing the three-fold world. His tresses of black hair stretch up skywards and with just the right proportion of fierceness he crushes all fiends to dust. With the golden vajra which he holds in his right hand, he repels the foes that converge from without. From the left hand he sends forth the phantom forms of black scorpions. For overpowering the serpents, he is adorned with serpents of all the five families. Since he makes the samsāra void, he is adorned with a garland of fifty heads. Since he is perfected in the ten powers of a buddha, he wears a fresh elephant-skin. Since he overpowers the mightiness of pride, he wears a tiger-skin. Since he leads the ḍākinīs to play, he wears the precious ornaments of bone. From every pore there emanate fierce little appearances of himself. In smoke and fire the three-fold world trembles like a star'.[a]

To the right of the window is the Lotus-Lord of Dance, who is the special *yi-dam* of the Rong-phu lamas and therefore both of Rong-phu and Jiwong Monasteries. He is known as Unity of All the Blessed (*bde-gshegs-kun-'dus*). Although originally a form of Śiva, this divinity was accepted into Buddhism as one of the many forms of Lokeśvara. He therefore becomes a special manifestation of Avalokiteśvara. In any case he belongs to the Lotus-Family, whose head is Amitābha, and thus he, like Avalokiteśvara, is an emanation of the *sambhoga-kāya*.[b] He therefore belongs directly to the spiritual lineage of Padmasambhava. He is red and four-armed. The left upper hand holds a lotus and the right upper arm a rosary. His two lower arms envelop his partner and between his joined hands he holds a golden vajra. The partner is of the same family-colour (al-

[a] *Union of the Precious Ones*, fol. 19*a*. [b] see p. 228.

though a lighter shade) and is called either just the Red Ḍākinī or else Pāṇḍuravāsinī, who is the goddess regularly assigned to the lotus-family (see pp. 82 and 230). She also is four-armed. In two hands she holds the knife and skull-cup, which are the normal equipment of ḍākinīs. In the second left hand she holds the sword of wisdom and in the right a yogin's wand in its gruesome form (*khaṭvānga*). The entourage which makes up this mandala is a simple affair, consisting of emanations of the central pair at the four points of the compass and of four animal-headed gate-keepers. There are two protectors, Hayagrīva, the horse-headed god, and Mahādeva (the great god), who is Śiva himself. Hayagrīva, who is completely Indian in origin, is summoned at the beginning of a ceremony in order to drive away all malevolent forces. He also appears elsewhere in the temple in his own right as one of the two door-protectors, where his function is the same. Śiva enters the Buddhist pantheon as one of those who have made the vow of active co-operation in return for his permitted existence (t'am-cen). He is red and appears as a fat and amorous yogin, surrounded by four red yoginīs. He is placed below Hayagrīva, for the latter is accepted as the fierce manifestation of the lotus-family, who plays his part without any compulsion. During the ritual the monks must conceive of themselves as Hayagrīva, but never as Mahādeva, who is a mere defender (see p. 79).

The wall to either side of the main entrance is covered inside with fierce protectors. On the left and right of the door, as one enters, are Hayagrīva and Swirler of Nectar (*bdud-rtsi-'khyil-ba*). On the far left is the Cemetery Goddess (*dur-khrod-lha-mo*) who is identified with Ekajaṭā, and on the far right is the Four-Armed Defender, namely Mahākāla. Both of these had been accepted early on as defenders by Indian Buddhists.

The upper temple is square and far smaller. It contains on one wall the thirty-five Confessional Buddhas (*ltung-bshags-sangs-rgyas*), on another the twenty-five Pundits, who according to the traditional accounts interpreted and translated texts under the guidance of Padma-sambhava. Their names occur in ritual as a form of litany. To the left of these is another set of divinities. of whom the central one is clearly Avalokiteśvara in a four-armed manifestation (pl. 37). The upper left hand holds the lotus and right the rosary, while the other two hands are joined in supplication. Above is a small figure of Amitābha, the head of the family, and arranged three on each side to form a circle are the buddhas of the six spheres of existence. They are therefore envisaged as emanations of Avalokiteśvara, who appears here under the name of 'Universal Saviour' (*'gro-ba-kun-sgrol*), for it is thought that he is active in the salvation of beings, wherever they may have been born. The mandala is completed with four feminine gate-keepers, all in tranquil form, seven graceful ḍākinīs (*ma-mo*) and the protector Thang-lha, who is a completely indigenous Tibetan divinity. Like Ma-ning and Mahādeva, he is one of those who is bound by oath (t'am-cen). Once again the significance of all these forms can only become clear from the ritual:

'OṂ ĀḤ HŪṂ HRĪḤ OṂ MAṆĪPADME HŪṂ
OṂ is the Body of all buddhas,
ĀḤ is the Speech of all buddhas,
HŪṂ is the Mind of all buddhas,

OM signifies possession of the five types of wisdom, by which the four types of activity are self-perfected.
MA represents the Body of the Great Compassionate One, who removes the sufferings of the beings in the six spheres.
ṆI means that with his tranquil nature he cleanses all evil defilement.
PAD means that he spreads good qualities far and wide.
ME means that by power of consecration he causes everyone to possess them.
HŪṂ means that by fierceness he overpowers all evil obstructions.

We beg you to serve the cause of living beings by means of the four types of activity, and to grant to us consecration and the perfect achievement!

O Avalokiteśvara of Great Compassion, whose form is white and emits rays of light, for you are untouched by the defect of any imperfection. You have one face and show a smiling countenance, for you are filled with love for all beings. Your two eyes look downwards with tranquillity, for you feel equal compassion for all. Two of your hands are placed palms together in front of your heart, for this indicates the unity of Wisdom and Method. Your other right hand holds a rosary and this is a sign that you draw beings forth from phenomenal existence. Your other left hand holds a lotus, as a sign that you serve the cause of living beings but are yet free from any attachment. You are adorned with jewelled ornaments, as a sign that while you are pure you have not abandoned pleasant things. You emit light rays of the five colours, as a sign that you remove the evils of the six spheres of existence. You have as your head-adornment a perfect buddha, as a sign that you are born of the lotus-family. You have the six buddhas as your emanations, as a sign that you close the doors to rebirth in the six spheres of existence. You have four goddesses as your gate-keepers, as a sign that you practice the four kinds of activity. To Avalokiteśvara salutation and praise!

From the cemetery of lotus-wrath there come these dark red companions of the yogins, keepers of the conquerors' doctrine. You are the seven mother-goddesses, phantom-forms of the Word of the Blessed, granters of consecration and performers of fierce acts. Salutation to you!

> Guardians of the mystery of Amitābha,
> Hearers of the word of Avalokiteśvara,
> Doers of the work of the Adamantine Lotus-Born,
> Keepers of the Word of the Blessed,
> Watchers of the word of us yogins,
> Companions of all who practice the doctrine,

O you seven mother-goddesses, who possess the power of consecration as guardians of the doctrine, accept these ornamented sacrificial cakes! Make to increase the doctrine of the Great

Compassionate One and bring to completion all your appointed tasks!'[a]

The invocation to the God of the Plain (*Thang-lha*), which follows straight on, is in a very different style of Tibetan, similar in fact to that of the old epic songs. It is an old non-Buddhist prayer, adapted to the new environment, just as the old God of the Plain had to be converted himself.

'Wisdom's mansion is vast—not small.
Set ready is the elephant and lion throne, high—not low.
Spread is the lotus-carpet of sun and moon, bright—not dull.
The splendid gods of wisdom stand in attendance, near—not far.
Fulfilling your function as guardian of the world, strong—not weak,
Come hither and take your place upon this lotus-throne, we beg!
O Power of the Blazing Vajra, thou who art born of the bond![b]
As for your divine father, he is Zenith Sovereignty of Light (*'od-gung-rgyal*).
As for your divine mother, she is the Single-Winged Turquoise-Bird (*gYu-bya gshog-gcig*).
As for your name, it is Ya-sh'ur, god of nyen.[c]
As for the name of the country where you dwell,
it is the Oblong Lower Marsh (*'dam-shod snar-mo*),
Bright turquoise-land of the vulture,
Green in summer, green in winter,
A joyful land to live in,

[a] *Meditation upon the Universal Saviour* (*thugs-rje chen-po 'gro-ba kun-sgrol-gyi bla-ma'i rnal-'byor brgyud-'debs*), fol. 15*b* ff.

[b] 'Born of the bond' (*san. samayaja*) is actually a spell, calling him to be present by reason of his bond. 'Power of the Blazing Vajra' is his initiatory (secret) name.

[c] The 'nyen' (*gnyen*) are a class of indigenous divinities, who in the following passage seem to be implicitly identified with the 'gandharvas' (*dri-za*) of Indian mythology. 'Ya-sh'ur' might be translated as 'Snub-nose'. One may note that Thang-lha is related by his exalted parentage to the line of Yar-lung Kings.

A happy and a sacred land.
As for your non-religious name, it is Ya-sh'ur, God of the Plain (*thang-lha*).
As for your religious name, it is *Pañcaśikha*, King of Gandharvas.
As for your secret name, it is Power of the Blazing Vajra.
As for what you have on your person, it is flowing white silk.
As for the horse you ride, it is the divine horse, White Goose.
You gallop through the three spheres,
White light-rays blazing forth,
Wielding a baton in the right hand,
You dispatch the seven mothers to their tasks.
Fingering a rosary in the left hand,
You recite mantras to the Tutelary Divinity.
As for the phantom-forms you send forth, they are divine armies a hundred thousand strong.
Together with your circle of followers,
Come hither and perform your task.
Lord of all who have taken the vow,
Slayer of all who refuse to submit,
Death to all perjurers,
Glory of all yogins,
Friend of us who now perform the ritual,
The command to action has now been given,
Subdue the raving fiends, cut down the hostile foe.
Quickly tether your horse. Let not the nails press into his hoofs.
Sharpen your weapons quite fine. Let the tips be nothing lacking.
It matters not to whom you bid defiance.
The suit is already decided.
It matters not with whom you race.
The finish is already decided.
Carry off the hostile foe. Protect us with affection.
The time has come, so think well on your bond.
It is time for action, O king of obstructive foes.
Perform therefore your appointed task.

You are the country-god of the four regions of Ü and Tsang.
You are the god of Trhi-song-deu-tsen, the Divine Son, the King who was Protector of the Doctrine.
You were bound to the bond of your word by Padma-sambhava of Urgyen.
So hearken now to what is required of you.
To all knowers of mantras who follow in the wake of Padma-sambhava of Urgyen in these last days of the doctrine,
To all those of noble birth who are descended from Trhi-song-deu-tsen, the Protector of the Doctrine,
To the mighty ones who touch the zenith,
To the lowly, as to a son, you must give protection!
Watch over the four regions of Tibet, as though it were wealth.
Watch over the temple of Sam-yä, as though it were treasure.
If you do not protect us living beings now in this last world-age,
Will you not perhaps be mindful of these happenings:
Firstly how Vajrapāṇi pressed the life from your heart on the way to the north,
Secondly how Padma-Heruka forced you into subjection on Mt. Hä-po by Sam-yä,
Thirdly how Vajra-kumāra, having collected together all gods and demons on the summit of the fair-formed king of mountains, forced them to take the vow.
I now am Padma-sambhava.
You are the great nyen, God of the Plain.
This place is Tibet of the four regions.
Grace envelops us like a cloud.
Compassion descends like a shower of rain.
The bond is lost to sight together with your exterior form.
O God of the Plain, we beg you to come.
You yourself and your following of nyen
We shall honour with the most splendid of excellent offerings.
We honour you with pure water from the rocks and from the snows,
With white clouds of sweet-smelling incense,

With silver and gold and the five kinds of precious things,
With adornments and silks and brocades,
With mutton from Tsang and with pure white rice.'

This invocation has been quoted in full, for apart from being a colourful example of the type of t'am-cen, it illustrates the special rôle that these converted gods have to play in the religion of Tibet and how they are treated alternately to threats and to offerings. In no way are they permitted to interfere with the Buddhist doctrine, to which they remain helplessly subject. In no sense can they be said to have perverted it or forced it to compromise. Their inclusion in the lowest ranks of the Buddhist pantheon has allowed the Tibetans to remember their ancient gods while still being faithful to the new doctrine. Different protectors have come to be attached to different cycles of divinities and so to their rituals. The reason for the connection could only be discovered by an historical study of the origin and development of these texts, which is a task still to be undertaken. The result of this is, however, that a group of protectors comes to receive attention, in so far as they are called upon in ones or twos or threes in the rituals that are constantly being performed in a monastery. These rituals are of course largely the same for any given order of monks. Thus at Jiwong and among the Nying-ma-pas generally the chief protectors are:

Nag-po chen-po	(Mahākāla)
Ma-ning	
gZa-lha	(Rāhula)
Khyab-'jug	(Vishnu)
lHa-chen	(Mahādeva)
rDo-rje Legs-pa	
Dur-khrod lha-mo	(Ekajaṭā)
rNam-thos-sras	(Vaiśravaṇa)
rDo-rje gzhon-nu	(Vajrakumāra).[45]

These have all once been divinities of universal power, who

therefore rank higher than those gods, whose sphere was only a local one, like the God of the Plain and the many mountain-gods. The latter are known as country-gods (*yul-lha*) or lords of the soil (*gzhi-bdag*). There is a special category of them, known as lords of (buried) treasure (*gter-bdag*), who are supposed to have watched over the texts that had been buried by Padma-sambhava. An example is Ham-trhang (*ham-'phrang*) who was the keeper of the ritual of *The Union of the Precious Ones*. He is therefore remembered in the ceremony.

'O keeper of the treasury, wide and deep, in the cave of the vajra-rock of Ham-trhang. Together with your entourage of serpents and demons and healing spirits of the lake, accept these desirable offerings and sacrificial cakes, which we now offer. Do as you have been commanded by Padma-sambhava, and as you have promised.'[a]

All these lesser gods are seldom depicted and certainly receive no daily attentions. The great t'am-cen, however, who occupy a considerable amount of space on the monastery-walls, are reminded every day of the bond they have made. A special room, known as the Protectors' Room (*srung-khang*) is reserved for this purpose. It seems to be the one place in a Tibetan monastery, to which a stranger is normally denied access, and in any case no woman or married man may enter there. At Ji-wong this room is on the first floor, adjoining the upper temple. The walls are completely black, except for the fearful figures in white outline of Mahākāla, Ekajaṭā and Rāhula. The only other colour is the red of their jaws and lolling tongues. From the ceiling hang a human-skin, an elephant-skin and a tiger-skin in quite convincing imitation. There is one life-size image of Mahākāla. Opposite this against the wall is the small raised seat for the keeper of the temple and suspended above it is the large drum, which accompanies his solitary invocations. Let into the wall is a small cupboard, containing a rather worn sacrificial cake. It is actually renewed after any large ceremony and serves as an offering for all the t'am-cen collectively (*dam-*

[a] *Union of the Precious Ones*, fol. 35*a*.

can spyi-gtor). Before he begins his invocation, the keeper of the temple opens the cupboard, thus exposing it to view, so that he may offer it up afresh. He recites an abbreviated version of the ritual as it is performed in the major ceremonies and will be described below.

There remains one other fresco in the upper temple, which has yet to be described. This is of Vajrasattva, but in a form different from that in which he has appeared above. Reference was made in Ch. 2 to the impossibility of making any final distinction between Vajradhara (Holder of the Vajra) and Vajrasattva (Vajra-Being), for both represent buddhahood in its adamantine aspect. It has been observed that any of the five buddhas may serve as the supreme symbol of buddhahood, and since buddhahood knows of no duality, they are all ultimately identical. Owing to the sameness of family and family-colour, Vajrasattva becomes equated with Akshobhya to the extent of replacing him as one of the five buddhas, as occurs in the set of tranquil divinities. Nevertheless they are distinguishable iconographically, for whereas Akhshobhya's posture is that of the 'earth-witness', sometimes with a vajra on his left palm, Vajrasattva holds bell and vajra (symbols of wisdom and method) in his crossed hands, retaining therefore the sign of his absolute nature. As a single supreme divinity his absolute nature is further emphasized by making him white, just as Avalokiteśvara and Tārā are white.[a] It is in this form that he appears here. Nor is the connection with the Vajra-sattva of the consecration-ritual lost. Thus at the beginning of the ceremony, following the taking of refuge and the raising of the thought of enlightenment, the practiser must conceive of himself as purified by and identified with Vajrasattva.

'Upon my lowly head rests the Body of Light of Vajrasattva, who comprehends all families. He is shining white, holds vajra and bell and is adorned with gems. He is seated cross-legged. He smiles. His nature is compassionate. At his heart is the syllable HŪṂ, encircled with 100 letters. Nectar trickles like

[a] see p. 115.

a flow of milk. From head to foot it cleanses my limbs of sickness and evil. Like a crystal vase, which is filled with curds, I become of pure brilliance of the nature of light.' (One should then recite the mantra of a hundred syllables or that of six syllables until the effect is achieved. Then end with the words:) 'Vajrasattva, dissolved in light, sinks into myself'.[a]

The monks themselves seldom know why any particular divinity is invoked for a special purpose, for they merely practise what they themselves have received from their teachers, and their acceptance is uncritical. The very nature of their religion makes this inevitable, at least for the majority, and much merriment was occasioned by my persistence in raising questions, of which they themselves had never thought. The best place to find the answer to such problems is in the texts themselves, but these are so many, that one hopes usually in vain for some short cut.[b]

The Preparation of the Offerings

The regular offerings to any divinity consist of seven small bowls (or several sets of seven small bowls), filled with water. Part of the daily duty of the keeper of the temple is to refill them with fresh water, as well as lighting lamps, burning incense and reciting a brief invocation. The water in this case represents the seven basic offerings such as should be presented to any honoured guest, namely: water for drinking, water for washing, flowers, incense, lamps, perfume and food.[46] For special ceremonies all these things are offered in kind. The food consists of an unbaked cake, made from ordinary parched flour (tsam-pa) and butter and mounded into a cone. Pats of butter, skilfully shaped into flat discs, are stuck onto the front. This is the regular form of sacrificial cake (*gtor-ma*). The bowls

[a] *Union of the Precious Ones*, fol. 3*a*.

[b] In this case one may assume a connection with the consecration-ritual quoted on p. 73, for the practiser desires to be consubstantiated in Vajrasattva.

for flowers and incense are first filled with rice and into this are stuck the sticks of incense and a single flower, sometimes of paper. The lamps are shaped like a chalice (pl. 38). They are filled with melted butter and burn in the manner of a candle. On big festivals the consumption of butter is enormous.

The seven offerings are known as the external worship (*phyi-mchod*) as distinct from the five offerings of internal worship (*nang-mchod*). These represent all pleasurable sense-perception, namely that of form, sound, smell, taste and touch. A sixth, mind, is added, but this is not part of the original set, to which constant reference is made in the texts. These six are represented by a mirror, a bell, a stick of incense, a sacrificial cake, a piece of silk and a page of text. These two kinds of offerings are all suitable for tranquil divinities. There are also offerings of a fierce kind, which needless to say are not actually represented in kind. The offerings of external worship should be seven to correspond with the tranquil set, but I have never seen more than six, namely: a 'cemetery-flower', incense of singed flesh, lamp of human fat, scent of bile, beverage of blood and food of human flesh. The last item is made of parched flour and butter, but sometimes modelled to show a human head and hands and feet. It is also coloured realistically. The other items are indicated in the same manner as the tranquil offerings. Internal worship is represented by the 'flower of the senses' (*dbang-po'i me-tog*). This again is made of the normal cake mixture, but it is modelled to represent a skull-cup containing a heart, a tongue, a nose, a pair of eyes and a pair of ears. It is very realistic and suitably coloured. The texts also refer to the offerings of 'secret worship' (*gsang-mchod*), which are listed as flesh, heart, blood, brain and entrails. They are never represented, and the monks who are usually rather vague about such niceties, understand the six listed above, cemetery-flower etc. as the items of secret-worship. These things sound far more gruesome when one attempts to list them methodically, than they actually are in practice. All that is important is to have fierce offerings of a kind for fierce divinities, and the detailed lists that occur in the rituals are usually in Sanskrit, which most of the monks just recite by rote without understanding the meaning. It would therefore be misleading to give the impression that these folk delight in horror for its own sake.

There remain three other special items, nectar, medicine and blood, which are represented by local beer or spirit. These three are in origin associated with the quest of Indian alchemists for eternal youth, which is one of the preoccupations attributed to the eighty-four siddhas. In any case such a quest represents a vulgarized aspect of the mystical seeking after the immortal condition (*amṛta*) of buddhahood. It is in this sense that they are understood in the ritual and they are therefore regarded as the supreme offerings.

As may well be imagined the preparation of all these things occupies a great deal of time, normally the whole day preceding the ceremony. They are prepared of course in accordance with the requirements of a particular ritual. Thus for 'The Union of the Precious Ones' all those described might be needed, but for the 'Universal Saviour' only the tranquil kind of offerings would be prepared. But this is only half the business for there are other sacrificial cakes (tor-ma) of a rather different kind. These are intended for specially named divinities and so have come to actually represent the divinity in some sense. They are far larger and often much more elaborate than the ordinary food-offerings. Thus the tor-ma of Padma-sambhava is shaped as an enormous lotus, beautifully modelled and suitably coloured. That of the Universal Saviour has a six-petalled lotus worked on the front of it. That of Ham-trhang is modelled with a serpent entwining it. That of Dorje-Lek-pa has a ram's head at its base. That of the seven mother-goddesses is modelled to appear sevenfold. That of the God of the Plain has a horse's head at its base and so on. The offerings are arranged in tiers on a specially prepared side-table, those of the chief divinities on the upper tier, the defenders and lesser divinities next below. Next come the offerings of internal worship and on the bottom tier the offerings of external worship (pl. 39*a*). Below the table on a raised platform are placed the impromptu offerings of the faithful, rice-cakes, long twisted biscuits, sweetmeats, any available fruits, dishes of cooked peas, sweet potatoes or other vegetables. After the ceremony these are distributed with some of the sacrificial cakes to all who are present. One's share may be quite formidable, but fortunately there is always someone else willing to receive it.

The Ordering of the Ceremony

The ceremony may begin at any agreed time, but usually, before midday, and it will last as long as the benefactor requires. A ritual such as that of 'The Union of the Precious Ones' is quite long enough if recited just once, but it is often greatly lengthened by the continual repetition of the essential part. The benefactor may well ask for it to be repeated a hundred times. Throughout the performance buttered tea is served so that one's cup is never empty, and at noon and in the evening a meal is served in the temple to all present. There are breaks of ten minutes or so at convenient stopping places throughout the day. The ritual is recited in the form of a deep-toned chanting, interspersed with clashes of music from drums, cymbals, trumpets, a type of oboe, conch-whistles and bells, whenever a divinity is called upon to be present. I used to sit with the text (previously prepared) spread before me, and since the windows are closed and a curtain hangs over the door, the only illumination comes from the flickering butter-lamps. There is no doubt of the impressiveness of the performance and it would need little further stretching of the imagination to believe that the divinities are actually present, for one learns to know them so well from the paintings and from the texts. The order of the ceremony in its simplest form is more or less as follows:

One clears the place of hostile forces.
One constructs a protective circle.
One recites the formula of taking refuge,

One makes confession and receives purification.
One rejoices in the accumulating of merit.
One realizes union with the divinity.
One consecrates the offerings.
One summons the divinity.
One makes the offering.
One sings the praises of the divinity.
One recognizes the benefits derived,
(i) perception of the unity of existence.
(ii) perfection of the four-fold activity.
One makes a final invocation.
One consecrates the ceremony to the welfare of all beings.

In practice a ceremony is never as simple as this, for there are all the lesser divinities, who require their share of attention. Little time is spent on those who do not belong fully to the cycle concerned. Thus the lesser gods, lords of the soil, lords of the treasure and similar spirits, are summoned, given their offering and dismissed together with the offering, which is placed outside. In the case of unwelcome guests, such as malignant sprites, the practisers adopt a fierce aspect, usually that of Hayagrīva, and the offering is thrown with threats from the door.

'One is momentarily consubstantiated with the mighty Hayagrīva in his blazing form:

OṂ HRĪḤ PADMĀNTAKṚTA VAJRA-KRODHA HAYAGRĪVA HULU HULU HŪṂ PHAṬ

(One scatters the offerings for the malignant spirits.)
May these offerings for malignant spirits be as a lake of nectar in a vessel of gems, which emanates from the pure condition of absolute voidness, where there is neither perceiver nor object of perception.
Burnt, purified and blown upon by Fire, by Water and by Air.
By pronouncing ĀḤ and HŪṂ they become the most desirable of desirable things.

OṂ ĀḤ HŪṂ OṂ ĀḤ HŪṂ etc.

Now you spirits, who have been honoured here today,
Stay not here. Be satisfied with these offerings and begone, each to your proper place.
If you fail to go and cause obstruction, I shall neigh like the mighty Lotus-Horse (Hayagrīva). The three spheres, the three worlds, will tremble and fear, and all malign spirits and demons will be crushed to dust.

OṂ PADMĀNTAKṚTA HŪṂ PHAṬ. Slay all harmful enemies.
Turn them away in tumult!'[a]

The construction of the protective circle is achieved with such words as: 'May this place be protected to all sides and all directions by rainbow-weapons. May it have an adamantine base and canopy of horns, surrounded by a ring of fire. OṂ VAJRA-RAKSHA JVALA HŪṂ.' The temple thereby assumes the character of a mandala, in the midst of which the practiser, the offerings, the divinity must lose all concepts of self-identity.

The divine power is therefore sometimes regarded as immanent and again sometimes as transcendent, depending upon the momentary view-point.

'The mandala is wisdom's most noble form,
Thus like the moon it cannot wax and wane.
But like the sun that shines equally on all,
In compassion it is everywhere the same.
Come hither, hearken to us, tarry here!
Ineffable Dharma-Body, Wisdom Imperturbable,
Enjoyment-Body of Great Bliss, Lord of the Five Families,
Body of Human Form, skilled in Method and Compassion,
Sometimes tranquil, sometimes fierce,
To thee we bow in salutation!
Produced in thought, envisaged in form,
Samanta-bhadra rests in the pure expanse of space,
Midst clouds of worship unsurpassable.
Thee we worship with an ocean of offerings,

[a] *Union of the Precious Ones*, fol. 2*b*.

The external, the internal and the secret.
In Samanta-bhadra's secret womb
Everything without exception, pervading all the buddha-spheres,
Has but a single flavour, for joining and separation are non-existent there.
Let us rejoice with the Thought of Enlightenment, where duality is unknown!'[a]

The formula for the taking of refuge and the purificatory meditation upon Vajrasattva have been quoted above, so we may continue the ritual with the act of dedicating merit.[b]

All elements are of the nature of the three-fold buddha-body
And I bow before them in the vaste expanse of non-duality.
I worship them in the sameness which is non-created and limitless.
I confess to non-recognition of my own mind's buddhahood.
I rejoice in existence as a condition of self-knowledge.
I will turn the wheel of the ineffable far-spreading doctrine.
I pray that samsāra and nirvāna may rest undifferentiated.
May this all be dedicated to the spontaneous manifestation of the mystery of the doctrine.
May we gain the great and excellent all-pervading bliss of two-in-one.

Union with the divinity

E MA HO. My own person in a blaze of light is the Vajra-Yoginī
Fire and light of pure lustre—the surpassing condition of the pure Void.
Space and the directions are the sphere of rainbow-rays.
On my head rests Guru Padma-sambhava and Avalokiteśvara
And the Head of our Family, the Buddha of Boundless Light
And all the wise masters of India and Tibet, perfected in sūtras and tantras and similar treatises.

[a] *ibid.*, fol. 40*a*. [b] *ibid.*, fol. 3*a* ff.

O Foremost Buddha, Samanta-bhadra Amitābha,
O Kesar-pāṇi, Guardian of our Land of Snows,
O Lotus-Born of rainbow-form, who dost convert the world,
We beseech you, grant us your consecration.
(There follows an invocation to the set of 25 pundits.)

Consecration of the offerings

RAṂ YAṂ KHAṂ

OṂ ĀḤ HŪṂ—thus one signs forehead, heart and throat with the three seed-syllables.

Then rays shoot forth in all the ten directions, and the offerings are scorched and blown and cleansed, so that they are purified of all discursive thought, inherited tendencies and evil, and they become as nectar.

The potion, the blood and the oblations quiver in a blaze of light, surpassing worship, ineffable, sublime.

OṂ ĀḤ HŪṂ—thus all elements of existence, both absolute and phenomenal, are eternally void like space, void of perceived and perceiving, of giving and taking, of done and doing, of all limitations, thus do I, the Lotus-Born, say.

DHARMADHĀTU-SVABHĀVA ĀḤ HŪṂ HRĪḤ

Calling upon the divinity

This uncreate mind of my wretched self is the brilliant lotus-body of the Precious Three in Unity. (The face) is white and lustrous in complexion and is adorned with smiling beauty. He holds a vajra and skull adorned with the precious vase of life. He wears the cornered hat with waving plume and clasps a *khaṭvānga* in the left hand. He wears a special flowing robe as his religious garb and on top of it a cloak of silk.

Adorned with his marks and characteristics, he is beauteous like a mandala of light. He sits cross-legged enveloped in the Great Bliss of the Universal Sameness.

In this body of light with its essence of wisdom, the rays of compassion of pure vacuity (shine) equally upon all.

Enveloped in the midst of the manifold rainbows of the ḍākinīs, he pervades with his physical manifestations all fields of activity. Since his body is like space, he meets nowhere obstruction.

He is perfect in form for he is the norm of all the Blessed,
And all are absorbed into the mandala of the buddhas.
Even the name of opposition and obstruction is unknown.
Samsāra and nirvāna are produced like a creation of magic.

Upon the forehead of this translucent body—OṂ
At the throat—ĀḤ
At the heart—HŪṂ

From here rays of light stream forth, and (reaching) the Lotus-Light Palace on the Glorious Copper Mountain, they draw forth from there the Guru of Urgyen, the Lotus-Born, together with his entourage of everywhere-pervading buddhas, exceedingly small and spherical like a sesame seed.

HRĪḤ—At the beginning of a previous world-age in the north-western region in the Land of Urgyen you acquired the most wonderfully excellent perfection upon a lotus-flower, and so you are famed as the Lotus-Born and are surrounded by an entourage of many ḍākinīs.
Now I beg you to approach and bless this my striving in your wake. Bestow blessing on this sacred place. Grant me the four consecrations for this my sacred striving. Remove all hindrances, false guides and obstructions, and grant me perfection of both sacred and a mundane kind.

OṂ ĀḤ HŪṂ VAJRAGURU PADMA Garlanded with Skulls.
VAJRASAMAYAJAH SIDDHI PHA LA HŪṂ ĀḤ

Salutation to the Lotus-Body of blazing light, which is free from origination, destruction and change, perfect in activity, saving all living-beings by means of self-existent compassion, and raining down perfections like wish-granting gems.

The offering of the oblations

OṂ ĀḤ HŪṂ—All quintessence that is worthy, in gross and subtle form,
Some mentally produced and some self-manifesting,
In the Universal Sameness of deep realization,
We offer to the Buddha Precious Three in One.

Now as for the various kinds of offerings:

For his head we offer lovely flowers,
For his nose we offer sweet-smelling incense,
For his body we offer food and fragrant water,
For his tongue we offer savoury oblations,
For his mind we offer pleasant-sounding music.
We offer worship of gesture and dance,
We offer worship of praise and song,
Contemning not desirable things, we present the external offerings,
Contemning not mental distractions, we present the internal offerings,
We present the secret offerings, where uniting and separation are unknown.
We present the offering of the medicine, which contains the eight fundamental and the thousand supplementary ingredients.
We offer the blood which brings release from the five poisons of existence.
We make the offering of cakes,
We make the offering of the sacred item, nectar.
We make these offerings with no thought of giving and taking.

To the Guru together with the Tutelary Divinity and the troupe of ḍākinīs
We make the glad offering of that sacred item, the excellent nectar,

That item which is perfected of the Five Wisdoms for the cleansing of the Five Evils.

Look upon us with compassion and grant us the consecrations and perfections.

Praises

HRĪḤ—Although all buddhas are one in the sphere of wisdom and the supreme truth possesses neither parts nor modes, yet by your skill in the use of right means you manifest a form suitable for those you intend to convert and because of your compassion you produce and send forth these phantom forms. So I salute and I praise you.

Unity of All Blessed in the form of an eight-year-old boy,
Protector of all beings, Lotus-Born,
Your changeless complexion resembles shining sun on snow,
Glistening slightly reddish. Salutation and praise to you!

Means and Wisdom are indistinguishable and so you hold vajra and skull.

You hold the Vase of Life—Life for Two-in-One and Vase for Wisdom.

The *khaṭvāṅga* cuts off at the root the three poisons. It is the Mother's perquisite.

You are both wrathful and smiling, for the converting of living beings.

Salutation and praise to you!

You wear a red religious garb with a criss-cross pattern of gold.

You wear the cornered hat with waving tastle and hanging ribbons.

On your lotus-throne you are resplendent with your marks and characteristics.

Perfect are you in all qualities, external and internal,

Salutation and praise to you.

There is no uniting or separating for your forms and their fields of activity.

The magical activity of the buddhas throughout all ten directions cannot be predicated as great or small, for they abide in the condition of the three-fold body. The lightning of your phantom-forms shoots through the void.

Salutation and praise to you.

With the light-rays of the 100,000 suns that characterize your splendour, you draw forth from its condition of self-nature the Power of Life. Like a wish-granting gem, which fulfils all wants and desires, eternal Vajra-Body, salutation and praise to you.

Although there can be no perceptual basis for this worship and praise, yet in order to remove these notions which are a kind of accidental defilement, you disport yourself in a non-dual state, Means and Wisdom indistinguable like water entering water.

Perception of the Unity of Existence

At my own heart at the centre of an eight-petalled lotus,
Upon a lunar disc is a five-pointed golden vajra,
Marked at its centre with the syllable HŪṂ which is white in colour.
Around the points of the vajra is a circle of syllables which are of the five colours and encircle it to the right.
From these light-rays stream forth and offer the highest form of worship to all the buddhas who completely pervade their fields of activity.
All blessings of Body, Speech and Mind concentrate upon myself.

In the intermediate sphere all gods and powerful demons are forced into subjection, and all orders that we give them are effortlessly performed.

In the lower sphere the sins of all the beings of the six spheres are cleansed and they are made to rejoice in happiness.

The rays that thus stream forth and returning concentrate again have become a vast interplay of the outer and inner world, of sacred mantras and of wisdom.

OṂ ĀḤ HŪṂ VAJRAGURU PADMASIDDHI HŪṂ

(As this is the basis of mantra-recitation, it should be performed as much as you can.)

The Fourfold Activity

(i) *Pacifying*. I am the Lotus-Born with HŪṂ as my inner life, white in colour. At my head there is a white lotus with 32 petals and at its centre upon a lunar disc is the syllable OM with the other syllables of the mantra at the ends (of the petals), giving forth white light-rays. Induce contact, produce efficacy! All evil and the eight fears are tranquillized, the inner and the outer world become Vajrasattva's sphere.

After 'VAJRAGURU' etc. 'OṂ ŚĀNTIṂ KURU YE SVĀHĀ May sickness, evil and all bad tendencies, enemies and all harmful obnoxious things, sharp weapons and concocted poison, all the one thousand and eighty demons, the four hundred and four kinds of illness, ill omens and bad dreams, may all these things be quickly tranquillized.

(ii) *Gaining Prosperity*. I am the Lotus-Born with HŪṂ as my inner life, yellow in colour. At my navel there is a yellow lotus with sixty-four petals and at its centre is a jewelled BHRŪṂ with the chain of other syllables, giving forth yellow light-rays. Force contact, produce efficacy! The two stocks of merit and the six kinds of wealth will prosper. the inner and the outer world become Ratnasattva's sphere.

The mantra is: BHRŪṂ PUSHTIṂ KURU YE SVĀHĀ
Long life and good fortune, fame and power, prosperous activity for followers and pupils, good destiny, enjoyable things and all good qualities, may these quickly prosper.

(iii) *Empowerment*. I am the Lotus-Born with HŪṂ as my inner life, red in colour. At my throat there is a red lotus with sixteen petals, and at its centre upon a solar disc is the syllable HRĪḤ with the chain of other syllables at the ends (of the petals), giving forth red light-rays. Force contact, produce efficacy! Samsāra and nirvāna are brought together, and the inner and the outer world become Padmasattva's sphere.

The mantra is: HRĪḤ VAŚAṂ KURU YE SVĀHĀ

May the compassionate blessing of the buddhas and all that living-beings see and hear and think and touch, in fact the triple world, all come within my power.

(iv) *Destroying*. I am the Lotus-Born with HŪṂ as my inner life, deep blue in colour. At my groin there is a dark-green lotus with (twenty-) eight petals and upon it a sword, marked with the syllable HŪṂ and with the mantra-chain, giving forth black rays. Force contact, produce efficacy! Enemies, demons, the five poisons will be destroyed and the inner and the outer world become Karmasattva's sphere.

The mantra is: HŪṂ MĀRAYA PHAṬ

All fiends and frightful creatures, foes of the doctrine and private foes, all the demons throughout space, may they all be destroyed.'

The rites of pacifying, prospering, empowerment and destroying were originally just four of the many different magical rites which one finds listed in earlier texts.[a] They were later endowed with a significance of a far higher order, namely as the four main types of Buddhist activity. The central concept of this later Buddhism is that enlightenment is a union of wisdom and means. Thus buddhahood cannot be just quiescent and nothing else, for it is active in overcoming evil, in bestowing good things upon all living beings, in bestowing the consecrating power by which buddhahood may be known and by destroying the foes of the doctrine. If some of these things seem at first to be rather un-buddhist activities, it must be remembered that

[a] see p. 77.

for the tantric Buddhists, buddhahood is no escape from the world, for it is engaged in the world, from which it is in no wise distinct. Hence the slaying of enemies, as in the case of King Lang-dar-ma, becomes a proper act, although the slayer is not thereby freed from the consequences. Whether one regards this as a degeneration or not, depends upon one's view of what a religion should be. It is certainly based upon an entirely different world-view from that of the early wandering ascetics, but of course it is not far removed from the ordinary Mahāyāna conception of the bodhisattva.

These four rites are fitted into the regular mandala-schemes, both external and internal:

Pacifying	Vajra-family	Head
Prospering	Jewel-family	Navel
Empowerment	Lotus-Family	Throat
Destroying	Karma-Family	Groin

The allocation is probably quite arbitrary, although as is often the case, reasons can be deduced after the event. The central position of the external mandala (Tathāgata-family) and the heart of the body remain unspecified, for all four rites concentrate at this point. The names Jewel-Being, Lotus-Being and Karma-Being are equivalents for the heads of these families just as Vajra-Being (*Vajra-sattva*) is for Akshobhya.

Nevertheless these four rites do not just remain the signs of a buddha's activity, for any of them may be performed in the name of a higher being, who has them at his disposal. Thus during my stay at Jiwong one of the main flag-poles in front of the entrance to the temple was struck by lightning and felled to the ground. Nga-wang Yön-ten chose to regard this as an evil portent and he spoke anxiously of the hostile forces that were ranged against the Buddhist doctrine in the region. The Lord of the Soil bore the chief responsibility, it seemed, but he was also thinking in terms of the Chinese communists across the frontier in Tibet and the political trouble-makers in the village below. Thus the fierce Rite of Destroying was ordered for the following day, and in the morning preparations began. A square raised hearth was set up in the centre of the courtyard in front of the temple. On the top surface a triangle was marked with its point directed towards the open gateway of the monastery, indicating the point of direction of the destructive force. Inside this triangle was drawn a smaller one with a sword along its centre line, both pointing in the same direction. This was all painstakingly drawn and coloured. The square top of the hearth was dark blue, the outer triangle dark brown and the inner triangle red. The sides of the triangle were decorated with vajras and gems in conventional design. On the top of this elaborate hearth sticks of equal length were piled up carefully, preserving the triangular shape. Meanwhile in the temple porch other monks were active over other preparations. Since the rite was to be performed in the name of the yi-dam Padma-Narteśvara ('Unity of All the Blessed'), his tor-ma was set up on one table, flanked by the Lord of the Soil (not the local one against whom the rite was partly directed) and the Lord of the Treasure, who are invoked in this ritual. In front of these three tor-mas were placed the seven regular external offerings and their fierce counterparts. On another side-table was placed the tor-ma of the God of Fire (Agni), flanked by little banners (*rgyal-mtshan*) to do him honour and with the seven regular offerings placed before him. A foul poisonous brew, which is the fierce oblation, was now mixed in a bowl. The directions in the manual name Indian leaves and juices, which are not available in Jiwong, but local substitutes were used. Human fat was likewise unobtainable, thus mutton-dripping served instead. The ingredients floated in black mustard oil and the resultant potion certainly looked sufficiently horrible. The actual ceremony, which was held in the afternoon, was the briefest of my experience, lasting a mere two hours. The regular invocation of the Unity of All the Blessed was first recited, so that mystical union with him once achieved, the practisers could dispose of his destructive power. Thereafter Agni was praised for his co-operation and the potion was poured ladle-full by ladle-full upon the blazing hearth, the monks meanwhile directing wrath and destruction upon all fiends and foes (pl. 39*b*).

Every ceremony ends with a final prayer and blessing, of which brief examples are given here:

'May all these beings, who are without protection and who have no protector, quickly gain the unsurpassable condition of supreme enlightenment. Let the twelve-fold causal nexus, which is the basis of all deluding existence, revolving like the wheel of a cart, be quickly destroyed.'

'May we have the blessing of our lamas that all stupidity may be dispersed with regard to the nature of existence!
May we have the blessing of our tutelary divinity, that we may achieve whatever we intend!
May we realize the blessing of the Great Symbol in the womb of Body, Speech and Mind!
The Blessing of the *Dharma-kāya*, Boundless Light,
Extending blessing through the realms of a thousand suns,
Foremost of perfecters of those glorious qualities, which are the best of all desirable things,
May blessing such as this descend upon us here today!
The blessing of the *Sambhoga-kāya*, the Great Compassionate One,
Extending blessing like the moon throughout the heavens,
Foremost of perfecters of the hopes of bodily beings,
May blessing such as this descend upon us here today!
The Blessing of the *Nirmāṇa-kāya*, Padma-sambhava,
Extending blessing far and wide as to the myriads of stars,
Teaching in a manner suitable to each place and to each person,
May blessing such as this descend upon us here today!'[a]

It will be apparent from the foregoing that the ceremonies consist mainly in the rhythmic and solemn recitation of texts. The only actor is the keeper of the temple, who in all things functions on behalf of the whole community. Thus during the recitation of the litanies of salutation, some of which are very

[a] *Union of the Precious Ones*, fol. 53*a*–53*b*.

lengthy, he takes his position in the centre of the aisle and continues to make full obeisances so long as the recitation lasts. When the divinities are summoned, he walks round the temple, swinging the censer, while the music crashes. While the verses of purification for the offerings are being recited, he sprinkles them with water from the ritual vase. When the offerings are presented, it is he who raises them in offering. If they are for unwanted guests, he steps backwards in time with the chanting, as though leading the spirit with him to the door. The pupils of the monks are meanwhile active in doing the rounds with pots of tea, in assisting the cook and in bringing in the food at the proper times. Any lay-folk who are present sit around the walls or behind the two rows of monks. Everybody is served with tea, if they produce a cup from their ample breast-pocket. Everybody receives food in quantities proportionate to their station and their sex. The solemn scene is pervaded with good-will and often touched by mirth. There is no doubt that a Tibetan religious festival is an event to be remembered.

Guiding the Consciousness after Death

One of the most interesting rites is the one performed on behalf of the consciousness of a deceased person. It was shown in Ch. 1 that although the doctrine of rebirth is fundamental to Buddhism in all its forms, there was yet considerable difficulty in identifying the actual transmigrating principle. The problem was finally (but only implicitly) solved by the development of the new philosophical theories, which taught the non-predicability of everything whatsoever. All names and forms assumed thereby a merely relative value, and so it was no more inaccurate to say that this person is reborn than to say that the person is the non-substantial manifestation of co-operating elements. The whole tantric theory is based upon the doctrine of absolute non-substantiality and thus all its forms and symbols are quite unreal in themselves. The after-death rites are of this kind. At first they might appear to imply belief in a real transmigrating element, identified as consciousness. In fact the whole aim is to eradicate belief in anything substantial and to show the identity of samsāra and nirvāna. It is for this reason that the Wheel of Life is represented as the mandala of Avalokiteśvara. His manifestation as the six buddhas of the six spheres of existence is merely a special application of the system of the five buddha-families to the six-fold wheel of existence. The spheres of existence are actually referred to as families. It is really rather a clumsy way of making five and six fit together and illustrates a certain indifference to the details of formal representation. All that is important is the idea, in this case the sameness of the phenomenal and the buddha-spheres. In order to achieve this effect the five evils are extended to six and one of the five types of wisdom is duplicated. But we are not so much concerned with upbraiding the Tibetans for their clumsiness, as with emphasizing that even when they appear to be claiming presumptuous powers in leading a person towards final beatitude, they are merely affirming through the rite the central belief that is fundamental to all their religious practice. This rite differs not at all in intention from that of their normal meditation, but the effects, instead of being applied universally are directed primarily to the benefit of one person. In the process they make use of all the ancient symbolism of the wheel of existence, forcing it to fit the new symbolism. In the event it does not quite fit, but as it is a mere symbol, which is literally thrown away at the end of the ceremony, this matters not at all.

In practice this ceremony is always performed at the instigation of the deceased's relatives, who may well be thinking in terms of actually influencing the course of rebirth of one of their number. Often, however, their intentions are far less noble, being merely concerned that the spirit of the deceased (conceived of in no Buddhist sense) should cause them no trouble in the future. All the presents (mentally produced it is true) which they promise him for the journey through the after-life serve no useful purpose according to Buddhist theory. In this ceremony two very different beliefs are combined, but because of their difference they are very easily disengaged. The whole theory of a journey through an intermediate state is non-Buddhist. It has not been included here since a translation and an adequate description are already available elsewhere.[a] One may note, however, that the divinities who are supposed to people it are the 'Tranquil and Fierce' ones listed above, who are all certainly of Indian origin. The chief reason of course for performing the ceremony is just that it is the custom, and thus it would be misleading to base our evaluation of it on the vague beliefs of many of the lay-folk. Our Nying-ma-pa authority, Kün-zang La-ma is quite adamant on the value of these performances: 'The great teacher of Urgyen said: "When you consecrate the name-card, it is already too late. The consciousness wanders in the intermediate state like a mad dog. Even if you could conduct it to heaven, it would still be in difficulty." The belief that it can be led up and down like a bridled horse can only actually apply to this very life. One virtuous action performed while one occupies the present body is more efficacious than all the rest.'[b]

The ceremony as described here, was instigated at Jiwong Monastery by the father of a boy who had died of small-pox. The body had been cremated down in the valley several days before. Hence there arises the need for a name-card as substitute for the person. This is quite normal Tibetan practice.[c] The monks mark out a mandala in the form of a lotus with six petals, in the centre of each of which is drawn one of the symbols of the six spheres of existence, marked with an identifying initial syllable.[d]

On the 1st a blue triangle with syllable DU to indicate the hells,

[a] Evans-Wentz, *The Tibetan Book of the Dead.*

[b] *Kun-bzang-bla-ma,* fol. 10*b*.

[c] The following extracts are taken from *Instruction in the Abodes of the Universal Saviour* (*thugs-rje chen-po 'gro-ba-kun-sgrol-gyi gnas-lung*).

[d] *du* for *duḥkha* (misery), *pre* for *preta* (departed spirit), *tir* for *tiryak* (*animal*), *nṛ* for *nṛ* (man), *a* for *asura* (titan) and *su* for *sura* (god).

on the 2nd a red semi-circle with PRE for the unhappy spirits,
on the 3rd a yellow square with TIR for the animals,
on the 4th Mount Meru and the four continents with NR for men,
on the 5th a green oblong with A for the titans,
on the 6th a white lotus with SU for the gods.

Then they prepare a name-card for the deceased. His effigy should be drawn in a kneeling position with hands raised in supplication. The following words are written:
'Tse-wang (or whatever may be his name), who has left this life for the beyond, makes salutation. He offers worship. He confesses his sins. He begs to be saved from the wheel of existence, especially evil rebirths, to be cleansed from all his evil and to be advanced towards supreme enlightenment.'

On his forehead is written SU

throat	A
heart	NṚ
navel	TIR
groin	PRE
soles	DU

Over his head is drawn an umbrella and underneath him an eight-petalled lotus. To his sides are silk pendants with five folds. If it is a man, he is given an arrow. If it is a woman, she is given a bamboo reed. On the forehead is fixed a mirror.

If he is a lama, he is given a throne.
If a man, some pieces of armour,
If a woman, some jewellery and a heap of spun wool,
If a child, some toy or anything that used to please him.

Then one should put ready food-offerings for the six buddhas who watch over the six spheres of existence and six small sacrificial cakes (ransom-offerings) for the beings of the six spheres.
At the head of the mandala one places a table marked out with a white eight-petalled lotus (representing the paradise of Avalo-

kiteśvara). One should empower the ritual vase by invoking Vajrasattva or the Great Compassionate One (Avalokiteśvara) in accordance with the prescribed rite.

Then one must call the deceased into the name-card.

One sprinkles it with the water of the ritual vase, calling on the deceased to present himself, wherever he may be. Then holding vajra and bell and motioning the hands in the HŪM-*kāra* gesture, one intones:

'By the truth of the perfect five-fold buddhahood,
By the grace of the great self-manifesting absolute,
By the truth of the mighty two-fold merit of the whole religious assembly,
By the truth of the Lord of Great Compassion,
By the truth of the six buddhas who convert the beings of the six spheres,
By the truth of the four immeasurable meditations,
By the bond of secret spells, of all the spells of the six families,
By the bond of the determined hand-gestures which are the essence of forms,
By the conjuration of sages who are masters of the spell (*vidyādhara*),
By the concentrated thought of us yogins and our assistants,
By the truth of all gods who are on the side of virtue,
By the power and the grace of this great truth,
Let the deceased come here, whose effigy is fixed to this card.
He who has passed from this world and is in process of changing his body,
Whether he is already born in one of the six spheres or still wanders in the intermediate state,
Wherever he may be, let his consciousness gather upon this symbol.
Let him come here, where entry to the spheres of existence is closed and the door to salvation wide-open.
Let him be mindful of his lama and his tutelary divinity.
Let him take his place gradually but firmly at this support of our mental production.'

Then the ransom-offerings are thrown to the evil spirits who have any claim upon the deceased, ordering them to be gone at their peril. If any of his bones are available, they are placed by the name-card. They are then purified by sprinkling with sand and black mustard, which have been rendered potent by purificatory spells. 'Wherever has been born or wherever may abide the consciousness of the deceased whose impure bones are with this card, by the compassion of Avalokiteśvara may he be freed from the sufferings of the three states of woe, which are accumulated karma in the form of illusory torments. May he be born where the Lord can convert him, and having been born in such a condition, may he know the truth of the Mahāyāna and achieve the state of knowledge.'

Then one explains to him the meaning of the symbols:

'Hearken, thou noble son, who has passed from hence!
Listen, thou who wanderest amidst the illusions of another world!
Come to this most delightful place in our human world!
This umbrella shall be your palace, your protection, your consecrated shrine.
This name-card is the symbol of your body,
This bone the symbol of your speech,
This jewellery the symbol of your mind,
This arrow is the symbol of your life-force,
This mirror is the symbol of your gaze,
These silk pendants are symbols of your five senses,
These five gems symbolize the essence of your being,
These scented garments symbolize your inherited propensities,
These little bells symbolize your adornments.
O make these symbols your abode!
Let your mind with its inherited propensities tarry in this place!
Uncertain, unsteady, you tremble elsewhere in the six spheres of existence,
Be mindful of your lama and your tutelary divinity, who are your refuge!

Direct, arouse your mental powers and come here to this place!
Here at the frontier of samsāra and nirvāna we shall guide you into the path of salvation.
So make the three-fold refuge, raise the thought of enlightenment and hold to the vow of the bond!'

The monks now on behalf of the deceased make homage to Avalokiteśvara, recite the taking of refuge formulas and express aspiration towards enlightenment.

The main part of the ceremony has now been reached. It is assumed that the deceased may take birth in any of the six spheres, and so he is released from each in turn, his name-card being moved around the lotus-petals, so that he progresses from the hells to the sphere of unhappy spirits, thence to the animals, men, titans and gods. In each sphere the same sequence of ritual is followed. Thus the name-card is first placed in the hells and the ritual proceeds thus:

(a) *Purification*

'The true nature of your master is the Compassionate One himself, and now assuming the form of the Buddha of the Hells, Dharmarāja, he appears clearly in the sky before you, dark blue in colour and holding a wand whence issues fire and water. O noble son, he will clear away all the evil effects and all the suffering of your birth in hell which has been occasioned by the fruition of the sin of wrath. Concentrate upon this fact.

HRĪḤ I am the Great Compassionate Avalokiteśvara. That I may encompass all beings with my compassion, I appear as the Buddha of Hell, Dharmarāja. I purify all evil wrath and anger. I hold the wand of fire and water and teach the doctrine of forbearance. I remove the sufferings of cold and heat from the body of the deceased. OṂ MAṆIPADME HŪṂ.'

(b) *The Leading Forth*

'O noble son, by the force of your selfish indulgence in wrath you have been born in hell and are exhausted by the unbearable sufferings of heat and cold, but even so by the power of your master's spell and mental concentration and symbolic gesture you are encompassed with compassion and are led forth from hell. Concentrate on this. One certain day you died, O noble son, and by force of all your former wrath you have been born in hell amidst heat and cold most terrible. Come hither! Beg for refuge! May you be encompassed with compassion!'

(c) *Washing away the evil effects*

(The officiant takes up the ritual vase)

'O noble son, all the impurities of the evil effects of wrath which attach to your life series, are washed away by the nectar of knowledge. Concentrate on this. HRĪḤ. From the wondrous ritual vase which is of the nature of the dharma-body there goes forth pure water full of virtues. May the deceased be cleansed by it, and the impurities of his wrath removed, may he realize the nature of the translucent mirror-like wisdom. OṂ Ā HŪṂ.'

(d) *Presentation of the food-offerings*

'RAṂ YAṂ KHAṂ. OṂ Ā HŪṂ. The Buddha of the Hells is presented with the food-offerings of eight flavours. Concentrate on this. May all these beings who offer to the Buddha of the Hells this most delicious well-made eight-flavoured offering, taste the luxurious food of deep meditation. NAIVEDYA-PŪJA HO.'

Giving the ransom-offering

'RAṂ YAṂ KHAṂ. OṂ Ā HŪṂ. May all your creditors of hell be appeased by these ransom-offerings and may you bring to fruition the two-fold stock of merit. Concentrate on this. This wondrous ransom-offering of the five desirable things is consecrated for the effacing of all debts to hell. May the deceased bring to fruition the two-fold stock of merit, practise the doctrine and experience the fruit of final release. OṂ SARVABALIṂ TA KHĀHI.'

(e) *Instruction*

'Be mindful of the meaning of my words. Ho deceased one! So great was your suffering, you thought you were dead, but since everything is impermanent, it partakes of the nature of death. The nature of existence is nought else but suffering. You fluttering consciousness, wandering in the intermediate state, come here and be mindful of your lama and your tutelary divinity. Practise virtue and shun evil. Free yourself from all attachment to self.'

(f) *Injunction to salutation*

'Imagine that you have produced phantom bodies as numerous as the atoms of the buddha-fields and that together with all your friends and relations you are making salutation to the divine assembly of the mandala. Concentrate on this. Listen, noble son, thou who hast left this life. Come to this delightful palace. This reed is your life's centre. Make this umbrella the abode that houses your body and this name-card the support for your form and your consciousness. Salute the gods of the mandala and go to them for protection. NAMAḤ SARVATATHĀGATAPURUSHA HO.'

(One makes three obeisances and places the name-card in the sphere of the unhappy spirits.)

(g) *Cutting off future connection with the hells*

'Listen, deceased. Although the fruit of the evil of wrath which attached to your life-series was a cause of your being born in the hells, yet by the power of this undefiled ritual the door of birth in hell has now been closed. Concentrate on this. HRĪḤ. This place is closed from now on. This sphere of hell is overwhelmingly great in its sufferings of heat and cold. Frightful are birth and death. Strict is the force of karmic effects. Be free of attachment. Be free of desires. Abandon the sufferings of existence. OṂ DAHA DAHA SARVA NARAKA GATA HADUNA HŪṂ PHAṬ.' The door of hell is closed.

The process is now repeated for each of the other spheres of existence. The admonitions and invocations are the same throughout, all that changes being the type of suffering, the name of the particular buddha, the relevant sin and the type of wisdom which is born when the sin is removed.

Sphere	*Buddha*	
Hell	*chos-kyi-rgyal-po*	= King of the Dharma
Unhappy spirits	*kha-'bar-rgyal-po*	= King of the Burning Mouth
Animals	*seng-ge-dam-brtan*	= Lion Firm in his Vow
Men	*shākya-thub-pa*	= Sage of the Śākyas
Titans	*thag-bzang-ris*	= Design of Excellent Weave
Gods	*lha-dbang-brgya-byin*	= Indra Lord of Gods

Sphere	*Suffering*	*Evil*	*Type of Wisdom*[a]
Hell	Heat and cold	Wrath	Mirror-like Wisdom
Unhappy spirits	Hunger and thirst	Avarice	Wisdom of Self-knowledge
Animals	Enforced labour	Stupidity	Wisdom of Self-knowledge
Men	Knowledge of life and death	Desire	Discriminating Wisdom
Titans	Discord and strife	Jealousy	Active Wisdom
Gods	Falling from high estate	Pride	Wisdom of Sameness

Having closed to him the sphere of the gods, the deceased is given final admonition to avoid attachment to phenomenal existence. The name-card is then placed together with the mandala of the eight-petalled lotus on a small table before the head-lama. The mandala of the six spheres is pushed together and thrown away. At this point the *Rite of the Intermediate State* may be recited. The relatives offer him, food, drink, clothes and all desirable things.

'Listen, noble son deceased, your parents, your brothers and sisters, your cousins and uncles and aunts, your devoted friends, are dedicating to you all these splendid things, food and drink and clothes and jewels, horses and elephants and foot-attendants, gold and silver, copper, iron, grain of all the different kinds, jewelled carriages, and platforms for mounting, couches, parks and castles, fields, implements, bright lamps for overcoming evil darkness, friends as protection against fear, in short all de-

[a] Compare this expanded set of six with the normal set of five as given on p. 67.

sirable things belonging to the categories of form, sound, smell, taste and touch. They are dedicated for ever as the property of your shrine. All desirable things and good qualities without limit, may they come just as you wish and in conformity with the doctrine.[a]

'O noble son deceased, just listen. If you are experiencing the intermediate state and suffer from the sickness of the three poisonous evils, then shall be dedicated to you the best of medicines, this inexhaustible nectar. If you are afflicted by foes and demons, then shall be dedicated to you armour and weapons, courage and skill and strength. If you suffer like an unhappy spirit from hunger and thirst, then shall be dedicated to you food and drink and limitless good things to remove the suffering of hunger and thirst. If you are cold, your clothes shall be warm and soft. If you are hot, they shall be light and cool. There shall be dedicated to you the finest of clothes of all sorts, just as you want them, beautiful, ravishing and pleasant to touch. If you are caught in the mass of darkness of false knowledge, these bright lamps shall be dedicated as your sun and moon. If you faint with exhaustion along the way, there shall be dedicated shade and water and means of transport.

Since everything is dedicated to you in this way so that you possess unalloyed happiness, even if you should assume another body and walk the path of existence, you must surely obtain the right circumstances of life and a suitable character with the seven good qualities. Thus may you meet with virtuous guides in the religious life and may you honour the lamas and the Three Precious Ones. May you support the monasteries and

[a] This list of good things is conceived in regal style and one remembers the offerings made at the tombs of the ancient kings. These are described in the *rgyal-po bka'i-thang-yig*, fol. 42 ff. The passage has been translated by Prof. Tucci in *Tombs*, pp. 9–10. It represents undoubtedly the origin of this part of the after-death ceremonies. The invocation that follows immediately, conceives of the deceased as being reborn as a lord of men ('May you care for all men in accordance with the doctrine'), and it may well be that we have here an early Buddhist version of a pre-Buddhist ceremony, clumsily changed to suit the tenets of the new doctrine.

temples, enjoy all desirable things, have good servants and followers and care for all men in accordance with the doctrine.

HRĪḤ. The best of wealth is the wealth that one gives away, for this makes an end of avarice. One enjoys without effort such wealth which is never exhausted. May this deceased and all living-beings rejoice in the wealth which is given away!

The best of adornments are the adornments of good conduct. They remove the evil countenance of attachment. It is proper that one should be honoured with such ravishing adornments. May the deceased and all living beings delight in the adornments of good qualities!

The best of garments are the garments of forbearance. They preserve against the pangs of wrath. They are pleasing to everyone and one's own mind is content. May the deceased and all living beings delight in the garments of forbearance.

The best of transport is the horse of effort. He quickly crosses the great plain of indolence and reaches the country of great and unalloyed bliss. May the deceased and all living beings delight in the horse of effort!

The best of food is the food of contemplation. It removes those sufferings of hunger and thirst which are a distracted mind. One's faculties are content with an unalloyed bliss. May the deceased and all living beings delight in the food of contemplation.

The best of friends is the friend that is wisdom. He teaches the manner of deliberation as one who knows both sides. He is a friend who removes the darkness of ignorance and from whom one is never parted. May the deceased and all living beings rejoice in the friend of wisdom!'

(The consciousness of the deceased is then shown the way.)

'Listen, deceased, O noble son! This realm that was closed to you has become from now on the buddha-field of Avalokiteśvara, where never sounds the name of life and death and transmigration. Your protector now is Avalokiteśvara. Your friends now are the bodhisattvas. Meditation is your food, deep concentration your enjoyment. You have as your wealth the nectar of knowledge. Ineffable clouds of worship rise to the All-Good. The pure-sounding doctrine resounds. The wheel of the doctrine turns in eternity. Come this way, the supreme one. Keep to these sacred precincts.

Your faculty of knowledge which had its abode in this name-card, has turned into a white A and relinquishing the name-card, it becomes one with your lama who is the heart of the mandala.'

(*The burning of the name-card.*)

'The former body of flesh and blood together with the image of the name-card of the deceased Tse-wang (or whatever his name), all the component parts and sense-spheres of this body of the four elements with its inherited tendencies is cleansed by the fire of that supra-sensual knowledge which pertains to the divine company of Avalokiteśvara. HRĪḤ. Listen deceased, O noble son. The fire of the Body, Speech and Mind of Avalokiteśvara has consumed the three poisonous evils.'

'The remaining bones and ashes are sprinkled with water from the ritual vase to the accompaniment of this mantra:

OṂ VAJRA PRAMARDANAYA SVĀHĀ

One imagines a lunar disc above the bones, on which there is a white A, whence flows a stream of nectar, which washes away all the evil defilements of the deceased.

With these ashes one makes little effigies, which are properly consecrated in due course. The certain effect of all this is that the deceased is released from existence, especially evil rebirths, and is born in the purity of the buddha-field.'

VII

REFLECTIONS

As a last act at Jiwong I asked for the ceremony of the Universal Saviour to be performed, which provided an opportunity for consuming a large quantity of butter, feasting the monks and thus making a general recognition in the terms they best understood for all the help and friendliness, which we had received during our stay. My assistant, Pasang, had spent several years at Jiwong as a boy, and this had accounted for our initial welcome, which soon began to pass the bounds of normal hospitality. What joy it was, therefore, for once to be the benefactor myself, although I remained in my accustomed seat, while Pasang played the part. I was also glad to hear the invocation of *Thang-lha,* 'God of the Plain', who is protector of the Saviour's entourage. The text has been quoted above (pp. 239 ff.) but a straight translation conveys nothing of the impressiveness of its rhythmic recitation in Tibetan with the accompanying clashes of drums, cymbals and bells and the blowings of trumpets and conch-shell. Three days later we set out on the twelve days' treck to Kathmandu, the first stage of the journey towards home. To tramp day after day across foothills and through valleys, sometimes tiring and monotonous, sometimes restful and exhilarating, is the best of endings to the experiences that have been described. There is time for reflection, for the drawing of conclusions, for the penetration to inner meanings. It is then that one may know the enjoyment that springs from the intuitions of knowledge.

It would be rash to argue any firm conclusions on the basis of our studies, but we may share with our readers some of the reflections which arise from them. For fragmentary as this account may be, it presents none the less a survey of the whole history of Buddhist developments, if indeed rather from a Tibetan point of view. It would be unwise for a westerner to predicate any particular type of Buddhism as true or false, as good or bad, for it may well be that he has only partly understood it. Remembering Aśoka's ancient dictum, that all that is well said, is the word of a buddha, we might also hesitate to formulate any limiting generalizations. At the same time we have noted vast changes in the doctrine, such as Aśoka and his contemporaries never dreamed of. Thus if we can identify any constantly recurring themes, we may also discover thereby the *élan vital* of Buddhism.

One fundamental theme concerns the *nature of existence*. The Buddhist view might be resumed for westerners with the words of an ancient Christian prayer: 'the changes and chances of this fleeting world'. It is this notion of impermanence and transitoriness, which is both the cause of universal sorrow and the incentive to bring it to an end. Thus the four-fold truth of sorrow, of its origin, of its ending and of the means to its end, provides the regular psychological and philosophical starting-point. The traditional pattern of life is that of the Wheel of Existence, which is depicted in the porch of every Tibetan temple. One may wonder perhaps how many people, as they move in and out, take to heart the lesson of its symbolism. After all, do they not often request the monks to perform ceremonies on their behalf; at best their motive is the desire for religious merit and often merely for prosperity and well-being in their present lives. But these questions are not especially relevant to Tibetan Buddhism, for one observes that in all the great religious traditions there are two main categories of practisers: those who are prepared to make all else subservient to their religious practice and those who wish to have their religion associated with success and happiness here and now. One might define these viewpoints simply as other-worldly (*jenseitig*) and this-worldly (*diesseitig*).

So long as a civilization is united in its adherence to a common religious tradition, one finds a working co-operation between these two main categories. The 'other-worldly' practisers function as the guides and assistants of those who are immersed in the affairs of this world, while these for their part bestow honour and material goods upon those whom they expect to support them in their higher aspirations. In spite of the obscuring effects of human passions, this relationship has worked in Europe in the past, and it still works in Tibet today. The two categories seem to be essential to one another: to-day the monastic orders of modern Europe appear as ineffectual members of a social body, which finds no use in them; on the other hand the credulous lay-folk of Nepal provide an example of would-be practisers of the Buddhist doctrine, who lack the guides that might direct their endeavours. Where, however, both categories are represented, we are justified in taking as our measure the aspirations of the 'other-worldly', for they set the standard, which is at least recognized, if not followed, by their countrymen. Thus the Wheel of Existence has not yet become an empty symbol for the Tibetans, and the mainspring of their religious practice remains the basic notion of impermanence.

There is also no change in the *conception of buddhahood*. It may seem absurd to speak of change in a condition which is universally described as essentially changeless. Still it might have been possible to detect one, just as between the goal of the early disciple (*śrāvaka*) and the goal of the bodhisattva. When we spoke in Chapter I of the goal having changed, it was this that we had in mind and not buddhahood itself. The term *nirvāṇa* is ambiguous, for it may refer to the goal of the disciple or to that of the perfect buddha. As we know now, the first indicates release from existence, whereas the second is knowledgeable participation in existence. Hence it is definable as the union of *saṃsāra* and *nirvāṇa*, of Wisdom and Means. Although all such definitions are the fruit of the Mahāyāna, they manifestly have their basis in the earlier teachings, for no Buddhist ever doubted that the Śākya-Sage preached the doctrine for the welfare of living-beings, when he might just as well have faded away into nirvāna. His life was the model for these later developments.

The basic change that occurred did not affect the nature of buddhahood itself, but the way in which its relationship to phenomenal existence was envisaged. This was represented by a shift from the historical to the idealistic view-point, which has been described above. Buddhas are no longer thought of as succeeding one another in time, but as being forms of one central principle. There is, therefore, only one buddha in essence, who historically is the Śākya-Sage and idealistically the buddha or whichever divinity appears at the centre of the mandala, e.g. Vairocana, Vajrasattva, Hevajra, Padmasambhava and all the rest. They are all equal in their consubstantiation in buddhahood. No well-instructed Buddhist has ever believed in a primordial buddha (*ādi-buddha*) as a sort of god-creator of the universe. But many Buddhists at all periods and in all places have clearly been liable to conceive of buddhas within the limited terms of their comprehension. Thus false notions of all kinds have continuously arisen, and Tibetan religion might be called the most debased of Buddhist traditions, just because it provides great scope for such falsifications. It is certainly the most complex of Buddhist traditions, but at the same time it is difficult to discover there anything which has not been worked to fit the Buddhist framework. The survey of tantric developments (Ch. II) has shown how very extended was this framework even before the Tibetans began to weave their patterns on it, and their elaborations do not so much distort the earlier forms as pervade them in a strangely subtle manner. Little as we know of the original p'ön-pos, there is sufficient evidence of the importance of celestial space in their religion (*gnam-gyi-chos*). It may seem too facile an association to recall the cold clear star-lit nights which are so typical of Tibetan travel. But it is this very notion of celestial space, which seems to colour the traditional Mahāyāna doctrine of the Universal Void. Thus proceeding one stage further, one observes that the divinities themselves, who become manifest in space and light, seem more than mere supports for meditation as allowed by orthodox belief, and assume the substance of those ancient gods, whom we have illustrated in the person of Thang-lha. It is this strange sense of real beings, who are conjured forth, which gives such impressiveness and fascination to Tibetan ceremonial. This impression is reflected in the mental disposition of many of the monks, who should 'know better', and is amply confirmed by the credulity of simple folk, who often have the most elementary grasp of the higher teachings. It is this credulity and a childlike delight in wonderment, which accounts for the popularity of stories of strange magical and psychic powers, which are attributed to renowned religious teachers, past and present.[a] But the influence works both ways, for if at one stage popular beliefs may suggest falsification of the higher concepts, at a later stage, when they are better integrated, they may themselves become the means for a new and equally valid expression of the same ideal. This had already been achieved in India by the tantric Buddhists, who had digested such heterogeneous material, that the indigenous beliefs of the Tibetans were afterwards absorbed with little difficulty. Thus it is often difficult to decide what elements in this religion are tantric Buddhist or just plain Tibetan. No other Buddhist tradition is so well integrated, and at the centre it preserves intact the essential notion of unpredicable buddhahood, which is the final goal of striving, to which all religious forms are ultimately subservient. The ideal of buddhahood has remained unchanged through the centuries. The changes which we have noted refer to the forms of expression and the means of realization, which have continually been elaborated and enriched. For those who are seriously interested in the practice of this doctrine, it would therefore be foolish to reject all later developments as spurious.

But although there has been so considerable a development in

[a] Mircea Eliade has demonstrated the confusion that exists popularly between spiritual perfection and the possession of super-human powers. He concludes by observing that 'at a certain "popular" level every master in the spiritual life comes to join the arch-type of the Great Magician, who has attained release in this very life (*jīvanmukta*) and is thus possessor of all powers (*siddhi*)'. *Le Yoga*, p. 294.

forms and methods of practice, the ideal life of a Buddhist still follows the same pattern. The counsel of perfection is always that of celibacy, of abandoning home for a homeless state. This is as true of the earliest period of the doctrine as of the Buddhists of Shar-Khumbu or anywhere in Tibet to this day.

Just as striking is the continuity in the cult which centres around the *stūpa* (chö-ten). From the earliest period to the present day, the stūpa has been the supreme symbol of the doctrine. Its form and its symbolism have developed: first a reliquary, then symbol of the sovereign-buddha, then expression of the immanence of buddhahood, identical in meaning with the mandala. It is found in all Buddhist countries in all periods, and if one might speak of Buddhist orthodoxy, its surest sign would be respect for the stūpa and a comprehension of its significance.

Buddhism has never been a kind of escapist philosophy, and rarely the kind of sage's paradise, as it is sometimes envisaged. Least of all is it the religion which is no religion, as some modernists have obtusely defined it, as though it could be divorced from the normal activities of this world as a sort of abstract quiescence. The council of Lhasa (see ch. IV) decided this question long ago, but the whole course of history provides an even more cogent argument, for Buddhism has moulded the traditions and customs of half the civilized world. Indeed a religion achieves very little unless it can permeate the whole life of a people, and I doubt if there is any country other than Tibet, where religion still exercizes so deep an influence. Civilization like culture cannot be a static condition. It depends for its existence upon an actively civilizing religious tradition, and that is the essential part that Buddhism has played. In this sense the Tibetans may be accounted the most civilized of men. Individually they may sometimes be brutal, unjust, self-seeking (as all men seem liable to be), but only by flouting the teachings that they know so well: 'The best of wealth is the wealth that one gives away' and all the other perfections besides. The significant fact is that they are individually capable of suddenly giving all away and pursuing the religious life. This is no uncommon event. Moreover a measure of the general sentiment is the vast generosity of these people where religion is concerned, and generosity is a preëminent virtue in a religion where the root-evil is selfish desire. There is no suggestion that the Tibetans are morally superior to other peoples, but rather that they are never lacking in a deep religious sense, which even in the case of the most villainous of characters expresses itself as fervent faith in the Three Precious Ones in time of trouble. This is no empty hypocrisy, but a religion working at its lower levels.

Tibet is often compared with the Europe of the Middle Ages simply on the basis of certain external resemblances, such as the power of the monasteries, the feudal nature of its society, the general conditions of life, 'the dirt, the disease, the poverty, the ignorance', but no one seems to have examined the root-cause of the resemblance. It is in short the acknowledged presence of a religious faith, which in both cases permeates the whole structure of society. The final expectation of society is directed towards another sphere of ineffable experience, and not, one might add, upon doubling one's standard of living within the next twenty years or so. Thus the dirt and disease, distressing as they are to any sensitive European, have no blighting effect upon the happiness of this people, for their joy springs from another level. One may also speak mistakenly of their poverty, for they are poor in the way that toilers of the soil have always been poor, and not in the sense of the soul-destroying poverty of nineteenth-century industrial England, which all too easily distorts our view of all that went before. As for their ignorance, one may observe that they still believe the world to be flat and arranged like a mandala with Mt. Meru at the centre and four continents at the four directions. One might compare the mediaeval conception of the world with its spacial conception of heaven and hell. There is a fundamental resemblance in the two systems, which somehow gets the better of the modern westerner with all his superior skill in the exact sciences. We might laugh at their curious and clumsy notions, but at least the Buddhists have never believed their schemes to be real. All that matters to them is not whether the world is round or square, but that it is transitory, relative through and through and so devoid of meaning in itself. It becomes endowed with meaning only in so far as by living in it one may attain to the condition of perfect changelessness, which is the source of all final happiness and the only worthy goal for man's higher striving. It is this faith in the changeless beyond the changing, which gives purpose to the life of man, and it is the existence of this faith that distinguishes what may be called a traditional civilization from the helpless instability of modern life, which (let it be confessed) remains civilized only so long as it may keep some slender hold upon the traditions of its own religious culture. This surely is the supreme service of studies such as ours. The life around us is becoming increasingly proficient in technological matters and increasingly indifferent to the art of living, as though it were something reserved for leisure time. If any balance in modern life is to be achieved, the wide-spread interest which now attends mechanical achievements must be matched by at least an equal interest and enthusiasm for the cultural and spiritual achievements of mankind.

APPENDIX

Spiti and Lahul, 1953

This appendix consists of two personal letters as written immediately after my return from this particular "adventure".

Manali
16th September 1953

I have returned to Manali after forty days of travel, having covered more than 300 miles on foot and on horse-back. Travel in these regions is very slow (15 miles is a very long day's journey), for the routes are no more than mountain-tracts while rivers are many and bridges are few. The only inhabited portions of Lahul and Spiti lie along the river valleys and it is these that the routes normally follow. The map of our travels [*see map p. 298*] does not show the many tributaries that pour into the main water-courses, and it is these that present most difficulty, for they are all fierce surging torrents. Sometimes it is possible to cross them by clinging to the pack animals and wading waist-deep in icy water; sometimes one must make a detour high up into the mountains until a suitable crossing-place is found; sometimes, but rarely in Spiti, there is a foot bridge, but a loaded pack-horse cannot cross, so these must be unloaded and everything man-handled, and then the horses led unwillingly across the narrow platform of planks and rushes. On one such occasion one of the horses took fright and struggled, then slipped and plunged into the torrent thirty feet below. It was carried far downstream before it succeeded in struggling onto the. rocks, and by then it lacked its harness and all its trappings. On another occasion when we were wading across, the horse to which I was clinging, wheeled and turned about in mid-stream, and the torrent was such that I could do no more than cling on, but he thus gave fright to the horse beside him, and this plunged and threw Ram Chand who was clinging to him, off his feet. He was completely drenched and terrified, but he managed to gain the other bank. Water was no friendly term in those days. The main river-valleys are linked by tracks across high passes. Thus in order to reach Spiti from Manali, one must either cross the Rohtang (13,000 ft) or the Hamtah (14,000 ft) Pass. Thence one must travel for three days up the uninhabited Chandra Valley, and then cross the Kunzang Pass of 14,900 ft to the head of the Spiti River, reaching Losar, the first village in Spiti on the sixth day of travel. To go from Spiti to Lahul there is but one pass to be crossed, but this is the Baralacha of 16,000 ft and this too takes six days from Losar to the first village in Lahul. Actually when one is once in Lahul or Spiti these heights are not so formidable, for the general level of the rivers themselves is above 10,000 ft and Dankhar, the most spectacular of Spiti villages is above 12,000 ft, while Kyibar lies at 13,400. All this is not without its affect upon the traveller, for the atmosphere is very rare, so that the sun burns with unmitigated fierceness by day, but as soon as it has set, it becomes suddenly very cold. I remember longing in the evenings that it would sink below the mountains, so there might be rest from its penetrating glare, and longing equally in the mornings that it would rise, so that once more we might be warm. It was therefore a fantastic journey, for these conditions are of course completely Tibetan. To the south beyond the main Himalayan Range, the monsoon rains have been falling in torrents, and the whole Beas Valley right up to the southern side of the Rohtang and Hamtah Passes is rich in luxurious vegetation. The atmosphere is hot and moist and everything teems with life. But once across these passes all is changed, for here very little rain can penetrate. In the Chandra Valley there is grass and there are shrubs and a few stocky trees, but along the Spiti River there is nothing, just sand and rocks and snow and sky. Sometimes the, erosive action of the water has produced fantastic shapes in the rocks and sand along the banks, so that one passes along rows of weird sentinel-like cones, and I used to wonder whether we were on the moon. At other times there was just dull monotony.

The villages appear wherever there is sufficient ground at a manageable slope along the river edge and where there are sufficient streams from above to provide irrigation. Barley is the staple crop, but wheat and maize are grown, in Losar and Hansi peas, in Kaze and Dankhar turnips and potatoes, and in Pho and Tabo little apricots. Again in the villages little willow-trees grow by the streams, and again in Pho and Tabo little firs and poplars. There is sufficient grazing for sheep and goats and dzos (an animal half-yak, half-cow) and horses. From these lists it may be deduced how meagre were the food-supplies available to my party—some vegetables, in two places peas, elsewhere turnips and potatoes, twice a cabbage (treat indeed) and once two eggs, provided by the only hen I saw in Spiti and presented by a kindly village headman, Meat was always difficult, because no one could afford to share an animal with me, and a whole sheep or goat was normally more that we could cope with. Once at DarLkhar the headman consented to go halves, and once at Losar, when we had six days of travel over the Baralacha Pass before us, I purchased the goat complete. These things were cooked with spices and butter and eaten with the rice and unleavened bread, prepared from the stocks we carried with us. When all else was lacking, there was always jam and a curry that could be prepared from dried peas. Then the villages used to present us with *tsamba*, barley roasted and ground and at its best not unlike "bemax", with curds and milk, with *chang*, a kind of barley-beer, and *arak*, a potent distillation of the latter, tea, salted and buttered in Tibetan style, was always being offered, and it was the normal drink in my own camp. We camped in Spiti all nights but three, for twice we were offered an empty house, and on one of the rare occasions when it rained, we used (with the headman's consent) a small temple. The buildings are all built of mud-bricks, supported by wooden struts and pillars, sometimes finely carved. The windows are just square holes, and there is never any chimney. For this reason alone my own tent was always to be preferred, for the smoke was intolerable. Everyone else however can converse happily in quite a dense concentration. The ground-floor consists of stables, pens and store-rooms, and above are the living-rooms, opening off a central courtyard. There is no need for a bathroom for it is not the custom to wash. This is a great pity, for how often are fine features ruined by sheer dirt. The men all wear long hair plaited in Tibetan style, and beads and ear-rings, so it was often difficult to distinguish a youth from a girl. They were all inquisitive, but friendly and very generous, and for them my camp served as a kind of travelling circus, for it was surrounded by onlookers during daylight hours, some of whom were ready to assist and fetch us things, seldom seeking for some reward. Old people would sit about and twirl their prayer-wheels, sometimes others would make music for me with a drum and trumpet, others would sit around the fire drinking *chang*, taking a simple interest in all our preparations.

So thus we travelled—along desolate tracks by day and halting every evening to camp alongside some village. My party consisted of Ram Chand, who was a disappointment, for he was very slow in thought and action, and of Kal Zang. After the first four days of travel I had no choice but to dismiss the monk from Lahul, whom I had engaged in Manali with his three packhorses. Both he and the animals were old, and quite unsuitable for such a journey (although he thought that the solution was to pay him extra because it caused him so much difficulty). I dismissed him nearby .i camp of nomads in the Chandra Valley, near which I ws camping, and accepted the proffered services of a younger fellow, who was camping there and had heard of the difficulties we had encountered that day through fault of the Lahuli monk. He had actually stranded Ram Chand and myself on the other side of a raging torrent, for while we were undressing and preparing to cross with the horses, he plunged with them into the water and was gone. Thereafter shouts were, of no avail, for they were drowned in the noise of the water. We had no choice but to make a long and weary detour up the mountain side, until a point was reached for a man to cross in safety: This detour took five hours, so the actual advance made in that day was negligible. This provided a just cause for terminating his services and taking on those of this Kal Zang. Nor have I ever made a more happy exchange, for he was perhaps the chief cause for the success of the whole trip. Apart from looking after his horses, he served as cook (and a very good one) and general servant. There was no task he would not undertake and he was never anything but cheerful. He was born in Kulu and his parents died when he was young, first his mother, then his father, when he was but twelve. So he ran away with his father's six horses (as he was an only son, they were rightfully his), joined other muleteers and engaged himself for transport work in their company. Thus he can neither read nor write and his world is limited to this region of transport. Yet I have never met a man, more intelligent, self-possessed and self-reliant. He is a Buddhist and his name means "Auspicious World-Age", and round his neck hangs a silver casket containing an image of Guru Rimpoche, who traditionally is supposed to have first established Buddhism in Tibet and is one of the chief "buddhas" of Tibetan religion.

I seem to have described adequately the general conditions of the trip and can now turn to specific happenings. Leaving Manali on August 1st, I crossed by the Rohtang Pass over to the Chandra Valley. For one proceeding towards Spiti, the Hamtah Pass offers a shorter route, but it is extremely steep on the southern side. Moreover if one crosses by the Rohtang, one can make use of the rest-house at Kote below the pass for one night and of that at Koksar the next night when one has crossed. We were in any case held up below the pass by 48 hrs of heavy and incessant rain (for until one crosses one is still at the mercy of the mosoon) and it would have been truly wretched if there had been no better shelter than my tent. From Koksar I moved up the Chandra River; the second day occurred the exchange of the Lahuli monk for Kal Zang, as above recounted. Owing to the shortness of this day's march, the next two were very long and tiring, so long indeed that we were forced to set up camp some three miles short of Losar, which we should properly have reached. We camped therefore close to some nomads who were able to supply us with some brushwood and some milk, our two chief daily requirements.

And thus the journey continued: through Losar to Kyoto, thence to Kyibar, which, is approached through a deep sandstone gorge, out of which one clambers to over 13,000 feet. In all these places there are small temples, which I systematically visited, but found nothing of special note.

From Kyibar, it is but three miles to the neighbouring village of Kyi, and here high above the village is the first monastery of importance. It is built on the crest of a ridge, the temples on the summit, and the cells of the monks, of whom there are some 125, placed higgledy-piggledy almost on top of one another down the steep incline. The whole compound is surrounded by a wall, so in past times it would have served as a very strong fortress. The buildings are all white-washed, and rising from the temple roofs are pinnacles in gold. I spent a long afternoon visiting the shrines and reading and talking with three of the elders. I now discovered that whereas it was very difficult to render myself comprehensible to then village-folk, to the monks my Tibetan was sufficiently intelligible. The dialect of Spiti differs very greatly from that of central Tibet, but many of the monks are widely travelled, have often studied at Lhasa or at Tashilünpo, and are therefore accustomed to ways of speech other than those of their own land. We drank tea, invocations were offered on my behalf, and then I departed.

Thence to Kaze, the chief village of Spiti; were dwells the Nono, for such is the title of the Prince of Spiti. My letter of introduction to him had proceeded me the previous day, and so that evening he called, and invited me to his house next day. His house lies across the Spiti River, which here spreads out into three wide and comparatively shallow streams. At this point it can therefore be forded and one need stiffer only the discomfort of cold water to ones thighs and some 300 yards of knobbly stones (rubber bathing sandals would be very useful in Spiti). But to spare us even this inconvenience, the Nono sent horses, and so we were able to splash happily through the water, led by his grooms. One of the pleasant features of being entertained in this land, is that ones followers are always entertained as well. I was simply provided with a more ample quantity of cushions, so that I there sat higher; my tea-cup would be provided with both silver-stand and lid, whereas Ram Chand's would have just a lid, and Kal Zang would have the bare cup. Food would be served to me on dishes of better quality and always in greater quantity. Apart from these marks of distinction, which applied of course to the Nono and his retinue as well, all conversed as equals together. And so we had the normal tea, then chang and arak, followed by rice, baked meat and mono. These last are the best of Tibetan dishes and we even made them on occasion in our camp. They are just minced meat (minced in these parts by grinding between stones), well spiced, then pressed into rounds of pastry, which are then sealed and steamed. We planned a festival at the nearby monastery of Tang-gyud for when I returned from my visit to Tabo, which would be in a week's time, and the Nono then proceeded to make use of this purely frivolous engagement to excuse himself from a court-case that he should have attended at Kyelang about that time. (Kyelang, the chief village of Lahul, is 20 days journey there and back from Kaze, and he just did not want to the bothered.) Moreover he asked me to write the letter of excuse. "It will have to be postponed, he said, and if they postpone it, it cannot be held until next year". This of course is quite true, for within a few weeks, snow and ice will close down on Spiti and all travel is stopped, but it well illustrates the tempo of life here, So after visiting his private temple and distributing presents to the children and the servants, we rode back through the water to our camp.

It was three days journey from Kaze to Tabo, for although the distance is but 31 miles, the last section from Pho onwards can be very troublesome. So was I told. On our return however we arrived in two days, but not without some effort. Such forcing of the pace never went without protest from Kal Zang, for it does not allow the horses time to graze sufficiently before dark. There was a tendency for both him and Ram Chand to keep the journeys short, and for me to attempt to reach the next objective as quickly as possible. Sometimes I would give way and sometimes insist on my plan, and all went well in the end. These routes are all defined in stages, which are known and accepted by all who travel, and one pays by the stage and not by the day, so the journey from Kaze to Tabo, whether completed in three days or two, still counts as three stages.

The goal of the next day's travel was Dankhar. This little village is built high up on the crest of a ridge overshadowing the Spiti River. It must owe its position to this fact alone, for it dominates the whole valley. The terraced fields are far far below, reaching down to the river. At the very summit is the old fort, now occupied by the village headman; below that are the ordinary houses, all built of mud and whitewashed in the normal style. On one side the ridge juts out over a precipice of some thousand feet or so, and on the top of this they have placed the monastery, so that one drops from one side of the courtyard into space. In past times the site would have been completely impregnable. It is approached from the Kaze side by a track that climbs up from the river and then traverses high up the side of the mountain, so that one moves round a great arc until the protruding ridge, on which the castle stands, is reached. The whole approach seemed so fantastic that for this occasion I was quite unaware of normal tiredness, and clambered up into the fort until progress was checked by a locked trap-door, then down again amongst the houses, now all quite deserted, for men and women alike were still at work in the fields far below. The track drops steeply down the other side of the ridge, and down below by a stream the others were already setting up camp. The head-man soon appeared and saw to it that we were brought milk and wood. He was a pleasant fellow whose features for once showed to advantage, for he was actually clean. He sat down by the fire to ask of our doings, and suddenly asked me how old I was, and his delight was extreme to find he was the same age as myself. So he send forthwith for a jar of *chang*, and by the time this was emptied, it was already dark, and my meal of curried potatoes and turnips and unleavened bread was eaten under the stars. He promised that meat should be found for us on our way back from Tabo. The next morning he escorted me up to the monastery; it is small, but the best I have seen so far, for its frescoes are of great age and beauty. I listed them and identified them as far as possible and photographed some, and then we clambered to an upper temple, up mud stairs, notched ladders and through trap-doors, as crazy a means ol access as one could imagine. This was an even more interesting visit and so the process of listing and photographing continued. Thence back to the camp-site, where all packing was done and the morning mal of rice, dried peas and curried potatoes awaited me. It was our regular practice to prepare two meals a day, and since we rose with first light at 5.30, a main meal was acceptable at 8.30 or so. Within an hour we would be on our way, usually reaching our destination between four and five, when an evening meal would be prepared. We usually halted half-way on the journey, made tea with the petrol-stove and I would eat a little *tsamba* or rice with milk. (It must be confessed on these occasions visions of other and more delicious picnic fare would sometimes appear to me, but in retrospect at least Spiti wins after all.)

From Dankhar one travels to Pho, remarkable for its many trees, willows and firs and poplars, in the shade of which we camped. We were visited at once by the village doctor (who relies for his cures on incantations and herbs) and invited to his home to drink tea. Carpeted seats were already prepared and Tibetan tea and biscuits (rare indeed in these parts) were served. Then followed the inevitable hang, cooked greens of two unidentifiable kinds, unleavened bread and apricots. Perhaps enough has now been written about food, and it will serve to show how one lives here.

The last section of the journey to Tabo is short but tiresome, as one has to unload the horses and man-handle all the baggage in order to get them along by the river, where the route presses against overhanging cliffs. So we took as travelling companions two monks who were going our way, and they were soon busy helping carry the boxes and bundles and bedding. The route here of course is most spectacular, but if one dwells on all these things in turn, this letter will never be finished.

We reached Tabo at midday and with the consent of the head-lama set up camp in the monastery enclosure, and while Kal Zang prepared refreshments, I went to have a preliminary inspection of the buildings. Now Tabo is the most important of all Spiti monasteries, for it was founded in the 11th century by one of the first great leaders of Buddhism in Tibet, Rinchen S'ang-po, and the original circle of divinities, used at that time in the ritual of mystic consecration, is still there intact. It is therefore an extraordinary sensation, when one knows this, to stand in the main temple amidst the Great Buddha Vairocana (Brilliance) and the 28 gods of his suite, who all sit cross-legged with individual expressions and gestures, around the four walls of the hall. Then at the end in a kind of sanctury sits the Great Buddha Amitabha (Boundless Light) with four standing attendants. The walls are all richly and wonderfully painted, suffering only from the effects of time. Nor is this all, for there is a large ante-chamber and elsewhere in the enclosure five smaller temples, all likewise painted. These buildings of course are all built of the normal mud-bricks with wooden supports, and there are many others, once the cells of the monks I suppose, which are now complete ruins. Elsewhere there are rows of *chotens*, also built of mud and in various stages of delapidation. The monks, 24 in number, seem to keep the main buildings in some kind of repair, but the rest must for long have been past all hope, and they now live outside the monastery enclosure. To be encamped within however made it possible for me to go round these temples again and again. Moreover morning and evening one heard the invocations to Vajrabhairava (the Fearful One), who is the tutelary divinity of the community. It was weird indeed to stand alone in that temple and listen to the rhythmical rising and falling of the recitations and the clashing of cymbals and thudding of drums. The second day of my stay nine of the monks danced for me in the parts of Vajrabhairava and his fearful following with hideous masks and gorgeous silks. This was by far the best of my visits.

The third day we left and returned via Dankhar (where the headman welcomed us at once with a large jar of *chang* and provided meat as he had provided, and the next evening, very tired, we reached Kaze. How tedious had been the last three hours of travel!

The next day was fixed for the visit with the Nono to the Tang-gyud Monastery nearby, nearby in the sense that it could be reached in some two hours of incredibly steep climbing. It was the steepest track that I have ever ascended (as distinct of course from real rock-climbing) and we used horses to do it, but this necessitated dismounting continually in order to lead them up difficult pitches. As we approached we were greeted by the sound of trumpets and cymbals and conch-shells from the monastery-roofs; then we entered through the gate-way, where the two chief lamas presented white-scarfs of greeting. We were conducted to one of the temples where carpets were spread and low tables set with tea-caps and bowls. Tea was served, and (to the laymen) *chang* and *arak* and then bowls of hot *momo* appeared. Fun as it might seem, this place was a great disappointment, for the monks, even the head-lama, seemed ignorant and unlettered, and of their own tutelary divinity Hevajra, in whom I have a special interest, they had not even an image. They could not answer simple questions and their spelling of names was so incorrect, that at my protesting, the Nono himself took over, and wrote, I was pleased to discover, most perfect Tibetan. A name, if but spoken and quite unfamiliar, needs also to be written, before it can be rightly understood, for in Tibetan, so many words are pronounced in similar fashion that only the spelling can give the real sense. One always knows if the spelling one is given is plausible or not; but here they produced impossible combinations of letters. Likewise the dance that followed, although entertaining enough, was without any ascertainable significance, and so pleasant as the day had been, it was in fact the most useless of visits.

From Kaze we returned to Losar in four days, this time south of the river. It was during this journey that we had our first rain and after a very wet night and miserable morning, we arrived in a light drizzle on the third evening at Hansi. Here we established ourselves on the headman's suggestion in a small secondary temple. I occupied the temple itself while the two men spread themselves in the circumambulatory passage, in the corner of which they did the cooking. It really was the most wretched of shelters, for the enormous prayer wheel and butter-lamps were of little consolation when billows of smoke come in from hitherto unnoticed (it was very dark inside) holes that pierced the wall between the temple and the passage. But by now the whole village seemed to have gathered without, awaiting my emergence, and this time I did not feel like being the centre of interest, but the smoke left no choice, so we sat in the passage, now packed tight by all who could manage to get in, and so the evening passed. It was by no means without interest, for they brought me books to see (and buy if I wanted them) and at my request a carpet too, over which we bargained hard, finally leaving the issue unsettled until the following day.

Early next morning an old man appeared who said he must see me alone, and when we were inside he produced from his cloak a beautiful little Śâkyamuni Buddha in moulded silver. This he wanted to sell, he said, but no one must know, and so the image passed into my possession at slightly more that half the price he first asked. We next went to drink tea with the village-headman and the carpet of last evening turned out to be his. On my expressing regret that the design was not greatly to my liking, a monk who was there said that he had a small carpet, much smaller than this, but that the design was far superior, and so he went and fetched it. It was a superb little thing, and so bargaining began all over gain. As we left the headman's house, a servant came from the doctor's, who said we must drink tea there before leaving, so thither we repaired, where between other conversation, an agreement was finally reached. So henceforth my tent has been resplendent with a Tibetan dragon-carpet of many colours.

The track takes one to the bank opposite Losar and then leaves one to wade unhappily through three wide streams, into which the river is here divided. While we were resting with the horses, contemplating this prospect, a black horse on the far bank, gave a loud neigh, plunged into the water and crossed to our side, where he tried—quite unsuccessfully—to make friends with our three. But he was determined to persist at all costs, and so when we started, I climbed on his back and holding his mane, crossed the water in comfort. Now I had decided to add a fourth horse to our party, for it was my intention to ride over the Baralacha and through Lahul, where the route is much better, so when it proved impossible to hire a horse in Losar, it was arranged that Kal Zang should buy the black horse. He was altogether a successful purchase, and he was of so friendly and yet independent a disposition, that I am sorry it has not been practicable to keep him. But all this anticipates. In any case no business of any kind could be done that day, for the villagers had been having a fair, and men and women alike were all too drunk to be serious, so that day not even milk and wood were procurable', let alone the other provisions we needed for the six days' journey over the pass. By twelve next day however a goat had been slain and cut into joints, sufficient firewood for five days had been brought and sufficient milk for two. Fortunately in Hansi we had been given potatoes and turnips, for here in Losar nothing else was to be had. For our lodging that night however we had used a small empty house, that stood alone by a willow-grove, just below the little temple, and apart from the smoke, which it was possible to keep away from my room, it proved a very pleasant situation.

Thus soon after twelve we left together with the black horse, who was happy to follow his new-found companions, whatever indifference they might show him. That day's journey was very short, for we camped at the place where the track forks, the route to the left leading up over the Kunzang Pass whence we had previously come and that to the right towards the Baralacha Pass, whither we were bound. It was pleasant to be camping right in the midst of the mountains with no spectators (however friendly) to cope with. And so this lonely journey continued; the next day we passed the desolate Chandratal (the Moon Lake) and there met some shepherds grazing vast numbers of sheep, until high up above the Chandra gorge we established camp on a small grassy stretch midst the smell of wild mint. This evening was even more pleasant than the last. The following day we continued up the valley until at 4 pm we were brought to a halt by a tributary torrent, which was too deep and fast-flowing to cross, so we decided to camp there, although the site was not good, hoping that in the early morning (before the sun had melted the snows and this new water had caused the rivers to rise) the flood would be less. Our hopes were fulfilled, for although there was still a great deal of water, it was possible to negotiate it, and so by 1.30 we gained the top of the pass. There is grass there and many kinds of beautiful flowers which live here between 14,000 and 16,000 feet, and there are high snow peaks to left and right. It is an exciting place, for three tracks join at the top, that to Ladakh, 10 days distant, that from Spiti and that to Lahul, where we were now going, but this begins another chapter.

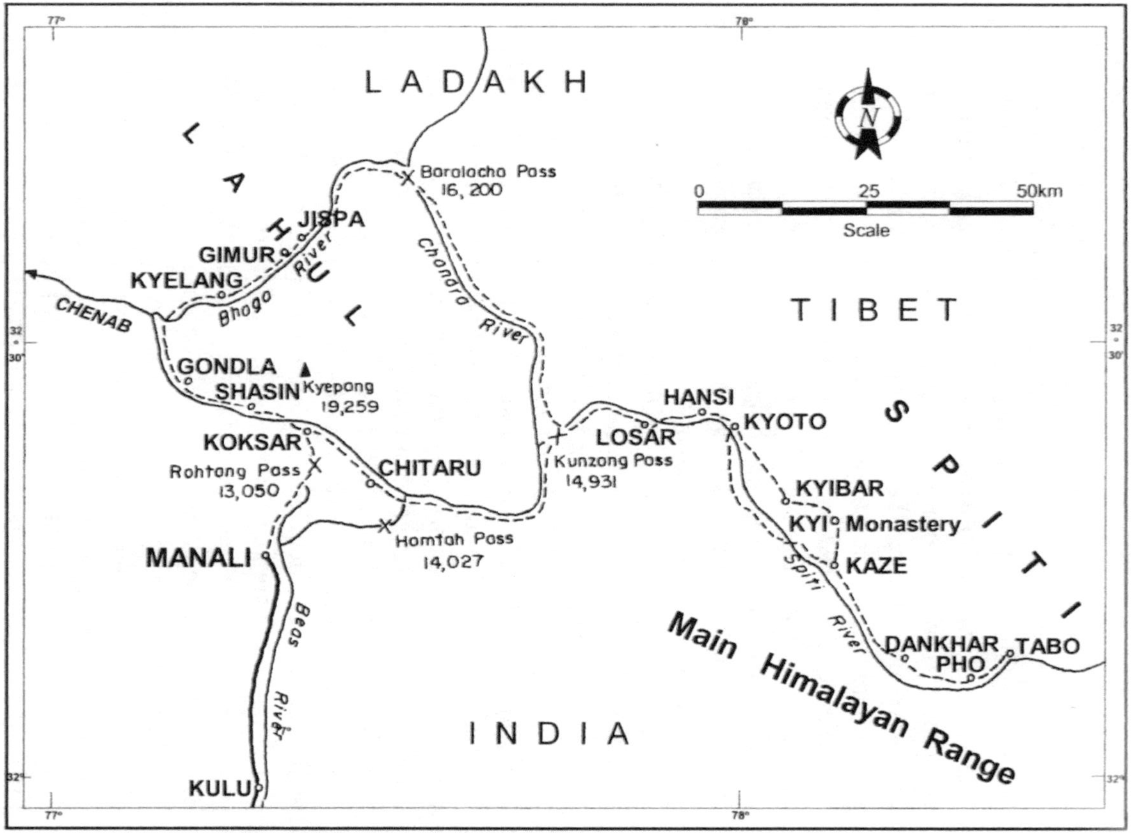

Journeys in Spiti and Lahul

SPITI AND LAHUL 1953

Hotel Cecil
Delhi
27th September 1953

The inhabited part of Lahul just consists of the valleys of the Bhaga and Chandra Rivers in their lower reaches, and of the Chenab River which those two unite to form. It is an interesting experience to enter a country side by side with one of its main water systems and to see the barren rocks gradually turning into grass slopes, then little juniper trees appearing, then the first little village surrounded by its fields, then more and even larger trees so that at last one was riding through a forest, then the villages of Jispa and Gimur and houses and fields on one side of the river or other most of the way to Kyelang. There was also a gradual increase in life and activity.

Lahul is quite different from Spiti and one climbs down into a more fertile world, where some of the amenities of modem life have found their way. For it is far more accessible from the Kulu Valley, from which it is separated only by the Rohtang Pass and some 40 miles of well-kept track. Down the Bhaga River and up the Chandra as far as Koksar there are situated government rest-houses, where one can put up in sufficient comfort for the night, so that our camping days were over. Food was obtained with far greater ease, for vegetables of several kinds were available and even eggs (which with the addition of wild thyme became delicious omelettes aux fines herbes), while in Kyelang there are actually shops (in Spiti there is no shop), where tea and sugar and biscuits and jam and other things to delight weary wanderers whose supplies are running low.

Our progress was very slow. Jispa had been reached on the 6th day since leaving Losar and all this time we had been high up amidst, desolate mountains, and now it was pleasant to gradually come back to human life again. Three miles below Jispa is the little village of Gimur and above it a monastery, the first when one comes from the north. As we were riding through the village we met the Thakur of Khangsa surrounded by a whole concourse of people, all on the way to some local election, where the five elders for the village were to be chosen. The Thakurs are the barons of Lahul, who until recent times were petty tyrants. They now continue to exist as the chief land-owners. They are all related, and I have met four of them out of a total of some six or seven. They have three main seats, great fortresses of mud and wood, gorgeously adorned in the main apartments with rugs and silks. The Thakur of Khangsa (one mile below Gimur) was the first to be met. He greeted me as a friend from whom he had been parted for years and invited me to stay that night at his house, suggesting that while he attended the elections, I should visit Gimur monastery, which I according did, while the luggage and horses proceeded to his house.

At the monastery I found his uncle, the Thakur of Gimur, who is of a very religious disposition, supervising the monks who were busy painting. I admired their work, which was spoiled only by the garishness of the paints they are now forced to use, for the proper Tibetan pigments cannot be obtained here. Their monastery was also notable for the possession of a very fine image of the Great Buddha Vajradhara, which I successfully photographed. Thence we clambered across to the Khangsa Fort, which externally is best illustrated by its photograph, up the crazy stairs and some four storeys or so, until I was shown into the main sitting room, spread with superb Tibetan carpets, and furnished with cushions and low Tibetan carved tabled. Everyone was still away, except for a few of the servants, and these brought me rice and spiced potatoes and peas, sugared apricots and a bottle of *arak*, which had the flavour of a passable brandy.

At six o'clock the Thakur himself (his name is Pratap Chand) returned from the elections, bringing with him some twelve guests. *Arak* was pressed upon them, musical instruments—a drum, a trumpet and a small harmonium were sent for, and soon every one was dancing the local folk-dances. This spontaneous jollification continued until 9 pm, where more food was served and so to bed.

The next day I continued to Kyelang, accompanied on my way by some of the dancing party. Here I stayed in the bungalow of the Thakur (apart from his Khansa Fort, he has houses of one kind or another at all convenient places); this he had lent me, for I had been warned that Kyelang was so filled with Indian police and officials, that the rest-house would be already full. This was quite true.

In Kyelang we tarried four days, and I visited the fort of the Gungrang Thakur nearby and the four chief monasteries of importance. Only the fort contained something of interest, for in the one of its chapels are figures from the same cycle of divinities that are to be found at Tabo, and they are certainly of very great age - probably 900 years. Elsewhere everything was well-kept and recently painted, so that traces of the past have disappeared. You will tire of accounts of the usual tea drinking that took place at these visits, and so I may pass briefly over our stay at Kyelang.

Thence we continued by steady stages. At Gondla I visited the Thakur in his fort, and at Shashin the god Kyephang in his temple. This last is an interesting character, for he is the one non-Buddhist divinity of power and importance, who survives from very ancient times. His real home is on the mountain-top above the village, but he has been given these quarters in the village at the foot, so that his paraphernalia is conveniently to hand. He has no image, but is represented by a stick with silk wrapped around it and with a small silver umbrella on top. In the course of the year he is offered a large number of goats, which provide a ceremonial banquet for all who care to be present.

We continued to Koksar, back across the Rohtang Pass, and down to Manali. One needs to descend but a short distance below the pass, and one is back in India once more. One is conscious so soon of heat and moisture, to which the thick vegetation bears witness. By comparison with Spiti, Lahul had seemed fertile, but in comparison with the valleys south of the main Himalayan Range, it becomes barren again.

This was the end of the journey, of which Spiti had been the chief and best part. Its discomforts were at once forgotten, and within 24 hours I was wondering if I might return there once more. But it would have to be another year. These two passes, the Rohtang and the Hamta, are open only from June to November. The rest of the year they are sealed with snow and ice and completely cut off from Manali. The Baralacha Pass is likewise scaled, so Spiti is separated for most of the year from Lahul as well.

I spent ten days at Manali to get things in order and deal with correspondence, and have arrived now in Delhi once more to prepare for fresh ventures.

AUTHOR'S LATER NOTE

Following upon Giuseppe Tucci's *Indo-Tibetica*, vol. III, part I (frequently referred to in my foot-notes, p. 174 onwards), the only later work of substance dealing with Lahul and Spiti is that of Romi Khosla, *Buddhist Monasteries in the Western Himalaya*, Ratna Pustak Bhandar, Kathmandu, Nepal 1979.

NOTES

For books mentioned see Bibliography pp. 303–5

1. Watters, *On Yuan Chwang's Travels in India*, I, 113 ff. On the spelling of Yuan Chwang's name see the introductory note by Rhys Davids, I, xi–xiii. Since W's edition is my main source of reference, I shall adhere to this spelling throughout except when other references are given. See also St. Julien, *Histoire de la vie de Hiouen Thsang* (Paris 1853); *idem*, *Mémoires sur les contrées occidentales*, 2 vols. (Paris 1857–8); S. Beal, *The Life of Hiuen Tsiang* (London 1911). For a generally informative presentation of Yuan Chwang's travels see R. Grousset, *In the Footsteps of the Buddha* (London 1932), being a translation of his *Sur les traces du Bouddha* (Paris 1929).

2. His experience of his first trance had occurred while his father was performing the ceremonial ploughing and he himself was seated nearby beneath a rose-apple tree. (Thomas, *Life*, pp. 44–5.) Mlle. Falk regards the extreme simplicity of this incident as a sign of its great age. 'Even if we cannot be absolutely sure of having before us an incident from the historical biography of Gotama, it would seem certain that it belonged to the proto-buddhistic biographical legend. Enlightenment did not spring from the spiritual conquests accumulated throughout innumerable aeons, but from the recapturing of a youthful experience; it did not spring from super-human powers, but from the spontaneous grace of joyous ecstasy' (*Il Mito Psicologico, p. 572*).

3. Belief in rebirth is axiomatic from the early doctrinal period onwards. There are, however, traces in early texts of another world-view, e.g. 'Faith, morality and charity, these are the things that wise men praise. This is the divine path, they say, and by means of it one reaches heaven' (*Udānavarga*, X. 1). See also the *Dhammapada* I. 17 and 18. This straight-forward morality, which promises a good future (*sugati*) for the good and a bad future (*durgati*) for all the bad one has done, is an essential part of the 'Good Law'. Good future and bad future are later interpreted as the upper and lower parts of the wheel of life (see pp. 15–17), but since the whole wheel is essentially wretched, there is a certain contradiction involved in calling part of it good. This contradiction persists throughout the whole history of the doctrine. We are told at the end of the after-death ceremony, as it is still performed in Tibet, that its sure effect will be to release the deceased one from existence and from an evil future (*durgati*). One can of course always interpret this last term to suit the context, but one is led to wonder what may have been the force of *sugati* and *durgati* in the earliest period, possibly before the doctrine of universal misery was formulated and certainly before the early philosophers set

to work. For a general summary of views on the pre-canonical period, see Schayer, 'New Contributions to the Problem of Pre-hīnayānist Buddhism'.

4. The early Buddhists inevitably engaged in polemics with the followers of other religious disciplines, admitting their ability to attain to all stages in the deepening of trance, but denying their experience of the final condition of nirvāna. The terms defining the types of practice (e.g. the four *brahma*-abodes) and the stages of trance (*dhyāna*) were in any case common property. Only *nirvāṇa* came to be accepted as a specifically Buddhist term, so that it was placed above and beyond those categories of religious experience, which were common property. In this sense it is purely a distinction of terminology. Mlle. Falk has conclusively demonstrated the origin of Buddhist religious experience in the general context of the Upanishads and nothing is to be discovered concerning the nature of nirvāna by a study of sets of stereotyped stages. Such a study is interesting but inconclusive. See Günther, *Seelenproblem*, e.g. pp. 94 ff. At all stages of its development, Buddhism has remained part of Indian religious experience. See Przyluski, 'Buddhisme et Upanishad', *BEFEO*, xxxii, 141 ff.; de la Vallée Poussin, 'Vedānta and Buddhism', *JRAS*, 1910–1, 129 ff.; *idem*, 'Le Bouddhisme et le Yoga de Patanjali', *MCB*, v, 223 ff., where a bibliography is given. Also Stcherbatsky 'Rapports entre la théorie bouddhique de la connaissance et l'enseignement des autres écoles philosophiques de l'Inde', *Muséon*, 1904, 129 ff. For a general discussion of Buddhist yoga see Eliade, *Le Yoga*, 862 ff. The only satisfactory attempt at demonstrating the superiority of the Buddhist nirvāna is that of Heiler (*Die Buddhistische Versenkung*). 'When one speaks of *nirvāṇa* in the west, one usually understands something which in its greatness is entirely other-worldly and transcendentally eschatological. But like the Christian conception of the Kingdom of God, the greatness of *nirvāṇa* is as much this-worldly as other-worldly. The religious hope which is directed towards the other world is ever the potential form of the salvation which is longed for in this world' (p. 37). This would certainly be an adequate interpretation of the religious aspirations of the Mahāyāna, but is it universally true of the nirvāna of the early disciples? There is a certain basis for the claim in the undeniably moral character of the earliest Buddhism which we know of (see note 3), for right conduct (*śīla*) is an essential part of the training. Although the same may be said of much non-Buddhist practice, all Buddhism is generally permeated by it (even after tantric notions had been incorporated) and in the theory of the bodhisattva, it certainly achieves its most noble form. See my discussion of Buddhist morality in *Springs of Morality* (Burns Oates, London 1956), Ch. XIX.

5. Absence of knowledge (*avidyā*) is understood by Foucher (*La Vie du Bouddha*, p. 166) in the sense of 'inconnaissabilité'. 'C'est du font de l'Inconnu—c'est de l'*Invu*, comme disent toujours les pandits.' One may well think of the famous 'Hymn of Creation' (Macdonnel, *Vedic Reader*, *OUP*, 207–

11): 'Who truly knows, who may here declare, whence it has been produced and whence is this creation?' But in fact the answer has already been given in a preceding verse: 'Sages seeking in their hearts with wisdom, etc.' Note the interpretation of Mlle. Falk (*Mito Psicologico*, p. 311): 'Searching in the profundity of his own heart, the sage has seen, what no divinity perhaps can see: it was not the cosmic power of *māyā* that was operative before the beginning of the cosmos, but the psychological power of *tapas*.' See also her comment on the instruction which Pañcaśikha gives to King Janaka (p. 352): 'But there are some who say that ignorance is the cause in a new existence of the karmic processes, and that like desire and agitation, it binds one to evil.' These, without any possibility of error, are the buddhists or their precursors, who saw in ignorance the immediate cause of the samsāra.' It would be odd indeed if the enthusiasm of nascent Buddhism were based upon a mere realization of final uncognizability. The agnosticism which characterizes some of the sayings attributed to the Śākya-Sage, is applicable only to the sphere of philosophical disputation. See following note.

6. See E. J. Thomas, *Early Buddhist Scriptures*, pp. 192–99. Of special interest is the story of Vacchagotta's enquiries concerning the existence or non-existence of a self (*ātman*) (*Saṃyuttanikāya*, iv. 400). He was greeted by silence, and afterwards the sage explained to Ānanda, that had he told Vacchagotta that it existed, it would not have assisted him in realizing that 'all the elements are self-less'. If on the other hand he had told him that it did not exist, his mental confusion would have been worse than before. Günther quotes this (*Seelenproblem*, pp. 25–6) as evidence for his argument that the Śākya-Sage denied the existence of a 'self' only in so far as it might be identified as a real thing in a phenomenal sense. This theory certainly becomes plausible in the light of the extremely materialistic nature of the philosophical categories of the early schools. Günther's study is most helpful in this slightly enlarged context.

7. For a discussion of this theory of time and the difficulties involved in it see Schayer, *Contributions to the Theory of Time in Indian Philosophy*, Krakow 1938, pp. 18 ff.

8. Again Günther has drawn attention to an early text, which manifestly presupposes later developments: 'That which is known as eye, ear, nose, tongue, body, that regarded as the self is inconstant, not firm, not eternal, subject to destruction; but that which is known as thought, mind, consciousness, that, regarded as self, is constant, firm, eternal and not subject to destruction, and will therefore always remain the same' (*Dīghanikāya* I. 21; *Seelenproblem*, p. 85).

9. see *Bu-tön*, II, 46 ff. The theory of the three philosophies has been propounded by Stcherbatsky: 'Die Drei Richtungen in der Philosophie des Buddhismus', *Roc. Or.*, vol. 10, pp. 1 ff. These categories are quite valid so far as they go, but they are referable only to the main philosophical develop-

ments of the first thousand years of canonical Buddhism. The history of Buddhism is not just a history of philosophy. See Schayer, 'Precanonical Buddhism', *Archiv Orientalní*, 7 (1935), 121–34.

10. see Eliade, *Histoire des Religions*, pp. 321 ff. For a comparison of the Buddhist and Christian 'centres' see de Lubac, *Aspects of Buddhism* (being a translation of his *Aspects du Bouddhisme*, Paris 1951), ch. 2. For the symbolism of the pillar see Przyluski, 'Le Pilier de Sarnāth', *Mélanges Linoissier*, II, 481–98. Also Mus, *Borobuḍur*, Part 4, ch. III, 145 ff.

11. It is all but impossible to find a satisfactory translation for *nirmāṇakāya* which means literally 'creation-body'. But the notion of creation has no part in Buddhism. It refers to any sort of body, physically manifest, which for practical purposes is always human. Translations such as manifestation-body, emanation-body, are unsatisfactory, for these define equally well the *sambhogakāya,* which is merely manifest in another sphere. The problem of *nirmāṇa* in fact illustrates the fact that the applied meaning of a term is not always to be discovered by philological means. Mus has attempted this in the case of *sambhoga* (*Borobuḍur,* Part 6, ch. VII, 648–62) and his discussion of the problem has influenced my choice of translation, 'Reciprocal Enjoyment', but I also have in mind its appropriateness, so far as the set of Five Buddhas is concerned. 'Theirs are *sambhoga*-bodies, free of apertures, flesh and bones, pure light and naught else, like reflections in a mirror and free from such concepts as truth and falsehood' (*Advayavajra-saṃgraha,* p. 42, ll. 5–7; *Buddhist Texts,* p. 251). They are of the nature of the other buddha-bodies just be implication. In practice the *sambhoga*-body comes to be equated with the divine nature of the great Indian gods, for Avalokiteśvara and Padmanarteśvara are its typical representatives. see pp. 228 and 235.

If comparisons are helpful, one might think in terms of the *dharma-kāya* as impersonal god-head, the *sambhoga-kāya* as personal god and the *nirmāṇa-kāya* as the divine saviour in human form, remembering always, however, that the whole context of Buddhism is essentially different from that of Christianity.

12. The actual discovery that Buddhism originated in India seems to be attributable to Jesuit missionaries of the late seventeenth century. See de Lubac, *La Rencontre du Bouddhisme et de l'Occident*, pp. 116–7.

13. see Bourda, 'Quelques réflections sur la pose assise à l'européenne dans l'art bouddhique', *Art. As.*, xii (1949), 302–13.

14. *MMK, skr.*, p. 133, *tib. Nr. Kj. rgyud,* xi, fol. 245*a* f. This buddha is actually named Tathāgata Ratnaketu (Jewel-Comet) and it might seem more suitable to relate him with Ratnasambhava of the Jewel Family. But the stage has not yet been reached for the definition of buddhahood as five-fold, and thus the constituent elements of sovereignty, light, power, are inevitably intermingled. It is important now merely to note that it is first Vairocana who comes to the fore as sovereign-buddha. See *Bu-tön*, II, 69.

15. From his conviction of the universality of certain basic religious concepts Przyluski has attempted to find in Maitreya a Buddhist version of Mitra, basing his argument largely on the title 'Invincible' that pertains to both of them ('La Croyance au messie dans l'Inde et l'Iran', *RHR*, vol. 100 (1929), pp. 1–12). Lévi has held to the same view ('Maitreya le Consolateur' *Mélanges Linoissier*, II, 355–402). Filliozat, however, has argued, I think conclusively, the basic Indian nature of Maitreya ('Maitreya, l'*Invaincu*', *JA*, 1950, pp. 145–9). In this as in other aspects of Buddhism, Iranian influence has not been so much formative as conditioning. India absorbs and reinterprets so readily, that it was difficult indeed to teach her anything essentially new. Thus while it may be possible that the conditioning idea of a saviour-hero came from Iran, the development of the idea proceeded entirely in accordance with Buddhist theory. Similarly a Buddha named Boundless Light suggests at once an Iranian origin, but he is a buddha none the less, and there is nothing in later developments to suggest anything heterodox in his nature or his function. One might identify the whole five-buddha system as non-Indian in origin, but it can be understood only within the terms of reference of Indian Buddhism. See also note 18.

16. Mlle. Lalou establishes a connection in myth between Mañjuśrī and the Gandharva Pañcaśikha and Kārttikeya Kumārabhūta (*Iconographie des étoffes peintes dans le Mañjuśrīmūlakalpa*, pp. 66 ff.). Mlle. Falk finds a plausible historical connection between the Pañcaśikha of the *Maitri-upanishad* and the earliest Buddhists (*Il Mito Psicologico*, p. 560).

17. see Takakusu, 'Le Voyage de Kanshin en orient (742–54)', *BEFEO* xxviii, 1–2, p. 24 fn.

18. Mlle. Mallmann has gathered together most usefully a great deal of information concerning Avalokiteśvara: *Introduction a l'étude d'A.*, but seemingly resolved to find an Iranian origin for him, she proposes an unlikely interpretation of his name, suggesting that he too is a solar divinity. Once again this has been countered by Filliozat, Avalokiteśvara d'après un livre récent', *RHR*, cxxxvii (1950), pp. 44–58.

19. The basic meaning of *maṇḍala* is circle or sphere. In the context of religious ritual it refers primarily to a circumscribed area which is rendered safe from hostile influence for the performance of the rite. Since the worshipper or practiser operates through his divinity, it represents the sphere into which the divinity is summoned. It is thus a centre of power. With the equating of divinity and sovereignty, it comes to be identified with the sovereign's palace and develops into the palace of the divinity, conventionally represented with gates to the four points of the compass. For a brief but complete study see Tucci, *Teoria e Pratica del Mandala*. See also note 10.

20. 'Guarantee', skr. *samaya*, tib. *dam-tshig*. This is a constantly recurring term in the tantras and it seems impossible to find a fixed translation for it.

The basic notion is that of a bond, that is to say between the divinity and his devotee. This is precisely how the four buddhas of the direction should be envisaged, for as heads of the families to which the practisers belong, they become the guarantees of consubstantiation in buddhahood. In ritual the divinity may be represented by a sacrificial offering. This too is a 'guarantee', and in this case the term might be better translated as 'sacrament'. It is convenient to note also two compound words based on *dam-tshig*, for which I know no proper Sanskrit equivalent. One is *yi-dam* (which stands for skr. *devatā*, divinity, or more explicitly, *ishtadevatā*, chosen divinity) meaning 'thought-guarantee', for it is by the concentrated direction of thought, that the monk seeks unity with his chosen divinity, who is for him the guarantee of buddhahood. The other word is *dam-can* (pron. t'am-cen), which refers to a very different class of divinity, those who 'possess the bond', viz. those who have bound themselves to serve the doctrine in the rôle of protector. See pp. 242–4.

21. In so far as she is the expression of Wisdom, she is also known as *vidyā* (knowledge), for she is the formal representation of the spell (*mantra*) of the divinity. Thus the spell is regularly feminine in form, e.g. *vajra-sattvī*, *ratna-sattvī*, etc. (p. 68). Moreover the spell itself is also given form as a hand-gesture. Thus it comes about that the yoginī is also known as the Symbol (*mudrā*) with which she is theoretically identical and which she actually replaces in the rite involving sexual symbolism. 'This is the "bond" (*samaya*) of all mantras, which is indefeasible. He becomes in that very moment the peer of Vajrasattva, a Sovereign, in whom reposes all *dharma*, one who achieves release through desire. Even thus with thought directed to the adamantine *dharma*, the practiser *should use as his effect* (*sādhayet*) this lovely maiden, fair-faced, wide-eyed.' (*Guhyasamāja-tantra*, p. 94, ll. 16–20.)

22. Lévi notes another name for this shrine, *viz*. *Khāsācaitya*. The name in use, however, seems to be *Khāsticaitya*. This was explained as meaning the Shrine of the Dew-Water (from *khasu*, dew; *ti*, water). While the building was in progress, the water for mixing became exhausted owing to drought, but by spreading a cloth at night and squeezing the dew from it in the morning, sufficient water was obtained to finish the stūpa. So much for a popular etymology.

23. This Tibetan text, also available at Bodhnāth, is the *bal-yul mchod-rten 'phags-pa-shing-kun dang de'i gnas gzhan rnams kyi dkar-chag*.

24. It is noteworthy that whereas Svayambhūnāth is mentioned in Tibetan historical works as an historical site, which was visited for instance by Atīśa in A.D. 1140, Bodhnāth is only mentioned in relationship with the legend which has been quoted. This suggests that it was founded as a Tibetan shrine at some later date, when Buddhism was so well established in their country, that the Tibetans could begin to take an interest in past traditions and found shrines in other lands. It is certainly the most recent

of all the great shrines of Nepal, being in existence some time before the fourteenth century.

25. Towards the end of the seventh century I-Tsing observed that 'in great monasteries in India, at the side of a pillar in the kitchen or before the porch, (there is) a figure of a deity carved in wood, two or three feet high, holding a golden bag and seated on a small chair with one foot hanging down towards the ground. Being always wiped with oil, its countenance is blackened, and the deity is called Mahākāla or the great black deity. The ancient tradition asserts that he belonged to the beings of the Great God (Maheśvara = Śiva). He naturally loves the Three Precious Ones and protects the five assemblies from misfortune' (I-Tsing, *A Record of the Buddhist Religion*, trsl. by J. Takakusu, Oxford 1896, p. 38). Subsidiary figures and divinities, which seem to have adorned the shrines from early times, came to be conceived of as worshippers and defenders. The *yaksha* were probably the first to be co-opted (see note 33), and clearly there was nothing to limit this convenient practice, which enables folk to remember the old gods, while paying their respect to the buddhas and the monastic communities.

26. This was indicated long ago by F. W. Thomas (*JRAS*, 1906, I, p. 464). and the discussion was carried further by Sten Konow (*JBORS*, 1925, pp. 1–13) who pointed out that this six-syllabled mantra is a *vidyā*, in the full sense of being represented as a feminine partner. See also note 21. In so far as Tārā becomes the partner of Avalokiteśvara, she becomes of course identifiable with the *vidyā*. This seems to be the solution of the problem, and there is no justification for splitting the compound into such a phrase as 'jewel in the lotus', for which a meaning can as always quite easily be found. The Tibetans know of several interpretations of these six syllables, one of which is quoted above (see p. 237), but these throw no light on the original significance. If questioned, they say it is just the mantra of Avalokiteśvara, which is certainly so, and with analogous feminine forms to compare it with, there is really no cause for surprise.

27. It is difficult to be precise about the significance of the term *bon-po*, when the Tibetans themselves use it in so general a sense. Tucci (*Ind-Tib.*, I, 69) and more recently Hoffmann ('Zur Literatur der Bon-po', *ZDMG*, 94, 1940, p. 174) have drawn attention to its different applications. In fact it is applied both to aboriginal religious practice, still extremely active in Himalayan districts, and to the developed form of the religion, which has organized itself by shameless borrowing from Buddhism. The former is nowadays chiefly characterized by belief in local and personal spirits of different kinds. Some people are liable to be 'possessed' by a spirit, which often remains unidentified and may even be unwanted by the person concerned. I had once a Tamang porter who was afflicted in this manner, and after such a bout, during which he sat gabbling and foaming at the mouth, he would be left weakened

and distraught. At Kumjung in Khumbu, there is a man who makes his living by such 'possession', for he is believed to be capable of giving advice in trouble, of diagnosing illness, of locating lost articles, etc. One may call this a type of shamanism, but to define the real basis of such beliefs is difficult, when the people themselves are so vague on the subject. During my stay in Khumbu, I was once asked by a villager to locate some turquoises which he had lost. 'But how should I be capable of that?'—'Because we know you are always looking at books' was the reply. The most prominent feature of this 'aboriginal' religion is the cult of mountain-gods and 'lords of the soil', (see page 176), and another firm connection with the past is found in the actual names of the different spirits, lu (*klu*), dre (*'dre*), pho-lha (*idem*), drap-lha (*dgra-lha*), shen-dre (*shi-'dre*). So far as the early Tibetan period is concerned, religious beliefs seem to centre round the divine origin of the king, but it is probably only later that these are stigmatized as *bon-po*. In the *Padma Thang-yig* (fol. 162*b*, ll. 5–6; Toussaint, pp. 311–2) tombs are said to be the *bon-po* practice, whereas chö-tens are buddhist. Another problem is presented by the early tradition, which relates that Shen-rap, the 'founder', was born in Sh'ang-sh'ung, and that *bon-po* practices first came from the west. The whole idea of a 'founder' is clearly suspect, for he would be quite superfluous where aboriginal beliefs and practices are concerned, and has all too obviously developed into a *bon-po* equivalent of Śākyamuni. Nevertheless the tradition itself is well worth investigating, for it is indeed likely that other religious beliefs reached central Tibet before the arrival of Buddhism, but one must note that Buddhism presented itself in very heterogeneous forms. (One will find for example in the *Havajratantra* the description of the necessary rite for finding that which is lost.) There still seems to be much material to be explored in Chinese sources concerning the early Tibetans whom they encountered on their frontiers. Here is clearly a vast field for research. In the meantime in using the term *bon-po,* I have in mind two general applications, aboriginal religion of whatsoever kind and the developed pseudo-Buddhist *Bon*. (In discussing the continent of Africa with Tibetans, I have been asked the nature of the religion of the inhabitants, and in telling them that it is *bon-po,* I think it has been characterized for them as well as may be.) I note that Stein ('Récentes Etudes Tibétaines', *JA*, 1952, pp. 98–100) would prefer to see the term employed in a more restricted manner, but this would conflict with Tibetan usage. It would presumably be justified if we could identify some early exclusive application. One must certainly agree with him in suspecting Hoffmann's interpretation of the word *bon* itself. See also the article by W. Simon in *Asia Major,* V, 1, pp. 5–8.

28. see Francke, 'The Kingdom of gNya-khri-btsan-po', *JASB,* vi, p. 94: 'sPu is a large village on the Sutlej in Upper Kunawar with vast ruins around and may well have been the seat of a petty king. . . . The spelling *spu* of this village is testified to by many stone inscriptions in the vicinity. On maps the

place is spelt Spooch.' The suggestion of a connection with the first king of Tibet has been firmly rejected by Petech (*A Study in the Chronicles of Ladakh*, p. 21) who argues that Mount Purgyul is by no means the same as Pu-gyel (*spu-rgyal*) and suggests that in any case the language of that area was non-Tibetan. The name of the mountain is not directly relevant, for it is sufficient that the name of the place is Pu (*spu*) and that there might reasonably have been a king of Pu (*spu-rgyal*). As far as language is concerned, we cannot be sure, but see note 36. Our knowledge of the early period is so vague, that it seems unwise to reject open possibilities. The rite of the rope-descent (see p. 133–4) suggests another possible connection with this general area. The alternative spelling of the name of the ancestor-king as *spur-rgyal* (thus giving the meaning 'Corpse-King') is presumably a scribal 'improvement'. If the initial head-letter of *rgyal* were pronounced, it would occur very easily.

29. *gnod-sbyin*, 'demon', literally 'giver of harm'. It is advisable to avoid the use of the translation *yaksha*, when there is reasonable certainty that the word is used in a pre-Buddhist sense. Compare note 33. Translations are found for the obscure names in this passage wherever possible, simply in order to render it as readable as may be. Thus the rendering of *srid-pa'i lha* as 'gods of the world' is a merely temporary expedient. The name *Yab-bla-bdal-drug* (Yap-la-däl-tr'uk) has been discussed by H. E. Richardson, 'A 9th Century Inscription from rKong-po', *JRAS*, 1954, pp. 163–4.

30. B. Laufer, 'Über ein Tibetisches Geschichtswerk der Bon-po', *T'oung Pao*, 1901, pp. 24 ff. Nya-trhi-tsen-po is said to be a descendant of the Pāṇḍavas, thus deliberately connecting him with the famous dynasty of the Mahābhārata, so that he might be shown to be non-Buddhist. This whole work is of great interest as a deliberate attempt at rewriting traditional Buddhist accounts. In many ways it probably comes nearer to historical accuracy. Thus we learn that the people clung to their old p'ön-po ways, and when they were forced to become Buddhists, they had p'ön in their hearts and Buddhism in their hands (pp. 38–9). One may also note that Yar-lha-sham-po, the mountain upon which the king is supposed to have manifested himself is named as the god of the west (p. 41).

31. The name of the king actually appears in this chronicle, spelt as *dri-gum*, but it is clearly interpreted as meaning Sword-Slain (*gri-gum*). Must one therefore deduce that already in the ninth century *dri* and *gri* were both pronounced tr'i, or at least with some similar sound that was identical? This question has already been raised by Stein ('Récentes Etudes Tibétaines', *JA*, 1952, pp. 82–3), who has drawn attention to its importance. See p. 170 and note 36.

32. Some uncertainty enters the list at the end of the reign of Trhi-song-deu-tsen. The problem has been discussed by Petech, *Chronicles*, pp. 74 ff.; Thomas, *Documents I*, 267–8; Tucci, *Tombs*, pp. 22 ff.; Richardson *JRAS*, 1952, pp. 138 ff. and *JRAS*, 1954, pp. 165–6. Evidence is certainly in

favour of the theory of Tucci and Richardson, that Trhi-song-deu-tsen withdrew from power some years before his death in 804, and that he was followed by two of his sons, the first one reigning for a short time and dying before his father.

33. These *yakshas* (*gnod-sbyin*) were placed around the temples, following the Indian custom, to serve as protectors. They are explicitly defined as such in the *Padma Thang-Yig* (fol. 179*a*5, Toussaint, p. 343).

34. The status of Ting-dzin S'ang-po has been discussed by Richardson, (*JRAS*, 1952, pp. 135–7). The title 'Belonging to the Great Command' (*bka chen-po la gtogs-pa*) is an active form of the expression 'bound to the authoritative word' (*bka la btags-pa*) of the inscription just quoted. The source of authority is the *chos-'khor*, which I have translated after some hesitation as 'religious assembly'. The normal translation would be 'wheel of the doctrine', but the other one is certainly justified, if we may argue back from later usage. Thus To-ling and Tabo Monasteries, two of the chief religious establishments founded by Ye-she-ö (see p. 179) about A.D. 1000 are known as *chos-'khor* (Tucci, *Ind-Tib.*, II, 72–3).

35. If we are to judge by what subsequently happened, this can only mean that no hīnayāna scriptures other than those of the (Mūla-) Sarvāstivādins were to be translated at all, and that the mantras were to be incorporated into the texts where they belonged, but in the original Sanskrit. It seems likely that through confusion of names, the later historians have attributed the initiative for this great task of systematic translation to Räl-pa-cen instead of to his predecessor Sä-na-lek. (see Tucci, *Tombs*, pp. 14–15.) It was observed above that this king suffers neglect in their brief references (pp. 158–9).

36. The capital of Sh'ang-Sh'ung was Khyung-lung on the head-waters of the Sutlej about forty-five miles west of Mt. Kailas. Guge is mentioned in the *Tun-huang Documents* (p. 156), where it might be understood just as another name for Sh'ang-Sh'ung. According to the *Blue Annals* (vol. I, 37) Sh'ang-Sh'ung forms part of Guge, but the author is writing in the fifteenth century, and since the application of these names was not constant, this does not help with the earlier period. With the establishing in the tenth century of a powerful dynasty at To-ling, some sixty miles west of Khyung-lung, the name Guge comes to be applied to the whole region eastwards as far as Pu-rang. All that is known about this region in the earlier period, is that it was a reputed centre of p'ön-po activity and the home-land of the supposed 'founder' of p'ön. Just as the translations of Buddhist texts were given duplicated titles in Sanskrit, so p'ön-po texts were given them in the 'Sh'ang-Sh'ung language'. It is in fact likely that these titles are entirely fictitious and that we have here just one more attempt at aping the Buddhists, but at least it indicates that this country was held in some prestige by the p'ön-pos. See Hoffmann, *Bon-Religion*, p. 220. F. W. Thomas seems to be of the opinion that this language was a form of Tibetan, for he suggests that

some MS. fragments, which show kinship to Tibetan, may be in the Sh'ang-Sh'ung language (*JRAS*, 1933, pp. 405–10). Petech says categorically that this is not so, but produces no cogent evidence (*Chronicles*, p. 51). Unless some other plausible suggestion can be put forward, likelihood is certainly in favour of Tibetan.

37. The Tibetan word yak (*gYag*) has come to be accepted in European languages, but the word which is available to us for designating that other common animal, which is a cross between a yak and cow, seems to have been misapplied. I mean the word 'zebu', derived from Tibetan dzo-po (*mdzo-pho*), which is the male of this species. It seems now to be applied quite wrongly to the humped Indian cow (*OED*). See, however, H. C. Wyld, *Universal Dictionary of the English Language*, p. 1415, where the derivation is correctly given.

38. A few scattered examples of pagoda-temples are still to be found in some western Himalayan districts. See *Punjab District Gazetteer*, vol. xxx A, 'Kangra District, Part II, KULU', pp. 37 ff. Also Francke, *Ant. Ind. Tib.*, I, p. 9. This style of architecture must once have been as common in these regions, as it still is in Nepal.

39. It is unexpectedly described in the *Punjab Gazetteer*, *op. cit.*, p. 204, as 'the largest and most noted monastery in Lahul'. In 1953 it presents itself as one of the smallest and certainly the most neglected of Lahauli monasteries, being in the charge of one solitary monk. There are remains of ancient woodwork without, and inside standing amongst images of recent workmanship on the altar is the head of a bodhisattva, which had been dug up in the valley below. See pl. 24. Is this a possible example preserved from the time when Kulu was a Buddhist land? It shows a striking resemblance to some Central Asian models.

40. Of such a kind is the temple of Kye-phang at Shashin below Kokshar in the Chandra Valley, and of Jam-la at Prīni just below Manālī at the head of the Kulu Valley. Purgyul's chief centre is at Nako in the Sutlej Valley. See Tucci, *Secrets*, p. 69. Under later Buddhist influence some of the more important Lords of the Soil came to be represented pictorially in the Buddhist temples. Thus Ka-rgyal, 'lord' of Tsaparang, is frequently depicted in that region (Tucci, *Secrets*, p. 174; *idem*, *Ind-Tib.*, III, Part 2, p. 168). Likewise at Tha-me (*thang-smad*) and Teng-po-che (*steng-po-che*) in Khumbu paintings of these 'local lords' are to be seen in the temples. In Gangtok (Sikkim) Yap-dü (*yab-bdud*), protector of the south, and Kang-chen-dzö-nga, protector of the north, are represented at the monastic dances.

41. Their knowledge was never general and discursive, but always directed towards the mastering of specific texts. Works on philosophy and logic required the exercise of discriminating thought, and the commentaries written later by the Tibetans themselves certainly prove their capability in this respect. The tantras on the other hand were the means towards the actual

realization of the *summum bonum* of Buddhist religion, for they are the manuals of the actual practice. They could therefore only be transmitted by one who was already initiated into the mystery. Hence their translation into Tibetan involved the acquisition of an Indian spiritual heritage in the full sense of the term.

42. As Tucci suggests, some of these images may have been carelessly repaired at some time. Thus Ratnasambhava's right hand is placed behind his right knee, and one might contend that the gesture is not correct. The colour, however, is conclusive. Amoghasiddhi is rather dark-blue than dark-green, but in this case the gesture of dauntlessness cannot leave one in doubt. The names of the sixteen attendant bodhisattvas are presumably those shown on the diagram of *Ind-Tib.*, III, Part 1, p. 60. One may note that the four mudrā, Vajrasattvī, etc. are not represented. (see note 21.)

43. This tribe seems to the Qarluq (tib. *gar-log*). H. Hoffmann, 'Die Qarluq in der tibetischen Literatur', *Oriens*, III (1950), pp. 190–208.

44. There are at least two 'yeti-heads' in Khumbu, for another in rather better condition reposes in the temple at Kum-jung. They are in fact pointed caps, made from what appears to be a section of hide from a wild boar (*ri-phag*). They are skilfully shaped without seams and so that the back-bristles run over the crest of the hat. In popular belief the yeti is an entirely mythological creature, identifiable with the *rākshasa* of Indian mythology. He belongs to the entourage of the 'Country-God' of Khumbu (*Khumbu-yul-lha*), who sends him forth as an emanation, when he intends harm to anyone. Thus to see a yeti is a very bad omen, only to be countered by directing effort forthwith towards accumulating merit. The yeti-caps are used once a year in the temple dances, when a monk masquerading as the yeti accompanies the 'country-god' on his reeling rounds. Mountaineers have on several occasions mentioned the existence of unexplained foot-prints, which their Sherpa assistants regularly identify as these of a yeti. Whatever these foot-prints may be, the only connection with the yeti exists as an extension of the popular imagination.

45. All these t'am-cen are of Indian origin, except perhaps for Dorje-lek-pa. Ma-ning is identified with Mahākāla in the invocations which are addressed to him. Hoffmann notes that 'the Dorje-lek-pas are just one of the many groups of demons, which Padmasambhava converted on his way through Tibet' (*Bon-Religion*, p. 164). In *The Acts of the Great T'am-cen Protectors of the Doctrine* (*bstan-skyong-ba'i dam-can chen-po-rnams-gyi phrin-las dngos-grub-kyi rol-mtsho*, Rin-chen gTer-mdzod, vol. TI) he appears as a minor divinity in the entourage of Mahākāla (fol. 11*a*–*b*). At the same time he is given higher rank than the *brtan-ma* and *sa-bdag*. I am inclined to regard him as non-Tibetan and as an early importation from the west. His name suggests an Indian origin and he has no non-religious name, as has Thang-lha. The only shrine of Dorje-lek-pa, which I have seen, is just beyond Jispa in northern Lahul. It is

built of stones around a tree and inside is a flat-stone with a painting on it showing the god seated on a ram.

46. The original set of seven included music (*śabda*) but this has been dropped and the group-name 'worthy offerings' (*arghya*) added instead as though it were a separate item. It is interpreted as 'drinking-water'.

MANDALAS

MANDALA OF THE UNION OF THE PRECIOUS ONES

(*see pl.* 36)

		I		
7	8		1	2
		II		
6				3
		III		
5				4
	VII		VIII	
IV		VI		V

I. Amitābha (Boundless Light).
II. Avalokiteśvara.
III. Padma-sambhava (Central Buddha).
IV. Guru Tr'ak-po, the Fierce Master (yi-dam).
V. Senge-Dong-ma, the Lion-headed Goddess (kandroma).
VI. Ma-ning (protector).
VII, VIII. Mandāravā and Goddess Ocean of Wisdom (wives of Padma-sambhava).

1. Sun-Ray.
2. Lotus-King.
3. Lion of the Śākyas.
4. Adamantine Sagging-Belly.
5. Roaring Lion.
6. Lotus-Born.
7. Thoughtful Coveter of the Best.
8. Guru Padma-sambhava.

} These are all special forms of Padma-sambhava (Central Buddha) see p. 228.

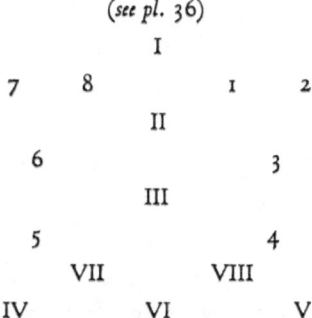

MANDALAS

Mandala of the Eighty-Four Perfect Ones

(*see pl.* 10)

Row I.	1	2	3	4	5	6	7	8	9
II.	10	11	12	13	14	15	16	17	18
					23				
III.	19	20	21	22		24	25	26	27
					32				
IV.	28	29	30	31		33	34	35	36
V.	37	38	39		Vajradhara		40	41	42
					and				
VI.	43	44	45		partner		46	47	48
VII.	49	50	51	52	53	54	55	56	57
VIII.	58	59	60	61	62	63	64	65	66
IX.	67	68	69	70	71	72	73	74	75
X.	76	77	78	79	80	81	82	83	84

Row I.

1. Pad-byung (Padma-sambhava).
2. Lohipa.
3. Saraha.
4. Dzokipa.
5. Lilapa.
6. Birvapa.
7. Ḍombipa.
8. Shavaripa.
9. Saraha the Younger.

Row II.

10. Kokalipa.
11. Minapa.
12. Kolarakshava.
13. Tsaurakhampa.
14. Vinapa.
15. Akarshinta.
16. Tog-tse-pa.
17. Tantripa.
18. Tsamaripa.

Row III.

19. Khaḍga-pa.
20. Nāgārdzuna.
21. Nag-po-pa (Krishna).
22. Āryadeva.
23. Thangepa.
24. Tilopa.
25. Naropa.
26. Shalampa.
27. Tsatapa.

Row IV.

28. Bhatrapa.
29. rDo-khan-ci (Dhoshanti).
30. Mekopa.
31. Adzuki.
32. Sakalipa.
33. Ḍom-gi-pa.
34. Kamaripa.
35. Dzalandara.
36. Rāhula.

Row V.
37. Dharmapa.
38. rDo-ka-ri-pa.
39. Medhenpa.
40. Sangadzala.
41. Dril-bu-pa.
42. Ayogipa.

Row VI.
43. Tsakolipa.
44. Gudhuripa.
45. Ludzikapa.
46. Kampalipa.
47. Bhadeva.
48. Tantapa.

Row VII.
49. Kukuripa.
50. Kudzñālipa.
51. Dharmapa.
52. Madhilapa.
53. Acinta.
54. Bhalakapa.
55. Nalipa.
56. Bhusukapa.
57. Indrabhutipa.

Row VIII.
58. lCam-legs-sming-dkar.
59. Dzalendra.
60. Nirguni.
61. Tsapari.
62. Tsampakari.
63. Bhikhana.
64. Til-sdungs-pa.
65. Kumaripa.
66. Du-med-pa.

Row IX.
67. Maṇibhadra.
68. Mekhalipa.
69. Kanakha.
70. Kanakipa.
71. Kantalipa.
72. Dhasuripa.
73. Udharipa.
74. Kapalipa.
75. Kiripa.

Row X.
76. mTsho-skyes-rdo-rje (Saroruhavajra).
77. Sarvabhagali.
78. Nāgabodhi.
79. Surali.
80. Sahani.
81. Kalipa.
82. Anangipa.
83. Samantra.
84. Byāripa.

These names are copied from the sketches used by the painter of this *thanka,* who lives at Jal-sa in Shar-Khumbu. Being an entirely Tibetan one, our list accords generally with Tucci's no: IV, that of Klong-rdol-bla-ma (TPS, p. 227 ff.), but there Pad-byung (1) is absent and the number is made up by a certain Kamkana, who comes between our No. 45 and 46. Most of these names are Sanskrit in form, but often so hopelessly corrupted in their Tibetan spelling, that the original form of the Sanskrit cannot be ascertained. A very few of the names are translations, e.g. Nag-po-pa (21) and mTsho-skyes (76).

MANDALA OF THE UNIVERSAL SAVIOUR

(*see pl.* 37)

			I				
10		6		1			7
	5		II		2		
		4		3			
			III				
9	14	15		11			8
	16	17	IV	12	13		

I. Amitābha (Boundless Light).
II. Avalokiteśvara (Universal Saviour).
III. Padma-sambhava.
IV. Thang-lha (God of the Plain).
1. Indra Lord of Gods. (East)
2. Śākya-Sage. (SE.)
3. King of the Burning Mouth. (SW.)
4. Lion Firm of Vow. (West)
5. Design of Excellent Weave. (NW.)
6. King of the Dharma. (NE.)
7. Guardian Goddess with the hook. (East)
8. Guardian Goddess with the noose. (South)
9. Guardian Goddess with the fetter. (West)
10. Guardian Goddess with the bell. (North)
11–17. The Seven Graceful Ḍākinīs (Ma-mo).

ON THE SPELLING OF TIBETAN AND SANSKRIT NAMES

In attempting to give phonetic spellings for Tibetan I am not trying out something new. Dr. E. Obermiller, whose untimely death every student of Tibetan must lament, regularly used similar spellings, and anyone who is aware of Tibetan as a living language, may legitimately record the ancient names in a form that represents the literary pronunciation. The classical spellings, whenever given, appear in italics.

In Sanskrit and Tibetan words one should pronounce:

a — like *u* in s*u*n,	ā — like *a* in br*a*nch,
e — like *ai* in r*ai*n,	ī — like *ea* in str*ea*m,
i — like *i* in tw*i*g,	ū — like *oo* in r*oo*t,
o — like *o* in c*o*ld,	ä — like *e* in sc*e*nt,
u — like *oo* in w*oo*d,	ö — like *er* in f*er*n,
	ü — like *u* in y*u*le.

Consonants may be pronounced as in English with the following exceptions

c — like *ch* in pit*ch*er,	th — like *t-h* in goa*t-h*erd,
ch — like *ch* in *ch*urn	ph — like *p-h* in to*p-h*eavy,
kh — like *k-h* in Yor*k-h*am,	tsh — like *ts-h* in ca*ts-h*ome,
trh — like *tr-h* in *Traherne*,	ś — like *sh* in *sheep*.

when pronounced as one syllable.

For some Tibetan words we must add one symbol to indicate low pitch as opposed to high. Unless we distinguish this pitch orthographically, the reader will frequently be confused by assuming that some words are the same when they are not. In Tibetan the aspirates: *kh ch th ph tsh trh* and the sibilants: *s sh* are regularly on a high pitch, whereas: *k' ch' t' p' ts' tr' s' sh'* are on a low pitch. These last represent the sounds of the classical spellings, *ga, ja, da, ba, dẓa, gra, dra, bra,* when they occur as initial letters, and of *ẓa* and *ẓha,* wherever they occur. This system of indicating pitch was also used by Obermiller and by Bell.

Although there is a great diversity of dialects within Tibetan lands, there is nevertheless a recognized literary pronunciation, with which all trained monks are acquainted. It has the advantage of a certain universality and consistency, and is therefore given here by the phonetic renderings.

TIBETAN AND SANSKRIT NAMES

The classical spellings of Tibetan names are represented in *italics* by means of the following syllabary:

ka	*kha*	*ga*	*nga*
ca	*cha*	*ja*	*nya*
ta	*tha*	*da*	*na*
pa	*pha*	*ba*	*ma*
tsa	*tsha*	*dza*	*wa*
zha	*za*	*'a*	*ya*
ra	*la*	*sha*	*sa*
ha	*a*		

I have taken certain liberties with Sanskrit terms, when the correct spelling cannot be in doubt. *sh* is used for the cerebral sibilant and so *ishtadevatā* and *Vishnu* are written without *ṭ* and *ṇ*. Similarly *ankuśa* is written without any marking of the guttural nasal, since its nature is made certain by the following guttural. It is hoped that this will cause no difficulty to students.

Certain terms of common occurrence, e.g. nirvāna (*nirvāṇa*), mandala (*maṇḍala*) are partially anglicized by the omission of diacritical marks except vowel length when they appear in roman type. *ś* has however been retained, e.g. Aśoka.

Also note chaitya for *caitya*.

CHRONOLOGICAL TABLE

B.C.	
c. 528	Enlightenment of the Śākya-Sage at Bodhgaya.
269–236	Reign of Aśoka, whose empire centres on Magadha. Buddhism reaches S. India and Ceylon, N.W. India and Nepal.
A.D.	
1st–2nd centuries	The Kushan Empire flourishes in N.W. India. Buddhism spreads across Central Asia to China.
4th–5th centuries	The Gupta Empire flourishes in Central India.
c. 450	Nālanda Monastery is founded by Kumāragupta I.
c. 454 onwards	NW. India is invaded by the Huns. Period of vandalism and destruction.
606–47	Harsha establishes a firm empire in Central India.
c. 625–855	Kashmir remains stable under the Karkoṭa dynasty.
629–645	The Chinese pilgrim, Yuan Chwang, travels through Central Asia and India.
c. 630	Thön-mi Sambhoṭa visits Kashmir; subsequently writing is introduced into Central Tibet.
650 onwards	Tibetan troops make conquests in Central Asia.
c. 765	The Pāla Dynasty is established in Bengal, maintaining a general hold over Magadha. Odantapuri Monastery is founded. Śāntarakshita and Padma-sambhava arrive in Central Tibet.
783	The Chinese are forced by the Tibetans to make terms.
787	The founding of Sam-yä Monastery.
794	The Council of Lhasa.
822–3	The Chinese are again forced to terms.
842	The murder of the last of the Yar-lung Kings.[a]
10th century	The establishing of new dynasties in W. Tibet and the pre-eminence of the Kingdom of Guge.
954–1055	Rin-chen S'ang-po, the Great Translator.
958–1054	Atīśa, the Great Teacher.
996 (?)	The founding of Tabo Monastery.
1001 onwards	NW. India is pillaged by Mahmud and his fellow-Moslems.
1073	The founding of Sa-kya Monastery.
1012–97	Life of Marpa, the Translator.
1042	Atīśa arrives in Guge.

[a] For the complete list of these kings see p. 135.

1197	Magadha is conquered by the Moslems. Final destruction of the great places of Buddhism in India.
1204	Śākya-śrī arrives in Tibet.
1357–1419	Tsong-kha-pa, the Great Reformer.
1418	The founding of Dre-pung Monastery.
1641	The Abbot of Drepung (fifth in the series) is made ruler of Central Tibet by the Mongols. Thus begins the rule of the Dalai Lamas. (This name is an English corruption of a title bestowed on the third Abbot of Dre-pung by the Mongol Chief, Altan Khagan.)
1646	Large areas of Western Tibet are annexed by the Tibetans of the Centre, supported by the Mongolians.
1715–21	Tibetan travels of the Jesuit missionary, Desideri, the first European to become proficient in Tibetan.
1827–30	The Hungarian scholar, Csoma de Körös, prepares his summary of the Tibetan Canon, and thus initiates modern Tibetan studies in the west.

BIBLIOGRAPHY

Advayavajrasaṃgraha, ed. B. Bhattacharyya, *GOS*, XL, Baroda.

Bacot, J. *Les Ślokas Grammaticaux de Thonmi Sambhoṭa*, Paris, 1928.

Bacot, Thomas and Toussaint. *Documents de Touen-Houang relatifs à l'histoire du Tibet*, Paris, 1940.

Bell, C. A. *Grammar of Colloquial Tibetan*, Bengal Government Press, 1939 (3rd edition).

— *The Religion of Tibet*, Oxford, 1931.

Bourda, M. G. 'Quelques réflexions sur la pose assise à l'européenne dans l'art bouddhique', *Art. As.*, xii (1949), pp. 302–13.

Briggs, G. W. *Gorakhnath and the Kanphata Yogis*, *OUP*, Calcutta, 1938.

Brough, J. 'Legends of Khotan and Nepal', *BSOAS*, xii, part 2, pp. 333 ff.

Conze, E. *Buddhism, Its Essence and Development*, Oxford, 1953 (3rd edition).

Conze, Horner, Snellgrove and Waley. *Buddhist Texts through the Ages*, Oxford, 1954.

Das, S. C. *Indian Pandits in the Land of Snow*, Calcutta, 1893.

Dasgupta, S. B. *An Introduction to Tantric Buddhism*, Calcutta, 1950.

David-Neel, Alexandra. *With Mystics and Magicians in Tibet*, London, 1931.

Demiéville, P. *Le Concile de Lhasa*, Paris, 1952.

Eliade, M. *Le Yoga, Immortalité et Liberté*, Paris, 1954.

— *Traité d'Histoire des Religions*, Paris, 1953.

Evans-Wentz, W. Y. *The Tibetan Book of the Dead*, London, 1927.

— *The Tibetan Book of the Great Liberation*, Oxford, 1954.

Falk, Marya. 'Il Mito Psicologico nell'India Antica', *Reale Accademia Nazionale dei Lincei*, Rome, 1939, Memorie della classe di scienze morali.

Filliozat, F. 'Avalokiteśvara d'après un livre récent', *RHR*, cxxxvii (1950), pp. 44–58.

— 'Maitreya, l'*Invaincu*', *JA*, 1950, pp. 145–9.

Foucher, A. *La Vie du Bouddha, d'après les textes et les monuments de l'Inde*, Paris, 1949.

Francke, A. H. *Antiquities of Indian Tibet*, 2 vols., Calcutta, 1914 and 1926.

— *A History of Western Tibet*, London, 1907.

— 'The Kingdom of gNya-khri-btsan-po', *JASB*, vi, pp. 93 ff.

Glasenapp, H. de. *Mystères Bouddhistes*, Paris, 1944.

Guhyasamāja-tantra, ed. B. Bhattacharyya, *GOS*, LIII, Baroda.

Günther, H. *Das Seelenproblem im älteren Buddhismus*, Konstanz, 1949.

Har Dayal. *The Bodhisattva Doctrine in Buddhist Sanskrit Literature*, London, 1932.

Heiler, F. *Die Buddhistische Versenkung*, München, 1922.

Hevajra-tantra, ed. and tr. D. L. Snellgrove, London Oriental Series, (1957).

Hoffmann, H. *Quellen zur Geschichte der tibetischen Bon-Religion*, Wiesbaden, 1950.

I-Tsing. *A Record of the Buddhist Religion as practised in India and the Malay Archipelago* (A.D. 671–695), tr. J. Takakusu, Oxford, 1896.

Lalou, Marcelle. *Iconographie des étoffes peintes dans le Mañjuśrīmūlakalpa*, Paris, 1930.

Lamotte, E. 'La Légende du Buddha', *RHR*, 1948, pp. 39 ff.

Landon, P. *Nepal*, London, 1928.

Laufer, B. 'Über ein tibetisches Geschichtswerk der Bon-po', *T'oung Pao*, 1901, pp. 24 ff.

— *Aus den Geschichten und Liedern des Milaraspa*, Wien, 1902.

Lévi, S. *Le Népal, Étude historique d'un royaume hindou*, 3 vols., Paris, 1905–8.

Mallmann, Mlle. de. *Introduction à l'étude de l'Avalokiteśvara*, Paris, 1948.

Lubac, H. de. *Aspects of Buddhism*, tr. G. R. Lamb, London, 1954.

— *La Rencontre du Bouddhisme et de l'Occident*, Paris, 1952.

Mus, P. *Borobuḍur*, Hanoi, 1935.

— *Les Buddhas Parés*, *BEFEO*, xxviii, nos. 1–2, pp. 153–280.

Nebesky-Wojkowitz, R. v. 'Die Tibetische Bön-Religion', *Archiv für Völkerkunde*, II (1947), pp. 26–68.

Obermiller, E. *History of Buddhism by Bu-ston*, 2 parts, Heidelberg, 1931–2.

Oldfield, H. A. *Sketches from Nipal*, 2 vols., London, 1880.

Petech, L. *A Study on the Chronicles of Ladakh*, Calcutta, 1939 (published as a suppl. to vols. 13 and 15 of the *Indian Historical Quarterly*).

Przyluski, J. 'Le Pilier de Sarnath', *Mélanges Linoissier*, Paris, 1932, II, pp. 481–98.

— 'Vêtements de religieux et vêtements de rois', *JA*, xiii, pp. 365 ff.

— 'Les Vidyārāja', *BEFEO*, 1923, pp. 301 ff.

— 'La Ville du Cakravartin', *Roc. Or.*, v, pp. 165 ff.

Punjab District Gazetteer, vol. xxx A, Kangra District, Parts II–IV, Lahore, 1918.

Richardson, H. E. *Ancient Historical Edicts at Lhasa and the Mu Tsung/Khri Gtsug Lde Brtsan Treaty of A.D. 821–2 from the Inscription at Lhasa*, *RAS*, Prize Publication Fund, XIX, 1952.

— 'Three Ancient Inscriptions from Tibet', *JRASB*, xv, no. 1, 1949.

— 'Tibetan Inscriptions at the Źva-ḥi Lha-khang,' *JRAS*, 1952, pp. 133–54 and *ibid.* 1953, pp. 1–12.

— 'A Ninth-Century Inscription from Rkong-po', *JRAS*, 1954, pp. 157–73.

Roerich, G. N. *The Blue Annals* of gŹon-nu-dpal, Calcutta, 1949 and 1953 (2 vols.).

Sāṅkṛtyāyana. 'Recherches Bouddhiques: L'Origine du Vajrayāna et les 84 siddhas', *JA*, 225 (1934), pp. 209–30.

Schayer, St. 'New Contributions to the Problem of Pre-hīnayānist Buddhism', *Pol. Bul. Oriental Studies*, I (1937), pp. 8–17.
— *Contributions to the Theory of Time in Indian Philosophy*, Krakow, 1938.
Schubert, J. *Tibetische Nationalgrammatik*, Leipzig, 1937.
Stcherbatsky, Th. *The Central Conception of Buddhism*, London, 1923.
— *The Conception of Buddhist Nirvāna*, Leningrad, 1923.
Tāranātha. *History of Buddhism in India, tib. tx.* ed. A. Schiefner, St. Petersburg, 1868; German tr. *idem*, 1869.
Thomas, E. J. *Early Buddhist Scriptures*, London, 1935.
— *The Life of Buddha as Legend and History*, London, 1949, 3rd edition.
Thomas, F. W. *Tibetan Literary Texts and Documents concerning Chinese Turkestan, RAS*, Oriental Translation Fund, Part I (1935), Part II (1951), Part III (1955).
— 'The Tibetan Alphabet', *Festschrift z. Feier d. 200-jähr. Bestehens d. Akademie d. Wissenschaften in Göttingen*, 1951, pp. 146–65.
Toussaint, G-C. *Le Dict de Padma (padma thang yig)*, Paris, 1933.
Tucci, G. *A Lhasa e Oltre*, Rome, 1950.
— *Indo-Tibetica*, vols. I–IV, Rome, 1932–41.
— 'On the validity of the Tibetan historical tradition', *India Antiqua*, Leiden, 1947, pp. 309–22.
— *Secrets of Tibet*, tr. Mary Johnstone, London and Glasgow, 1935.
— *Teoria e Pratica del Mandala*, Rome, 1949.
— *Tibetan Painted Scrolls*, 3 vols., Rome, 1949.
— *The Tombs of the Tibetan Kings*, Rome, 1950.
— *Tra Giungle e Pagode*, Rome, 1954.
— *Travels of Tibetan Pilgrims in the Swat Valley*, Calcutta, 1940.
Uray, G. 'On the Tibetan Letters *Ba* and *Wa*,' *Acta Orient. Hung.* (Budapest), vol. v (1955), pp. 101–21.
Vallée Poussin, L. de la. *Études et Matériaux*, London, 1898.
— *L'Inde aux temps des Mauryas*, Paris, 1930.
Vogel, J. Ph. 'Triloknāth', *JASB*, lxx (1902), part 1, no. 1, pp. 35 ff.
Waddell, L. A. *The Buddhism of Tibet or Lamaism*, London, 1895.
Watters, Th. *On Yuan Chwang's Travels in India*, 2 vols., London, 1904 and 1905.

quoted in the text

1. བཀའ་ཐང་སྡེ་ལྔ་

རྒྱལ་པོ་བཀའི་ཐང་ཡིག་དང་། བློན་པོ་བཀའི་ཐང་ཡིག་

2. བཀའ་རྫོགས་པ་ཆེན་པོ་ཡང་ཟབ་དགོན་མཆོག་སྤྱི་འདུས་དང་དེའི་ཆ་ལག་ཞི་ཁྲོ་ངེས་དོན་སྙིང་པོའི་ལས་བྱང་དོན་གསལ་ལ་ཁྲིར་བདེར་བསྒྲིགས་པ་པདྨའི་དགོངས་རྒྱན་

3. ཆོས་སྤྱོད་ཀྱི་རིམ་པ་ཐར་ལམ་རབ་གསལ་

4. ཐུགས་རྗེ་ཆེན་པོ་འགྲོ་བ་ཀུན་སྒྲོལ་གྱི་བླ་མའི་རྣལ་འབྱོར་བརྒྱུད་འདེབས་བྱིན་རླབས་མྱུར་འཇུག་དང་ཕྱིན་ལས་ཚོགས་ཁྲིགས་སུ་བསྒྲིགས་པ་

5. དུས་མཐར་ཆོས་སྨྲ་བའི་བཙུན་པ་ངག་དབང་བསྟན་འཛིན་ནོར་བུའི་རྣམ་ཐར་འཆི་མེད་བདུད་རྩི་འི་རོལ་མཚོ་

6. བལ་ཡུལ་གྱི་མཆོད་རྟེན་བྱ་རུང་ཁ་ཤོར་གྱི་ལོ་རྒྱུས་

7. བྱང་གཏེར་ཐུགས་རྗེ་ཆེན་པོ་འགྲོ་བ་ཀུན་སྒྲོལ་གྱི་གནས་ལུང་ཚོ་ག་བླ་མའི་ཞལ་ལུང་ལྟར་ཁྲིགས་སུ་བྱས་པ་གསལ་བྱེད་ཉི་མ་

8. རྫོགས་པ་ཆེན་པོ་ཀློང་ཆེན་སྙིང་ཐིག་གི་སྔོན་འགྲོའི་ཁྲིད་ཡིག་ཀུན་བཟང་བླ་མའི་ཞལ་ལུང་

9. ཨོ་རྒྱན་གུ་རུ་པདྨ་འབྱུང་གནས་ཀྱི་སྐྱེས་རབས་རྣམ་ཐར་རྒྱས་པར་བཀོད་པ་པདྨ་བཀའི་ཐང་ཡིག།

ABBREVIATIONS

For References see Bibliography, p. 303–5.)

Art. As.	*Artibus Asiae*, Leipzig.
AHE	Richardson, 'Ancient Historical Edicts'.
Ant. Ind. Tib.	see Francke, *Antiquities of Indian Tibet.*
BEFEO	*Bulletin de l'École française de l'Extrême-Orient*, Hanoi.
Blue Annals	see Roerich.
BSOAS	*Bulletin of the School of Oriental and African Studies*, London.
Buddhist Texts	see Conze etc.
Bu-tön	see Obermiller.
GOS	Gaekwad's Oriental Series, Baroda.
Ind-Tib.	see Tucci, *Indo-Tibetica.*
JA	*Journal Asiatique*, Paris.
JRAS	*Journal of the Royal Asiatic Society*, London.
JRASB	*JRAS* of Bengal, Calcutta.
JBORS	*Journal of the Bihar and Orissa Research Society.*
MCB	*Mélanges chinois et bouddhiques*, Brussels.
MMK	*Mañjuśrī-mūla-kalpa*, ed. Gaṇapati Śāstri, Trivandrum Sanskrit Series, vols. LXX, LXXVI, LXXXIV.
Nr. Kj.	*Narthang Kanjur.*
Nr. Tj.	*Narthang Tenjur.*
OSI	Ordnance Survey of India.
PDG	*Punjab District Gazetteer.*
RAS	*Royal Asiatic Society.*
RHR	*Revue de l'Histoire des Religions*, Paris.
Roc. Or.	*Rocznik Orjentalistyczny*, Krakow.
skr.	Sanskrit.
STTS	*Sarva-tathāgata-tattva-saṃgraha, Nr. Kj. rgyud*, vii, fol. 213–440.
tib.	Tibetan.
tr.	translation.
Tun-Huang Documents	see Bacot, etc.
tx.	text.
TPS	see Tucci, *Tibetan Painted Scrolls.*
ZDMG	*Zeitschrift der deutschen Morgenländischen Gesellschaft.*

GENERAL INDEX

When a term requires definition, the first entry will normally give direct access to it. Thus in the case of some entries a higher page-number will come first. Figures in brackets indicate relevant subject-matter, where the term itself is unnamed.

abhaya (dauntlessness) *see* Gestures
abhidharma (systematic philosophy), 28, 180, 224
abhisheka see Consecration
activity (four kinds) *see* Rites
Adamantine Sagging Belly, 228
Adamantine Youth *see* Vajra-kumāra
ādi-buddha, 96–7, 114, 278
Advayavajra *see* Avadhūtipa
Agni, 260
Ajanta, 42, 45–6
Ākāśadhātvīśvarī, 82
Ākāśagarbha, 186
Akshobhya, 60, 66, 74–5, 78, 103–4, 113, 186, 203–4, 206
Amideva (= Amitābha), 124
Amitābha, 60–1, 66, 115, 186–7, 227, 228, 233
Amitāyus, 60
Amoghasiddhi, 50, 66
amṛta (nectar, elixir of immortality), 247, (60, 86)
anātmatā (absence of self or personality), 25–8, 52, 285
animals, 17, 216
anuttarayoga-tantra, 202 ff, 90
arhat ('worthy', *viz.* early disciples who had experienced nirvāna), 227
A-sh'a, 139
Aśoka, 3, 7, 18, 50, 93, 167–8
āśravas, 18 *fn.*
asura (titan), 17; *see* Wheel of Existence
Atīśa, 179, 180, 192–8, 202
ātman (self) *see anātmatā*, Personality
Avadhūtī ('she who is rejected'), 88, 90
Avadhūtipa (*alias* Advayavajra, Maitripa), 104, 194
Avalokiteśvara, 62–3, 67, 78, 114–6, 144, 187, 191, 228, 287; 'Universal Saviour', 237–8, 265–74 *passim*; Legends, 98, 124–6
avidyā (absence of knowledge *or* ignorance), 284–5

Baltistān, 140, 172
Bāmiyān, 172
banra, 108, 110
Baralacha, 171
Beas, 171
Bhagavān see Buddha the Lord
Bhagavatī ('Lady'), 115
Bhairava ('Fearful') 78, 118; *see* Vajra-bhairava
Bhairava-kāla-rātrī ('Fearful goddess of the black night')= Kālī, 210
Bhaja, 42–3
Bhedsa, 42–3
Bhutān, 213
Bodhgaya, 1–5, 194; Tibetan Monastery, 4–5, 19
bodhicitta see Thought of Enlightenment
Bodhipathapradīpa, 195
bodhisattva 11–12, 26, 35–6, 54, 61–64, 181
Bodhnāth, 98–100, 114, 150
Body of Enjoyment *see* Buddha-bodies
Body, Speech and Mind *see* Threefold Formula of Personality
bon see p'ön-po
bond *see samaya*
brahma-abodes, 208, 284
Buddha, definition, 9–12, 22, 277–278; quasi-historical *see* Śākya-Sage; the Lord (*Bhagavān*) 55, 56–9, 66, 74, 96–7, 186, 278

Buddhas, former, 190 *fn.*; confessional, 236; of the Six Spheres, 229, 263, 271
Buddhahood as Fivefold, 59, 64 ff, 74–5, 96–7, 103, 184, 186, 230–231; fierce forms, 79, 232; feminine partners, 82, 230, 232
Buddha-Bodies, 37, 89, 234, 250, 261
Buddha-Families, 62–3, 65–6, 74–5, 259, 263; *see also* Family Protectors
Buddha-Heruka, 79, 205
Buddha-Master of Medicine, 190–1

caitya, 38; *see* chaitya
cakra (psychic centres), 89; *see* Internal Maṇḍala
Caṇḍālī ('outcast'), 88, 90; compare *Avadhūtī*
Caṇḍaroshaṇa ('Fierce and Wrathful'), 78
Canons, 29; *see pāli*, Tibetan
caryā-tantra, 202
caste, 108–10
Caurī, 200, 232
cave-temples, 40 ff.
Cemetery-Goddess, 236, 242
Central Asia, 52, 140, 142, 157, 168–9, 186
Ceylon, 52; *see also* Theravādin
chaitya, 41, 42, 47, 111; *see also* stūpa
Chandra, 171
Ch'ang-chup-ö, 179, 184, 194
Chenab, 171
Chim-bu, 153
Ching-wa, 134, 153
chö-ten ('basis of worship') *see* stūpa
Circle of Existence *see* Wheel of Existence
Circle of Idealized Existence *see* Maṇḍala
Components of Personality (*skandha*), 23, 65, 67
concentration (*samādhi*), 21, 60, 80, 208 ff., 234, 244–5, 256–7, 274
consciousness, 15, 23, 26, 67, 85, 263, 285
'Consciousness-Only' *see* 'Mind-Only'
consecration, 68 ff.; four stages, 89, 206
cosmic body *see* Internal Maṇḍala
'country-gods' *see* Lords of the Soil
Csoma de Körös, 182

Da-me-ma, 200
ḍākinī, 175, 203–4, 228, 233–4
Dalai-Lama, 134, 137, 187
Dam-pa, 207
Dankhar, 189
Dārika, 104
dauntlessness (*abhaya*) *see* Gestures
De, 131 ff., 136
Decorative motifs, 43, 188
'Design of Excellent Weave', 229, 271
Dharma, Doctrine, 20–37; 'Law', 93, 283; 'Religion', 144; *see* Three Precious Ones
dharmas see Elements of existence
dharma-cakra see Wheel of the Doctrine
dharma-kāya see Buddha-Bodies
Dharma-rāja *see* King of the Dharma
Dharma-vajrī, 68
dhyāni-buddha, 103; *see* Buddhahood as Five-Fold
Diamond-Seat, 1–4, 35
Dīpankara-śrī-jñāna, 194; *see* Atīśa
discipline, monastic (*vinaya*), 20–21, 29, 152, 180
Discourses *see* Sūtras
Ḍombhipa, 194
Ḍombhi-Heruka, 199
Dorje-Jik-ch'e *see* Vajra- bhairava
Dorje-lek-pa, 242, 247, 294
Dro-wa-kün-dröl *see* 'Universal Saviour'
Drok-mi, 198–200
Drom, 196–8
Drugu, 139
Dudh-kosi, 213

Durgā, 81
Dü-song, 135, 138, 147
dzo, 293; *see* zebu

earth-witness gesture *see* Gestures
eight-fold path, 20
Ekajaṭā, 82, 236, 242, 243
elements (gross), 23, 209
elements of existence, 23–5, 26, 75
Evils, three, 15, 65; five, 65, 75; six, 263, 271

Families *see* Buddha-Families
Family-Protectors, 65, 116, 163
Fierce divinities, of buddha-rank, 78–9, 203–11, 232; *see also yi-dam*; protectors, 68, 230, 232; *see also* t'am-cen
Five Buddhas *see* Buddhahood as Five-Fold
Five Evils *see* Evils
Five-fold personality *see* Components (*skandhas*)
Five Wisdoms *see* Wisdom as Five-fold
'Flower of the Senses', 246
Four kinds of ritual action *see* Rites
Four Truths, 20
Former Buddhas *see* Buddhas

Gandhāra, 45
Gandhi, 8
Gandhola, 174, 293
Gaṇeśa, 102, 118
Gangtok, 213
Gar Clan, 138–9, 147
Gaurī, 200, 232
Gayadhara, 199
Ge-luk-pa ('Virtuous Order'), 4, 183, 187, 189
'Gem-Moon', 190
Gestures, 49, 67; earth-witness, 18, 60; dauntlessness, 44, 47; giving, 45; meditation, 45; preaching, 37, 45, 47, 48, 57; ritual gestures, 68, 70–3 *passim*, 269
Ghasmarī, 200, 232
Gilgit (*bru-zha*), 140, 147, 152, 162, 172
'God of the Plain' (*thang-lha*), 239–242, 247
'Goddess Ocean of Wisdom', 229
Goddesses, 80–4, 114–5, 116, 229–232; *see also* ḍākinī, yoginī
Goddesses of the Offerings, 67, 184, 230
Gods, early Buddhist conception, 16; introduced into Buddhism, 78–83; *see also* bodhisattvas, 61–4
'Good Characteristics', 190
Gorakhnāth, 113, 118, 151
Gotama, 1, 107, 283
Great Vehicle *or* Way *see* Mahāyāna
Guarantee *see* Samaya
Guardian divinities *see* Fierce divinities
Guge, 171, 178–9, 189–94 *passim*
Guhya-samāja-tantra, 90, 195, 204
Gupta Dynasty, 45
guru (master), 196–7
Guru Tr'ak-po (*yi-dam*), 228, 234–5

Hālāhala, 78
Halumantha, 124
Hamta Pass, 171
Ham-trhang, 243, 247
Hayagrīva (Horse-Neck), 78, 230, 249–50
'Heart-Drop' practice, 162
Hells, 17
Heruka, 205, 78, 79, 80, 103, 203, 205–9 *passim*
Hevajra, fierce divinity, 103, 203–205; invocation, 73
Hevajra-tantra, 64, 77 *fn*, 80, 89, 90, 193, 198, 199–200
Himālaya *or* Himalayas, ix *fn*.
Hīnayāna (Lesser Vehicle), 10, 12, 28, 194
Hinduism, compared with Buddhism, 77, 106–9, 119
Hodgson, 51, 103
homa-sacrifice, 112; *see* Rites

'Horse-Neck' (Hayagrīva), 230
Hūṃ-kāra, 203, 205
Hundred Thousand Tantras of the Old Sect, 161–2

I Tsing, 101
images, 44 ff, 185, 227; Nepalese tradition, 53–4
Incarnate Lama, 218; *see also* Dalai-Lama
Indra, Lord of Gods, 43, 98, 168, 229, 271
Indrabhūti, 151
Indus, 172
'Intermediate State', 264, 271
Internal maṇḍala, 88–90, 234, 253, 256
Islam, 2, 3; *see* Moslems

Jains, 10, 43, 45
Jālandhara, 171–2
Jam-la, 176
Jambhala, 78
jar, 69, 73, 80; *see* vase
Jewels, three *see* Three Precious Ones
Jiwong, 217–20 and *passim*
Jñānaśrī, 193
Jñānendra *see* Säl-nang of Ba
Jo-wo *see* Precious Prince

Ka-dam-pa, 198, 202
Ka-gyü-pa, 104, 213
Kailas, Mt., 170, 172, 178; *see* Meru
Kālacakra, 105
Kamalaśīla, 157–8, 181
Kandroma, 175, 228; *see* ḍākinī
Kanjur ('Translated Word') *see* Tibetan Canon
Kāṇha (= Kṛshna), 194
Kanheri, 48
Kanishka, 167–8
Kar-chung, 153, 159
Karla, 42–3
Karma-Heruka, 79, 232
Karma-vajrī, 68
Kashmir, 106, 140, 141, 152, 167–9, 171–2, 180, 186, 191–2

Kāśyapa, 99, 190 *fn.*
Kathmandu, 96, 102
Kesarpāṇi (= Avalokiteśvara), 252
Kha-rag, 129
Khāsācaitya, 288
Khasarpaṇa 186
khaṭvānga, 76 *fn*, 255
Khotan, 139, 140, 144, 147, 152, 172
Khu-tön, 197
Khumbu, 213–6 *passim*, 290, 293; 'country-god', 294
Khyap-juk *see* Vishnu
Khyung-lung, 292
'King of the Burning Mouth', 229, 271
'King of the Dharma', 229, 271
Knowledge, three-fold, 13, 22
Kön-cho-ci-dü *see* 'Union of the Precious Ones'
kriyā-tantra, 202
Krodheśvarī ('Lady of Wrath'), 82, 232
Kshānti, 168
Kshitigarbha, 186
Kshitipāṇi, 64
Kulu, 140, 171–2
Kumārī, 115, 118
Kün-tu-s'ang-po *see* Samanta-bhadra
Kun-zang Pass, 171
Kurukullā, 78
Kushans, 45, 60, 168, 301
Kuśinagara, 6, 7, 37
Kye-phang, 176
Kye-s'ang-dong-tsap, 149
Kyi, 189–190
Kyi-rong, 199

Ladakh, 170, 171, 178, 189
Lahul, 170, 171, 293
Lalanā (skr. 'wanton woman', tib. *brkyang-ma* 'she who is alone'), 88, 90
lama (skr. *guru*, 'master'), 196–7, 201
Lama-Yidam-Kandroma, 175; *see* Three Precious Ones

Lang-dar-ma, 99, 135, 165, 177, 259
Lankāvatāra-sūtra, 158
Lek-pa'i-she-rap, 180, 193, 197
Lesser Vehicle *see* Hīnayāna
Lha-chen (Mahādeva) *see* Śiva
Lha-de, 179, 192
lingam (phallic symbol), 114
'Lion Firm of Vow', 229, 271
Lion of the Śākyas, 228
Lion-Throne, 47, 186
Locanā, 82, 114, 230
Lokanāth, 78
Lokeśvara, 114, 63, 78, 102, 113, 115, 152
Lokeśvararāja, 66, 68
Lokottaravādins, 10
Lo-ngam, 132
Lord Buddha *see* Buddha the Lord
'Lords of the Soil' (country-gods), 176, 241, 243, 249, 260, 294
'Lords of the Treasure', 243, 249, 260
lotus, 62, 66, 84, 116, 186; psychic centres, 89
Lotus-Born *see* Padma-sambhava
lotus-holders (*padma-pāṇi*), 47, 116
Lotus of the Good Law, 57–9 *passim*
Lumbini (Rummindei), 6, 7

Mādhyamika ('followers of the mean', *viz.* Doctrine of Relativity; *see* Perfection of Wisdom), 47, 224
Magadha, 2, 45, 54, 106, 168, 172, 187, 193
Mahādeva *see* Śiva
Mahākāla, 79, 102, 242, 243, 289
Mahāsanghika, 46, 105
Mahāsthāmaprāpta, 64, 186
mahāsukha-kāya ('Body of Great Bliss' = Self-Existent Body, 89–90), 234
Mahāvīra, 10
Mahāyāna (Great Vehicle *or* Way), 11, 12, 33 ff, 75, 115, 152
Mahāyāna (Chinese teacher), 156–8
Maitreya, 4, 19, 189, 191, 287
Maitribala, 169
Maitripa *see* Avadhūtipa
Māmakī, 82, 114, 230
Ma-mo (mother-goddesses), 237, 238–9
maṇḍala, definition, 287 (34–5); application, 64–77 *passim,* 79–80, 209, 250, 264, 265; Sam-yä, 154; Tranquil Divinities, 230–1; in praise of the maṇḍala, 250; *see also* Vajra-dhātu-maṇḍala
Mandāravā, 173, 229
Mandi, 173–4
Mang-song-mang-tsen, 135
Mang-yül, 148
Ma-ning, 229, 242
Mañjuśrī, origin, 61–2 and *note* 16; change of family, 67; his partner, 81; Nepal legend, 92; Family-Protector, 116; fierce manifestation, 205; human manifestations, 149, 187
Mañjuśrī-mūla-kalpa, 55 *fn,* 57, 62, 63, 112, 116
mantra (spell), 68, 69, 74, 83
Mantrayāna, 51 *fn,* 56
Māra, 13–14, 18, 44, 60, 103
Marpa, 199–200, 207
Ma-sh'ang trhom-pa-kye, 99, 148–9
master (skr. *guru,* tib. *blama*), 86, 87, 196–7, 220; *see* Vajra-master
Mathurā, 44–5
Matsyendranāth, 113–4, 116–8, 151–2
Me-ak-tsom, 135, 147–8
Medicine, 247, 254
Medicine-buddhas, 189, 190–1
Meru (Kailas), 133, 281
Mila Räpa, 87, 104, 121
Mind *see* Threefold Formula of Personality
'Mind-Only', 31–2, 34
Min-dröl-ling, 219
Monasteries, 2, 18, 40–9 *passim,* 85, 95, 102–3, 108, 147, 179, 215; definition, 201; *see also* Jiwong, Sam-yä, Tabo, *vihāra*

Monks, 201–2, 222–4
Morals, 20, 75–6, 273, 283
Moslems, 106, 119, 141, 147, 168, 189
'Most Noble Sorrowless One', 190
Mu (spirit-sphere associated with early Tibetan belief in divine kingship), 127, 130
mudrā, Gestures, *q.v.*; Symbol, 82, 261, 288
Mūla-sarvāstivādin, 20–1, 292
Mu-ne-tsen-po, 135
Mus, 39–40
mystical philosophy *see* Perfection of Wisdom

nāga (serpent), 44
Nag-po chen-po *see* Mahākāla
Nairātmya, 82; *see also* Da-me-ma ('Selflessness'), 200
Nako, 185
näl-jor-pa *see* yogin
nāma-rūpa see personality
Nam-ri-song-tsen, 135, 138, 139
Nang-sh'er-s'u-tsen, 149
Nāropa, 104, 194
Narteśvara, 78; *see* Padma-narteśvaı
Nāsik, 42, 47–8, 57
Nāyikā, 82
Nepal, 92–3 and *passim*, 140, 141, 148, 150, 164, 172
Newāri, 92–3
Nga-ri (Western Tibet), 179
Nga-wang Yön-ten, 221–2, 259
Ngog, 197
Nīlakaṇṭha, 78
nirmāṇa-kāya, 286; *see* Buddha-bodies
nirvāṇa, 12–13, 26–7, 32–3, 75, 80, 284
Nyang-ro, 132
Nya-trhi-tsen-po, 127–133 *passim*, 291
nyen, 129, 239
Nye-thang, 198
Nying-ma-pa, 151, 219
Nyu-gu-lung, 199

'Ocean Melody of the Sound of the Doctrine', 190
Ö-de, 179
Ö-de-p'e-de, 132
Ö-de-pu-gyel, 128–9, 130, 134, 136
Ö-gung-gyel, 239
Odantapuri, 106, 154, 194, 301
Oḍiviśa, 101, 106
offerings, 40, 111, 245–8, 252, 254, 269, 295
Oṃ Maṇipadme Hūṃ, 116, 237, 289
Ön-chang-do, 163

Padma-Heruka, 79, 232, 241
Padma-k'ang-tsen of Gö, 99; *see* Trhi-s'ang of Gö
Padma-Narteśvara (Lotus-Lord of Dance), 187, 233, 235–6, 260; *see* Narteśvara
Padma-sambhava, 2, 150, 155–6, 198; legends, 6, 98–9, 150–2, 173–4, 177, 241; liturgy, 175, 247, 251–6; his manifestations, 228
pagoda-temples, 53, 94, 102
Pāla Dynasty, 54, 101, 301
Päl-gyi-dorje, 99, 165
pāli (early Indian language in which the canon of the Theravādins is preserved), 5, 29, 152
Pañcaśikha (the sage), 285
Pañcaśikha (*gandharva*), 240
Pañcaśikha mañjughosha, 61–2, 287
Pāṇḍuravāsinī, 82, 114, 230, 236
Pang-bo-che, 214
P'ar-lha-tshik-dün, 130
partners, 80–4, 200–2, 203–4, 206–7, 210, 229–32
Parvatī, 81
Pāśupatas, 113
Paśupati, 113
Pāṭaliputra, 168
Pātan, 94, 102–3, 108, 119
Perfect Ones *see* Siddhas

Perfection of Wisdom (*prajñāpāramitā*), 31, 33, 75, 121, 158, 180; as supreme feminine divinity, 81; *see also prajñā*, Wisdom and Means
person (*pudgala*), 26, 27, 85
personality, 15, 23, 25–6, 65; *see* Components (*skandha*), Threefold Formula
Peshawar, 172
Piprawa, 7
p'ön-po, 122, 127–8, 131, 137, 289–90, 291
Potala, 105, 124–5; residence of the Dalai Lama 133
Prajāpati, 81
prajñā, partner, 81–2, 206, 207, 210; wisdom, *q.v.*
prajñāpāramitā see Perfection of Wisdom
Prajñendraruci, 198
pratimoksha (rules of monastic discipline), 20, 227
pratītyasamutpāda see Twelve-fold causal nexus
preaching gesture *see* Gestures
Precious Prince, 145–7
Prīni, 293
Protectors *see* Fierce divinities, Family Protectors
Pu (OSI: Poo), 129, 290–1
Pu-De Zenith Sovereignty, 134
pudgala see person
Pu-gyel, 129, 131
Pukkasī, 200, 232
Pu-rang, 178, 189
Pur-gyul, 176, 293

Rāhula, 79, 242, 243
Rāhulagupta, 193
Rājgir (ancient name: Rājagṛha), 2, 54, 94
Räl-pa-cen, 135, 145, 163–4, 172
Ra-mo-che, 145
rap-ch'ung-wa (skr. *pravrajita*), 201
Rasanā (skr. 'girdle', tib. *ro-ma* 'corpse'), 88, 90
ratna (jewel), 66
Ratna-Heruka, 79, 232
Ratnaketu, 286
Ratnapāṇi, 64, 67
Ratnarakshita, 104, 105–6
Ratnasambhava, 66–7
Ratna-vajrī, 68
Red Crag, 152, 155
Richardson, x–xi, 142, 159, 161
Rin-chen S'ang-po, 87, 180–5, 192–193
rites, of magic, 76–7, 161–2, 279 *fn*; four kinds of ritual action, 77, 257–61
Riwalsar, 173–4
'Roaring Lion', 228
Roerich, 193 *fn.*
Rohtang Pass, 171
Rong-phu (OSI: Rongbuk), 213, 218, 219
Rope-descent, 127–34 *passim*
Rummindei *see* Lumbini

Saddharmapuṇḍarīka see Lotus of the Good Law
S'a-hor, 154, 173
śakti, 81
Śākya-Sage (Śākya-muni), quasi-historical, 1–3, 5–9, 20, 22–3, 37–8, 227, 278; mythical associations, 9–11, 43–4; supra-mundane conception, 54, 58, 59; as family-head, 62–3; as one among many, 102, 103, 229; Lion of the Śākyas, 228
Sa-kya-pa, 199
Śākya-śrī, 105–6
Säl-nang of Ba (Jñānendra), 148, 150, 157, 158
samādhi see concentration
Samanta-bhadra, bodhisattva, 64; buddha, 232–4, 252
Samatha, 195
samaya (bond, guarantee), 287–8, 71, 74, 239
sambhoga-kāya, 286; *see* Buddha-Bodies

Sambhoṭa of Thön, 141–2, 143, 167, 169, 171
saṃsāra ('moving on together', *viz.* phenomenal existence), 27, 31–2
saṃskāra (impulses), 15, 23, 67
Śamvara, 205–6, 78, 103, 105, 204
Sam-yä, 152–3, 158, 196, 198, 241
Sä-na-lek, 135, 136, 138, 158–63, 292
Sānchi, 40
Sanga Dorje, 213–4
sañjñā (perceptions), 23, 67
Śāntarakshita, 99, 148, 149–50, 152, 156, 173, 181
Śāntipa, 198
Sarasvatī, 81
Sarnāth, 18 ff.
Sarvadharma-pravṛtti-nirdeśa, 158
Sarvanivaraṇavishkambin, 64
Sarvāstivādin, 26–7, 46, 152, 164
Sarva-tathāgata-tattva-saṃgraha, 58; *see* 'Symposium of Truth'
sattva-vajrī, 68, 71–4 *passim*
Śavarī, 200
Self-Existent Body, 89–90; *see also* Buddha-Bodies
Senge-dong-ma, 228
Senge-nam-gyel, 189
Se-tsün, 196
sexual symbolism, 83–4, 88–90
Sh'a, 162
Sh'a-ma, 206–7
Sham-po, 132
Sh'ang-sh'ung, 139, 170–1, 290, 292–3
Shar-Khumbu, 97, 213–6
Shashin, 293
Sherpa, 215–6
Sh'i-wa-ö, 179
Siddhas ('Perfect Ones'), 85–7, 104–105, 151–2, 178, 296–7
Sikkim, 213
Śiva, 63, 79, 107, 113–4, 176, 191, 203, 205, 289
skandha see Components of Personality
'Slayer of Death' (Yamāntaka), 230
Śmaśālī, 200, 232
Song-tsen-gam-po, 135, 138, 139, 141, 144, 150, 170
soul *see* personality
Sovereign-Buddha *see* Buddha the Lord
Speech *see* Threefold Formula of Personality
spells *see Mantra*
spheres of existence, 15–17, 263–5, 271
Spiti, 171, 176, 178, 182, 188
śrāvakas ('hearers', *viz.* those who claim to follow the early teachings), 61 *fn*, 277
Śrī-ghosha *see* Trhi-sh'er of Ba
stūpa (tib. chö-ten), 37 ff, 44, 49, 96–7, 100, 103, 114, 167, 280; *see also* Svayambhūnāth, Bodhnāth
Śuddhodana, 6
Sum-pa-khen-po, 127
'Sun-Ray', 228
'Supreme De Zenith-Sovereignty, 132–3
Sutlej, 171, 178, 182
sūtras, definition, 54–6; new ones, 29, 30, 61
Suvarṇaprabhāsottama-sūtra, 55 *fn*, 158
Suzuki, 157
Svayambhūnāth, 95–8, 99, 114, 195
Symbol, *see Mudrā*
symbols of Śākya-Sage, 39–40
'Symposium of Truth', 58, 69, 80, 182, 202
Swāt Valley (Uḍḍiyāna, *q.v.*), 172
sword, 66
'Swirler of Nectar', 230, 236

Tabo, 183–7, 190–1
t'am-cen (*dam-can*), 288, 242–4 (63, 79, 256)
tantras, texts, 54–6, 81–2, 224, 293–4; extra-canonical, 161–2; categories, 202–4, 181
tantric, defined, 51 *fn*

Tārā, 78, 82, 114–6, 230
Tāranātha, 101, 105
tathāgata, 9–10; family name, 62-3, 66
Taxila, 172
Teng-bo-che (*steng-bo-che*, 'great high-place', OSI incorrectly: Thyang-bo-che), 214, 293
ten powers (of a buddha), 22
Tha-me (*thang-smad*, 'lower plain'), 293
Thang-lha *see* God of the Plain
Theravādin, 10, 12, 19, 27–8, 52, 152
Thomas, E. J., 5
Thomas, F. W., 292–3
Thön-mi Sambhoṭa *see* Sambhoṭa
'Thorough-Knowing King', 190
Thought of Enlightenment, 35–6, 55, 75, 89–90, 227, 251
'Thoughtful Coveter of the Best', 228
Three Evils *see* Evils
Threefold Formula of Personality (Body, Speech and Mind), 68, 214, 237, 256, 274
Threefold knowledge of a buddha, 13, 22
Three Jewels (Buddha, Law/Doctrine, Assembly), 155, 160; tantric form, 175, 226, 228
Three Precious Ones (*dkon-mchog-gsum*)= Three Jewels (*triratna*)
Tibetan canon, 29, 53, 105, 152, 161, 163–4, 180–2
— early literature, 122–32 *passim*, 153–4, 239–42, 271–2
— language, 142–4, 291
— tea, 195
Ting-dzin S'ang-po of Nyang, 159, 160–3
Ti-se (Meru, Kailas) 132–3
titans, 17; *see* Wheel of Existence
tombs, 132, 290
Tong-tsen of Gar, 138
tor-ma, 245–8
Tr'ak-shing-do (OSI: Takshindo), 214–5
'Tranquil and Fierce Divinities', 229–32
tr'a-pa, 201
tree, 1, 4, 39, 44
Trhan-tr'uk, 144
Trhi-de-song-tsen, 135, 136; *see* Sä-na-lek
Trhi-de-tsuk-tsen, 135; *see* Me-ak-tsom
Trhi-mang-long, 135
Trhi-ring, 138
Trhi-s'ang of Gö, 148–9
Trhi-sh'er of Ba, 99, 156
Trhi-song-deu-tsen, 98–9, 135, 136, 138, 148–58, 241, 291–2
Trhi-song-tsen, 135; *see* Song-tsen-gam-po
Trhi-tsen-po, 131
Trhi-tsuk-de-tsen, 135; *see* Räl-pa-cen
Trhi-U-dum-tsen, 135; *see* Lang-dar-ma
Trhül-nang, 145
Tr'i-Gum, 131–2, 137
tr'up-thop (*siddha*), 201
Tsang, 179, 196, 198
— King of, 133–4
Tsang-po, 133
Tsaparang, 185
Tsen-nya of Gar, 138
Tsong-kha-pa, 4, 19, 187, 189, 202
Tucci, xi, 134, 136, 145, 174, 185
Tun-Huang, 137, 150
Twelve-fold causal nexus, 13–15, 261; *see also* Wheel of Existence
'Two-in-One' (tib. *zung-'jug*), 83, 88–90, 96, 251

U-shang-do, 153
Udayana, 127
Uḍḍiyāna, 140, 151, 168, 172–5 *passim*, 203
'Union of the Precious Ones', 175, 204, 228–34; liturgy, 249–58, 261, 295

'Unity of All the Blessed', 204, 235–6, 255
'Universal Saviour', 237–8, 264–75 *passim*, 298
Urgyen (tibetanized form of *Uḍḍiyāna*), 214, 253
Ushnīsha-sitātapatrā, 116 *fn*.
Ushnīshavijayā, 101

Vāc, 81
Vairocana, 58, 59, 66, 74, 182, 191, 202, 206, 286
Vairocana (Translator), 218
Vaiśravaṇa, 242
vajra, 62, 66, 74, 84, 186, Pl. 38
Vajra-bhairava, 183, 205
vajrācārya see Vajra-master
Vajra-ḍāka, 205, 207–10
Vajra-ḍākinī, 210
Vajradhara, 74, 86
Vajradharma, 71
vajra-dhātu-maṇḍala, 66 ff, 74, 76, 97, 159, 182, 184, 229–31
Vajradhātvīśvarī, 82
Vajragarbha, 70
Vajra-Heruka, 79, 232
Vajrakarma, 71
Vajra-kumāra, 234, 241, 242
Vajralocana, 70
Vajra-master, 71–2, 112, 160, 192
Vajrānkuśa, 68
Vajrapāṇi, 62–7 *passim*, 116, 163, 241
Vajrapāśa, 68
Vajraratna, 71
Vajra-samādhi-sūtra, 158
Vajrāsana see Diamond-Seat
Vajrasattva (Adamantine Being), 68–74 *passim*, 244–5, 259
Vajrasphoṭa, 68
Vajra-Vārāhī, 207, 210
Vajrāveśa, 68
Vajrayāna, 51 *fn*, 76
Vajra-yoginī, 251
Vase of Life (vase containing the nectar, 247), 255
—, ritual, 262, 266, 269, Pl. 38; *see also* 245
Vasubandhu, 30, 101
Vasudharā, 78
Vātsīputrīyas, 26
'Victorious' (Vijaya), 230
vidyā, 288, 289
vidyādhara (*lit*. 'holders of the spell' —both human and non-human), 62, 233, 266
vihāra ('monastery'), 96, 102, 108–9, 111, 119
vijñāna see consciousness
Vikramaśīla, 85, 103, 105–6, 172, 194, 196, 198
Vimalamitra, 161–2
Virūpa, 198
Vishnu, 107, 242

Wheel of Existence, 13–17, 23, 224–5, 263–71 *passim*
wheel (of the Doctrine), 39, 44, 57, 66, 70, 120, 251, 274
Wisdom, in the early schools, 21–2, 27; as a 'Great Perfection' *see* Perfection of Wisdom; as 'feminine partner' *see prajñā*; 'Wisdom and Compassion/Means', 83–4, 255, 256, 258; *see also* 'Two-in-One'
Wisdom as Fivefold (*pañcajñāna*), 65, 67, 255; as sixfold, 263, 271
Wise Man and Fool, 169
'worship', external, internal and secret, 245–7

yaksha, 154, 289, 291, 292
Ya-sh'ur, 239–40
Yamāntaka, 'Slayer of Death', 204–205, 105, 230
Yar-lha-sham-po, 127
Yar-lung, 127, 134, 135, 136, 141, 169, 172
Yer-pa, 156, 198

Ye-she-ö, 179, 180, 181, 184, 194
yeti, 214, 294
yi-dam, 288, 79–80, 105, 228, 234–236, (203–11)
Yogācāra ('practice of yoga', *viz*. the Doctrine of 'Mind-Only', *q.v.*), 30 *fn*, 47, 101
yoga-tantra, 202–3
yogin, 85–9, 113–4, 119–20, 161
yoginī, 82, 88, 206; eight of low caste, 200, 232
yoginī-tantra, 203–4, 206
Yön-ten of Tr'en-ka, 164
Yuan Chwang, 3, 18, 30 *fn*, 101, 140, 168, 174

zebu (tib. *mdzo*), 293, 170, 215
Zen, 157
Zenith Sovereignty of Light, 239

TIBETAN INDEX

Except where page numbers are given, references will be found through the General Index

Ka-rgyal	293
Kun-tu-bzang-po	Samanta-bhadra
Klu	290 (serpents)
dKon-mchog-spyi-'dus	'Union of the Precious Ones'
bKa-'gyur	Tibetan canon
bKa-rgyud-pa	Ka-gyü-pa
bKa-gdams-pa	Ka-dam-pa
sKar-chung	Kar-chung
sKor-bon	130
Kha-'bar-rgyal-po	King of the Burning Mouth
Khum-bu yul-lha	Khumbu 'country-god'
Khyab-'jug	Vishṇu
Khra-'brug	Trhan-tr'uk
Khri-'dus-srong	Trhi-dü-song
Khri-lde-gtsug-brtsan	Trhi-de-tsuk-tsen
Khri-lde-srong-brtsan	Trhi-de-song-tsen
Khri-dbu-dum-brtsan	Trhi-U-dum-tsen
Khri-'bring	Trhi-ring
Khri-mang-slong	Trhi-mang-long
Khri-gtsug-lde-brtsan	Trhi-tsuk-de-tsen
Khri-btsan-po	Trhi-tsen-po
Khri-srong-lde'u-btsan	Trhi-song-deu-tsen
Khri-srong-brtsan	Trhi-song-tsen
mKha-'gro-ma	ḍākinī
Gar-log	294
Grva-pa	tr'a-pa
Gri-gum	Tr'i-gum
Grub-thob	Tr'up-thop
dGe-lugs-pa	Ge-luk-pa
dGra-lha	290, (drap-lha)
mGos-Khri-bzang	Trhi-s'ang of Gö
'Gar sTong-btsan	Tong-tsen of Gar
'Gar bTsan-snya-ldom-bu	Tsen-nya of Gar
'Gro-ba-kun-sgrol	'Univeral Saviour'

TIBETAN INDEX

mNgon-mkhyen-rgyal-po	'Thorough-knowing King'
bCen-po	129
Chos-kyi rgyal-po	King of the Dharma
Chos-'khor	292
Chos-sgra rgya-mtsho dbyangs	'Ocean Melody of the Sound of the Doctrine'
mChod-rten	chö-ten, *see* stūpa
Nyi-ma-'od-zer	'Sun-Ray'
gNya-khri-btsan-po	Nya-trhi-tsen-po
gNyen-po	129, 239
rNying-ma-pa	Nying-ma-pa
rNying-ma'i rgyud-'bum	'Hundred Thousand Tantras of the Old Sect'
sNying-thig	'Heart-Drop'
gTer-bdag	Lord of the Treasure
gTor-ma	tor-ma
Thag-bzang-ris	'Design of Excellent Weave'
Thang-lha	'God of the Plain'
The-brang	127
Thon-mi sam-bho-ṭa	Sambhoṭa of Thön
Dam-can	t'am-cen
Dam-can-spyi-gtor	243–4
Dur-khrod-lha-mo	Cemetery-Goddess
bDag-med-ma	Da-me-ma
bDud	Māra
bDud-rtsi-'khyil-ba	Swirler of Nectar
bDe-mchog	Śamvara
bDe-gshegs-kun-'dus	'Unity of All the Blessed'
'Dre	290
rDo-rje	Vajra
rDo-rje 'jigs-byed	Vajra-bhairava
rDo-rje grod-lod	Adamantine Sagging Belly
rDo-rje legs-pa	Dorje-lek-pa
rDo-rje gzhon-nu	Vajra-kumāra
lDe	De

Nag-po chen-po	Mahākāla
Nang-mchod	246
gNam-gyi khri	131
gNam-gyi chos	136
gNam-ri-srong-btsan	Nam-ri-song-tsen
rNam-thos-sras	Vaiśrāvaṇa
rNal-'byor-pa	näl-jor-pa (yogin)
Pad-ma-mtsho	Riwalsar
sPu	Pu
sPu-de-gung-rgyal	Pu-de Zenith-Sovereignty
sPu-hrangs	Pu-rang
Pho-lha	290
Phyi-mchod	246
Phying-ba	Ching-wa
'Phrul-gyi lha btsan-po	128
'Phrul-snang	Trhül-nang
Bar-lha-tshigs-bdun	P'ar-lha-tshik-dün
Bon	P'ön
Bya-rung-kha-shor	98
Byang-chub-'od	Ch'ang-chup-ö
Brag-dmar	Red Crag
Bran-ka Yon-tan	Yön-ten of Tr'en-ka
Bru-zha	Gilgit
'Brog-mi	Drok-mi
'Brom	Drom
Bla-lde-gung-rgyal	Supreme De Zenith-Sovereignty
Blo-ldan-mchog-sred	Thoughtful Coveter of the Best
dBang-po'i me-tog	Flower of the senses
dBa-gsal-snang	Säl-nang of Ba (Jñānendra)
dBa-snang-bzher-zu-brtsan	Nang-sh'er-s'u-tsen
'Bal-skye-zang-ldong-tshab	Kye-s'ang-dong-tsap of Bäl
sBa-mi-khri-gzher	Trhi-sh'er of Ba
Ma-ning	Ma-ning
Ma-mo	Ma-mo
Ma-zhang khrom-pa-skyes	Ma-sh'ang trhom-pa-kye
Ma-sangs	129
Mu-ne-btsan-po	Mu-ne-tsen-po
Mes-'ag-tshoms	Me-ak-tshom

Myang-ngan-med mchog-dpal	Most Noble Sorrowless One
Myang ting-nge-'dzin bzang-po	Ting-dzin S'ang-po of Nyang
dMu-gZa lda-me-bcun	130
rMu or *dMu*	Mu
gTsug-lag	136
bTsan	129, 136
bTsan(-po)	127–8
bTsan-thang-sgo-bzhi	127
mTshan-legs-pa	'Good Characteristics'
mDzangs-blun	'Wise Man and Fool'
Wal-wal-sras-po	130
Zhang-zhung	Sh'ang-sh'ung
Zhi-khro	'Tranquil and Fierce Divinities'
Zhi-ba-'od	Sh'i-wa-ö
Zhva	Sh'a
gZhi-bdag	Lords of the Soil
Za-ram	129
Za-hor	S'a-hor
Zung-'jug	'Two in One'
gZa-lha	Rāhula
'Od-gung-rgyal	239
'Od-lde-bed-de	Ö-de-p'e-de
'Od-lde-spu-rgyal	Ö-de-pu-gyel
'On-chang-rdo	Ön-chang-do
Ya-zhur	Ya-sh'ur
Yab-lha-bdal-drug	130
Yar-klungs	Yar-lung
Yar-lha-sham-po	127
Yi-dam	Yi-dam
Ye-shes-mtsho-rgyal	'Goddess Ocean of Wisdom'
Ye-shes-'od	Ye-she-ö
Yer-pa	Yer-pa
gYu-bya gshog-gcig	239
gYung-drung	128, 136

Ra-mo-che	Ra-mo-che
Rab-byung-ba	rap-ch'ung-wa
Ral-pa-can	Räl-pa-cen
Rigs-gsum-dgon-po	Family-Protectors
Rin-chen zla-ba	'Gem-Moon'
Rin-chen bzang-po	Rin-chen S'ang-po
Ru-bzhi	130, 170 *fn.*
Rol-rtse	127
Lam-'bras	199
Legs-pa'i shes-rab	Lek-pai-she-rap
Shi-'dre	290
Shā-kya seng-ge	Lion of the Śākyas
Sa-skya-pa	Sa-kya-pa
Sa-bdag	Lords of the Soil
Sangs-rgyas sman-gyi lha	Buddha Master of Medicine
Sad-na-legs	Sä-ne-lek
Seng-ge sgra-sgrogs	Roaring Lion
Seng-ge dam-brtan	Lion Firm of Vow
Srid-pa'i lha	130
Srung-khang	243
Srong-btsan-sgam-po	Song-tsen-gam-po
gSang-mchod	246
gSer-bzang dri-med rin-chen	Immaculate Gem of Excellent Gold
Ham-'phrang	Ham-trhang
lHa-chen	Mahādeva
lHa-lde	Lha-de
lHa-dbang brgya-byin	Indra Lord of Gods

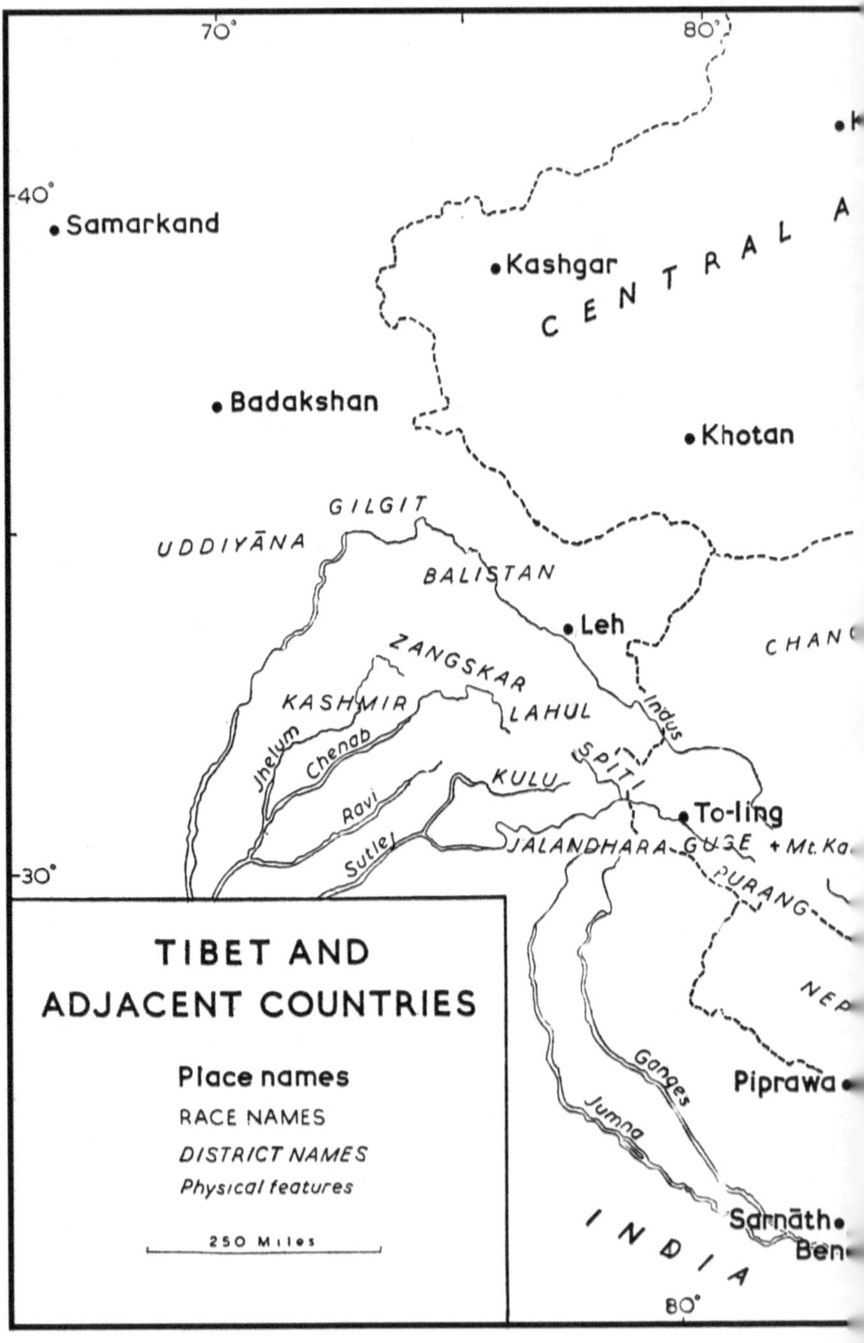

TIBET AND ADJACENT COUNTRIES
Place names
RACE NAMES
DISTRICT NAMES
Physical features
250 Miles
70°
80°
40°
30°
Samarkand
Kashgar
CENTRAL A
Badakshan
Khotan
GILGIT
UDDIYĀNA
BALISTAN
Leh
ZANGSKAR
KASHMIR
LAHUL
Indus
Jhelum
Chenab
SPITI
KULU
Ravi
To-ling
Sutlej
JALANDHARA
GUGE
Mt. Ka
PURANG
Ganges
Jumna
Piprawa
Sarnāth
Ben
INDIA

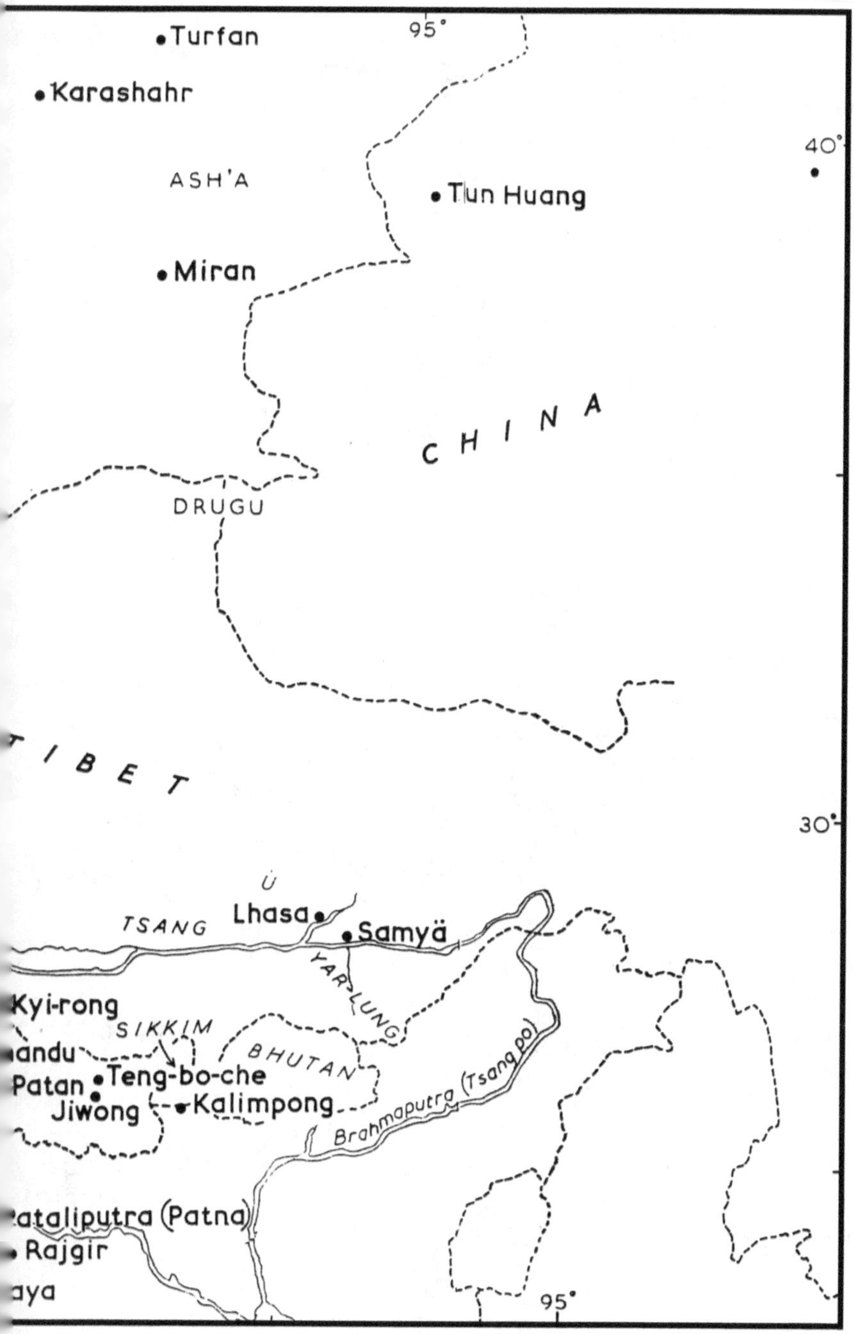

Turfan
Karashahr
95°
40°
ASH'A
Tun Huang
Miran
CHINA
DRUGU
TIBET
30°
Ü
Lhasa
TSANG
Samyä
YARLUNG
Kyi-rong
SIKKIM
BHUTAN
Teng-bo-che
Patan
Jiwong
Kalimpong
Brahmaputra (Tsang po)
ataliputra (Patna)
Rajgir
aya
95°

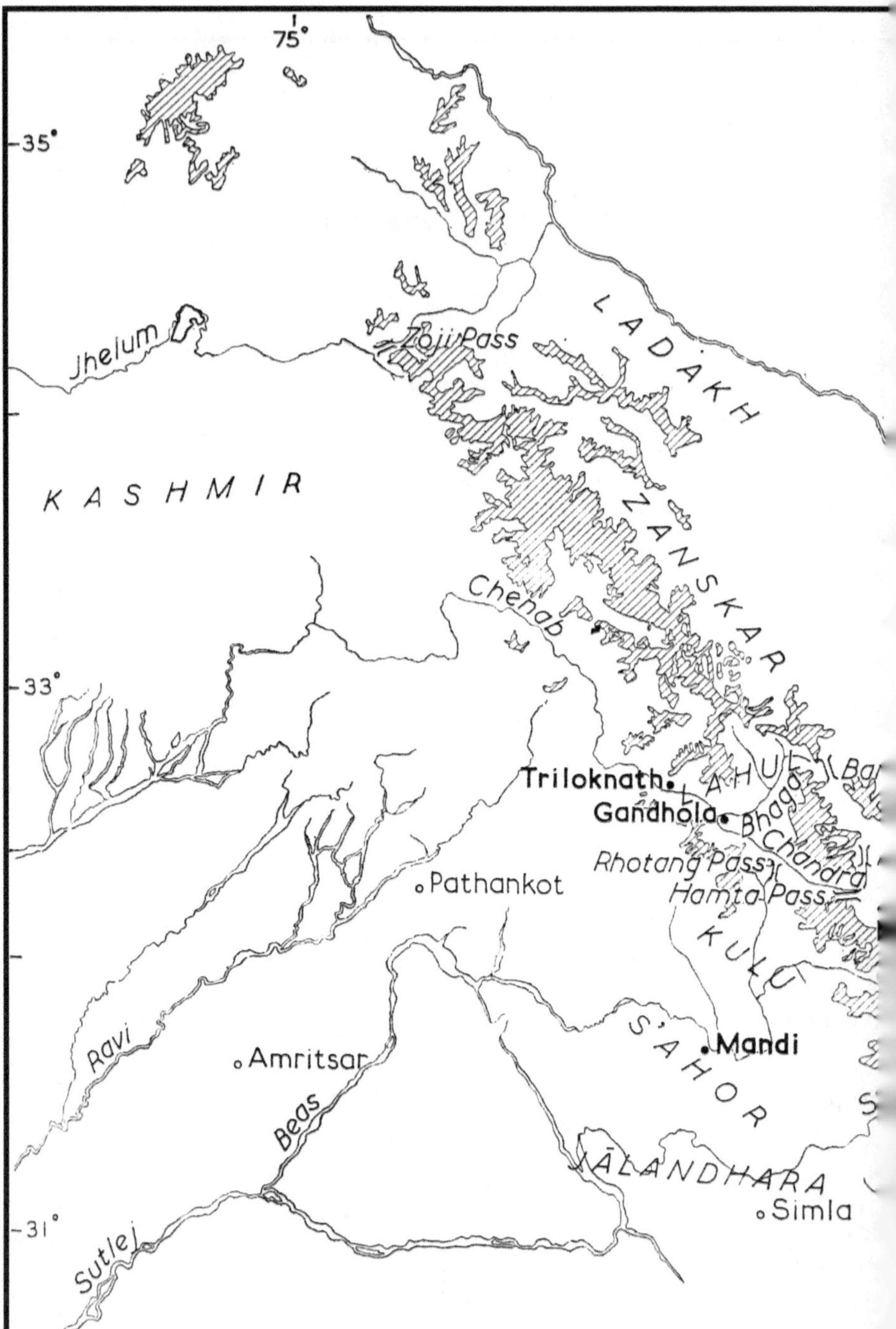

75°
35°
33°
31°
75°
77°
Jhelum
Zoji Pass
LADAKH
KASHMIR
ZANSKAR
Chenab
Triloknath
LAHUL
Gandhola
Bhaga
Chandra
Rhotang Pass
Hamta Pass
Pathankot
KULU
Mandi
ŚAHOR
Ravi
Amritsar
Beas
JĀLANDHARA
Simla
Sutlej

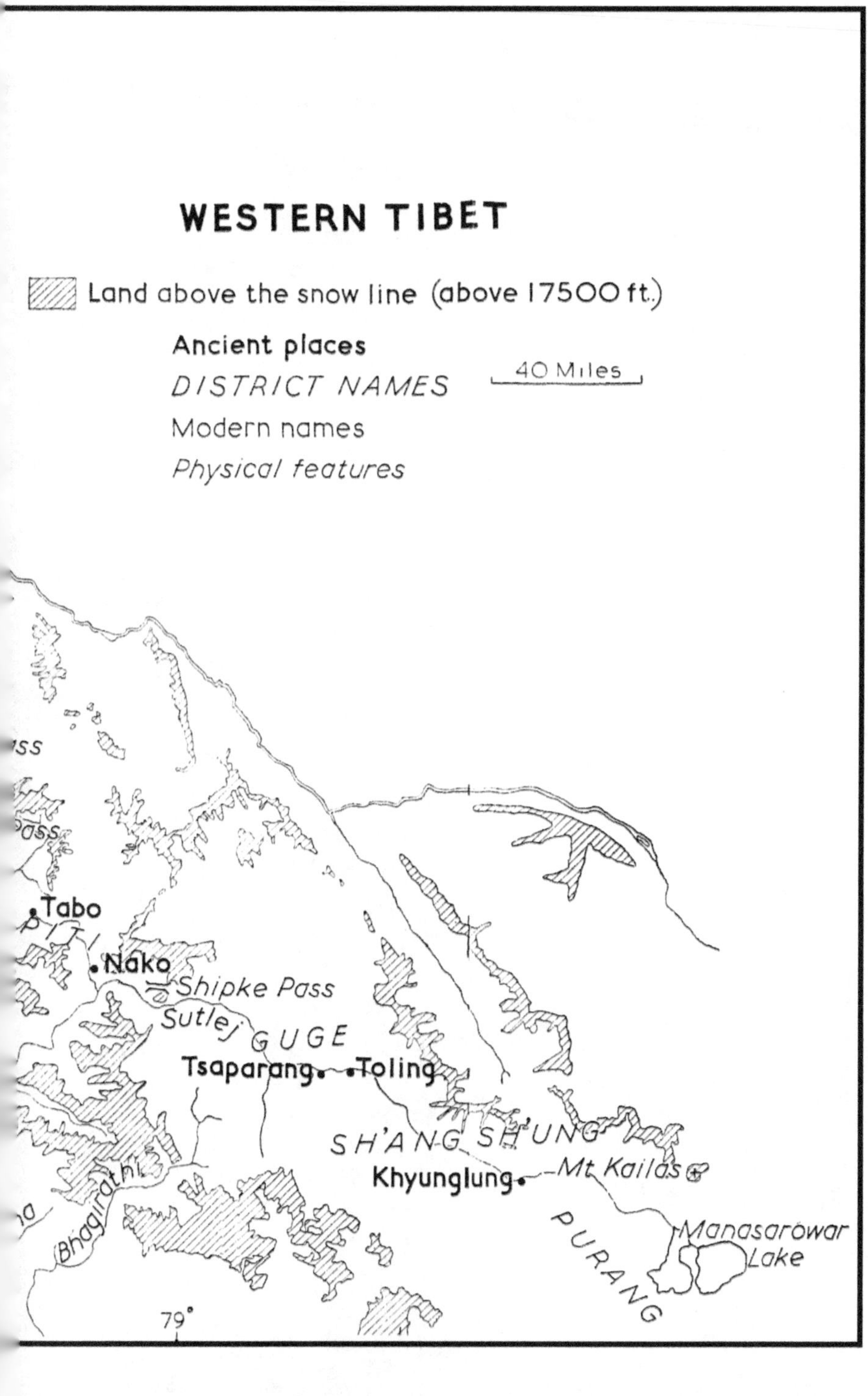
WESTERN TIBET
Land above the snow line (above 17500 ft.)
Ancient places
DISTRICT NAMES
40 Miles
Modern names
Physical features
Tabo
PITI
Nako
Shipke Pass
Sutlej
GUGE
Tsaparang
Toling
SH'ANG SH'UNG
Khyunglung
Mt Kailas
PURANG
Manasarowar
Lake
Bhagirathi
79°

ABOUT THE AUTHOR

David Snellgrove is renowned for his ability to convey the spirit as well as the textual interpretation of Sanskrit and Tibetan texts relating to the history of Buddhism. Following his retirement from teaching commitments in 1982, and a career-long interest in Tibetan peoples and cultures, Dr. Snellgrove transferred his scholarly focus to South-East Asia, primarily Indonesia and Cambodia, where he resided for over ten years.

David Snellgrove is a Doctor of Literature in the University of Cambridge, Professor Emeritus of the University of London and a Fellow of the British Academy. Dr Snellgrove currently resides in Italy.

David Snellgrove has been a prolific author throughout his long career. In addition to the present volume, Orchid Press is proud to have published the following partial list of his works :

Asian Commitment: Travels and Studies in the Indian Sub-Continent and South-East Asia (1st ed., 2000)

Khmer Civilisation and Angkor (1st ed., 2001/03)

(with Hugh E. Richardson) The Cultural History of Tibet (3rd ed., 2003)

Indo-Tibetan Buddhism (2nd ed., 2004)

Angkor Before and After: A Cultural History of the Khmers (1st ed., 2004)

Religion as History – Religion as Myth (1st ed., 2005)

The Nine Ways of Bon: Excerpts from the *gZi-brjid* (2nd ed., 2010)

The Hevajra Tantra (2nd ed., 2010)

Himalayan Pilgrimage (3rd ed., 2011)

Four Lamas of Dolpo (3rd ed., Vol. I & 2nd ed., Vol. II, 2011)

www.ingramcontent.com/pod-product-compliance
Lightning Source LLC
Chambersburg PA
CBHW021148230426
43667CB00006B/303
* 9 7 8 9 7 4 5 2 4 1 4 1 1 *